to Systemic Functional
Linguistics

Also Available from Continuum:

Collected Works of M.A.K. Halliday
Edited by Jonathan J. Webster

Volume 1: *On Grammar*
Volume 2: *Linguistic Studies of Text and Discourse*
Volume 3: *On Language and Linguistics*
Volume 4: *Language of Early Childhood*
Volume 5: *The Language of Science*
Volume 6: *Computational and Quantitative Studies*
Volume 7: *Studies in English Language*
Volume 8: *Studies in Chinese Language*
Volume 9: *Language and Education*
Volume 10: *Language and Society*

The Essential Halliday
Edited by Jonathan J. Webster

Key Terms in Systemic Functional Linguistics
Christian Matthiessen, Kazuhiro Teruya and Marvin Lam

Halliday: A Guide for the Perplexed
Jonathan J. Webster

Continuum Companion to Systemic Functional Linguistics

Edited by
M.A.K. Halliday
and
Jonathan J. Webster

continuum

Continuum International Publishing Group
The Tower Building   80 Maiden Lane, Suite 704
11 York Road   New York
London SE1 7NX   NY 10038

© M.A.K. Halliday, Jonathan J. Webster and contributors 2009

All rights reserved. No part of this publication may be reproduced or transmitted in any form or by any means, electronic or mechanical, including photocopying, recording, or any information storage or retrieval system, without prior permission in writing from the publishers.

British Library Cataloguing-in-Publication Data
A catalogue record for this book is available from the British Library.

ISBN: 978-0-8264-9447-4 (Hardback)
      978-0-8264-9448-1 (Paperback)

Library of Congress Cataloging-in-Publication Data
The Publisher has applied for CIP data.

Typeset by Newgen Imaging Systems Pvt Ltd, Chennai, India
Printed and bound in Great Britain by CPI Antony Rowe, Chippenham, Wiltshire

Contents

Preface by M.A.K. Halliday	vii
1. Introduction *Jonathan J. Webster*	1
2. Ideas & new directions *Christian M.I.M. Matthiessen*	12
3. Methods – techniques – problems *M.A.K. Halliday*	59
4. Language development *Clare Painter*	87
5. Language and other primate species *James D. Benson & Paul J. Thibault*	104
6. Linguistic computing *Elke Teich*	113
7. Corpus-based research *Canzhong Wu*	128
8. Clinical applications *Elizabeth Armstrong*	143
9. Discourse studies *J. R. Martin*	154
10. The place of context in a systemic functional model *Ruqaiya Hasan*	166
11. Stylistic analysis: construing aesthetic organisation *David G. Butt & Annabelle Lukin*	190
12. Resources and courses *Mick O'Donnell*	216
13. Keywords	229
References	254
Index	293

Preface to
Continuum Companion to Systemic Functional Linguistics

M.A.K. Halliday
University of Sydney

It is always difficult to achieve, and to maintain, a balanced perspective on language, because one is constantly having to shift one's depth of focus. This is true, of course, with any phenomenon that is being investigated in theory, since the focus will always have to shift between the instance and the system that "lies behind" it; if this seems to present a special problem in the case of language, this is because language is a system of meaning – a semiotic system – and so the relation between system and instance is a complex of physical, physiological and social-semiotic factors.

But there is another aspect of the problem that faces a student of language: namely, the very broad range of human activities in which language is the key component. Again, of course, all the major disciplines, the domains of organized knowledge, ramify into branches and sub-branches each with its own special methodology and its own specialist practitioners; there is the same problem everywhere of keeping all corners of the forest, and the trees, in focus of attention. But again this can present an added difficulty where the theory derives its main impetus from outside, from its application to very varied problems, both practical problems and research problems. Language is likely to appear in very different guises when it is operating in such varied contexts as a classroom, a law court and a surgery; yet its effectiveness – and therefore the effectiveness of any attempt we may make to intervene in the processes in which language is involved – always depends on the functional integrity of the system as a whole.

It is a characteristic of a functional theory of language, especially one that seeks to be "appliable", that it brings into relief those features of a language that resonate with the cultural and situational context, and so shows up the part, or parts, that language is playing in any particular environment, in all the varied facets of people's lives. If we observe an infant learning its first language, we can track in detail the emergence of the phonological, semantic and lexicogrammatical resources which will enable the child to act effectively in, and on, its environment of people and of things. If a system of verbal communication breaks down, we can identify its weak points, the disjunctions and sources of misunderstanding within the text. If language is being used to deceive, we can suggest what may be the warning signs. A functional description such as those developed in systemic functional linguistics offers ways in to investigations such as these. They are strategies to be pursued, of course, not rules of procedure – still less guarantees of success! The theory provides something to think with, a framework of related concepts that can be drawn on in many different contexts where there are problems that turn out to be, when investigated, essentially problems of language.

Examples of the deployment of systemic functional linguistics in many different spheres of action can be found throughout recent publications, all of which figure in the references cited in this volume. The two volumes of *Continuing Discourse on Language,* edited by Hasan, Matthiessen & Webster (Equinox, 2005, 2007), provide a highly informative and well-documented survey of the field. The present book is not intended to duplicate the purpose or the coverage of those two volumes. They are concerned with the applications – with the work that has been and is being done, in these various spheres, with systemic functional linguistics as a working tool. This volume, as a "Companion", sets out to describe and explain the different aspects of the theory in relation to the contexts for its application, more in the spirit of "how to . . .", with the aim of showing what is involved when the theory is being said to be "applied".

We have wanted to keep the book to a manageable size, even at the expense of omitting one or two possible further headings. In particular, there is no separate section on language in education, which is the one field in which systemic functional linguistics has been most widely deployed throughout the decades of its evolution; partly because, for that very reason, it would have demanded a great deal of extra space, but also because this work involves every aspect of language, and the ongoing contact and exchange of ideas with educators has implicated more or less all the dimensions of the theory. Other topics have been omitted because the work is still rather specialized and new. We hope the book will serve its particular purpose, and we are grateful to our publishers for accommodating a volume of this design within the scope of their publication programme. It certainly seemed to us to be a gap that needed to be filled.

1

An Introduction to *Continuum Companion to Systemic Functional Linguistics*

Jonathan J. Webster
City University of Hong Kong

Why Systemic Functional Linguistics is the *theory of choice* for students of language?

Perhaps because he is a language teacher turned linguist, M.A.K. Halliday has been able to maintain a perspective on language that is grounded in how we actually use language to construe reality and enact social relationships. What began as a "laundry card grammar" – "being written on the beautiful white cards that laundries inserted in one's shirts in the days before washing machines took over" – eventually developed into systemic-functional linguistics, which has become the *theory of choice* (in more ways than one) for those interested in achieving an 'appliable' description leading to an understanding of the enabling power of language.

For Halliday, the underlying quest has always been about description rather than theory. He maintains that it is "not so much new theories but new descriptions" that will enable us to engage more effectively with language. Theory becomes pertinent only insofar as it lays the foundation for grammatical description which embraces the complexity of language.

The most telling statement comes from a previously unpublished account (see Halliday 1950), dating back to 1950, of Halliday's investigation into the varieties of Cantonese of the Pearl River Delta region of central Guangdong. In this paper entitled, 'Some Lexico-grammatical Features of the Dialects of the Pearl River Delta', he writes, "The Chinese language works, and the task of the descriptive linguist is to show how it works." At the time, Halliday was then a student working under Professor Wang Li who was conducting a phonetic survey of these same dialects, attempting "to gain a complete picture of their phonetic structure, synchronically and diachronically: that is, including the phonology of the present sound-system and the historical development of each syllabic sound-group". Because of the chaos brought about by the civil war raging at the time, however, they could not do their survey work in the surrounding villages. Instead, they surveyed university students who were natives of these small towns and villages, and who spoke their own local dialects in addition to standard Cantonese. Complementary to the ongoing phonetic survey, Halliday developed a grammar questionnaire which he used to get the same university students to give him their versions of the Cantonese sentences in their own local dialects. Not only was Halliday interested in investigating the differences between Mandarin and Cantonese grammar, but also in looking at how these local dialects differed in their grammar from Cantonese.

Halliday's first published work was the paper on 'Grammatical Categories in Chinese', which appeared in the *Transactions of the Philological Society* in 1956, one year after he completed his Ph.D. at Cambridge, but three years before the subsequent publication of his Ph.D. dissertation 'The Language of the Chinese "Secret History of the Mongols 元朝秘史"'. In this paper, he put forward a scheme of grammatical categories for the description of "Modern Pekingese formal colloquial", or as he described it, "the type of Chinese which a foreigner learns". The textual basis for this description came from a small corpus of spoken material, which he recorded in Peking and elsewhere. Three types of grammatical categories served as the basis for description, including units, elements and classes, with the largest unit being the "sentence", and the lower limit of grammatical description being the character, as the unit of word structure.

When asked to compare his own approach with those of other linguists who helped shape not only his own thinking but also the discipline of linguistics as a whole, Halliday notes Firth's interest in varieties of a language, Hjelmslev's focus on a language as a whole and Jakobson's search for universals across all languages. Halliday's early work with what he called "New Chinese" or Modern Pekingese builds on and extends the general linguistic principles established by these scholars. He recalls, however, that it was a struggle to fit the frameworks which were then available with what he actually encountered in Chinese and later English:

> Struggling with the grammar of Chinese, and then of English, in the conceptual-categorial frameworks which were then available (traditional grammar, linguist's descriptions of languages, Jespersen and Wang Li, Firth's system–structure theory, Pike, Fries, Hill, Hockett, etc.), I was constantly finding that the categories were unclear: you would find a label attached to some patch or other, but with no indication of what kind of category it was supposed to be and the whole battery of technical statements never added up to a coherent picture of the whole. I felt I needed to know where I was at any moment and where any descriptive statement that I made fitted in to the overall account.

Such inadequacies in previous grammatical descriptions provided the motivation for Halliday to construct his "own mapping, or projection, of the design and traffic flow of language". It was something he entered into, however, as he puts it, "with many misgivings, because I never thought of myself as being a theorist".

Description and theory

Description must be grounded in a theory of how language works at the level of grammar. A grammar is that abstract stratum of coding between meaning and expression; it is a resource for making meaning. The grammar "transforms experience into meaning"; the grammar is itself "a theory of experience." Grammatics is theorizing about a theory of grammar; it is a theory for explaining how the grammar works and enables one to unconsciously construe experience.

Halliday gives the following example to illustrate how we use language to construe our experience: "Glass cracks more quickly the harder you press on it." There are two processes – *cracks* and *press* – along with their associated participants and circumstances. The elements of this sentence are as follows:

glass - participant;
cracks - process;
more quickly - circumstance;
the harder - circumstance;
you - participant;
press - process;
on it - circumstance (it = participant)

Just because we have construed this event in this way, it does not mean it is necessarily the only way to construe it. Rather, as Halliday (2005b: 64) notes, "Once given this construal we can re-theorize it at a different level, referring to materials, and structures, and forces, all of which can be accurately measured, and computing the mathematical relations among them." When we re-theorize experience, we re-make the language. What Halliday calls the more congruent statement: "Glass cracks more quickly the harder you press on it", in which we have processes stated as verbs and participant(s) as nouns, may be re-worded in the language of science as: "The rate of glass crack growth depends on the magnitude of stress." Nominalization is the means by which the processes (e.g. *cracks* and *press*) are turned into 'things', that is, into nouns. Halliday calls this 'grammatical metaphor'.

Grammatical metaphor

Grammatical metaphor involves the junction of category meanings, not simply word meanings. Examples of grammatical metaphor include *length*, which is 'a junction of (the quality) "long" and the category meaning of a noun, which is "entity" or "thing"', and *motion*, which is 'a junction of the (the process) "move" and the category meaning, again of a noun'. With grammatical metaphor, the scientist can make the world stand still, or turn it into one consisting only of things, or even create new, virtual realities.

Why does science require nominalization? The answer has to do with the structure of the scientific argument. As Halliday explains, "The core of a scientific text was the development of a chain of reasoning (ultimately based on experiments) in which each step led on to the next. But in order to lead on to the next step you have to be able to repeat what has gone before and is now being used as a springboard for the next move." The grammar 'packages' what has gone before, the preceding step in the experiment, by nominalizing the process (attribute or event), and making the Medium of that Process a 'possessive' modifier. Halliday illustrates with the following example: "The weather is constantly changing; but its changes have a definite pattern." Here the Process – *changing* – is nominalized into a noun – *changes*, and the Medium of that process – *the weather* – becomes the possessive modifier – *its*.

Science needs to turn the world into things; as Halliday explains, "Newtonian science has to hold the world still . . . while dissecting it – if you are trying to understand something, then in the early stages of your inquiry it is helpful if it does not change while you are examining it . . . scientists had to create a universe that was made of things." The scientist possesses an ideology, and as Halliday points out, "If we examine the discourse of science we can become aware of the ideology that is enshrined in the way scientific language construes the world."

All human adults and all human languages possess this ability to shift from the clausal to the nominal construal of experience, but this inherent potential in the grammar, which enables us to de-couple the lexicogrammatical/semantic interface and to re-couple it with a different ordering, is most characteristic of scientific discourse and the need to construct technical taxonomies and sequential argument.

In the following example, the process, *exposed*, becomes a noun, *exposure*, and the process *deteriorate* becomes *deterioration*. The adverbial modifiers of the

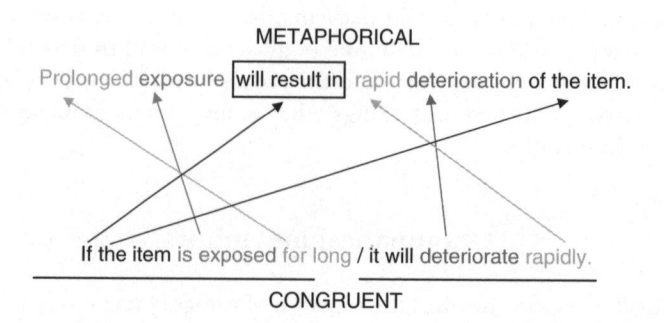

METAPHORICAL

Prolonged exposure will result in rapid deterioration of the item.

If the item is exposed for long / it will deteriorate rapidly.

CONGRUENT

processes become adjectival modifiers. The medium, *the item*, becomes a possessive modifier, *of the item*. Between the two nominalizations is a relational verb, *will result in*, expressing what the clausal relation denoted by the conjunction, *if*, in the congruent statement.

In order to understand better the meaning of whatever discourse we encounter, we need an approach to studying language which will help us understand how meaning materializes in language, and how language works to construe experience and enact social relationships.

Language as a systemic resource

Language, like other semiotic systems, is a systemic resource for making and exchanging meaning. Language is a particular kind of semiotic system which is based on grammar, characterized by both a stratal organization and functional diversity. Both this stratal organization and metafunctional diversity in language combine to form what M.A.K. Halliday refers to as a semiotic of higher-order consciousness, the basis for the human activity of meaning.

Language is the instantiation of an indefinitely large meaning potential through acts of meaning which simultaneously construe experience and enact social relationships. Acts of meaning are the linguistic instances of the linguistic system of meaning potential. Acts of meaning are a subclass of semiotic acts that are semantic.

A semantic system is a system of meaning which is distinguished from other semiotic systems by the fact that it is founded on grammar. It is a system of meaning of a natural language, a system of wordings. The semantic system is one of three levels, or strata, which together comprise the whole linguistic system. Between the semantic system above and the phonological and morphological realization below is the lexicogrammar.

The grammarian comes at the task of describing language from three perspectives, each of which corresponds to a different stratum. Corresponding to the stratum of semantics, the higher level, is the perspective from above, looking at what each category realizes or how it relates to meaning. Second is the stratum of lexicogrammar itself, where the perspective is from roundabout. The third perspective which looks at each category from below deals with the morphological and phonological realization of a given category. In a functional grammar, priority is given to the perspective from above, as form follows function, and the meaning of an expression will decide its phonological and morphological realization.

A semantic system is organized into three main functional components, or "metafunctions". The three components are: ideational, including logical and experiential; interpersonal; and textual. Corresponding to each component is a small number of discrete systemic clusters of systems with strong interconnections within each cluster, but weak associations outside the cluster with the rest of the grammar. The three metafunctions operate in parallel with the other two. A clause is the complex realization of options from these three functional-semantic components: ideational, interpersonal and textual.

Each metafunctional component produces its own distinct dimension of structure, with experiential meaning, i.e. the 'construing experience' function, realized as the structural configuration of process, participant(s), circumstance(s); textual meaning, i.e. the 'creating discourse' function, in terms of theme and information structures; and interpersonal meaning, i.e. the 'enacting social relationships' function, in structural terms closer to the syntactic tradition, i.e. Subject, Predicator, Complement(s), Adjunct(s).

The grammar of a language is thus represented in terms of features defined as terms in systems, with interrelated systems represented in the form of a system network, specifying the total systemic potential in terms of contrasting features and possible paths through the network. Each possible path through the network describes a class of linguistic items. In other words, "class is a statement of potential: if you are a nominal group, you may function either as Subject or Complement within the clause, and you may select for NUMBER: singular/plural" (Halliday 2005b: xvii). The specific role which each element of structure plays is its meaning, and may be stated in terms of a selection expression, or, in other words, "the set of features that delineate its path through the network" (Halliday 2005b: xix).

Clause and text

The point of origin into the system network is the clause. Halliday writes, "It was clear to me already, when I taught my first Chinese class on 13 May 1945, that the clause was the centre of action in the grammar" (2005b: xv). It was "the place, or the locus, where fundamental choices of meaning were made" (Ibid.). The clause as most basic lexicogrammatical unit creates and gives meaning to the text of which it is a constituent. But there is more to this relationship than constituency alone. Not only is the clause a constituent of the text, it is also the actualization of the text, inheriting properties from the text-as-model which is itself realized in relation to the context of situation. Clauses, like other semiotic units, may be said to "obey the Gestalt principle of having overall properties transcending the mere sum of their parts, and functioning in their contexts as integrated wholes" (Garvin 1985: 57). Clauses create text, explains Halliday, because a clause "has itself evolved by analogy with the text as model, and can thus represent the meanings of a text in a rich variety of different ways" (1981a: 44).

The difference between a text and a clause is that a text is a semantic entity, i.e. a construct of meaning, whereas a clause is a lexicogrammatical entity, i.e a construct of wording. A text is an intersubjective event, in which speaker and listener exchange meaning in a context of situation.

Context of situation is specified with respect to field, tenor and mode. The nature of the activity – *field* – is a determinant in the selection of options from experiential systems, including choices related to transitivity structure, or process, participant, circumstance. Role relationships – *tenor* – have a hand in determining the selection of interpersonal options, such as those from the systems of mood and modality. The symbolic organization of the text – *mode* – is involved in the selection of options in *textual* systems, which relate to the overall texture of the text, including choices involving cohesion, and thematic and information structures.

Any text is accessible to objective linguistic analysis through the categories of description for language as a whole, preferably functional and semantic in its orientation, 'with the grammatical categories explained as the realization of semantic patterns' (Halliday 1985a: xvii). In other words, language is treated as a system of meanings which has evolved out of speech encounters in which 'people create meaning by exchanging symbols in shared contexts of situation' (Halliday 1984c, 2002–2007 volume 1: 303). By means of my "text", I participate in an act of interpersonal exchange, communicating my sense of my own identity, my world view, my interpretation of experience. The investigation of the situation focuses on three main dimensions: (a) field — what is happening? (b) tenor — who is involved? (c) mode — how is it taking place? Likewise when analyzing the text/utterance, we pose similar questions: what is happening? who is involved? how is it taking place? Corresponding to each question is a component of meaning or semantic metafunction: ideational, interpersonal and textual. Again, corresponding to each functional component is a kind of structural representation. While the three metafunctions are arguably universal, the structures which realize them are not necessarily so. Systemic-functional grammar (SFG) seeks to identify the language-specific structures that contribute to the meaning of a text. Analysis along the lines proposed by Halliday is intended to show how and why a text means what it does.

Texture is what makes a text into a coherent piece of language, as opposed to simply being an unorganized string of sentences. One aspect of texture is cohesion, which deals with how successive sentences are integrated to form a whole. The other aspect of texture has to do with fit to context, or those choices based on what the speaker wants to say (Theme), and those choices related to the flow of information (Given-New). In both Chinese and English, the speaker is presented with a choice about how to order the elements both at the beginning and at the end of the clause. As a teacher of Chinese trying to teach his students how to start off a Chinese clause, Halliday initially thought that what occurs at the beginning of the clause is the "Given" part of the Given + New configuration. Subsequently, however, Halliday and others working within the systemic-functional framework, most notably Fang Yan (1993, 1995), observed that both English and Chinese make use of the initial position in the clause to identify the Theme, or the point of departure for the clause as message.

The distinction between Given and New information is but one consideration on the part of the speaker when it comes to deciding how best to convey the message in a particular linguistic and situational context. While what occurs at the end of the clause is typically the new and noteworthy information, the choice of what comes first is significant for reasons independent of this distinction between Given and New. The organization of the message to fit the context comprises two aspects: one aspect, what Halliday refers to as the "hearer angle", relates to the organization of the message so that it ties up with the preceding text, with that which the hearer has already heard about, i.e. the Given; the second aspect, the "speaker angle", relates to how the message is organized around what the speaker wants to say, or what Halliday calls "Theme".

Systemic Functional Linguistics provides a handle on language

M.A.K. Halliday's Systemic Functional Theory, with its emphasis on exploring the semogenic ('meaning-making') power of language, provides the handle we need to understand texts as intentional acts of meaning. Unlike the strongly framed vision of language and linguistics which characterizes the dominant paradigm in modern mainstream linguistics, Halliday advocates a broader understanding of language as "a meaning potential", and a theory of language "rather closely analogous to what it is theorizing about." Instead of theorizing about language "as an autonomous intellectual game", the goal should be to describe the grammatical resources available in language for making meaning. Meaning serves as a function of the description.

What's inside *The Continuum Companion to Systemic Functional Linguistics?*

The *Continuum Companion to Systemic Functional Linguistics* brings together some of the leading scholars working in SFL, including its founder, M.A.K. Halliday, to provide readers with a comprehensive introduction to key issues and research areas in SFL today.

Christian M.I.M. Matthiessen explores "Ideas and new directions" emerging in SFL, including

- in relation to "language as knowledge": the continued expansion of cognitive science as a macro-discipline;

- in relation to "language as behaviour" and "language as system": the development of the field of social semiotics, and also of cultural studies;
- in relation to "language as behaviour": the development of large-scale, systematic discourse analysis, and also of translation studies involving discourse analysis;
- in relation to "language as system": the development of the study of complex adaptive systems (providing a new approach to a general systems science), and also the acceleration in the development of the computational modelling of language as system.

Beyond the theory itself, Matthiessen notes how systemic functional metatheory – a theory of what systemic functional theory is like – has already proven to be an important resource for those working in computational modeling and intelligent computing.

In the "Method – techniques – problems", M.A.K. Halliday discusses the "architecture" of language as a system of meaning, "one among a wider class of systems called "semiotic" systems". Not only is SFL a general linguistic theory for "particular, comparative and typological" descriptions of language, it is also a theory which has neutralized the boundary between theoretical and applied linguistics. It is an appliable theory, whose "evolution has tended to be driven by the ongoing experience of its use and by its constant extension to new areas of enquiry and of action." Priority is given to the notion of system, or as Halliday describes it, "a set of features which stand in contrast with each other in a specified environment – of which one will be chosen whenever the environmental conditions obtain." Language occurs in context, and Halliday notes in particular the advances made by Hasan and Martin in extending the notion of system to the contextual stratum.

Claire Painter, in "Language development", explores language development research in terms of three themes: "first, the phases of language development proposed within the theory, secondly, the social dimensions of language development indicated by SFL research and finally the dynamic relation between learning language, learning through language and learning about language, long proposed by Halliday (1980) as three facets to the single process of developing one's mother tongue."

James D. Benson and Paul J. Thibault address the issue of whether language is an exclusively human phenomenon in "Language and other primate species". Following up on Benson's discussion of the implications of the bonobo Kanzi's use of a lexigram keyboard to communicate with humans, Thibault notes that it is not so much a question of whether bonobos and humans share a common code, but rather what is significant is how their repeated interactions, irrespective of the modality used, lead to a convergence of move-types, involving initiating and responding.

Elke Teich, in "Linguistic computing" reports on various tools and techniques for the computer processing of language. Teich also discusses a new and open initiative, the *Initiative for a Repository of SFL Resources* (IRSFL), for creating "an e-science infrastructure for SFL by building up a multilingual text archive, collecting corpora of various languages, registers and genres as well as providing tools for linguistic data processing and working out guidelines for building up SFL-based resources and recommendations for best practices." In the last section of this chapter, Teich refers readers to useful websites related to linguistic computing.

Corpus-based studies of language use in systemic functional linguistics are discussed by Wu Canzhong in "Corpus-based research". Wu also updates readers on various computational tools in corpus linguistics, in particular, a concordance tool called SysConc.

In "Clinical applications" Elizabeth Armstrong deals with developments in the investigation of speech and language disorders, including aphasia and dementia in adults, and developmental problems in children. Such studies of disordered language not only provide some perspective on normal language function, but also may contribute to efforts at improving treatment of such disorders.

James R. Martin, in the chapter on "Discourse studies", credits Halliday's modeling of social context in terms of field, tenor and mode for stimulating subsequent work on register and genre, noting in particular the development of genre analysis within Australian educational linguistics. Martin identifies the strength of SFL work on discourse with "its relatively well developed descriptions of genre and functional grammar, and the adaptability of SFL modeling across modalities (to image, music and action for example)."

In "The place of context in a systemic functional model", Ruqaiya Hasan argues for including context as a theoretical category, particularly if the goal of linguistics is concerned with achieving "a coherent and viable account of 'the architecture of language' as system", and also accounting for the practices of language maintenance and language change. Hasan also illustrates how a paradigmatic description of context is possible, and how contextual options may be shown to be realizationally related to lexicogrammatical choices via semantics.

In "Stylistic analysis: construing aesthetic organisation", David G. Butt and Annabelle Lukin note how Stylistic analysis is defined by its concern for the semantic consequences of linguistic patterns; but it can never be just an analysis of language in a written text or in an individual situation or performance. For this reason, students of linguistics can find the process of stylistic analysis doubly challenging: it soon becomes clear that analysis demands more than the accurate application of linguistic tools. One has to relate the linguistic analysis to such configurations of lived experience, to the 'problems' of the "speech fellowship" living the experience (Firth discussed in Butt 2001: 1809).

In addition to Michael O'Donnell's detailed summary of resources for those working in Systemic Functional Linguistics (SFL), ranging from online information sources to universities where one can pursue further study in SFL, there is also an extensive bibliography of key readings.

Finally, students and scholars of SFL will find an invaluable resource in M.A.K. Halliday's definitions of key terms in SFL, which includes a graphical representation of the relations between key terms.

2
Ideas and new directions

Christian M.I.M. Matthiessen
The Hong Kong Polytechnic University

1 Sources of ideas and new directions

In this chapter, I will be concerned with ideas and new directions in systemic functional linguistics (SFL). I have designed the chapter so that it will complement the discussion of new directions in systemic functional theory in Matthiessen (2007a) and in the description of lexicogrammar in Matthiessen (2007b). Here I will foreground developments that are closely related to applications and potentially fundable research projects, which means that I will pay attention to investigations focussing on particular registers or sets of registers mid-way along the cline of instantiation.

Like language itself, SFL has always been an open dynamic system serving as a **resource** for both **reflection** and **action** (see e.g. Halliday, 1985c). It is a system for reflecting on language and also on other semiotic systems — for analysing texts, for describing and comparing particular semiotic systems, and for theorizing language as a kind of semiotic system and by a further step for theorizing semiotic systems as a system of a particular kind; and it is also a resource for engaging with language in action — for intervening in social and semiotic processes, for developing plans of activity such as educational curricula and syllabi and communication networks in workplaces, for implementing models in working computational systems.

SFL is a **dynamic** system: it keeps changing in step with the environment in which it is operating. In this way, it has been remarkably stable since its beginnings in the 1960s; it has remained stable because it has kept changing. Like language, it is thus a meta-stable system. SFL is also an **open** system: as it changes, new features are added in response to new needs. In this way, the potential of SFL for reflection and action has been expanding since the 1960s; the rate of expansion has sometimes been faster, sometimes slower, but expansion has been a constant property of the development of SFL.

As SFL has expanded in new directions, into new territories, new ideas have thus tended to be added to the total resources that constitute SFL's potential for reflection and action. There have been ongoing movements within the theoretical model of language in context itself, ranging over different strata during the different phases of the development of SFL, as shown in Figure 1 below.[1] The overall effect of these movements has been to expand the domain of operation of SFL as an open dynamic system and to extend the descriptive coverage of the phenomenon under investigation, first language in context and now other semiotic systems in context. This coverage has been extended in the same way that cartographers have extended their coverage of areas around the world over the centuries — by **gradual approximation**, slowly increasing the scale. First they sketch the outlines of an area, and then they gradually fill in the details, thereby changing the scale of the map. This is a **holistic** approach to the development of maps. Of course, as they fill in the details, they may also change the overall outlines, adjusting them as they got access to new data. In the case of SFL, the approach of starting with the outlines of language and gradually filling in the details has been made possible by the **relational** and **dimensional** nature of the "architecture" of the theoretical model of language — the "scales" of scale-&-category theory, the first phase in the development of systemic functional theory (cf. Halliday, 1961). This is illustrated by the work on filling out the details in movements up and down the dimension of stratification, as indicated in Figure 1. Another good illustration is the work by Tucker (e.g. 2007; cf. also 1998) and a number of other systemic functional linguists (e.g. Neale, 2006) on filling in the details in the mid region along the cline of delicacy between the grammatical zone and the lexical one. As Tucker has pointed out, this work has been possible precisely because lexicogrammar is modelled "dimensionally" as a continuum extending from low delicacy (high generality) to high delicacy (low generality).

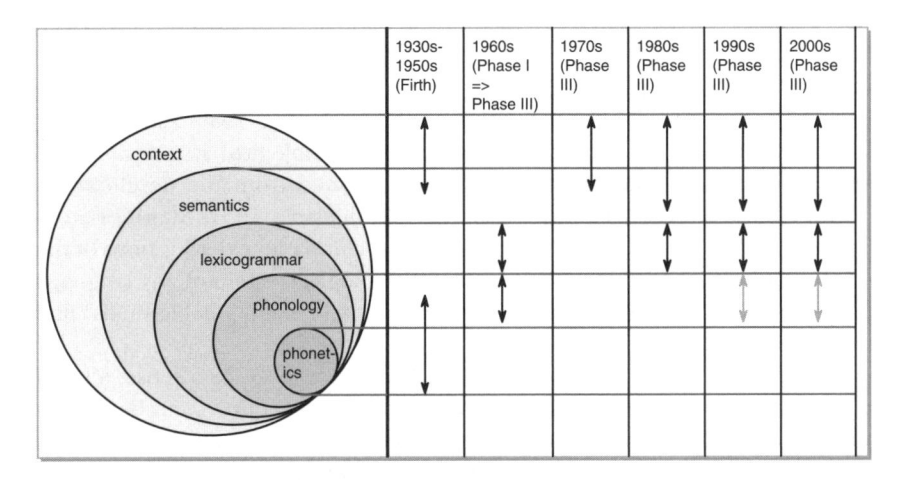

FIGURE 1 Phases in the development of SFL out of Firthian linguistics, represented as expansion of coverage of the strata of language in context

The expansion of the stratal domain of operation of SFL represented in Figure 1 was partly internally driven, partly externally driven. **Internal pressures** came from within systemic functional linguistics and were due to the orientation towards systems thinking and a holistic approach to scientific exploration. High value was placed on comprehensive accounts. **External pressures** came from the environment in which researchers operated with SFL — from considerations of the contexts of research and application. For example, the development of semantics that started in the second half of the 1960s was driven by the social perspective on language and socially oriented research projects (in particular work directed by Basil Bernstein at the Sociological Research Unit), leading to what Hasan et al. (2007: 699) call "pressure on the semantic sciences": "it was in a climate of meeting the needs of research that functional semantics which, up to that stage, had been a neglected field in SFL, received a kick-start". This pressure resulted in early proposals for semantic system networks by Ruqaiya Hasan, M.A.K. Halliday and Geoffrey Turner. Similarly, the growing body of research since the 1990s into the expression planes of semiotic systems other than language — systems operating alongside phonology and phonetics in spoken language, and alongside graphology and graphetics in written language, and the analogous systems in signed language — has been produced in contexts where multimodality is critical (cf. Martinec, 2005), including those of education, media studies, website development and information technology.

The development of the early semantic networks, discussed by Hasan et al. (2007: 702–709), also illustrates another principle in the expansion of the stratal coverage of language in context in SFL: experience gained in modelling and describing one stratal subsystem informs the modelling and description of new stratal subsystems. Thus system networks were originally developed by Halliday in the description of intonation (e.g. Halliday, 1963) and grammar (e.g. Halliday, 1964a, 1966), so it made good heuristic sense to apply them also to the task of mapping out the meaning potential of a language at the semantic stratum. Similarly, when I sketched a description of the phonology of Akan (mainly at the ranks of syllable and phoneme) in the mid 1980s (Matthiessen, 1987b), I based my explicit representation of phonological system networks and realization statements on what we had learned from the development of the computational Nigel grammar (cf. Matthiessen, 1981; Matthiessen & Bateman, 1991), since I hadn't got access to any comparable descriptions of the syllabic and phonemic subsystems of the phonological system of any language (Halliday's, 1992c, pioneering systemic account of "Peking syllable finals" had not yet been written at the time).

We can treat this approach as a purely heuristic strategy. In a sense, a good deal of linguistics in general in the first half of the 20th century can be seen as a heuristic expansion out of phonology. However, we can also reinterpret this approach as one based on a deep principle — the principle that language in context is subject to **fractal patterns**. In other words, certain patterns are manifested in different environments throughout all stratal subsystems of language in context. One such fractal pattern is the axial pattern of system networks with realizations statements specifying structural fragments underlying the stratal organization not only of phonology and lexicogrammar, where they were first explored, but also of semantics and context. In addition, this axial principle of stratal organization has also been used to explore the stratal subsystems of other semiotic systems, as in Kress & van Leeuwen (1996), with informal discursive realization statements, and Matthiessen et al. (1998), with formalized realization statements in a computational system capable of generating multimodal texts (health reports with accompanying maps showing outbreaks of communicable diseases).

The fact that SFL is an open dynamic system also means that ideas and new directions in SFL have originated not only within SFL itself, but also in **metalinguistic contact situations** in the many different environments in which SFL has operated since the 1960s. These are situations where the same or similar phenomena are being explored by scholars using different metalanguages, or theoretical frameworks; for example:

- In studying and modelling supported learning, systemic functional linguists drew on Jerome Bruner's notion of scaffolding, developed within cognitive psychology since the 1950s (see e.g. Unsworth, 1997; Painter, 1999a; Gibbons, 2002; Martin & Rose, 2005; cf. also Halliday, 1993b).
- In investigation the probabilistic nature of language, systemic functional linguists have drawn on information theory, as developed by Claude Shannon and others since the 1940s (e.g. Halliday, 1959, 1991a).
- In modelling systemic functional linguistics as a metalanguage, systemic functional linguists have drawn on Ron Brachman's work on knowledge representation in the 1970s (e.g. Matthiessen & Nesbitt, 1996; Halliday & Matthiessen, 1999; Teich, 1999).

Numerous other examples can be given, including e.g. the sociology of Bernstein (in relation to social structure and "codes", e.g. Hasan, 1989; Halliday, 1995b; in relation to the organization of knowledge, e.g. Christie & Martin, 2007) and the anthropology of Malinowski (in relation to context, e.g. Hasan, 1985a; and in relation to translation, e.g. Steiner, 2005).

Many systemic functional linguists have been bi- or multi-metalingual, combining the systemic functional metalanguage with other metalanguages derived from their background in fields such as education, translation, computer science, and speech pathology. In this way, systemic functional linguistics has been enriched by experts from other fields first undertaking Ph.D. research in systemic functional linguistics and then going on to supervise new areas of research.

2 The study of language: areas of investigation and disciplines

2.1 Frame of reference: 1978

In SFL, ideas and new directions thus emerge in different areas of research on language in exchange with different fields of investigation within a wide range of disciplines. Let's take as our point of reference Halliday's (1978a: 11) disciplinary map of the academic territory around language from about thirty years ago (reproduced here as Figure 2). He commented (pp. 10–11):

> A diagrammatic representation of the nature of linguistic studies and their relation to other fields of scholarship will serve as a point of reference for the subsequent discussion (figure 1 [Figure 2]). The diagram shows the domain of language study — of linguistics, to give it its subject title — by a broken line; everything within that line is an aspect or a branch of linguistic studies.
>
> In the centre is a triangle, shown by a solid line, which marks off what is the central area of language study, that of language as system. One way of saying what is meant by 'central' here is that if a student is taking linguistics as a university subject he will have to cover this area as a compulsory part of his course, whatever other aspects he may choose to take up. There are then certain projections from the triangle, representing special sub-disciplines within this central area: phonetics, historical linguistics and dialectology — the last of these best thought of in broader terms, as the study of language varieties. These sometimes get excluded from the central region, but probably most linguists would agree in placing them within it; if one could give a three-dimensional representation they would not look like excrescences.
>
> Then, outside this triangle, are the principal perspectives on language that take us beyond a consideration solely of language as system, and, in so doing, impinge on other disciplines. Any study of language involves some attention to other disciplines; one cannot draw a boundary round the subject and insulate it from others. The question is whether the aims go beyond the elucidation of language itself; and once one goes outside the central area, one is inquiring not only into language but into language in relation to something else. The diagram summarizes these wider fields under the three headings, 'language as knowledge', 'language as behaviour', 'language as art'.
>
> The last of these takes us into the realm of literature, which is all too often treated as if it was something insulated from and even opposed to language: 'we concentrate mainly on literature here — we don't do much on language', as if 'concentrating on literature' made it possible to ignore the fact that literature is made of language. Similarly the undergraduate is invited to 'choose between lang. and lit.'. In fact the distinction that is being implied is a

perfectly meaningful one between two different emphases or orientations, one in which the centre of attention is the linguistic system and the other having a focus elsewhere; but it is wrongly named, and therefore, perhaps, liable to misinterpretation. One can hardly take literature seriously without taking language seriously; but language is being looked at from a special point of view.

The two other headings derive from the distinction we have just been drawing between the intra-organism perspective, language as knowledge, and the inter-organism perspective, language as behaviour. These both lead us outward from language as system, the former into the region of psychological studies, the latter into sociology and related fields. So in putting language

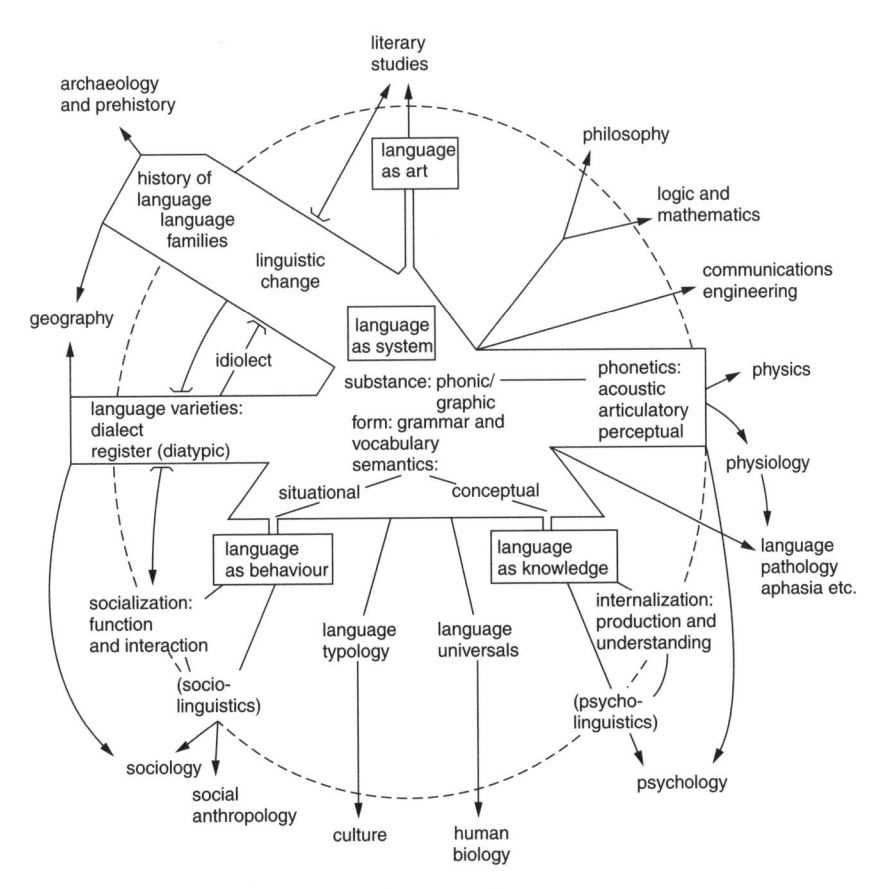

FIGURE 2 Linguistic studies in relation to other fields of scholarship around thirty years ago (Halliday, 1978a: 11)

into the context of 'language and social man', we are taking up one of the options that are open for relating language study to other fields of inquiry. This, broadly, is the sociolinguistic option; and the new subject of sociolinguistics that has come into prominence lately is a recognition of the fact that language and society — or, as we prefer to think of it, language and social man — is a unified conception, and needs to be understood and investigated as a whole. Neither of these exists without the other: there can be no social man without language, and no language without social man. To recognize this is no mere academic exercise; the whole theory and practice of education depends on it, and it is no exaggeration to suggest that much of our failure in recent years — the failure of the schools to come to grips with social pollution — can be traced to a lack of insight into the nature of the relationships between language and society: specifically of the processes, which are very largely linguistic processes, whereby a human organism turns into a social being.

2.2 New directions since 1978

The map of the academic territory around language in Figure 2 is still largely representative of today's academic landscape of engagement with different manifestations of language — as system, as behaviour, as knowledge, and as art. However, to take account of a number of new developments that have been consequential for SFL and its working environment, we can try to update the map by reviewing activities undertaken in relation to the different manifestations of language:

- in relational to "language as knowledge": the continued expansion of cognitive science as a macro-discipline;
- in relation to "language as behaviour" and "language as system": the development of the field of social semiotics, and also of cultural studies;
- in relation to "language as behaviour": the development of large-scale, systematic discourse analysis, and also of translation studies involving discourse analysis;
- in relation to "language as system": the development of the study of complex adaptive systems (providing a new approach to a general systems science), and also the acceleration in the development of the computational modelling of language as system;

2.2.1 *In relation to "language as knowledge"*

In relation to "language as knowledge", the most significant disciplinary formation is **cognitive science**, a macro-discipline (that is, a discipline consisting of component parts of other disciplines) emerging out of developments originating in the 1950s. Since the 1970s, it has continued to expand (e.g. Hirst, 1988; Posner, 1989; Baumgartner & Payr, 1995), with a growing number of research centres, journals and publications being devoted to it.

While systemic functional linguists in general have not worked with **mainstream** cognitive science, computational systemic functional linguists (see e.g. O'Donnell & Bateman, 2005; and *Computational linguistics* in this volume) have usually carried out their computational modelling of language in an environment where many researchers are oriented towards cognitive science. Consequently, a number of contributions to computational SFL have taken this environment into account (e.g. Matthiessen, 1987a; and, with an explicitly cognitive orientation, Fawcett, 1980, and the "Cardiff Grammar" work building on this foundation).

As an alternative to the conception of knowledge in mainstream cognitive science, systemic functional linguists have offered a language-based approach, developing an account of how experience is construed as meaning in the semantic system of a language (see Halliday & Martin, 1993; Martin & Veel, 1998; Halliday & Matthiessen, 1999; Kappagoda, 2005; Christie & Martin, 2007) and related this semiotic perspective (cf. Hasan, 1992c) to the new insights into language and the brain coming from advances in **neuroscience**, especially the work (inspired) by Gerald Edelman, Terrence Deacon and Michael Arbib (see e.g. Halliday, 1995a, 1995c; Thibault, 2000; Williams, 2005a, and contributions to the special issue of *Linguistics and the Human Sciences* edited by Williams). This systemic functional alternative to mainstream cognitive science is a direction for further development that resonates with non-mainstream cognitive science exploring conceptions of the "embodied mind" (e.g. Varela, Thompson & Rosch, 1991), of intersubjectivity (e.g. Trevarthen, 1979, 1987), of interaction (e.g. Lantolf & Thorne, 2006). The orientation is towards Vygotsky rather than towards cognitive science, and the potential for new developments in this area of dialogue has been explored by scholars relating to Halliday and Vygotsky brought together by Byrnes (2006).

2.2.2 In relation to "language as behaviour" and "language as system": social semiotics, cultural studies

In relation to "language as behaviour" and "language as system", Halliday's (e.g. 1978a) interpretation of language as **social semiotic** has had a profound effect on the academic landscape — including the growth of social semiotics as a thematic field of activity in its own right (cf. Kress & Hodge, 1988) and the launch of the journal *Social Semiotics* in the early 1990s. In Halliday's conception of language as a social semiotic system, language is seen as both system and behaviour (cf. Halliday, 1984a), and this perspective complements that of cognitive science, providing an account of the social construction of meaning. Social semiotics has fed into the development of "cultural studies", and, in its systemic functional interpretation, has also informed the development of clinical linguistics (see Armstrong, this volume) and of multisemiotic studies (see Thibault, this volume), discourse analysis (see Martin, this volume), and the continued development of educational linguistics.

In the 1980s, **cultural studies** emerged as a new disciplinary area relating also to "language as art" (in English-speaking countries, sometimes combined with English but sometimes replacing, or splitting off from, traditional English literature; cf. Christie & Macken-Horarik, 2007: 164–5), providing new opportunities for the analysis of texts that are highly valued by segments of the community other than the cultural elite (for SFL studies contributing to this area, see e.g. Cranny-Francis & Martin, 1994, on popular films, and Veloso, 2006, on comics). See further below on "artistic linguistics".

2.2.3 In relation to "language as behaviour": discourse analysis, translation studies

Language as "behaviour" (cf. Halliday, 1984a) takes the form of spoken, written or signed text, or discourse, and the analysis of text was central to the systemic functional research agenda from the start (see e.g. Halliday, 1964a; Hasan, 1964). As an area of investigation, **discourse analysis** really took off in the 1980s, partly as an area within linguistics (where it has also been explored under the heading of "text linguistics", particularly in work undertaken in continental Europe) and partly as an activity at the interfaces of different disciplines (cf. van Dijk, 1985, 1997; Titscher et al., 2000; Schiffrin, Tannen & Hamilton, 2001). Discourse analysis relates to both social semiotics and cultural studies, and it relates to developments in SFL — including the "Birmingham School" of discourse analysis (e.g. Coulthard, 1994; Coulthard & Montgomery, 2001) — but also to other currents; for overviews of systemic functional approaches to discourse analysis, see e.g. Martin's chapter on *Discourse studies* in this volume and Cloran, Stuart-Smith & Young (2007).

One orientation within the broad area of discourse analysis is **Critical Discourse Analysis** (CDA; see e.g. van Dijk, 2001, for an overview of the origins of CDA and the different strands it is made up of; see also e.g. Caldas-Coulthard & Coulthard, 1996), which was influenced partly by the pioneering work in Australia and the UK in the 1970s concerned with language and power and drawing on SFL (e.g. Fowler et al., 1979; Kress & Hodge, 1979). CDA and SFL thus overlap, and continue to develop in "dialogue" with one another (see e.g. Martin & Wodak, 2003; Young & Harrison, 2004).

Within SFL, one important contribution complementing CDA has been Martin's (e.g. 2002, 2004) programme of **Positive Discourse Analysis** (PDA), which is concerned with language and solidarity (rather than with language and power), with an emphasis of positive models for constructive socio-semiotic change such as the voices of reconciliation in South Africa.

The purposes of both CDA and PDA can be characterized in relation to the tenor variable of power (status) within context — in relation to difference in power and in relation to solidarity, respectively. However, there are of course many other purposes for undertaking discourse analysis, and we might develop an approach of appliable discourse analysis designed to be employable in a wide range of institutional settings where problems arise that can be explored through discourse analysis. Such an approach might be called **Strategic Discourse Analysis** (SDA, although this acronym also stands for "soap and detergent association", "small dead animals", and many other unrelated notions!). For example, SDA would include the methods for sampling discourse in an institution in order to shed light on problems in the operation of the institution relating to the flow of meaning through its semiotic networks ("communication networks"), the techniques for analysing the sample of discourse (including computational tools; cf. the chapters by Teich and Wu, this volume), strategies for developing interpretations based on the analysis e.g. through visualization (cf. Matthiessen, 2002a), and approaches to the development of solutions based in the analytical and interpretative findings (e.g. training materials, computer programmes).

Thus SDA should support the application of discourse analysis to **translation and interpreting**, and discourse analysis has increasingly been applied to tasks associated with this area — the training of translators and interpreters, the investigation of translation and interpreting and other activities relating to the analysis of both original and translated texts. Here discourse analysis has been based on various functional traditions (cf. Munday, 2001: Ch. 6), including Nord's (e.g. 2005) functional approach, Hatim & Mason's (e.g. 1990) functional approach, which draws of SFL. After a long period of a fairly low level of systemic functional activity (going back to the 1960s), this is now emerging as an important area of increasing activity. I will return to it below in Section 3.5.1.

In addition to these variants of discourse analysis relating to the purpose for carrying out the analysis, we can also recognize a range of different methodologies. The most important distinction is between manual analysis and automated analysis: I will return to this distinction below in Section 4.1. However, it is important to note here the development of **corpus linguistics** as a growing field of investigation — going back to the 1950s (with precursors in the 1940s, as in C.C. Fries's sampling of everyday discourse for his accounts of English) but taking off in the 1980s thanks to computational developments. Corpus linguistics is a set of methods for assembling and analysing large samples of text, complementing manual discourse analysis, but it has also been treated as a separate branch of linguistics, and the contributions in Hunston & Thompson (2006) explore the connections between corpus linguistics and SFL (see also Wu's chapter, *Corpus-based research*, this volume). In the late 1980s, there was a parallel development in natural language processing (NLP; also computational linguistics), which has often been referred to as **statistical NLP** (see Manning & Schütze, 1999). Here more powerful and sophisticated computational techniques than those traditionally used in corpus linguistics have been applied to large corpora to address a range of research problems in NLP. This now led to a reconceptualization of the linguistic system itself as inherently probabilistic (recalling Halliday's, 1959, insights into the nature of language that have informed SFL from the start, but with a syntagmatic rather than paradigmatic orientation): see Bod, Hay & Jannedy (2003).

2.2.4 In relation to "language as system"

In relation to "language as system", there have been important developments since the 1970s, helping create an environment conducive to dialogue with SFL. These developments include the study of complex adaptive systems, the computational engagement with language, and language typology:

- The boost to general system theory (which goes back to the 1940s) through the emergence of the study of **complex adaptive systems** as a meta-discipline — that is, a discipline based on the identification of complexity as a theme relevant to a wide range of systems of different kinds (see e.g. Gell-Mann, 1994, 1995, who suggests the term "plectics" for this "transdisciplinary subject"), resonating with systemic holistic thinking in systemic theory (going back to Malinowski's contextualism), as shown in the work by Chris Cléirigh (e.g. 1998); see also Thibault (e.g. 2004b).
- The continued expansion of both the hard and the soft sides of **computer science**, the development of **information technology** and the continued expansion of **computational linguistics** (natural language processing, language technology), including systemic functional computational linguistics with modelling of text generation, parsing and text analysis, and translation, and of **linguistic computing** involving the development of tools and techniques aiding linguists in text analysis (for a recent overview, see O'Donnell & Bateman, 2005, and Teich, *Linguistic computing* in this volume).
- The coming of age of empirical **language typology** based on large-scale comparison of categories of linguistic systems, usually taken to have started with Joseph Greenberg's seminal work in the 1960s (but also relatable to the Prague School approach to typology from the 1920s and 1930s, in particular Trubetzkoy's work in the area of phonology), with the four volumes on *universals of human language* representing research at Stanford University as a landmark in the late 1970s and the subsequent explosion of research, resource development and publications in this area — a recent landmark being Haspelmath et al. (2005). Against the background of empirical typological work in this tradition, systemic functional work on comparison and typology has gained momentum over the last decade or decade and a half

(see Caffarel, Martin & Matthiessen, 2004; Teruya et al., 2007) as part of multilingual studies. One important aspect of this is the systemic functional conceptualisation of grammaticalization (cf. Matthiessen, 1995b: 49-50): see Halliday (2008).

2.2.5 Multilingual studies

The field of **multilingual studies** has been proposed within SFL (see Matthiessen, Teruya & Wu, 2008) as an attempt to bring together multilingual concerns that have tended to be developed by distinct communities of scholars since the 1960s (in spite of the unifying efforts within SFL by Catford, 1965, and Ellis, 1966). It includes **description**, **comparison** and **typology** (e.g. Caffarel, Martin & Matthiessen, 2004; Teruya et al., 2007; and see Teruya, *Cross-language survey* in this volume), **translation studies** (e.g. Steiner & Yallop, 2001; Steiner, 2005a) and **second language education** (e.g. Byrnes, 2006, in press; Schleppegrell & Colombi, 2002; Teruya, in press).

These fields have tended to be insulated from one another for various reasons, including the focus on "language as system" (description, comparison and typology), the focus on "language as behaviour" (translation studies), and the focus (in "mainstream" work) on "language as knowledge" (second language education). However, the conditions now seem right for promoting collaboration among these different multilingual strands.

2.3 Language as a higher-order semiotic system

In relation to the map of manifestations of language and different disciplines engaging with these set out in Figure 2, one important development in SFL has been the ordered typology of systems operating in different phenomenal realms proposed by Halliday, and elaborated by Halliday and by myself (e.g. Halliday & Matthiessen, 1999: Ch. 13; Halliday, 1995a, 2005a; Matthiessen, 2007a: 545–547).

These systems are, in order of increasing complexity: (i) **material** systems: (1) **physical** systems, (2) **biological** systems; (ii) **immaterial** systems: (3) **social** systems, (4) **semiotic** systems. They are ordered in complexity in a number of respects, one key respect being that higher-order systems are also manifested as lower-order ones: biological systems are also physical systems, with the added property of "life" (ability to self-replicate, with individuation and with evolution as the mode of genesis); social systems are also biological (so also physical), with the added property of "value" (social order: networks of roles, division of labour, and so on); and semiotic systems are also social (so also biological, and also physical), with the added property of "meaning" (stratification into content and expression). Language is interpreted as a higher-order semiotic system — one which is not only stratified into content and expression but which is also further stratified within content into semantics and lexicogrammar and within expression into phonology and phonetics, and also organized metafunctionally into a spectrum of simultaneous modes of meaning.

This ordered typology of systems is important for new directions of research because it makes it possible for us to view language in the light of other systems as part of general systems thinking (cf. above) and to reason about the complementary contributions made by representatives coming from disciplines focussed on systems of different orders in solving problems that arise in the contexts of research and application. For example, in exploring medical risk jeopardizing patient safety in emergency departments of large hospitals, we have been able to differentiate different kinds of risk based on the ordered typology of systems, focussing on semiotic medical risk (see Slade et al., 2008). The typology also makes it possible to investigate and model correlations across systems of different orders more systematically, as when a context of situation unfolds through phases that alternate between semiotic processes and purely social processes or through phases that involve both (see Hasan, *The place of context in a systemic functional model,* this volume). Thus Steiner (1991) has already demonstrated recurrent patterns in the organization of semiotic action and social action.

3 The study of language: areas of investigation and registers

Complementing the update given above of areas of investigation in relation to the disciplinary map in Figure 2, we can also explore new developments in different areas of investigation in terms of what aspects of language and other semiotic systems they have been concerned with. This can take the form of a mapping from areas of ***study*** of the phenomenon of language, or of semiotic systems in general, to the phenomenon itself. The point of this is to get a clearer picture of what aspects of language are studied in particular areas of investigation so that it becomes possible to characterize and then also to assess coverage of linguistic (and more generally, semiotic) phenomena in different areas of investigation. Such a picture would allow us to identify gaps, each gap representing a potential opportunity for new developments.

3.1 Ways of characterizing the focus of different areas of investigation

To produce such a picture, we could use any of the dimensions of organization embodied in language (or those embodied in any other semiotic system). If we focus on global dimensions of organization (as opposed to local ones organizing any of the stratal subsystems), we can explore and determine the phenomenal focus of areas of investigation in terms of the global dimensions of the

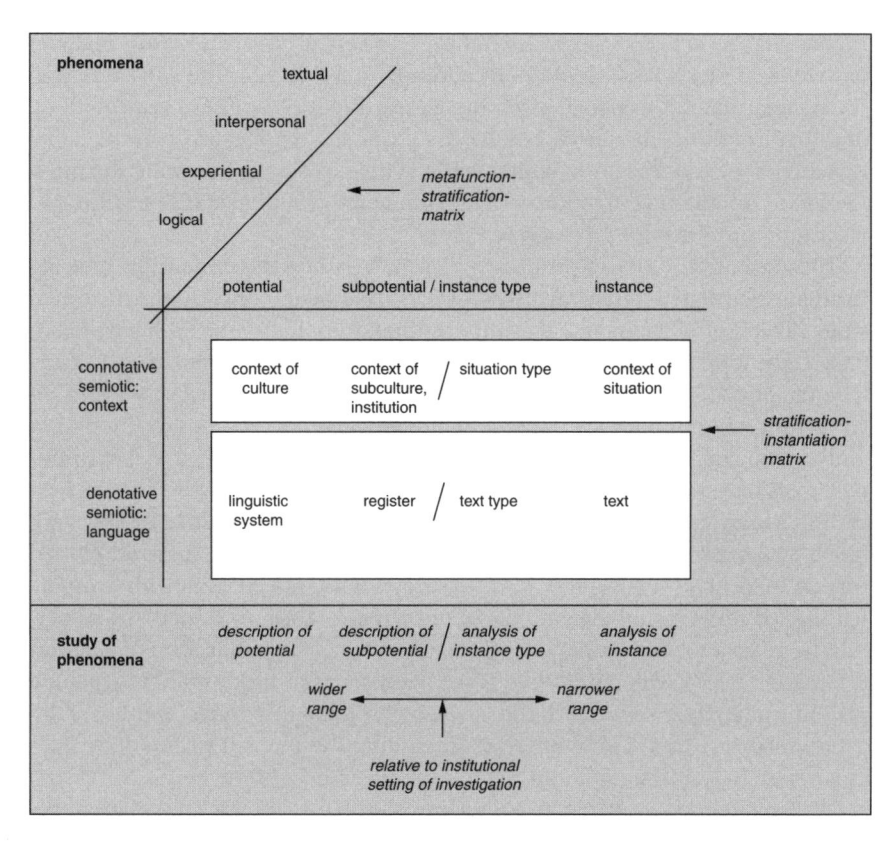

FIGURE 3 Determining the focus of the study of phenomena according to the dimensions of the organization of the phenomena

organization of language in context: (i) the spectrum of metafunction, (ii) the hierarchy of stratification, and/or (iii) the cline of instantiation: see Figure 3.

(i) Thus, we can explore and determine the phenomenal focus of areas of investigation in terms of **metafunction**, asking where the different metafunctions have been given particular attention. This would show, for example, that systemic functional translation studies have so far been more concerned with the textual metafunction than with the other metafunctions, focussing in particular on translation shifts involving the choice of theme, but that systemic functional media studies have concentrated more on the interpersonal metafunction, illuminating the significance of choices within the system of appraisal in relation to different "media voices" (cf. Martin & White, 2005: 164-184). It would also reveal imbalances of attention given to systems within a particular metafunction. For example, within the textual metafunction, THEME and COHESION have been given a great deal of attention in discourse analysis, but

INFORMATION (in the sense of the contrast between given and new information) has received much less attention. In addition, it would show how the interpersonal metafunction has been given increasing attention over the last couple of decades, resulting in new accounts, in particular of English interpersonal resources (see e.g. Martin & White, 2005). Thus a picture of showing the intersection of areas of investigation with metafunction would certainly be helpful in indicating opportunities for new research.

(ii) Alternatively, we can produce a picture based on the dimension of **stratification**, asking what areas of investigation have been concerned with which strata. This would again reveal an interestingly varied picture, with significant gaps, indicating areas where future work is needed. For example, studies of any type of spoken discourse have largely focussed on the content plane and on context, leaving phonology in general and the prosodic systems of intonation and rhythm in particular off the research agenda. However, the descriptive resources have long been in place to undertake prosodic analysis (see Greaves, 2007), going back to the work in the 1960s by Halliday (1967, 1970a) and, based on his work, by Elmenoufy (1969), and this tradition has been developed further by Tench (1990, 1996). Various studies have indeed dealt with prosodic features of spoken language as part of discourse analysis, and such efforts may now be given a boost for two general reasons. One is the publication of Halliday & Greaves (2008), which will serve as the key resource for new efforts to include prosodic analysis as a strand in the analysis of spoken discourse. Another is the growing body of multi-semiotic work, including the interest in "semiotic margins"; hopefully, intonation and rhythm can also find a home here.

(iii) Finally, another alternative is to base our picture on the cline of **instantiation**, asking what areas of investigation of have concerned with which "phases" of instantiation[2]. This would help us determine in what areas investigators tend to be system observers, instance observers, or some combination of both. Basing the picture on the cline of instantiation is helpful in sorting out "multilingual studies" as a diverse yet coherent area of investigation (see Matthiessen, Teruya & Wu, 2008). This is close to what Ellis (1966) called "a general comparative linguistics" many years ago (cf. also Ellis, 1987), and it includes typological and comparative linguistics, contrastive analysis, translation and interpreting studies, studies of language contact and of multilingualism (with bilingualism as a special case) in community and individual, language contact, language planning, and second/ foreign language education. For example, translation and interpreting studies have tended to focus on the instance pole of the cline of instantiation, whereas typological and comparative studies have generally focussed on the potential pole of the cline.

Putting together the hierarchy of stratification and the cline of instantiation, we can construct an instantiation-stratification matrix (cf. Halliday, 1995a) to characterize different areas of **specialization** of linguists and the **activities** they undertake in these areas (cf. Halliday, 2008: 188): see Table 1.

Table 1 Linguist's (semiotician's) specialization and activities in relation to stratification and instantiation

			specialization:	potential	subpotential/ instance type	instance
context			*contextologist [semanticist]*	cultural description	subcultural description/institutional analysis	situational analysis
language	content	semantics	*semanticist (text linguist)*	semantic description	register description/text type analysis	text (discourse) [including corpus] analysis
		lexicogrammar	*grammarian, lexicographer*	lexico-grammatical description		
	expression	phonology	*phonologist*	phonological description		intonation & rhythm analysis
		phonetics	*phonetician*	phonetic description		speech analysis
			activity:	*describe*	*describe / analyse*	*analyse*

Specialization tends to be determined by stratum: semantics — semanticist, text linguist; lexicogrammar — grammarian (syntactician and morphologist), lexicographer; phonology — phonologist; and phonetics — phonetician. Within lexicogrammar, there tends to be further differentiation in terms of delicacy (grammarian, lexicographer) and rank (syntactician, morphologist); but these distinctions are a feature more of theories that do not operate with a unified system of lexicogrammar, and systemic functional lexicogrammarians shunt along both the rank scale and the cline of delicacy (e.g. Tucker, 1998; Neale, 2006). Context is more problematic in terms of specialization; it is of course a domain explored from different vantage points by anthropologists, sociologists, social psychologists and also by AI researchers and philosophers, but in SFL, researchers working on context have naturally tended to be those who are concerned with semantics (as in the work on context by Hasan and by Butt, and by Martin), but in anticipation of an expansion of the field of description of context, we can imagine that this will be the task of contextologists.

Activity tends to be determined by instantiation: researchers **describe** systems of a language in its context of culture (at the potential pole of the cline of instantiation) and they **analyse** texts in their contexts of situation (at the instance pole of the cline). Thus we have descriptive linguists developing descriptions of (parts of) different languages (see e.g. Caffarel, Martin & Matthiessen, 2004), and discourse analysts analysing (sets of) texts (see e.g. Martin & Rose, 2003; Eggins & Slade, 1997; Stillar, 1998). Researchers concerned with the mid region between potential and instance may adopt either a system-based approach involving description of registerial subsystems (as in descriptions of register-specific semantic systems, e.g. Halliday, 1973a; Patten, 1988) or a text-based approach involving analysis of texts leading to generalizations about text type (as in e.g. Ghadessy, 1993b).

Specialists in all stratal areas can in principle undertake activities relating to all regions of the cline of instantiation. However, in practice, certain specialists tend to focus on some regions but not on others. For example, phonologists have not on the whole worked on phonology for the purpose of characterizing a register or text type, nor based their accounts on frequency in text[3], but there are certain important exceptions that show that at least higher-ranking phonology ("prosodic": intonation and rhythm) can be illuminated through a registerial focus: see e.g. Bowcher (2001) on intonation in sports commentary, Martinec (1995) on rhythm in news broadcasts, van Leeuwen (1985) on intonation in radio commercials, and Smith (2008) on intonation and register in general (including an overview of work on particular registers). And "corpus linguists" have tended to define their area of work in terms of what is currently possible to extract from large corpora with the kinds of computational tools used in corpus linguistics. This has meant that they have tended to work on lexis in lexicogrammar and on the region intermediate between lexis and grammar rather than on grammar or on semantics, or on phonology, for that matter (for discussion and possible new directions, see Hunston & Thompson, 2006). In general, new directions in research are likely to emerge as "stratal specialists" increasingly engage in description and analysis along all the phases of the cline of instantiation.

3.2 Different fields of investigation in relation to register

Here I will try to sketch a picture showing what different areas of investigation involving some type of text analysis have been concerned with in terms of the region of registerial variation along the cline of instantiation, as shown in Figure 3 above. In other words, we are exploring the mapping between fields of investigation in the study of language and the range of registers within language, as shown in Figure 4.

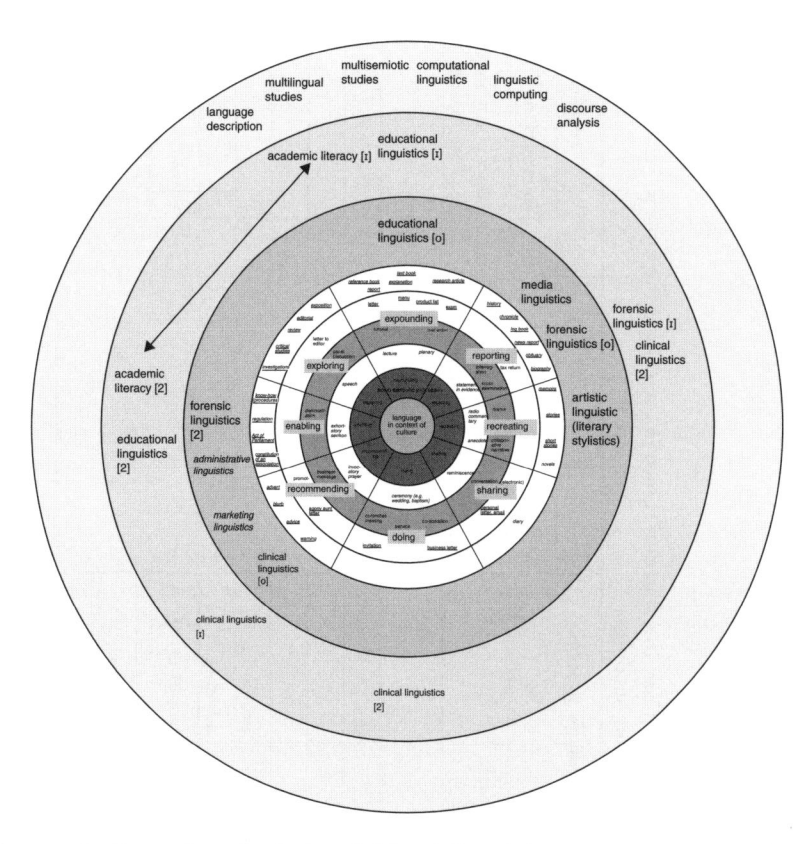

FIGURE 4 Examples of relating fields of linguistics investigation to different registers differentiated according to the contextual parameters of field and mode (see Matthiessen, Teruya & Wu, in prep., for this context-based register typology/ topological, adapted from a tabular display of context-based register typology designed by Jean Ure)

Table 2 Fields of linguistic investigation shown in the cells of the table in relation to socio-semiotic process (row headings) and register focus (column headings)

field: socio-semiotic process		wide	register focus intermediate	narrow
expounding		language description, multilingual studies, multisemiotic studies, computational linguistics, linguistic computing, discourse analysis	educational linguistics [1] *academic literacy*	educational linguistics [0] *epistemological linguistics*
reporting				media linguistics forensic linguistics
recreating				artistic linguistics (literary stylistics)
sharing				
doing				
recommending	promoting			*marketing linguistics*
	advising			clinical linguistics [0]
enabling	empowering		educational linguistics [2] *academic literacy*	
	regulating			organizational linguistics
exploring			*academic literacy*	*ethical linguistics*

The diagram represents a cline from fields of activity within linguistics that have a fairly narrow registerial focus to those linguistic fields that in principle engage with registers of any kind; this sorting of fields of activity is also set out in Table 2.

The typology of registers is based on aspects of field and mode within context; to complete the contextual typology, we would need to add tenor as well, transforming the circles at the centre of Figure 4 into a sphere. (Field is represented here by activity or "socio-semiotic process" rather than by experiential domain or "subject matter"; for a recent investigation of field, see also Hasan, 1999b.)

(i) **Mode**. The four inner concentric circles of the diagram represent different mode values — from inner to outer: **spoken monologic, spoken dialogic, written dialogic**, and **written monologic**. (These are clearly prototypes; there are various further possible elaborations of the kind identified by Gregory, 1967, and technologically enabled new possibilities that have appeared since then with advances in the development of new channels (cf. Martin, 1992a).)

(ii) **Field**. The sectors dividing the four inner circles represent different socio-semiotic processes within field. The socio-semiotic processes are (clockwise, starting at the top): expounding, reporting, recreating, sharing, doing, recommending, enabling, and exploring. They can be characterized briefly as follows:

- **first-order (social)**
  - **doing:** undertaking some course of action, facilitated by — but typically not constituted in — language ["language in action"].
- **second-order (semiotic [so also social]):**
  - **expounding** some general domain of experience by describing it, classifying (taxonomizing) it, explaining it and so on.
  - **reporting** some particular experiences, chronicling a flow of particular events, or surveying some particular region of space.
  - **recreating** some particular experiences — often imaginary, including the recreation of other socio-semiotic processes (sharing, doing, recommending, and so on).
  - **sharing** typically personal values and experiences as a way of "calibrating" interpersonal relationships.
  - **recommending** some course of action, either promoting it (either benefiting the speaker [demanding]) or advising the addressee to undertake the course of action [giving]).
  - **enabling** some course of action, either empowering the addressee or regulating him/her.
  - **exploring** typically public values or hypotheses, often comparing alternative ones and arguing in favour of one.

Drawing on Halliday's (1978a) distinction between first order and second order features of context, we have differentiated between the first-order social process of 'doing', where language is ancillary ("language in action"), and the second-order semiotic processes of 'expounding', 'reporting', 'recreating', 'sharing', 'recommending', 'enabling' and 'exploring', where language is constitutive.

Short texts can usually be located within a single region of the text topology in Figure 4, but extended **macro-texts** such as conversations in the course of a coffee break at a work place or a meal shared by family or friends (cf. Eggins & Slade, 1997), news papers and text books, can be analysed as rhetorical complexes formed out of rhetorical relations as modelled in Rhetorical Structure Theory (see e.g. Mann, Matthiessen & Thompson, 1992); compare the work on macro-genres by Martin (e.g. 1994) and other scholars building on his work (e.g. Christie, 1997). For example, the discursive nucleus of a quality newspaper lies in the written reporting region (news reports of different kinds, media interviews), but there are supporting discursive satellites in other sectors — exploring (editorials, letters to the editor, reviews), enabling (e.g. recipes), recommending (promotion: advertisements; advising: advice columns such as agony aunt letters), and recreating (e.g. cartoons).

The three outer concentric circles in Figure 4 represent the registerial location of different "hyphenated" fields of investigation within, or on the borders of, linguistics — combinations of some institutional domain with "linguistics" (e.g. "forensic linguistics"), "discourse" (e.g. "professional discourse"), "literacy" (e.g. "academic literacy"), "communication" (e.g. "health communication"), "studies" (e.g. "multimodal studies") or "science" (e.g. "cognitive science"). As already noted, these three circles represent a cline of register-specificity (cf. Table 2 above), ranging from fields of investigation being focussed on one particular sector in Figure 4 to fields of investigation ranging across all registers (at least in principle).

I will now comment on new developments in relation to the fields of activity within these three circles, starting with the one representing most register-specific activities. In terms of the cline of instantiation, we will thus move from particular (field-based) families of registers towards the potential pole of the line.

3.3 The first circle of investigation: narrow register focus

The first outer circle represents those fields that have tended to focus on registers within particular sectors of Figure 4 — that is, fields of investigation with a narrow register focus. These include both well-established sub-disciplines and potential sub-disciplines that may emerge as areas of concentrated and co-ordinated work in the near future:

- **Artistic linguistics** — focus on 'recreating' texts
- **Media linguistics** — focus on 'reporting' texts

- **Organizational linguistics** — focus on 'enabling' texts
- **Marketing linguistics** — focus on 'recommending: promotional' texts

(Some of the fields of investigation in clinical, educational and forensic linguistics include a narrow register focus; however, they also range over other registers, so they will be discussed in Section 3.4 below.)

3.3.1 Artistic linguistics

Artistic linguistics is the study of verbal art — of language as art. It is concerned with the 'recreating' sector of the diagram in Figure 4 (the 'recreating' row in Table 2) in the first instance, although poetry is a special case. Since poetry can be characterized "from below" in terms of patterns on the expression plane of language, it is not tied to any one sector. There are different types of poetry: narrative and epic poetry belong to the recreating sector, as do ballads and verse dramas; but lyric poetry, elegies and hymns belong to the 'sharing' sector, oral history (typically in preliterate societies) belong to the 'reporting' sector, and chants, spells and incantations belong to the 'doing' sector (language as magic). The same applies to song.

In the 'recreating' sector, field-based chronology is usually the central principle for organizing texts, but this narrative principle is also used in other sectors — chiefly in the 'reporting' sector, so 'recreating' shades into 'reporting' (as in the now popular cross-over between biography and fiction in works where the lives of typically well-known people are recreated), and narrative is manifested in both the 'recreating' and the 'reporting' sector (cf. Toolan, 2001).

"Artistic linguistics" is of course not a term generally used in English as the label for the linguistic study of verbal art (though there is an equivalent in Chinese, which is translated as "artistic linguistics"). However, it would be a useful term since the term that is often used, "stylistics", can also be seen as representing a methodology that is not restricted to verbal art.

Stylistics has been characterized as the study of "the study of varieties of language whose properties position that language in context" (Wikipedia entry), and has been on the systemic functional research agenda from the early days (see e.g. Hasan, 1964). It is in principle applicable to texts within registers of any kind in any location on the map in Figure 4 and could thus be seen as a branch of discourse analysis offering theory and techniques applicable to any text for revealing movements in meaning as a text unfolds (see e.g. Butt, 1983), for bringing out additional layering of meaning (see e.g. Halliday, 1971, 1982), and for exploring higher-level motifs, or "symbolic articulation" (see e.g. Hasan, 1985b). However, in practice, stylistics has tended to be concerned with the study of verbal art (see Hasan, 1985b): literary texts (see Butt & Lukin, *Literary Stylistics* in this volume) or highly valued texts not normally considered literature[4] — but most typically with high-valued ones of the "high culture"

Table 3 The expanding domain of artistic SFL

	elite	popular
verbal art	Hasan (1985b), Lukin & Webster (2005), Butt & Lukin (*Literary Stylistics*), Birch & O'Toole (1988), Thibault (1991); Miller & Turci (2007)	Hasan (1984b), Thoma (2006)
multisemiotic art	O'Toole (1994)	Steiner (1988); Cranny-Francis & Martin (1991, 1994); Unsworth (2006); Veloso (2006)

variety of literature (see e.g. Lukin & Webster, 2005; Birch & O'Toole, 1988; Thibault, 1991; Toolan, 1998; Prakasam, 1999). In view of this focus, we might also call this area of investigation "aesthetic linguistics", relating it to Mukarovsky's seminal work within the Prague School on the aesthetic use of language in verbal art.[5]

One important development in artistic linguistics within SFL has been the expansion of the domain of investigation along two dimensions: (i) from the high culture variety of literature to more popular literature and (ii) from verbal art to semiotic art in general. (The first dimension we might call the cline of brows, from high-brow via middle-brow to low-brow; but the notion of brows is arguably loaded against popular culture.) To get a sense of the future potential of artistic linguistics — or perhaps more generally "artistic semiotics", we can represent the two dimensions in tabular form, with references to key works in SFL: see Table 3. The entries in the "elite" column represent contributions that illustrate the framework and methodology of artistic linguistics in reference to elite art, but the framework and methodology can of course be applied to the investigation of popular art as well. The entries in the popular verbal art cell include work on traditional folk tales, and here we could also include work on literature for and by children (e.g. Toolan, 2001: Ch. 7; Williams, 1995, 2000; Rothery, 1990; Unsworth, 2006). However, most work on popular semiotic art in SFL seems to have been on multisemiotic art, including folk and rock songs, e-literature, and comic books.

3.3.2 Media linguistics

Media linguistics (to use this as a provisional term for an emerging area of study) is concerned with discourses in the media, and has developed as an area of research activity within systemic functional linguistics in recent years.

In principle, media linguistics could be concerned with texts within all registers that operate within the media, but in practice, the centre of gravity has been the 'reporting' sector in Figure 4: news reports of different kinds, although editorials have also been investigated within the 'exploring' sector.

While there are important examples of early work within the "East Anglia" tradition in the 1970s, including Trew (1979) and other contributions in Fowler et al. (1979) and research into the "media interview" in the 1980s and into the 1990s (including multimodal features, e.g. van Leeuwen, 1985; Bell & van Leeuwen, 1994), it was in the 1990s that "media linguistics" began to gain momentum and critical mass (e.g. Nanri, 2003; Iedema, Feez & White, 1994; White, 1997, 1998), and the first decade of the 21st century has seen sustained research in this area, including research projects in the Department of Linguistics at Macquarie University — like the "Bias in the news" project at the Centre for Language in Social Life with Annabelle Lukin[6], the research on multimodality in online news by Knox (e.g. 2007, forthc.) — and the multilingual news project reported on in Thomson & White (2008), including e.g. Knox & Patpong (2008).

3.3.3 Organizational linguistics

Organizational (or administrative) linguistics (to use this as a provisional name) has also developed as an area of research within systemic functional linguistics in recent years. It is concerned with administrative, bureaucratic or organizational discourse, which has a centre of gravity in the 'enabling' sector of the diagram in Figure 4. It overlaps with the interest in language in the workplace in applied linguistics, which has been informed by various theoretical approaches, including SFL.

Iedema (1996) lays a foundation for text-based research into administrative processes in workplaces — "organizational discourse", and has followed this up with further publications, showing for example how obligation may be construed or enacted in enabling discourse of the regulatory kind (e.g. Iedema, 1997a,c, 2000, 2003) , with "health communication" emerging at the intersection of clinical linguistics and organizational linguistics[7] (e.g. Iedema, 2007). Harrison & Young (2004) analyse bureaucratic discourse from a critical perspective, and Lavid (2000) compares forms designed for the public in English, German and Italian.

At the same time, there was considerable activity relating to "language in the workplace" at UTS with contributions by Di Slade, Hermine Scheeres, and others. In joint work, Iedema and Scheeres (e.g. 2003) show how "work" at workplaces has become increasingly semioticized, with employees having to take on roles in semiotic processes in addition to the their roles in more traditional material processes.

3.3.4 Marketing linguistics

Marketing linguistics (to use this as a provisional name for an area of investigation that may emerge as a focus of activities) is concerned with texts marketing commodities. Such texts fall within the 'recommending' sector of the diagram in Figure 4, more specifically within the 'promotional' subtype (recommending for the benefit of the speaker rather than for the benefit of the addressee). They include many different kinds of advertisement, product blurbs, fund raising letters, and other types of promotional text, and also "cross-over" registers such as infomercials (on the borderline between 'recommending' and 'reporting'). (These are texts persuading the addressee to do something, so the nucleus of such a text is typically a proposal, and the text as a whole can be interpreted as a macro-proposal, as in Martin, 1992b. They contrast with texts persuading the addressee of a proposition; such texts fall within the 'exploring' sector.)

There is potential here for a systemic functional development of marketing linguistics, but while there have been a number of accounts of different aspects of recommending texts of the promotional subtype over the years (e.g. Martin, 1992b; Fries, 2002; McAndrew, 2003; and in the context of translation, Taylor & Baldry, 2001; Steiner, 2004), these separate efforts have not yet come together as field of activity within SFL. However, a research project in Mendoza by a team led by Ana Hansen demonstrates the potential through the research into the promotion of wine; and texts within the tourism industry are increasingly being analysed within SFL. Research in this area has been given a boost by the development of the description of the system of appraisal in English (see Martin & White, 2005).

3.3.5 Other possible developments

In addition to the sectors in focus in media linguistics, administrative linguistics and marketing linguistics, it is possible to imagine that other register sectors will become the focus of dedicated fields of linguistic activity. For instance:

- **Epistemological linguistics**: while educational linguistics is concerned with 'expounding' texts within the institution of education, "epistemological linguistics" could emerge as a field of investigation dedicated to the study of the discursive construction and dissemination of knowledge in support of a wide range of applications (e.g. within education, within information technology, within the "knowledge industry"). It is possible to see Christie & Martin (2007) and Halliday & Matthiessen (1999) as complementary contributions towards the development of epistemological linguistics. The contributions in Christie & Martin (2007) investigate knowledge in relation to key distinctions in Bernstein's work, including centrally the distinction between vertical and horizontal organization. Halliday & Matthiessen (1999) reinterpret the cognitive notion of "knowledge" semiotically as experience construed as meaning within the ideational semantics of language, developing an account that is detailed and explicit enough to be modelled computationally.

- **Aesthetic linguistics:** "aesthetic linguistics" could emerge as a field of investigation dealing with 'exploring' texts concerned with the negotiation in a community of the value of works of art (and other artefacts evaluated in terms of aesthetic considerations), focussing perhaps in particular on the resources of APPRECIATION within the system of APPRAISAL (see Martin & White, 2005). Aesthetic linguistics would include literary criticism (see Lukin, 2003) and criticism of visual art (see Rada, 1989; and cf. O'Toole, 1994), reviews of performing arts and of film.
- **Ethical linguistics:** similarly, "ethical linguistics" could emerge as a field of investigation focussed on 'exploring' texts concerned with the exploration in a community of moral values, focussing perhaps in particular on the resources of JUDGEMENT within the system of APPRAISAL (see Martin & White, 2005). One aspect of such ethical concerns would be our environment, an aspect which is now being explored in ecolinguistics.
- **Ecolinguistics:** Ecolinguistics has in fact already been established as a new area of activity, relating linguistic work to ecological concerns. The Wikipedia entry is worth quoting: "Ecolinguistics emerged in the 1990's as a new paradigm of linguistic research which took into account not only the social context in which language is embedded, but also the ecological context in which societies are embedded. Michael Halliday's 1990 paper *New ways of Meaning: the challenge to applied linguistics* [Halliday, 1992b] is often credited as a seminal work which provided the stimulus for linguists to consider the ecological context and consequences of language." Ecolinguistics has been pursued by a growing number of linguists, including researchers such as Andrew Goatly drawing on SFL.

Both aesthetic linguistics and ethical linguistics would investigate 'exploring' texts, trying to reveal how aesthetic and moral values are negotiated publicly in a community, typically in the media. They could also include more private contexts of people 'sharing' personal values, prototypically in casual conversations, as part of the negotiation of interpersonal relations (cf. Eggins & Slade, 1997: Ch. 4; Horvath & Eggins, 1995). Sharing and exploring may shade into one another in technologically enabled contexts such as postings of reviews on websites (like that of the internet movie database) and exchanges in internet forums.

In addition, we can see the emergence of linguistic research centred on texts in the 'doing' sector, in particular on texts operating in service encounters. While service encounters have been an important site for systemic functional investigation for a long time (see Hasan, 1978; Ventola, 1987; Matthiessen et al., 2005), technological developments have created the conditions for a new kind of service institution — call centres. Call centres have mushroomed in a number of countries, including India, China and the Philippines. They are semiotically very interesting along a number of dimensions, and they are being explored in systemic functional terms in the Department of English language studies, the Hong Kong Polytechnic University, with links to researchers in other locations (see e.g. Forey & Lockwood (2007) and Lockwood, Forey & Elias, forthc.). Call centres bring together, as server and customer, interactants from potentially very different cultural and linguistic backgrounds. Their services are very often provided on an out-sourced basis, which creates an additional distance between the service provider and the company whose products the services are concerned with. These factors put special pressures on interpersonal relations between server and customer (see Hood & Forey, 2008), especially since customers not infrequently call up with complaints and stored-up negative affect.

3.4 The second circle of investigation: intermediate register focus

The second circle of fields of investigation represents those areas of systemic functional investigation that have been concerned with certain registers in particular but which can also range across several, many or even potentially all of the different register types:

- **Educational linguistics** — focus on registers of content subjects, in particular on 'expounding' (e.g. physics, chemistry, mathematics, biology), on 'enabling' (e.g. laboratory procedures in experimental subjects), on 'reporting' (history), and on 'exploring' (e.g. literary criticism in English; argumentative and comparative expositions in any subject).
- **Clinical linguistics** — focus on 'recommending: advising' texts in clinical consultations (and on 'doing' texts in surgery and other medical procedures), but also on other types of text when these texts themselves are used for diagnosis and treatment, as in speech pathology (traditionally narratives in the 'recreating' sector, but increasingly other types as well, such as letters (see Mortensen, e.g. 2005)).
- **Forensic linguistics** — focus on 'enabling: regulating' texts (in discourses of the law) and on 'reporting' texts (in the courtroom), but also on other types of text when these texts themselves are used for investigative purposes, as in investigations of authorship.

3.4.1 Educational linguistics

Educational linguistics (see chapters 9–12 in Hasan et al. (eds), 2005; for a recent overview of educational linguistics, see also Christie & Unsworth, 2005; for a recent overview of literacy pedagogy, see Martin & Rose, 2005; for recent contributions to second/ foreign language education, see Byrnes, 2006, in press) deals with many aspects of language in education and has been part of the systemic functional research agenda since the very early days (see e.g. Pearce, Thornton & Mackay, 1989).

Educational linguistics is, in principle, concerned with texts instantiating all registers since one key aspect of education is precisely giving pupils and students access to an ever-increasing range of registers, enabling them to expand their personal repertoires of registers so that they can master registers operating in a growing range of institutional contexts, thus removing barriers for them to access these contexts. There is an ordered registerial progression here in terms of learning and curriculum (e.g. Martin & Rothery, 1981), both across the major sectors of the diagram in Figure 4 and within these major sections, as discussed for science education by e.g. Rose (1997). The principle of an ordered registerial progression also applies to second/foreign language education. Rinner & Weigert (2006) show the significance of developing and using a curriculum for second/foreign language education based on register (genre).

At the same time, educational linguistics will focus on those registers that play a central role in particular subjects (cf. Shum, 2006, for recent work in the Hong Kong context) — e.g. explanations and reports (expounding) in secondary school physics (e.g. Veel, 1997), historical recounts (reporting) and argumentative expositions (exploring) in secondary school history (e.g. Eggins, Wignell & Martin, 1991; Martin, 2003), story writing (recreating) in primary school (e.g. Rothery, 1990).

The phenomena explored in educational linguistics are thus registerially composite, involving different motifs — the "content" of a discipline, pedagogic concerns, and also the regulation of behaviour in educational institutions. Contributions in Christie & Martin (2007) shed light on the composite registerial nature of educational discourse based on Bernstein's (e.g. 1996) work.

One new area for educational research and development lies at the intersection of educational linguistics and translation studies; this is the field of translator training. This field has emerged as a new focus in academic institutions, as translation has increasingly become professionalised and the training of translators and interpreters is being given academic status in undergraduate and postgraduate programmes around the world. Taylor (1998) is an important contribution to translator training (and Baker, 1992, a widely used text book in translation courses, contains key insights from SFL, particularly in the area of the textual metafunction), and a number of studies have focussed on translator education, including Shore (2001) and the recent work by Mira Kim (e.g. Kim, 2007; Burns, Kim & Matthiessen, in press).

3.4.2 Clinical linguistics

Clinical linguistics can be seen as an emerging formation of research and application relating to clinical and medical work, and more generally to health care.

It includes speech pathology (see Armstrong, *Clinical Applications*, in this volume; for a recent overview of speech pathology, see also Armstrong et al. 2005, and of language breakdown in a broad sense, including autism, see also Asp & de Villiers, forthc.), psychotherapeutic studies (e.g. Martin & Rochester, 1979; Butt et al., 2003; Meares et al., 2005; Fine, 2006), patient counselling, and other areas within the institution of health care.

These forms of clinical linguistics have 'recommending' contexts as their base in the sense that a good deal of clinical linguistics has been concerned with either the register of consultation, as in the EDCOM research project investigating communication in emergency departments of hospitals (e.g. Slade et al., 2008)[8], or with other registers that get activated as part of consultation. Such other registers that are "embedded" within consultations as part of diagnosis and treatment are of course not spread evenly across the registerial map in Figure 4, but in speech pathology the selection has expanded beyond the traditional descriptive and narrative tasks to include written letters of different kinds (see Mortensen, 2003, 2005) and spoken dialogue within different contexts.

In addition, the emerging field of "clinical" linguistics also includes 'doing' contexts such as those in which surgery is conducted in operating theatres, investigated within the "systemic safety" project at the Centre for Language in Social Life, Linguistics, Macquarie University (cf. Butt, 2008).

3.4.3 Forensic linguistics

Forensic linguistics is like clinical linguistics in that texts from any register can in principle serve as part of a "diagnostic" phase, as when the identity of the author of a particular text becomes a legal issue (e.g. Coulthard, 2004). Systemic functional linguistics has been a source of insight in forensic work, as is evident from the work by leading linguists in the field, e.g. John Gibbons (e.g., 2003, with references to registers (genres) in the legal context, including valuable work by Yon Maley) and Malcolm Coulthard.

However, at the same time, forensic linguistics has at least two institutional bases — one being geared towards goods-&-services (proposals) and the other towards information (propositions). On the one hand, it is concerned with texts instantiating registers associated with 'enabling' contexts of a regulating kind — laws and acts of parliament, constitutions, legally binding agreements and the like. Here one important concern has been with the accessibility of legal texts to people without training in this area (see e.g. Hansen-Schirra & Neumann, 2004). On the other hand, it is concerned with texts instantiating registers associated with 'reporting' contexts — police interrogations (e.g. Hall, 1998, forthc.), statements in evidence, cross-examinations in trials, and so on.

In current research at Sydney University, restorative justice in "Youth Justice Conferences" is being investigated from the point of view of multisemiotic systems.

3.5 The third circle: wide register focus

The third circle of fields of investigation represents those areas of systemic functional investigation that could in principle be concerned with registers of any kind but which have in practice been developed through investigations focussing on certain registers. This circle includes "multi-" studies — multilingual studies and multisemiotic studies. Both fields of investigation have benefited significantly from research projects focussed on particular registers or sets of registers.

3.5.1 Multilingual studies: translation and interpreting studies

The concept of multilingual studies in general was discussed briefly above in Section 2.2.5; here I will focus on one area within multilingual studies, viz. translation and interpreting studies. Translation has been on the systemic functional research agenda for a long time (for a recent overview, see Steiner, 2005a). Halliday (1956) drew attention to the significance of choice in translation, highlighting the value of the thesaurus as a lexical resource supporting choices in machine translation, and Catford's (1965) "linguistic theory of translation", based on the systemic functional theory of that period, has become a classic. In that sense, translation studies is not a "new direction" in SFL. However, on the one hand, interpreting studies is now being added to translation studies (e.g. Taylor Torsello, 1996, 1997), with a growing number of contributions in the last couple of years (e.g. Tebble, 1999, who has contributed to our understanding of tenor relations in medical interpreting), including work on interpreting between Chinese and English at universities in China, and at Macquarie University, e.g. Wang (2008); and on the other hand, the body of work in translation studies is now expanding rapidly in many places around the world, reflected in research projects, publications and also in translation courses informed by SFL.

Translation and interpreting are semiotic processes concerned with recreating meanings derived from a source language text in a target language. The source text and the target text are of course located at the instance pole of the cline of instantiation, but translation and interpreting always operate against the background of a meaning potential higher up the cline of instantiation. This potential is typically that of a particular register: translators and interpreters translate and interpret text as text belonging to some register or other; their acts of recreating meaning are informed by registerial meaning potentials.

The distinction between translation and interpreting is of course a registerial one based on the mode variable of context: translation operates on texts in the written mode, whereas interpreting operates on texts in the spoken mode (or in the signed and spoken modes in the case of interpreters working with sign languages). There are interesting intermediate cases involving cross-over in mode: sight translation (written source text, spoken translated text) and subtitling (spoken source text, written translated text); these embody considerations pertaining to both modes. Subtitling has been investigated from a systemic functional point of view by Taylor (e.g. 2003).

In addition to this basic mode-based distinction between translators and interpreters, translators and interpreters also tend to specialize in terms of register in other respects as well (cf. Steiner, 2005b) — for example, community interpreters, conference interpreters, court room interpreters, legal translators, medical translators all work with different registerial repertoires. Thus a number of studies have been concerned with the translation of texts within particular registers or with the investigation of original texts in two or more languages within the same register, e.g. Steiner (2004) on the translation of advertisements (recommending: promoting texts), Neumann (2003) on guide books in German and English, Hansen (2003) on translation of narrative text, Lavid (2000) on instructions in bureaucratic forms in English, German and Italian, Murcia-Bielsa (2000) on directives in English and Spanish, Mason (2003) on translation of organizational discourse.

Translation and interpreting studies drawing on SFL typically involve text analysis, and attention has increasingly been given to the construction of multilingual corpora and to techniques for automated analysis of such corpora (see e.g. Teich, 2003; Neumann & Hansen-Schirra, 2005; Pagano, Magalhães & Alves, 2004), as in the CroCo project at the Universität des Saarlandes in Saarbrücken[9]. Another important development is being pioneered by researchers led by Adriana Pagano and Fábio Alves at the Universidade Federal de Minas Gerais. This is research into the process of translation, combining methods for recording patterns in the unfolding of the translation of a text with systemic functional analysis. This approach has the potential to illuminate process-oriented accounts of texts in general, supplementing the product-oriented accounts that have come to dominate in the analysis of text (for process-oriented accounts, cf. also Martin, 1985b; Ravelli, 1995; Matthiessen, 2002a; and in the area of text generation, Matthiessen & Bateman, 1991).

3.5.2 Multisemiotic studies

Multisemiotic studies (for recent overviews and collections, see Martinec, 2005, and Royce & Bowcher, 2006; Ventola, Charles & Kaltenbacher, 2004,

Ventola & Moya Guijarro, in press; see also e.g. Kress & van Leeuwen, 2001) are characterized contextually in terms of mode (rather than field and tenor), so registerial focus relates to the mode-based concentric circles of the diagram in Figure 4 rather than to the field-based sectors: there is naturally a clear distinction between multimodality in the written mode and multimodality in the spoken mode, or of course in the signed mode (in the case of sign languages). The same principle applies to multisemiotic studies concerned with particular "channels" such as the web, as in Djonov (2007).

As far as the field-based registerial sectors of the diagram are concerned, multisemiotic studies do in principle range over all registers. However, certain registers have attracted more attention in research than others; for example, there are natural connections between multisemiotic studies and other areas discussed here such as educational linguistics (cf. Mohan, 1986, for pioneering work on 'expounding' texts; and Unsworth, 2006, on the new phenomenon of "e-literature" for children).

For general explorations of multisemiotic systems and register, see Bateman (2008) and Matthiessen (in press).

3.6 Institutional perspective

The different areas of investigation mentioned above were discussed in terms of particular registers or sets of registers. Complementing this kind of registerial map, we can also characterize areas of investigation in terms of institutional focus — in terms of institutions such as the institutions of education, healthcare and the law and in terms of the registerial ranges associated with institutions (see e.g. Christie & Martin, 1997). A given institution may be focussed on a particular registerial sector — e.g. media institutions will be focussed on the 'reporting' sector, health care institutions on the 'recommending: advising' sector, service institutions on the 'doing' sector, and educational institutions on the 'expounding' sector; but the overall operation of a given institution will cover a wider range of complementary registers concerned with different aspects of the workings of the institution. Following Hill (1958), we could call investigations taking institutions as their frame of reference **institutional linguistics** (cf. also e.g. Ellis, 1966: 17-18; Halliday, 1978a: 110). Since institution-based research is likely to play an increasingly important role in the future and since job opportunities may open up for systemic functional linguists within certain institutions, let me say a little bit more about institutions, relating the study of institutions to one of the key scholars informing the development of systemic functional linguistics out of Firthian linguistics — Bronislaw Malinowski (see e.g. Hasan, 1985a).

Institutions are of course social constructs — that is, patterns of organization within third-order, social systems, but they are also semiotic constructs — that is, patterns of organizations within fourth-order, semiotic systems (cf. Section 2.3 above). Institutions were central in Malinowski's theory of society and culture, having evolved to serve certain essential human needs ("biological or derived"), and for him they thus also served as a way into the study of a culture. Malinowski (1944: 154–155) characterizes institutions as follows:

> An ethnographer taking a rapid survey of various types of human culture, from the most primitive to highly developed ones, would make an interesting discovery. He would find that the work of culture is not done by any community as a whole, nor yet by individuals, but by smaller organized groups, that is, institutions, which are organized and integrated to form the community. The significance of this discovery is due to two facts, first, that an institution always presents the same structure, and second, that institutions are of universal occurrence; thus the institution is the real isolate of culture. It is possible to indicate the structure of such a system of organized activities: they are always carried on by a group in a definite manner, using a certain type of material outfit, and obeying norms which bind the members of that group and that group only. Thus equipped with a material outfit, with specific norms of conduct, and with a social organization, including central authority, the members of the institution carry out a type of behavior through which they achieve a definite purpose and contribute in a definite manner to the work of the culture as a whole. In the family and the state, in an occupational group, a factory, a trade union, a church, or a gang, we have to study exactly the same main factors and the relations thereof.
>
> The study of any culture must therefore be carried out in terms of institutions. This means in other words that an object or artifact, a custom, an idea or an artistic product, is significant only when placed within the institution to which it belongs. Certain institutions are to be found in all human societies; other types of institutions, though less universal, can be found in many cultures although some of them are more characteristic of highly developed societies. As culture advances we find that various organized activities, which on the primitive level were carried out as a by-product of other institutions, become organized in their own right. First and foremost perhaps appear military groups, administrative organizations and the political state. Later on courts of law, professional leaders and judges become detached and organized. Economic institutions multiply into the various guilds of artisans and craftsmen. Since the Industrial Revolution, factories, banking systems and large mercantile enterprises have multiplied almost indefinitely.

Malinowski then goes on to list eight main types of institution (family and derived kinship organizations, municipality, tribe as the political organization based on the territorial principle, tribe as a culturally integrated unit, age-group, voluntary associations, occupational groups, status groups based on the principle of rank, caste, and economic class), and to model institutions in terms of purpose, charter, personnel, norms, material apparatus, activities, implemented action, function and results. His work on institutions is well worth reviewing further in the current context of systemic investigations with an institutional focus; for example, his "occupational groups" can be related to current work on professional discourse. However, at this point, I will leave Malinowski and go on to locate the notion of institution in the systemic functional "architecture" of semiotic systems since this will make it easier to identify potential new directions of research.

In terms of the different orders of system — physical, biological, social and semiotic, institutions are, as already noted, both social and semiotic: as discussed by Malinowski, and more generally in social sciences, institutions are units of social organization characterizable in terms of distinctive systems of institutional roles and distinctive patterns of behaviour (social activity). Such social institutions are also manifested in terms of lower-order, material patterns (cf. Malinowski's notion of "material apparatus"): biologically, they may be manifested as ecosystems, and physically as habitats (including the various artefacts that accompany designed habitats). At the same time, social institutions are also interpretable at a higher order of abstraction as semiotic constructs — as patterns of meaning. Semiotically, institutions are locatable within context (as a connotative semiotic system) rather than within language and other denotative semiotic systems (cf. Martin, 1992a). They can be characterized in terms of ranges of values of field, tenor and mode.

In relation to the cline of instantiation, institutions are located midway between system and instance, and they can be interpreted as a system-based view of this region of the cline — that is, they can be modelled as subsystems or subpotentials (cf. Halliday, 1995a). This accords well with Malinowski's characterization of institutions. Viewed in semiotic terms, institutions are regions within the overall cultural potential of a society; they are cultural subsystems, ranging over certain field, tenor and mode values. At the same time, looking downwards towards the instance pole of the cline of instantiation, we can also characterize institutions as aggregates of situation types; that is, as situation types operate together within the "charter" of an institution (to borrow Malinowski's terms — the "collective purpose", the "doctrine on which an institution is based" (Malinowski, 1944: 157)).

The location of institutions in terms of the cline of instantiation and the order of systems (and stratification within semiotic systems) is represented diagrammatically in Figure 5. Figure 5 shows how we can approach the characterization of institutions by moving along the cline of instantiation and along the

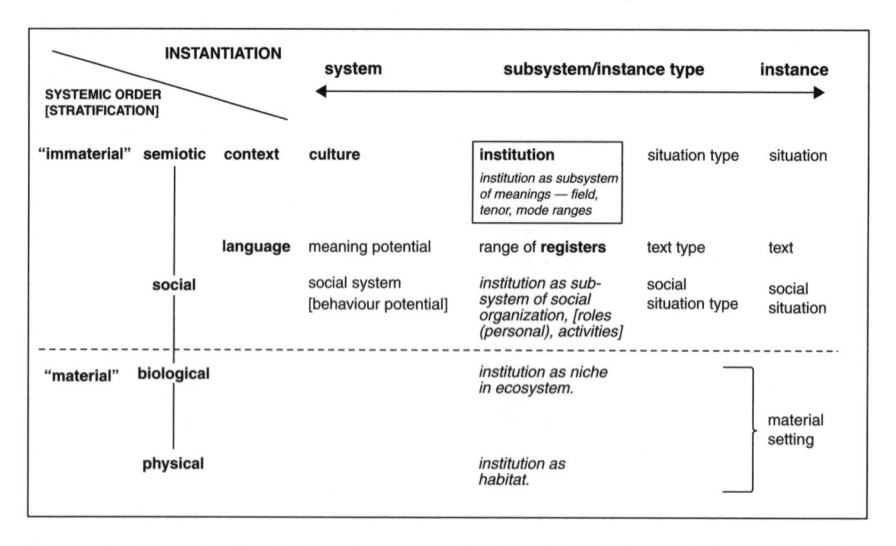

	INSTANTIATION			
SYSTEMIC ORDER [STRATIFICATION]		system	subsystem/instance type	instance
"immaterial" semiotic context		culture	**institution** *institution as subsystem of meanings — field, tenor, mode ranges*	situation type situation
language		meaning potential	range of **registers**	text type text
social		social system [behaviour potential]	institution as subsystem of social organization, [roles (personal), activities]	social situation type / social situation
"material" biological			institution as niche in ecosystem.	material setting
physical			institution as habitat.	

FIGURE 5 Locating institutions in terms of (i) the cline of instantiation and (ii) the ordered typology of systems

ordered typology of systems. Thus, moving along the ordered typology of systems and the hierarchy of stratification within semiotic systems:

- We can characterize institutions "from below" in terms of their **manifestation in social systems**, drawing on research into institutional role networks, social behaviour, situations within sociology, social psychology, ethnography and anthropology and organizational studies. Interpreting characterizations of institutions from these disciplines in systemic functional terms would be a very valuable foundation for future research.
- We can characterize institutions "from below" within the semiotic order, approaching them in terms of the **ranges of registers** that collectively define the (denotative) semiotic work being done within institutions. One example would be Gu's (e.g. 1999, 2002) "discourse geography" (or, using my own related metaphor, "discourse cartography") and his long-term project of mapping out Beijing in terms of a vast corpus of situated discourse. While this work is not specifically cast in terms of SFL, it serves as a very interesting compatible model. The same applies to the corpus-based "Language in the Work Place" project directed by Janet Holmes at the University of Wellington[10]. Within SFL, Ravelli's (2006, 2007) discursive window on the institution of museums serves as a helpful model for future research with an institutional focus. She documents the registerial range of museum exhibitions — including not only the 'reporting' and 'expounding' type of socio-semiotic

processes discussed above, but also the 'exploring' type, and emphasizing the multisemiotic nature of such exhibitions.

Similarly, staying within the systemic order of semiotic systems but moving along the cline of instantiation:

- We can characterize institutions "from above" in terms of the **cultural potential** of a society — that is, in terms of the systems of field, tenor and mode that jointly define this cultural potential. This approach remains a theoretical possibility rather than a practical one at present simply because we have not yet got a "reference description" of the cultural potential of any society. Developing such a description is the task for contextologists (cf. Table 2 above), but it is a daunting one! Nevertheless, conceiving of institutions as ranges of values within a cultural potential — as regions within the total cultural space of a community — is a helpful way of profiling them.
- We can characterize institutions "from below" in terms of the **aggregate of situation types** that instantiate an institution, by focussing on the situation types themselves (systemically, in terms of their field, tenor and mode values, and/or structurally, in terms of contextual (generic, schematic) structures) or on the registers / text types that operate within them. For a number of institutions, it is now possible to compile the accounts produced over the years of quite a few situation types, or genres, that can be located within a given institution. The point of this kind of compilation would be to take stock of the work that has already been done, to determine what situation types still need to be investigated, and to arrive at a more comprehensive understanding of the workings of particular institutions. Institutions for which may be possible include the institutions of the family (illuminated in particular through studies with developmental focus), of friendship, of the work place, of health care, and of education. For example, we could ask how much of the institution of a primary or secondary school has been mapped out so far in educational linguistics through the accumulation of accounts of different situation types (genres) at work in schools. We would probably find that situation types in and around the class room and text book materials are well documented, we would need to work on situation types relating to educational work outside the classroom — both within the school (study groups, personal library work) and outside the school (personal study, study groups, pupil-parent interaction), and to processes that accompany and support educational work (negotiating social relationships, managing the school, interfacing with other agencies and with parents).

In describing institutions in semiotic terms, we must of course take all contextual variables into consideration — field, tenor and mode. A comprehensive description of an institution will include all three perspectives; but we can also describe the institution selectively in terms of only one of these perspectives. Thus we can create a map of an institution based on the social and semiotic processes (the "activity sequences" — cf. Martin, 1992a) undertaken within it, and on the domains of experience that these relate to (field), or a map based on the network of roles that the "personnel" of the institution take on and the relationships they enter into (tenor), or a map based on the complementarity of semiotic and social systems contributing to the work achieved within the institution (mode).

A number of studies have demonstrated the value of examining institutions from the point of view of **institutional roles** and the **registerial repertoires** associated with these roles, now often discussed under the heading of "professional discourse". Here the basic question is: "what repertoire of registers does a person have to master to take on a particular institutional role?". An important example within systemic functional linguistics is Jill Kealley's (e.g. 2007) research into the language of nurses within the institution of health-care. Another is the work on different **voices** in media institutions (see e.g. Iedema, Feez & White, 1994; Martin & White, 2005: 164-184).

4 Metatheoretical, theoretical, descriptive and analytical developments

4.1 Analysis, description, comparison, theory and metatheory

As shown in Figure 3, there are many ways of exploring domains of investigation and new developments in SFL. In the preceding section, I used the cline of instantiation, focussing on registerial ranges within different fields of activity. Let me now review the location of these fields of activity relative to the different primary processes undertaken in linguistics — the analysis of particular texts, the description of the systems of particular languages, and comparison of a number of different linguistics systems, and the theorizing of language as a kind of semiotic system (or of semiotic systems in general): see Figure 6.

In the diagram in Figure 6, I have differentiated analysis, description, comparison and theory as distinct "phases" of processing of language in linguistics (cf. Hjelmslev, 1943; Halliday, 1992a; Matthiessen & Nesbitt, 1996).

- **Analysis** operates on instances of a language in its context: we analyse particular texts in their contexts of situation, assigning the analysis to them based on the description of the system of language.
- **Description** operates on the potential of a language in its context: we describe a particular linguistic system in its context of culture, basing the description on evidence from the investigation of instances.
- **Analysis** and **description** complement one another: they are concerned with different poles of the cline of instantiation (cf. Halliday, 2008). When we

Ideas and New Directions 49

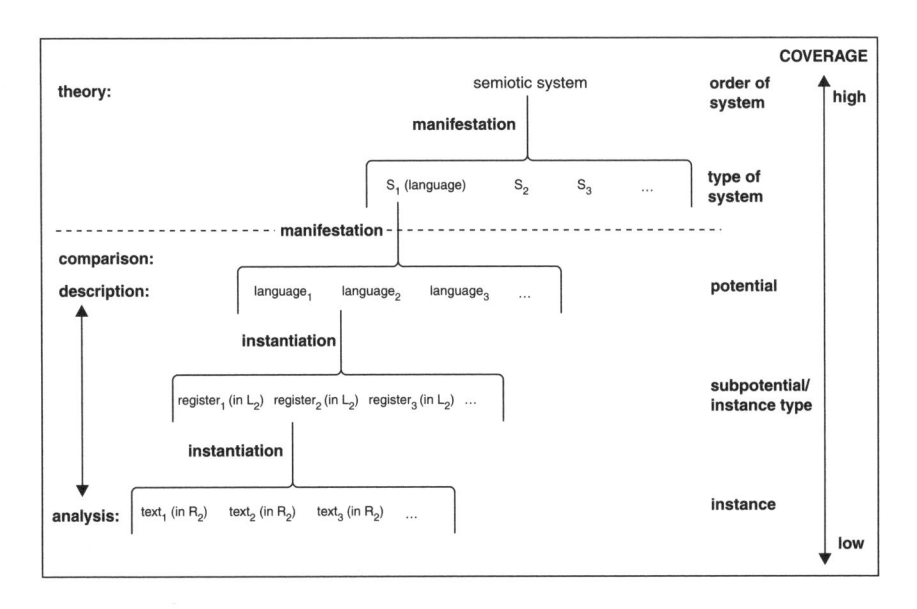

```
                                    COVERAGE
                    semiotic system        order of      ↑
theory:                                    system        high
                        manifestation

                    S₁ (language)  S₂  S₃  ...    type of
                                                  system
- - - - - - - - - - - - manifestation - - - - - - - - - - - -
comparison:
description:        language₁  language₂  language₃  ...    potential

                        instantiation

            register₁ (in L₂)  register₂ (in L₂)  register₃ (in L₂)  ...   subpotential/
                                                                           instance type

                        instantiation

analysis:   text₁ (in R₂)  text₂ (in R₂)  text₃ (in R₂)  ...    instance
                                                                           ↓
                                                                           low
```

FIGURE 6 Analysis, description, comparison and theory

focus on the region intermediate between the outer poles of potential and instance, we can either describe this region as sub-potentials or analyse it as instance types.

- **Comparison** operates on the potentials of two or more languages in their contexts of culture. If the sample of languages is representative of languages around the world (however we determine what constitutes a representative sample), then the comparison is highly generalized: it is typology (cf. Teruya et al., 2007; Matthiessen, Teruya & Wu, 2008; Ellis, 1966).
- **Theory** operates on language as a kind of semiotic system, or on semiotic systems in general; it serves to differentiate between higher-order semiotic systems (language) and primary semiotic systems (many other, perhaps all, semiotic systems).

As the diagram in Figure 6 shows, there is an increase of coverage of "information" as we move from single instances to the general category of semiotic systems. In analysis, we are only responsible for single instances — texts in their contexts of situation. Even if the texts are very long or we collect a considerable number of texts, they will only instantiate a small part of the total system of a language in its context of culture. In contrast, in description, we are responsible for the potential of a language in its context of culture. Such a potential is obviously quite vast, and when we try to back it up through the analysis of instances, we need huge samples — larger even than the current corpora of a few hundred million words. In comparison, we go beyond the description of particular languages in order to compare these descriptions; we are, in principle, responsible for the total potential of anything from a small handful of languages to large samples of hundreds of languages designed to be representative of the languages around the world.

Analysis, description and comparison are all concerned with the same order of abstraction — particular languages or collections of particular languages, and as the diagram shows we can locate the three processes of analysis, description and comparison at different points along the cline of instantiation. All three are thus ultimately grounded in "data" — in observable instances; and they operate with descriptive categories that have to be justified for each language under investigation.

In contrast, theory operates at a higher level of abstraction: it is concerned not with particular languages but with language in general as a type of semiotic system and with semiotic systems in general as an order of system in an ordered typology of systems (see Halliday, 1996; Halliday & Matthiessen, 1999: Ch. 13; Matthiessen, 2007a). Theory operates with theoretical categories (rather than descriptive ones) — categories such as (the cline of) instantiation, (the hierarchy of) stratification, realization, (the cline of) delicacy, (the spectrum of) metafunction. These come together in the theoretical model of the "architecture" of language. The theory makes it possible to characterize language as a higher-order semiotic (see Halliday, 1995c) — a semiotic system embodying the metafunctional spectrum and stratified within both the content plane (semantics and lexicogrammar) and the expression plane (phonology and phonetics). Particular languages are manifestations of language as a higher-order human semiotic.

When we develop theory, we must, in principle, cover everything in the realm of semiotic systems: we are responsible for information accumulated in the move up the cline of instantiation from instance to system, and for information accumulated from descriptions of particular languages. The general theory of language must thus have a very extensive coverage — otherwise it would not be a general theory of language. Therefore we cannot construct a general theory of language — or of any part of language — based only on one particular language. There is a real sense in which analysis, description, comparison, and theory are ordered in difficulty:

analysis < description < comparison < theory

This scale is typically reflected in academic programmes where SFL is taught: students doing undergraduate programmes or masters post-graduate programmes will learn to do text analysis and if they also do an undergraduate thesis or a masters thesis, this thesis is likely to be based on a research project involving text analysis. However, while students will master text analysis, they will probably not learn how to develop descriptions of languages, let alone how to do systematic comparison or construct general theory[11]. The challenge is to develop university curricula where it is possible to learn not only text analysis but also system description — curricula where one can learn to become a descriptivist. This would be a very significant new direction in SFL in terms of the training of future generations of students.

The focus on text analysis in university programmes is of course a relatively recent development — starting around 30 years ago but becoming more prevalent in the last two decades or so. Before text analysis came into focus in university programmes, description or theory was given prominence in linguistics programmes — which of the two was given more prominence depended on the orientation of a given programme. Up through the early 1960s, many programmes focussed on training "descriptivists". This tradition has continued, of course, in certain places; but as formal generative linguistics came to dominate in many linguistics or language studies departments, the focus shifted to theory — more specifically, to theory in the guise of theoretical representations. There was a long period when new theories, or new versions of existing theories, were developed in rapid succession.

This would seem to contradict my claim above that theory is the most challenging process of all because it presupposes comparison, description, and analysis — because it is responsible not just for a particular language but for language in general as a higher-order semiotic. However, the formal generative theory of this period was very different from the kind of theory we are concerned with in this book, systemic functional theory. On the one hand, the formal generative theory of this period was really based on one language — English (just as the missionary work in traditional grammar up through the 19th century was based on Latin or Greek). More specifically, it was based on relatively small fragments of English (compare Gross's, 1979, comments on the attempt to put together a more comprehensive description of English, the "UCLA" grammar). On the other hand, "theory" really meant theoretical representation (cf. Matthiessen & Nesbitt, 1996; Teich, 1999) — the rule systems devised at the time. Many of the findings — e.g. the principle of feeding and bleeding rule ordering — were comparable to what a programmer would deal with in developing (non-declarative) programmes in the 1960s and 1970s.

Theory in SFL is thus quite a substantial undertaking. However, there is one step beyond systemic functional theory (a step not shown in Figure 6). This is systemic functional metatheory: a theory of what systemic functional theory is like (cf. Halliday & Matthiessen, 1999; Teich, 1999; Matthiessen, 2007a). Systemic functional metatheory developed first in the context of computational linguistic research because there was a pressing need to understand the distinction between theory and representation (cf. Matthiessen, 1988a) and to understand the relationship between the deployment of systemic functional linguistics and the context of deployment (cf. Halliday, 1964a). However, it certainly has important roots in the work by Hjelmslev (in particular on connotative semiotic systems), Firth (his notion of linguistics as language turned back on itself) and Halliday (e.g. 1964a, 1977a). Systemic functional metatheory has served as an important resource in work involving computational modelling, but it is relevant across all fields of systemic functional activity, and future research, application and development can hopefully be based on and supported by systemic functional metatheory as well as systemic functional theory. This would certainly be a very valuable new direction of activity.

4.2 Text analysis

As the diagram in Figure 6 above indicates, the evidential or empirical basis of any work involving language is text (in context), and the fields of linguistic investigation discussed in Section 3 are typically grounded in the analysis of particular texts, but the research focus is usually locatable mid-way up the cline of instantiation on a register or set of registers. For instance, in the investigation of a given work place in organizational linguistics, the investigators are likely to sample a large number of texts and then to analyse them, but their focus will be on the register or registers that these texts instantiate, like the register of administrative directives. Given large enough samples of text, text analysis thus allows us to move up the cline of instantiation from instance towards potential. How far up we are able to move really depends on how large a sample the analysis can cope with. If the sample is large enough and covers an interesting range of registers, text analysis can help support the description of the systemic potential of a language. Let me comment briefly on methodology in text analysis, since this is very much part of the trajectory of current developments.

While "text analysis" (or "discourse analysis"[12]) is often seen as based on manual, human analysis, it can of course also be based on automated, computational analysis, or on a combination of manual and automated analysis (see Wu, 2000; Matthiessen, 2006; Hoey, 2006). Automated, computational analysis has been developed within corpus linguistics and linguistic computing (see Teich, *Linguistic computing*, this volume). The complementarity of manual analysis and automated analysis can be characterized in reference to the size of the sample of texts and the "level" (stratum, rank) of analysis (see Matthiessen, 2006: 108-113; Wu, 2000): see Figure 7. Here the horizontal axis represents the sample size (measured in terms of words, as is customary for languages with an alphabetic writing system operating with graphological words corresponding roughly to grammatical words, as in English, and shown schematically on a logarithmic scale), ranging from small samples of single short texts via medium-size samples — register corpora of tens of thousands of words — to very large samples — reference corpora of hundreds of millions of words.

Manual analysis can range over all the "levels" — all strata, and all ranks within a given stratum such as lexicogrammar, as long as descriptions are available, but

Ideas and New Directions 53

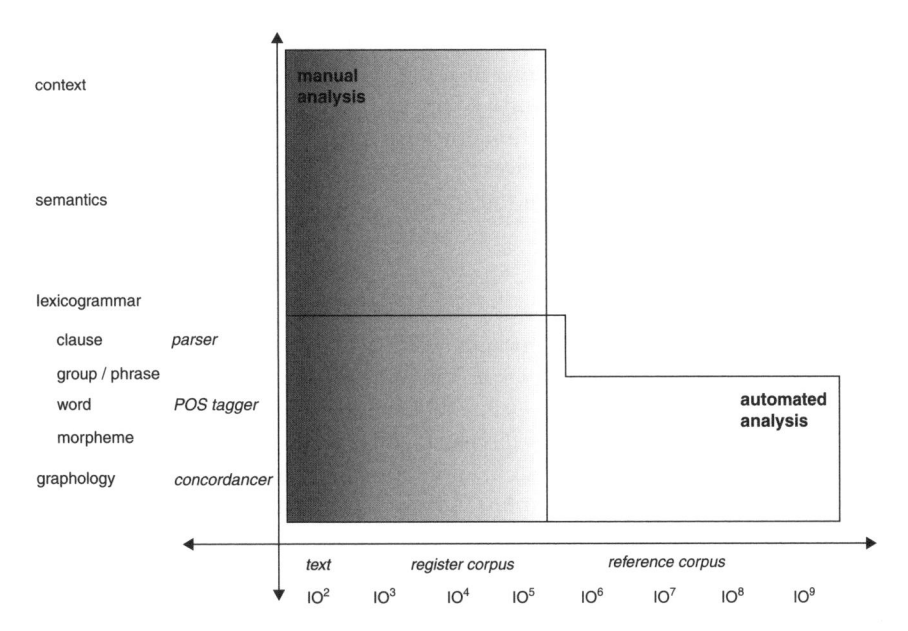

FIGURE 7 Modes of text analysis — manual and automated analysis in relation to "level" and sample size

it is severely constrained in terms of the sample size since it is very labour intensive and therefore expensive. The upper bound of the sample size is thus determined by funding: if research into language was funded at levels comparable to those of "hard sciences", much larger samples of text could be analysed manually.

In contrast, automated analysis can range over text samples of all sizes; here the upper bound is determined by computing power and has thus constantly been extended since the first systematic samples of electronically represented texts for computational processing were developed in the 1960s. Large corpora are now up to hundreds of millions of words, but even samples of this magnitude may not be extensive enough. The World Wide Web can be treated as a huge open and dynamic archive of texts, and this sample can be searched by means of search engines; but the sample is registerially quite skewed and the registerial make-up is not so easy to determine. The real constraint on automated analysis has to do with the "level" of analysis, however; the upper bound is still located somewhere within the stratum of lexicogrammar. For smaller samples, it is possible to "tune" parsers according to the registerial characteristics of the texts in the sample, but huge samples of registerially widely varied texts still pose a considerable challenge. Corpora that have been grammatically annotated through parsing, so-called "tree banks", are now available for research, but they tend to be small (a couple of million words) and registerially narrow, like the annotated versions of the Brown Corpus, the LOB Corpus and the Penn Treebank of one million words of texts from the Wall Street Journal. The "trees" are syntagms rather than function structures, but, in an additional cycle of parsing, such trees can themselves be analysed to produce (partial) function structures, as shown by Honnibal (2004a).

4.3 Time-frames

Text analysis is located at the instance pole of the cline of instantiation (cf. Figure 6) — although it is of course always based on a prior description of a potential located further up the cline of instantiation. Let me now relate text analysis and the other processes discussed above — description, comparison, theory — to time-frames in research, application and development.

Since texts vary considerably a length (given the fact that they are defined "from above" as language functioning in context; see Halliday & Hasan, 1976), the analysis of a particular text can take anything from a few minutes to a few days or even weeks, or quite possibly months. For instance, one hour of casual conversation may take ten hours to transcribe, and forty hours to analyse prosodically (in terms of rhythm and intonation).

Languages may vary in size (although finding reliable measures of the size of a langauge is very difficult), but there is no doubt that describing a linguistic system takes orders of magnitude longer than analysing a text. Dixon (1997) suggests that it would take three years to develop the first description of a language (given a budget of around 200 K US dollars) and this is the quantum of research undertaken within a Ph.D. candidature; but his estimate is based on his notion of description based on "basic theory", so I would multiply his estimate by three for a systemic functional description — that is, on the order of nine years for the first systemic functional description of a language (i.e. a description grounded in extensive text analysis, oriented towards meaning and designed to be a resource for the community of speakers as well as for linguists). This is equivalent to somewhere between 2-3 Ph.D. research projects (if we disregard the potential for research assistance). I think this is approximately right: researchers manage to squeeze outlines of languages into a single Ph.D. thesis — there have been a good number of systemic functional ones since the 1960s, but these are heroic efforts undertaken within a period of 4+ years and they often have to leave significant areas out (such as phonology, or at least prosodic phonology, grammar below the clause, semantics — not to mention context). So if a text takes say 4 weeks to analyse, a linguistic system takes on the order of 470 weeks to describe.

So much for analysis and description, but how long does it take to develop theory (setting comparison of descriptions of linguistic systems aside)? This is actually much harder to measure. One reason for this is that the development of theory is not usually the focus of research projects — neither of Ph.D. research projects nor of funded multi-person projects. Instead, systemic functional theory has been developed over a long period of time, around five decades by now, in the contexts of many projects of research, application and development and also in the contexts of many teaching programmes. Another reason why it is difficult to measure the time it takes to develop a certain quantum of theory is of course that like semiotic systems in general, theory never stands still; it is always changing. However, it is reasonable to say that the development of theory can be measured in terms of decades and generations of scholars. Here we are in the domain of scientific paradigms.

The considerations of different time-frames for the development of systemic functional linguistics are summarized schematically in Figure 8. Funded research projects typically last from a year to three years, or up to five years (depending on the size of the funding and the number of researchers involved); an individual Ph.D. research project lasts between three and five years. Such projects can thus deal with analysis of texts quite effectively, and there are innumerable examples of such projects. Longer projects of between three and five years may be able to produce descriptions of a particular language; above, I suggested that it would take on the order of nine years for a single senior researcher

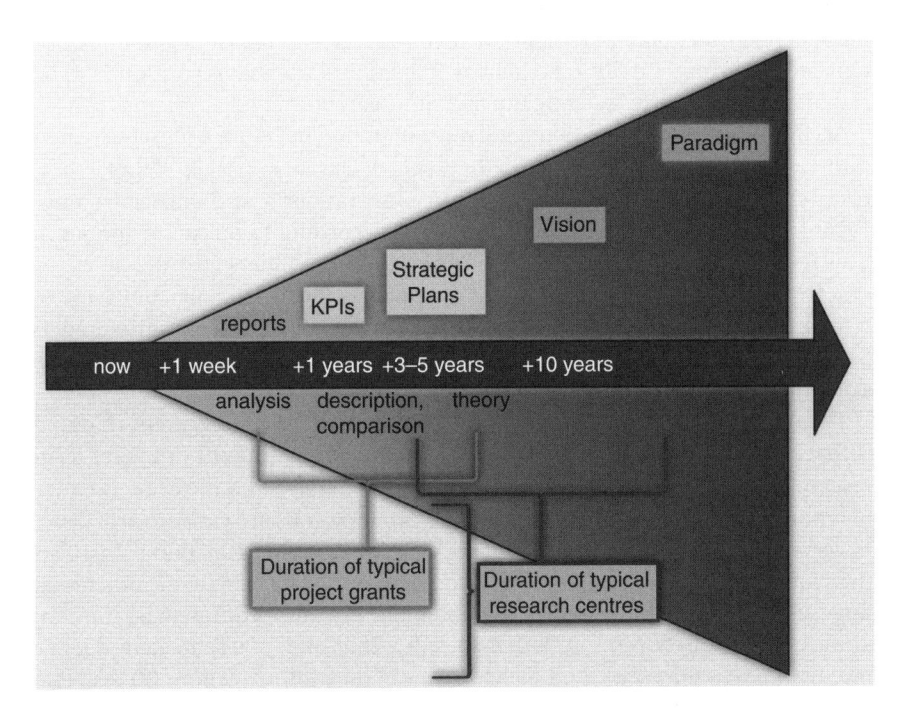

FIGURE 8 Development and time-frames

with research assistants to complete round one of a comprehensive systemic functional description of a particular language not previously described in systemic functional terms. The development of theory may fall within the scope of a research centre or laboratory within which a number of research projects are co-ordinated[13]. Such research centres may have a life-span of five to ten years — probably of at least two cycles of funding of typical research projects. Research centres would thus be well suited to the development of theory — not only because of the time-frame but also because they involve several or even many research projects. The challenge is to build this kind of development into the vision statement for a research centre and into shorter-term strategic plans.

Above the timeline in Figure 8, I have included some "buzz words" used in documents concerned with the planning and management of research. Research reports may be produced at different intervals, ranging from weekly to annual; and they will be expected at the end of a research project (maybe in the form of a Ph.D. thesis). Nowadays researchers likely to be measured in terms of KPIs, "key performance indicators", probably on an annual basis. Strategic plans operate over longer periods of time, probably extending beyond the duration of a single research project. They are in turn informed by vision statements, intended to give general direction to the development of research. Such vision statements are in turn informed by a research paradigm, such as the systemic functional paradigm for text-based research that began to be formulated in the early 1960s (cf. Halliday, 1964a) and which has continued to be elaborated and inform systemic functional research.

Accounts such as the diagrammatic representation in Figure 8 must be treated with caution: they can sit uneasily between declarative models ("this is how research has developed according to our observations") and imperative ones ("this is how research ought to be developed according to our prescriptions"). This tension can be recognized from work within the philosophy of science — much of it has been imperative in nature, produced in arm chairs, but some of it has been declarative in nature, produced in the field; and imperative models from the philosophy of science must be reviewed in the light of declarative accounts developed within the sociology of science[14].

The danger in today's academic world dominated by management thinking is that shorter-term research will be favoured to the detriment of longer-term research since shorter-term research is easier to manage and measure, is easier to report on, and is easier to get funding for since pay-offs are easier to articulate. However, the outlook is arguably brighter for systemic functional linguists than for many other colleagues for a number of reasons. (1) Systemic functional linguists have the skills to analyse the dominant discourses influencing the conditions for research (cf. e.g. Iedeman, Feez & White, 1994) to gain deeper insight into how they work, and such insight can then inform action. (2) Systemic functional linguists have a powerful multidimensional model to work with.

Ideas and New Directions   57

This makes is much easier to locate fundable quanta of research within the total map of the semiotic landscape, and to use the systemic model to look ahead into the future beyond the next funding cycle. (3) Systemic functional linguists operate within many different institutional contexts and many countries around the world, so they are well placed to develop collaborative networks of mutual support.

Notes

[1] This diagram only represents one aspect of the development of SFL in different phases. Complementary diagrams would show other aspects — like the development of coverage of metafunction, like the development of coverage of axis, like the development of coverage of the cline of delicacy, and like the development of coverage of the cline of instantiation. At the same time, even this stratal diagram needs to be supplemented to take into account the work in the last two decades or so on semiotic systems other than language.

[2] In the diagram in Figure 3 and elsewhere in this chapter, I use the term "register" in the sense established in the 1960s to refer to a functional variety of language (cf. Halliday, McIntosh & Strevens, 1964; Gregory, 1967; Hasan, 1973c; Halliday, 1978a; Matthiessen, 1993). A register is associated with contextual values of field, tenor and mode (cf. Hasan, 1973c: 272; Halliday, 1978a). In the work by Martin (e.g. 1992) and scholars drawing on this work, the term "register" has been used instead to refer to the contextual variables of field, tenor and mode (cf. also Martin, 2007, for discussion).

[3] For a discussion of probability in non-systemic phonology, see Pierrehumbert's (2001) overview of "stochastic phonology" and her (2003) overview of "probabilistic phonology". At a special colloquium on the history of approaches to phonology organized by Goldsmith at a phonology conference at Abbaye de Royaumont outside Paris in June 1998 (Current Trends in Phonology II), Halliday gave an overview of systemic phonology (see Halliday, 2000). Goldsmith presented a paper advocating revisiting the issue of probabilistic information in phonological accounts (going back to information theory). In the question period, Pierrehumbert commented that she would have thought systemic phonology was best suited to the incorporation of probabilistic information. This is an important insight and highlights the potential for future research in systemic phonology based on samples of texts at the instance pole of the cline of instantiation.

[4] Cf. the award of the Nobel Prize for Literature by the Swedish Academy to Bertrand Russell in 1950 and to Winston Churchill in 1953.

[5] Alternatively, we could use the term "aesthetic linguistics" for the investigation of literary criticism (cf. Lukin, 2003), which is located in the 'exploring' sector: 'recreating' texts are explored in aesthetic terms by means of the resources of APPRECIATION within the system of APPRAISAL (see Martin & White, 2005), sometimes tending in the direction of creating a kind of "metaliterature", echoing the aesthetic values of verbal art.

[6] Website: http://www.ling.mq.edu.au/clsl/reporting_war.htm

7 See e.g. Iedema's website: http://research.hss.uts.edu.au/health-communication-research/Health%20Communication%20Research.html
8 See e.g. http://www.newsroom.uts.edu.au/news/detail.cfm?ItemId=6400
9 Website: http://fr46.uni-saarland.de/croco/index_en.html
10 See http://www.victoria.ac.nz/lals/lwp/index.aspx
11 This applies to any of the strata of the theoretical metalanguage (cf. Halliday & Matthiessen, 1999; Teich, 1999), including the strata of "theoretical representation" and "computational representation". These areas need urgent attention, as emphasized by e.g. John Bateman and Elke Teich in recent plenary talks: for example, we need more "powerful" representations of structure — representations suitable for computational representation in systems capable of parsing large volumes of text.
12 For discussion of "text analysis" and "discourse analysis", see the section on terms in this volume.
13 There have been a number of these during the course of the development of SFL. A current example is the Multimodal Analysis Lab, directed by Kay O'Halloran at the National University of Singapore: http://multimodal-analysis-lab.org/ Another is the Halliday Centre for Intelligent Applications of Language Studies, directed by Jonathan Webster at Hong Kong City University: http://www.hallidaycentre.cityu.edu.hk/index.html
14 In sociology, Harold Garfinkel used to send his Ph.D. students planning to work on the sociology of science to do Ph.D.s in other disciplines so that as participant observers they would have the empirical based for developing a sociological account of how research is actually conducted.

3

Methods – techniques – problems

M.A.K. Halliday
University of Sydney

1 The design of language: finding your way around

1.1 General linguistic theory

Systemic functional linguistics falls within the definition of a general linguistic theory. It is "general" in the sense that it is a general theory for particular descriptions (Firth, 1957). But since "particular" suggests just individual languages, we should extend this to read "particular, comparative and typological" descriptions: that is, those which compare two or more languages, and those which explore similarities and differences among language types.

It is "linguistic" in the sense that it takes language as its object of enquiry. This does not mean, of course, that descriptions have to cover whole languages: most descriptive studies, especially comparative and typological, will be concerned with certain features of a language rather than with a language as a whole. At the same time, in order to be established as comparable in any significant sense, such features need to be located and understood in their context within the totality of the language. This means that comparison will involve systems, not single features. We may label some grammatical feature "passive" in languages a, b and c, but if we want to compare them we will first identify the system within which these features are located, then compare the relevant functions of these systems (are they all systems of "voice", which distribute the participants in a process into different discourse roles, e.g. Actor vs. Goal as Theme?), and only then look for partial analogies among the individual features.

Taking language as the object of enquiry means that the questions being investigated are questions to do with language. It does not mean that only language and nothing else is under scrutiny. Exploring questions of language will often require us to investigate other phenomena: if we want to understand functional variation in language, for example, we will need to know something about the sociological foundations of human relationships and interaction.

Equally, of course, scholars exploring questions which are not questions about language may need to gain some theoretical insight into language as an essential component in their own enquiries.

1.2 Language as a semiotic system

SFL locates language, in its turn, as one among a wider class of systems called "semiotic" systems – systems of meaning. The opposition here is that between semiotic and material: systems of meaning and systems of matter (Halliday, 2005a).

Language has the further property that it is a **semogenic** system: a system that **creates** meaning. Not all semiotic systems are also semogenic: a system of traffic signals, for example, is a system of meaning, but its **meaning potential** is fixed – it cannot create meanings that are not built into it. By contrast, the meaning potential of a language is openended: new meanings always can be, and often are being, created. Compare what a literate English-speaking adult could have meant in Chaucer's time with what you yourself are capable of meaning now.

When we refer to language as a semiotic system, the term "system" here is a shorthand for "system-&-process". In other words, language includes both the potential to mean and the act of meaning which brings that potential to life. A general linguistic theory encompasses both. For analogy, music is a semiotic system; and musicology is concerned not only with possible melodic and harmonic compositions but also with the production and reception of musical text.

At the same time, language is unique among our semiotic systems in that language is capable of describing itself. Whether or not anything that can be meant in every other human semiotic can also be meant in language (and there is no way of evaluating such a suggestion), those who operate with any of the others **also** operate with language; thus language serves as the general interpreter of all the rest (Matthiessen, 2001).

Semiotic systems, of course, have also their material mode of being: language is activated in social contexts, by the human body and brain, in the form of sound waves travelling through the air. Likewise systems of matter have their mode of being as meaning. Meaning needs matter to realize it – but matter needs meaning to organize it. Meaning in language is the most complex web of meaning that we know of.

1.3 SFL as problem-oriented theory

A **theory** is also a semiotic system: it is a system of interrelated meanings, mutually dependent and mutually defining. But whereas a language is an **evolved** system, and so represents a compromise among numerous different and potentially conflicting goals, a theory is a **designed** system, and as such it is oriented selectively towards specific and potentially explicit goals.

Systemic functional linguistics may be characterized as a **problem-oriented** theory, in the sense that it is designed to assist towards identifying and tackling problems that arise from outside itself – that is, not problems that the theory identifies for itself. Typically therefore the questions it sets out to answer are questions faced by people who are not linguists but are engaged in, or at least interested in, some activity in which language plays a key role. They might be translators or psychiatrists or teachers (of language or of anything else – all teaching depends on working effectively with language). The questions that arise may be research questions or questions of practical action; and language may have a central or a peripheral role in what they are engaged with; but in some way or other language is coming under their attention.

For these reasons SFL tends to neutralize the boundary between (theoretical) linguistics and applied linguistics. It has been called an "appliable" theory, and its evolution has tended to be driven by the ongoing experience of its use and by its constant extension to new areas of enquiry and of action (see especially Hasan, Matthiessen & Webster, eds, 2005, 2007). Every context of application brings with it new demands on the theory; and the lessons gained from facing up to these demands feed back into the theory and enrich it.

You will often hear the complaint that SFL is too complicated: it has too much descriptive apparatus. It is complicated – because language is complicated, and there is no point in pretending that it is simple. The problem is to recognize which aspects of the theory are relevant to a given task; and that does entail having some acquaintance with the whole.

1.4 The "architecture" of language

Because of its goal, of being useful, and usable, in a wide variety of contexts, rather than dedicated to just one or two, SFL has had to develop an explicit model of what we might call the "architecture" of language. Those using the theory in different contexts need to make reference to different architectural features – but preferably with an awareness of where their particular concerns fit in and relate to the design of language as a whole.

Actually, the "architecture" metaphor is a little too static; we should perhaps think rather in terms of a flow of traffic guided by an urban plan – or rather an urban complex, where all routes are open, some are more favoured than others, and the guiding principles (regarding precedence, motive power, speed and so on) have evolved over a long time and along with other features such as population density, advances in technology and so on.

The guiding principles in language are the dimensions of organization that define the system. There are various ways of specifying these; this is a possible framework for thinking about them (see Matthiessen, 2007a):

realization (the relation defining a hierarchy of strata)
metafunction (the modes of meaning in the system)

axis: paradigmatic (systems related in delicacy)
axis: syntagmatic (structures related in rank)
instantiation (the relation between system and text)

Given any task which consists in, or includes, engaging with language, the demands of the job can be stated in terms of these dimensions. For example, teaching pronunciation involves the two strata of expression (phonetics and phonology), and the relation between them; the two axes (system and structure) in phonology; and the concept of instantiation – pronunciation as (acceptable) instances of some specifiable systemic category. Such a task analysis gives a sense of the data and other resources needed for the job. Training translators, on the other hand, involves the strata of content (lexicogrammar and semantics), the relation of these to context, attention to delicacy in the system, and an awareness of the metafunctions and their interplay in the creation of meaning.

1.5 Realization, metafunction, axis and instantiation

1. All semiotic systems are based on realization. Where material systems are governed by causation (the relation between cause and effect), semiotic systems are governed by realization (the relation between token and value, or signifier and signified). Infant speech, or protolanguage, is made up of simple signs, with just one cycle of token and value: e.g. the token <u>nananana</u> means 'I want, give me'; and so on. Post-infancy, adult-like language is **stratified**: that is, it embodies cycles of realization:

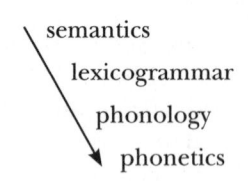

```
    semantics
      lexicogrammar
        phonology
          ↓ phonetics
```

– a cycle which then extends to the relation between language and its context of operation (Hasan, this volume; Butt & Wegener, 2007).

2. Possibly alone among semiotic systems, language is organized **metafunctionally**. Having evolved simultaneously as the means of making sense of our experience (construing "reality") and of getting along with each other (enacting our social relationships), language manages these as complementary modes of meaning (**ideational, interpersonal**) – along with a third functional component (the **textual**) which maps these on to each other and on to the context in which meanings are being exchanged. This pattern can be readily observed in the structure of the lexicogrammar of any language (see especially Caffarel, Martin & Matthiessen, eds, 2004).

3. Like every form of patterned activity language sets up relations on two axes, **paradigmatic** and **syntagmatic**. Syntagmatic relations are those between an element and what it goes together with, like Actor + Process + Goal in a clause, or Onset + Rhyme in a syllable; these are modelled in linguistics as relations of **structure**. Paradigmatic relations are those between an element and what could have occurred in place of it (but did not), like positive / negative ('yes/no'), first / second / third person ('me/you/him,her,it'). These are modelled in systemic functional linguistics as relations of **system**. SFL treats paradigmatic relations as the most abstract in terms of the theory, since they enable languages to be described and compared in terms of their meaning potential, irrespective of the vagaries of their realizations in structure.

Structures at any one stratum are organized in a compositional hierarchy known as "rank" (a part-whole relationship in which a structural unit of a given rank consists of one or more whole members of the next rank in the hierarchy); see Section 3 below. Systems at any one rank are organized in a dependency hierarchy known as "delicacy" (a taxonomic relationship in which any feature in a system, or combination of features, may be the **condition of entry** to a further system or systems); see Section 2 below.

4. At the most abstract level, "a language" is a vast network of systems, which we refer to collectively as "the system of the language". "Language as system" is then set against "language as text", the two being related by **instantiation**. Every text is an **instance** of some language system.

But system and instance are not two separate phenomena; rather, they are two **perspectives** on the same phenomenon (like "climate" and "weather" as two different perspectives on the same meteorological phenomena). We may choose either perspective according to whether we are collecting and organizing data (the "instance" angle) or we are constructing a general theory (the "system" angle). A rounded picture of language (as of everything else!) requires that we adopt both.

1.6 System - structure theories

SFL is a variety of a **system – structure theory**, which is a class of theories taking system and structure as primary organizing concepts. Such a theory takes seriously the Saussurean project of describing both syntagmatic and paradigmatic relations in language, including their relationship to each other. Other theories have treated the paradigmatic axis as secondary, or else ignored it altogether.

The leading originators of this kind of biaxial thinking in the mid-twentieth century were Trubetzkoy, Hjelmslev and Firth, together with their colleagues in what were sometimes referred to as the Prague school, the Copenhagen school and the London school. In the case of SFL the key figure was J.R. Firth, who had clearly enunciated the system - structure principle (see the two volumes of Firth's papers, Firth 1959 and Firth (ed. Palmer) 1968; see also Butt, 2001). In 'A synopsis of linguistic theory 1930 - 1955' (Firth et al., 1957; reprinted in Firth (ed. Palmer), 1968), Firth wrote:

> The first principle of phonological and grammatical analysis is to distinguish between *structure* and *system.*
> (Firth et al., 1957, p.17; Firth's italics)

In language as in other semiotic systems, meaning is the product of the interplay of system and structure – of syntagmatic and paradigmatic relations. But there are different ways of modelling the relationship between the two, including the relative priority accorded to one or the other. Firth did not describe the grammar of any one language; in describing phonology, he and his colleagues treated the two as equal and moved between them at any rank where they could be shown to intersect (see articles in Firth et al., 1957). Firth summarized the relationship by saying "system gives value to the elements of structure".

Sydney Lamb's relational network theory (formerly "stratificational grammar"), deriving most closely from the inspiration of Hjelmslev, likewise intersects system and structure as equal partners in the semogenic process, and therefore also in the linguist's descriptive enterprise. Lamb refers to "OR - relations" and "AND - relations"; he sees their interplay as an inherent property of the neural processes involved in semiotic activity, and hence extends the scope of the networks above phonology and lexicogrammar (Lamb's "lexological stratum") to the semantic ("semological") stratum that is next higher in the stratal hierarchy (Lamb, 1999).

2 System in systemic functional theory

2.1 System "realized in" structure

SFL differs from Firth, and also from Lamb, in that priority is given to the **system**. This does not mean that system is regarded as "more important" than structure (there is no evaluation involved!); it means that system is taken as the more abstract category, with structure as deriving from it. The two are shown to be interrelated – brought together in the description – at each **rank** at the strata of phonology and lexicogrammar: in a typical case there will be clause systems and clause structures, group systems and group structures, systems and structures of the tone unit and so on. Systems are said to be "realized in" the form of structure.*

---

* In the work of Halliday, Hasan, Martin, Matthiessen and colleagues this takes the form of a system / structure cycle at each rank in the lexicogrammar and the phonology (for other strata, see Section 6 below). In the work of Fawcett and colleagues the lexicogrammar is a syntax, defined structurally, with the systems located at the higher stratum of semantics (Fawcett, 2000). This reflects the different priorities in what are taken as the goals of the description.

The reasoning which led to this orientation was as follows. The theory seeks to be appliable to varied purposes, in varied contexts and in the description of any languages, particular, comparative or typological. This means that we need to be able to represent the meaning potential in a way which frees it from the constraints of structure. For example, it is likely that every language will have a system of **voice**, assigning different textual status to the participants in a process. But the structural resources for doing this are extremely varied: there may be formal distinctions in the verbal and / or nominal group, different ordering of elements in the clause, particles of various kinds, difference in the degree or kind of phonological prominence, and any combination of the above. It is virtually impossible to compare these, across languages or even within one language, if they have to be matched together as structures. But systemically they can all be brought within the compass of one comparable system. Many other grammatical systems, such as transitivity, modality, time (tense / aspect / phase), forms of appraisal, and speech function, show a similar variation in their deployment of structural resources.

When language is viewed as a resource for making meaning, which is the view that lies behind the appliability of the theory, the system represents the overall meaning potential – with "meaning" interpreted, as Firth regarded it, as a property of the totality of relations on all linguistic strata. (See Matthiessen, this volume.)

2.2 Representing the system

A system, then, is a set of features which stand in contrast with each other in a specified environment – of which one will be chosen whenever the environmental conditions obtain. Viewed as process, it is the name of the choice to be made. The system of POLARITY, which can be thought of as the prototype of all grammatical systems, is the set of features "positive / negative"; it is the name of the choice between the two. We show this as

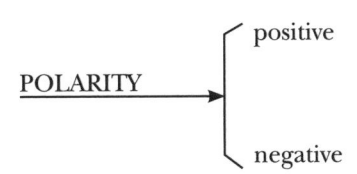

$$\text{POLARITY} \longrightarrow \begin{cases} \text{positive} \\ \text{negative} \end{cases}$$

The purpose of the arrowhead is to symbolize the "process" aspect of systems.

The environment of the choice is known as the "entry condition" of the system. Here it might be "major clause"; that is, if major clause, then select either positive or negative (stated procedurally), or every major clause is either positive or negative (stated descriptively).

A complete representation will show two further properties of the system: (1) the realization of each feature, and (2) the relative probabilities. An idealized version of the above would look like this:

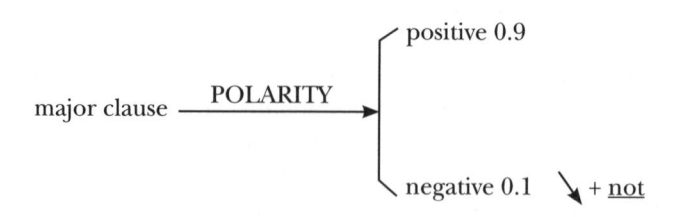

```
                                         ┌─ positive 0.9
        major clause ──POLARITY──▶       │
                                         └─ negative 0.1  ↘ + not
```

The probabilities shown here are, as it happens, based on observed frequencies in a corpus of modern English. The actual realizations are, of course, considerably more complex.

The paradigmatic principle means that features are not explained in isolation from their systemic context. We do not describe "negative", or "negation"; the object of description is the system – we describe POLARITY. We do not describe "passive"; we describe VOICE. We do not describe the "definite article"; we describe the system of NOMINAL DEIXIS. And so on.

This principle becomes particularly relevant when it comes to comparative studies. It makes little sense to compare "passive" across languages; but it makes good sense to compare systems of VOICE.

Some systems operate as "clines": there is continuous gradation, rather than a set of discrete terms. We return to these in Section 2.4 below.

2.3 Systemic domains

Each system has its domain, or **point of origin**: the location in the lexicogrammar or the phonology where the choice among the options is made.

This may be different from the place where the choice becomes manifested in the structure – where the features are actually **realized**. The point of origin may be at a higher rank, or on the same rank but at another location. Systems of TRANSITIVITY, MOOD & MODALITY, THEME and INFORMATION are always going to be associated with some unit that manages processes and propositions – that maps experiential and interpersonal meanings on to each other (typically the clause). They may be realized in the clause structure: by the order of elements, or by particles whose placing is clausally determined; but they may equally well be realized in the structure of groups or words (for example, cases in the nominal group), or in a unit on the phonological stratum related to the clause by default (for example, INFORMATION in the tone unit, which is in unmarked association with the clause).

Phonological systems may have their point of origin defined in terms of the phonological rank scale (for example, systems of TONE in the tone unit, the system of VOICING in the syllable onset). But they may be in terms of a unit in the lexicogrammar. The prototypical example of this is VOWEL HARMONY, where the phonological system of "y / w" is a system of the word; but there are many varied examples of this throughout prosodic phonology. An example from English is the system of RELATIVE DURATION of syllables in the foot, realizing the contrast of "+ / – group boundary" in the grammar, first observed by N. C. Scott in 1940 and described in detail by Abercrombie (1964) nearly half a century ago.

A few systems appear at more than one location. The system of TAXIS (parataxis / hypotaxis) is found in many languages at the rank of the clause complex; but it may extend to other "complex" ranks as well. It represents a choice between two degrees of interdependency (equal or unequal status) which in principle is available to any grammatical nexus. There may also be the option of positive versus negative polarity in other units than just the clause, where double negatives cancel each other out (as in *nobody doesn't know* meaning 'everybody knows'). If they don't cancel each other out, so that the meaning is the same as *nobody knows*, there is only one system here, with compound realization in the structure.

2.4 System networks

Systems are organized in **system networks**. These are clusters of associated systems, related to one another in simultaneity or dependency. In the lexicogrammar, system networks are typically within one metafunction (this is one of the principal demonstrations of the metafunctional principle). Thus mood and appraisal systems are interpersonal, those of transitivity are experiential (ideational), those of theme and information are textual. Systems of voice are mixed: their **potential** is defined experientially, by dependence on transitivity; but the choice within that potential is textual – the elements of transitivity structure are mapped into those of theme and information, assigning them kinds of value in the discourse. System networks have been extensively used throughout SFL writings; see especially Matthiessen 1996, Martin 1992a, Tench ed. 1992, Halliday 1985a – third edition (revised by Matthiessen). An early venture was Halliday's 'English system networks' (1976a).

Constructing a network means identifying a systemic potential at some location in the language: deixis in the nominal group, logical-semantic relationships in the clause nexus, structures of the monosyllable and so on. This defines the point of origin of the network, which then becomes a hypothesis about a designated area within lexicogrammar or phonology. There are now many computational resources to aid in the construction of networks; see Teich (this volume), O'Donnell (this volume).

Testing a system network involves three steps. (1) Generate the total paradigm of selection expressions from the network to ensure it says what you want it to say: that it is not too constraining (prohibiting combinations that are in fact possible) or too permissive (allowing combinations that are in fact not possible). (2) Generate the **realizations** of these selection expressions and test their accuracy. (3) Check the **proportionalities**: does replacing feature 1 by feature 2 mean the same thing in all environments? – or, if not, is the variation a predictable effect of the environmental shift? Networks of any complexity soon become too large to run through all the possibilities, and have to be tested by sampling.

The conventions for system network notation are set out on p. 84.

2.5 Problems with system networks

System networks soon become very complicated, and they pose the special problem that if you make any changes (as you always have to do, because you never get it right the first time) the whole network has to be formatted over again. This is less of a problem than it used to be, now that there are sophisticated computational resources to come to your help; but it is still a very demanding task to design and test them. To put this into perspective: the whole of a language, as far as we can conceive of it, is one vast system network. This resolves into a set of networks each for a different stratum; and, within that, a set of networks each for a different rank and metafunction (i.e. a cell in the metafunction / rank matrix). But when we move even a few steps in delicacy they still get very complex; so in practice one isolates a particular sub-domain (e.g. initials in the syllable, or temporal categories in the verbal group, or most general types of appraisal) and draws up a network for that.*

Two other problems arise both of which are problems of continuity: of resolving continuous contrasts, or "clines", into discrete categories. On the one hand, the system itself may be continuous: not just 'a or b' but some location on a scale from a to b. With the present conventions such systems have to be digitalized. There will often turn out to be good grounds for doing so. To give one example, in the English intonation system, in most varieties of English, the falling tone ("tone 1") always falls to low; but it may start at any height above that lowest point. However, if there is a pre-tonic segment to the tone unit the fall can be resolved into a system of three terms according to whether the tonic

---

* Two very large system networks for the grammar of English have been compiled in the course of computational linguistic (text generation) projects; see Fawcett (1997), Matthiessen & Bateman (1991), Bateman (1989).
These have proved valuable as research tools; but not (yet?) as resources for any practical applications.

fall starts above, on a level with or below the final pretonic pitch; so we can recognize "high falling / mid falling / low falling". When tested against natural discourse this proves to be the significant variable.

And on the other hand, the network recognizes only two states for the relationship between a pair of associated systems: either one system is fully dependent on the other, as in (a), or the two are simultaneous but fully independent, as in (b). Often however there is partial association between them such that, say, ax ay bx by are all possible but ax, by are favoured while ay, bx are very unlikely. Such degrees of association can be shown by spelling out the combinations and attaching probabilities to them (see next section, Section 2.6 below).

2.6 Probabilities in systems

The pattern described at the end of the last section is the effect of a general property of linguistic systems: that they are characterized by probabilities. If we recognize a systemic contrast between positive and negative in the clause, seeing this contrast as a feature of the meaning potential of the language, then we have to recognize that an essential property of this contrast is that it is **skew**: that positive is very much more frequent in discourse than negative.

We find in a reasonable sized corpus of English that about 90% of all clauses are positive. Frequency in the corpus (that is, of **instances** in the text) is the manifestation of probability in the system; we represent this as shown in Section 2.2 above. Suppose then that we find that, in the same set of clauses, there is a similar preponderance of indicative over imperative (these have not yet been counted, as far as I know). Then, if polarity and mood are

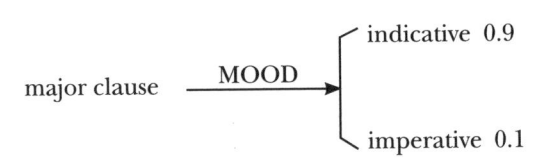

```
                                        ┌ indicative 0.9
major clause  ─── MOOD ──▶
                                        └ imperative 0.1
```

freely associated we shall predict:

positive indicative 0.81   positive imperative 0.09

negative indicative 0.09   negative imperative 0.01

To judge the significance of the different frequencies of ax, ay, bx, by we need to know the probabilities of a / b and x / y.

Halliday hypothesized that for two-term (binary) systems of primary delicacy there would be a tendency towards one or other of two probability profiles: the "equi" (roughly 0.5/0.5) and the "skew" (roughly 0.9 / 0.1). These would correspond in information theory to zero redundancy (H = 1, R = 0) and 50% redundancy (H = R = 0.5) respectively. This needs to be tested against data from a large-scale corpus.

Initial studies by Matthiessen showed an association between the frequency of a systemic feature and its elaboration into more delicate systemic options, at least in certain functional regions of the grammar. This seems highly plausible, and again will repay further investigation. (See Halliday & James, 1993; Halliday, 1992e; Matthiessen, 1999, 2006).

For relations between SFL and corpus studies see Hunston and Thompson (eds), 2006, passim.

3 Structure in systemic functional theory

3.1 Structure in phonology

We distinguish between a **structure** and a **syntagm** (in a way that is analogous to the distinction between a **system** and a **paradigm** in its traditional sense).

A syntagm is a sequence of classes: for example, consonant + vowel + consonant as the make-up of a syllable, or strong (salient) and weak syllable(s) in the make-up of a foot.

A structure is a configuration of functional elements (or simply "functions") at a given rank: for example, Onset ^ Rhyme as structure of the syllable, or Ictus ^ Remiss as structure of the foot. The elements of a structure may be shown as unordered: e.g. Ictus • Remiss, which states that they may occur in either sequence (as in traditional metrics, which recognizes both an iambic and a trochaic foot). The symbol ^ indicates that the ordering is an intrinsic feature of the structure itself.

Structures are associated with the units, at each rank, that are set up for the phonology of each particular language (Tench, ed., 1992). In English phonology, we identify a tone unit (or "tone group"), a foot (or "rhythm group"), and a syllable. Below the syllable there is the hemisyllable (the initial and final parts of the syllable, realizing Onset and Rhyme). The minimal units that make up the hemisyllable, whether represented as phonemes (Firth's "phonematic units") or as features, of course have no further phonological structure. We may choose to omit any reference to the hemisyllable, or to Onset and Rhyme, and model the syllable as a structure realized directly by sequences of phonemes; this is simpler for some purposes, but ignores certain aspects of phonological patterning – for example rhyming in verse, and the phenomenon of **phonaesthesia**.

It should be possible to establish a higher unit (either a "phonological paragraph" or a "tone unit complex") above the tone unit as at present described. (See Tench, 1990; Halliday & Greaves, 2008).

3.2 Structure in lexicogrammar

As in phonology, we distinguish between a structure and a syntagm, where a syntagm is a sequence of classes. A clause, for example, may consist of nominal group + verbal group + nominal group + prepositional phrase. A verbal group may consist of auxiliary verb + (lexical) verb + adverb.

A structure, again as in phonology, is a configuration of functional elements, e.g. (in a clause) Actor /Agent • Process • Goal/ Medium • Extent/ Time; (in a verbal group) Finite (operator) ^ Event. In grammar, however, structure is organized as a matrix of rank and metafunction. This appears most clearly at the rank of the clause, where the grammar integrates the three metafunctional components (experiential, interpersonal and textual) into a single integrated structure. The configuration of Agent • Process • Medium is experiential; it will be mapped into some kind of interpersonal structure, perhaps involving a Subject and some kind of predicating element (e.g. Subject • Finite • Predicator • Complement); and also into a textual configuration such as Theme ^ Rheme. Any constituent of the syntagm will thus have three simultaneous values in the structure; the prototypical case of this multivalence is the nominal group functioning simultaneously as Actor, Subject and Theme (see Halliday 1985a – third edition (revised by Matthiessen), chap.2).

The remaining metafunction, the logical, generates a different set of structures which realize systems of logical-semantic relations obtaining between pairs or longer sequences of elements having the same functional location, such as a nexus of two nominal groups functioning as Subject in the clause, or a nexus of clauses forming a clause complex. Here the structure of each nexus consists of a primary and a secondary element; the relation between the two will be either **hypotactic** (one dominant and one dependent element, occurring in either sequence) or **paratactic** (where the two are of equal status and the only primacy is that of the sequence in which they occur). A hypotactic structure is symbolized by letters of the Greek alphabet (α • β • ...), a paratactic structure by Arabic numerals (1 ^ 2 ^ ...).

The metafunction / rank matrix shows the rank at which the systems within each metafunction have their point of origin in the structure: their "address" in the system as a whole. The fact that each rank has its own systemic potential is a key principle of the management of complexity at the formal strata of phonology and grammar. See p. 85.

3.3 Types of structure

In phonology, where the expressive resources of a language are organized to form a speech chain, the variation among different kinds of structure is brought about by the potential that is inherent in different contrasting sound patterns. This has been represented in phonological theory as an opposition between

segmental and **prosodic** (between features that don't persist through time and those that do). At one time the prosodic were seen as the "marked" variant (called "suprasegmental" to suggest this); now we would see the distinction as a cline, with (if anything) the prosodic mode as the more fundamental (cf. Firth's original "prosodic phonology": Firth et al. 1957; Firth, 1959). Many features are in themselves quite variable in extension: for example pitch variation, whose domain is the tone unit in "intonation languages" but the syllable in "tone languages"; resonance (the contrast of oral / nasal); posture (palatal / velar, or "y/w"); voice quality (breathy / creaky) – all these are variable in their domain of operation. Only plosion (in plosives and affricates) inherently figures as a minimal segment.

In grammar, the situation is different. Here all structures can be (and traditionally have been) reduced to a single type, that of constituency – in other words, digitalized as parts of wholes. But this form of reductionism obscures the fact that there are four distinct types of structural organization in the "content plane" of language, which we can set out most simply as follows:

structural type	physical analogue	metafunction with which associated
configurational	particle	experiential
prosodic	field	interpersonal
periodic	wave	textual
iterative (serial)	string	logical

The payoff in evolutionary terms is clear. Given that different strands of meaning (different sets of systemic features) are being combined into a single syntagmatic time line, the more varied the structural resources the more freely they can be brought together. The speaker can put any spin (interpersonal) on any topic (experiential) at any discursive moment (textual) – and keep the story going along indefinitely (logical). Such a pattern is more likely to be viable – to be favoured in the evolution of language – than one in which every component of the meaning (every metafunction) is realized in just the same way (Halliday, 1979; Martin, 1996b).

3.4 Structural boundaries

So the structure-forming resources in a language are very varied, with variable range of operation. At the same time, there has to be some overriding order – some defining of bounded units as the domains of systemic choice. This, as has been said, is provided by the rank scale (Sections 1.1, 3.2): the emergence of a hierarchy of units serving as points of origin for meaning-making events.

These tend to be fuzzy at the edges. You can tell how many units there are in a given instance (how many tone units, for example, in a stretch of spoken English), and where their centres of gravity are – where the meaningful choices are activated (for example, the tonic foot); but you cannot say exactly where each tone unit begins and ends. The same could be true of a grammatical unit such as the clause, where the boundaries of the different metafunctional lines may not coincide.

Languages vary, obviously, both in how they exploit the various structural resources and in where they display greater or less indeterminacy. For analytic purposes, one takes certain more or less arbitrary decisions, e.g. about clause or syllable boundaries – especially in quantitative and comparative studies, where the critical factor is consistency: making explicit the criteria on which analytic decisions are taken.

In SFL the rank scale provides a robust criterion: each unit is said to consist of a whole number (one or more) of units next below in rank. For example, in English a tone unit always consists of one or more rhythmic units or "feet" (see Halliday & Greaves 2008 for illustration of this principle).

SFL places a high value on comprehensiveness in description. The scale of rank plays an important part in lexicogrammar and in phonology. This does not mean, of course, that there is no departing from this principle; language will always wriggle out from under any restraining mesh. It means that it is the default condition to which any departure is referred, for example in modelling the category of "ellipsis", or the status of clausal particles.

It is worth pointing out, perhaps, that the much derided popular adage that "the exception proves the rule" is in fact a useful tactic for reasoning with. If something is said to be an "exception", this is a way of proclaiming that there is a rule for it to be exception to. That rule can therefore be stated, as a generalization that holds good in principle, and that may have a significant place in some network of explanation. The "exception" then stands to be further explained, perhaps by limiting the domain of application of the rule.

On indeterminacy in language, see Halliday & Matthiessen (1999, chap.13), Matthiessen (1995a & b), Halliday (1995d).

4 Complexity in language

4.1 Grammar and lexis

SFL operates with the general concept of "lexicogrammar" rather than with a triad of syntax, morphology and lexicon. There are two main reasons for this. One is that the distinction between syntax and morphology has always been ill-defined – and however it is defined it will apply only to certain languages; so we use the more traditional term "grammar". The other is that the boundary between grammar (or syntax) and lexicon is extremely fuzzy; the two are joined in a continuum, and they are of the same order of abstraction, so that while we do need to recognize the distinct categories of grammar and lexis we also need to model them as a unity on a single stratum. The idea of words as bricks held together by grammar as mortar is not helpful. Rather, we think of a unified region where meaning is fashioned and organized (Hjelmslev's "form of the content"), but where the kind of organization changes, gradually but significantly, as you go from one end to the other (See Tucker, 1997, 2007; Neale, 2006).

We can think of the job of the lexicogrammar as that of managing the complexity of human existence; more specifically, the complexity of our experience and the complexity of our social relationships. Both these aspects of the human condition have become vastly more complicated over the life of the human species; this has been the driving force in the evolution of the brain, which is simultaneous with the evolution of language – language and brain have in fact been co-evolving, as facets of a single process (see Deacon, 1997; Melrose, 2006).

The lexicogrammar is thus a **theory** of the human condition – a construal of experience and an enactment of the social process. In the second of these (meta)functions most of the meanings (apart from individual personal names) are those of the interactive engagement of speaker and listener, not arranged into clearly defined pieces – they are the semantic prosodies characteristic of the interpersonal metafunction. But the construing of experience calls for the semioticizing of the material environment; and this demands on the one hand **common** names for the events and the particular things that participate in them, and on the other hand a range of very general properties of these phenomena and of the relations that appear among them. These get semioticized in two different ways, that we call "lexical" and "grammatical".

Meanings that are lexicalized are those which are construed as specific, in open sets (often highly taxonomized, especially the entities), and restricted to particular domains and contexts of appearance. Meanings which are grammaticalized are construed as general, in closed systems, and turning up in almost every semioticization of experience. And there is a region that is intermediate between the two, with highly generalized lexical items (like *thing, stuff, way* &c. in English) and less firmly systemized grammatical categories such as facet (*side, front* &c.), temporal aspect (*soon, just,* &c.) and many others. It is this intermediate region that is occupied by many of the interpersonal meanings, which are less polarized between the lexical and the grammatical (see Martin & White, 2005).

There are certain especially complex areas of experience which challenge the lexicogrammatical resources of any language. One such example is the phenomenon of pain, which is at best unpleasant and at worst unbearable and frightening. Such areas call for the interplay of lexis and grammar in elaborated ways which give particular insight into the semogenic powers of language; see for example Halliday (1998b), Hori (2006). On a different scale, the evolution of the discourses of science, with their massive deployment of the resources of grammatical metaphor, shows very clearly how language, and each particular language, totally regroups itself when experience comes to be **reconstrued** in new and significantly different ways (Halliday, 2002–2007, volume 5).

4.2 Complexity in lexicogrammar (1): lexical density

When we examine more closely the way complexity is organized and managed in language, we find that the lexis and the grammar do this in two rather different ways. In the lexis, complexity takes the form of increasing density; in the grammar, it takes the form of greater intricacy.

Lexical density is, essentially, the quantity of lexicalized information packed into a given unit in the grammar. The optimum unit for measuring lexical density is the **ranking clause**: that is, all clauses other than those that are rankshifted (or "embedded") – such clauses form part of (some constituent of) another clause and so are already included in the count for their host (or "matrix") clause. The variable to be counted is the **lexical item** (or "lexeme"). The lexical density of a text can be measured as the mean number of lexical items per ranking clause (Halliday, 1987).

Identifying the lexical item is of course problematic, since there is a great deal of indeterminacy (in any one language; much more of course in any comparison between languages). It can be thought of as a "content word", and so treated as if always just one word (in English, defined orthographically), with the line between it and the grammatical item (the "function word") drawn more or less arbitrarily provided it is kept consistent (as it must be for any comparative study).

Identifying the ranking clause demands some expertise in analysing grammar; an alternative tactic, devised by Jean Ure (1971), was to count the number of lexical items and the number of grammatical items and express this as a simple proportion. This can be done for, say, the first thousand words in any text, and it will give some idea of the variation among different registers. But the count per clause is more accurate and more revealing, since it can be related to other features in the grammar; and it can be used for comparison among languages, which the simple ratio cannot.

The main interest in assessing lexical density lies in the comparison of different registers within a language. High lexical density is a feature of written (as opposed to spoken) language, and in particular of its more technical and bureaucratic varieties. Comparing elaborated written with informal spoken English Halliday found a mean lexical density of 5 to 6 with the former and rather under 2 with the latter. The written varieties had a much greater tendency towards the lexicalization of complex meanings – and, as a corollary, a notably simpler clausal grammar. For a more sophisticated measure of lexical density it would be desirable to take account of the frequency ranking of the lexical items of the language. Clearly in some sense, at least, using items of very low frequency increases the complexity of the text. But this factor has not yet been incorporated into lexical density studies.

4.3 Complexity in lexicogrammar (2): grammatical intricacy

Grammatical intricacy is the measure of tactic complexity in the clause complex. (In principle it can be applied to complexes of any rank, but the clause complex is the most significant for the text as a whole.) In its simplest manifestation this means just counting the number of ranking clauses that are conjoined, either paratactically or hypotactically, into each single clause complex.

This can be computed as a mean value for any text. But there is likely to be a distortion here in the case of informal spoken texts (which is where the grammatical intricacy tends to be highest), because spontaneous dialogue is characterized by a mixture of some sustained and some very short turns, with the latter seldom exceeding a single clause; so any intricacy in the monologic moments gets obscured.

The main problem that arises in studying grammatical intricacy is that of deciding when a clause complex is finished. Again, in a written text one can go by the orthography: a clause complex is equated with a written sentence (which is the written surrogate of the clause complex to start with). But in the spoken language two problems arise. On the one hand, many speakers insert a conjunction (usually *and*) merely as a way of holding the floor, without maintaining any logical-semantic relation; and on the other hand, the logical-semantic relation may be maintained with no overt segmental marker (especially in a paratactic nexus of elaboration, usually realized as tone concord, which does not appear in orthographic transcription – though this can be overcome by using the SFL transcription as in Halliday & Greaves, 2008).

For a more sophisticated measure of grammatical intricacy it might be desirable to take account of the difference between the two forms of **taxis** (or "interdependency"), since it is usually assumed that hypotaxis adds more to structural complexity than does parataxis. In any case high grammatical intricacy will appear as a characteristic of spoken language, especially speech that is informal and spontaneous. The more intricate the structure of a clause complex, the more likely it is that this occurred in natural speech.

Thus in everyday spoken varieties of language, complexity in the meaning potential is typically managed by grammaticalizing: spreading out the lexical information across intricately constructed skeins of related clauses (See Halliday, 1985b).

4.4 Nominal and clausal styles

Of course the lexicalized information has to go somewhere in the grammar – it is not left in the air. Typically in English and other standard written languages it goes into the nominal group, which often becomes quite intricate in its own turn; thus discourse with high lexical density is sometimes called "nominal (or "nominalized") style". Discourse with high grammatical intricacy has been referred to as "verbal style"; but this is a misnomer: the opposition is not between nominal and verbal, but between nominal and clausal.

It seems the difference between the two styles is not that the clausal style has fewer lexical items, but that those there are are distributed among more clauses. This is true – but it is not the whole story. Many elements that turn up lexicalized in the "nominal" style do appear also in the clausal, often in a different word class; but if one "translates" from the nominal to the clausal, some disappear altogether. For example,

Nominal (high lexical density)	Clausal (low lexical density)
fire intensity has a **profound effect** on **smoke injection**	the more **intense** the **fire** the more **smoke** it **injects**
(one clause, six lexemes)	(two clauses, four lexemes)

– where *has a profound effect on* is grammaticalized as *the more . . . the more.*

The difference between the two forms of complexity relates first and foremost to the different properties of speech and writing. Speech flows along in a temporal sequence; spoken discourse is like a moving current – or, to vary the metaphor, its mode of complexity is choreographic, like the movement of a dance. Writing exists in linearized space; written discourse is like a river of ice, frozen in time – its mode of complexity is crystalline and highly compacted. In their relation to the construal of experience, each one makes reality look like itself.

In any assessment of complexity, such as in the context of evaluating teaching materials, there will always be the issue that complexity takes different forms. Density and intricacy are one illustration of this. But the complexity will be relative to the context, which includes the nature of the discourse and its place in the wider semiotic process. Formulations such as "passive is more complex than active", or "longer sentences are more difficult to process than short ones", are without any value, and not to be taken seriously – it is easy to find contexts where the opposite is the case. A "difficult" text is one that is complex in the wrong way, unrelated to what the situation demands; or, perhaps, addressed to the wrong audience – such as the wrong age group (cf. the next section).

4.5 The ontogenesis of complexity

How does the human brain develop to support this construction of complexity? We do not know how the brain evolved, in the species; but we can track its development in the history of the individual child, insofar as concerns the brain's ability to mean (for more detail see Painter, this volume).

The infant's protolanguage is not a referential system. Reference comes in as the beginning of the child's move into the mother tongue (into "language" in its usual sense). It begins with "proper" (individualized) naming, and then develops from "proper" to include "common" naming (reference to classes, typically in the first part of the second year of life). This is the first step in a three-stage progression in the modes of reference, which we can summarize as follows:

1. generalization (proper –> common)   1 - 4 years approx.
2. abstractness (concrete –> abstract)   5 – 10 „   „
3. metaphor (congruent –> metaphorical)   10 - adulthood

Common terms at stage 1 are those for concrete entities and processes, those that can be apprehended through the senses: people, animals, objects, and institutions with perceptible form (like shops). The next step, taken at the beginning of literacy and numeracy, is the move from concrete, perceptible referents to include abstract and symbolic entities (enabling the child to go into the primary school and take on educational knowledge). Any good textbooks and writings for children in this age range will show what kinds of reference are accessible to them.

Up to this time, meanings are construed **congruently**: processes are verbs, entities are nouns, qualities are adjectives (which in some languages, such as English, are a kind of noun; in others, such as Chinese, a kind of verb), and logical-semantic relations are conjunctions. But some metaphorical forms of reference have already come in, especially in maths with terms like *length, motion, subtraction, follows, results from*. Here there is a **cross-coupling** between the semantics and the grammar: a process or quality becomes a noun, a logical-semantic relation becomes a verb.

It is only as an adolescent, in the secondary school, that the developing brain is able to cope with discourse where the entire text is metaphorized in this way. These processes of **grammatical metaphor**, where the crossover is not between lexical items, as in metaphor in its traditional sense, but between grammatical categories, now take over as the purveyors of the technical, subject-based knowledge of our literate culture. By the end of adolescence the brain can handle all the modes of complexity that have evolved in the fully-developed adult semiotics. See Derewianka (2003); Painter, Derewianka & Torr (2007).

5 Thinking about language

5.1 3-M thinking (m → M → μ)

We think about language in order to be able to act: to act on language (perhaps by analysing discourse), and through language on other issues, both theoretical and practical. To be effective, all such action relies on our theoretical understanding of language.

One strategy for thinking about language is to consider how language itself "thinks about" (construes) the human condition. We saw in the last section how children move through different phases in relating language to the phenomena of experience: first naming particulars, then moving "up" to naming classes of sensible entities, then moving "out" from the sensible to the abstract and virtual – a progression from micro to macro to meta. We find the same thing happening in the development of functionality in language: the child starts with a small set of microfunctions (contexts of language use, in the protolanguage); then generalizes these to a simple set of two "macrofunctions" (mathetic/pragmatic, in the transition to the mother tongue); then transforms these into the intrinsic metafunctions of the content plane. In this analogous move, from micro to macro to meta, functionality has evolved from 'used in various contexts' to becoming the basic organizing principle of the language system.

We may become aware of this progression if we look over the "macrotext" of an evolving technical discipline – because it is a familiar strategy in the construction of a scientific theory. We find meronymy (the 'is a part of' relation) as the trademark of technical discourse, and hyponymy ('is a kind of') as that of the discourse of science (Martin & Veel eds, 1998); the latter is what takes us from the macro to the meta – to a higher order of abstraction (see Matthiessen, this volume). This principle is clearly at work in our own thinking about language, when we move from smaller to larger units in the structure and then from the structure to the system in search of explanations. For example, to understand *the* (the "definite article") in English, we first locate it in the structure of the nominal group, and then set up the system of NOMINAL DEIXIS – which may in turn lead us into another cycle in our investigation.

But how do we contextualize a problem – and ourselves in relation to it – in the first place? This means taking up a descriptive stance – or rather, moving among a number of different stances, to achieve a "trinocular" perspective on various dimensions, as these were outlined in Section 1 above.

5.2 Trinocularity

On any of the dimensions along which language is organized, there is room for a trinocular perspective. Given any phenomenon as an object of study, it can be looked at from three angles: from above, from below, and from round about. The metaphor of "above" and "below" is traditional in linguistics for the scales of realization (higher and lower strata) and composition (higher and lower ranks). Other scales are usually represented as "left to right", such as system to instance, and delicacy in the system network. The trinocular vision applies, of course, to these dimensions also.

Suppose for example we are investigating the systems of intonation in English. Stratally, this is located in phonology; we examine it "from above" (its role in the lexicogrammar), "from below" (its realization in the phonetics), and "from round about" (as a system in relation to other systems in the phonology). It is manifested structurally at the rank of "tone unit"; we examine it "from above", in larger patterns of tone unit sequences (perhaps there is a "tone unit complex"?), "from below", its composition in terms of feet or some other form of syllabic organization, and "from round about", its nature as a phonological unit with its own structures and boundaries. It can be analysed at various degrees of delicacy: most grossly (least delicately) in terms of the simple opposition between a falling and a rising tone; much more delicately as a system of some twenty contrasting tone patterns in the tonic and pre-tonic components; and, probably for most purposes, at medium delicacy as a system of five tones. It can be viewed from the "instance" end, as text in which certain patterns are found to recur (perhaps as shown instrumentally, with sound spectrography), and from the "system" end as an essential element in the overall organization of the language as a semogenic system – in its contribution to the making of meaning.

We will not attempt to describe all these things at once! But whatever it is that is on the agenda, as the current object of the description, has its location in this multidimensional space, providing multiple perspectives any of which can be adopted in order to validate the interpretation given.

5.3 Complementarity

Complementarity is the principle of having things both ways – of thinking in terms of 'both + and' rather than 'either / or'. Again, this is the way language "thinks about" the world: if our grammar can't decide whether time is a current flowing out of future through present into past or a translation out of virtual into actual, it says "well it's both" and construes temporal systems which embody some mixture of tense and aspect. In the same way the grammar's theory of events is a mixture of transitive and ergative: either one party is doing something which may or may not extend to another party (Actor ± Goal), or one party is involved in something which may or may not be caused by another party (Affected ± Agent); the two seem to be contradictory, but the grammar accommodates both.

Such situations arise in language when the grammar has to make sense of experiential phenomena that are not uniform but ranged along a cline of variation, such that the two ends seem quite distinct even though there is a broad region in the middle. We have to accommodate this vision in our own description – to take it from the grammar into the grammatics. So we set up, say, ergative structures and transitive structures; and we may call those processes which are better described ergatively "ergative processes" and the ones better described transitively we call "transitive processes" (Davidse, 1992, 1999). There will always be room for disagreement; thus, Halliday follows traditional grammar in regarding all the finite tenses of English as serial tenses ("past in present", "future in past" and so on), recognizing aspect in the non-finite distinction between infinitive and participle, whereas the structuralist grammarians treat the composite finite forms as aspect. Such disagreements arise because the facts are complex and linguists have different goals and place different values on the criteria involved (e.g. SFL places a high value on evidence from function in discourse).

Certain complementarities are fundamental to linguistics because they represent features that are intrinsic to language as a whole; these have already figured in the preceding sections. One of these is instantiation, the complementarity of language as system and language as text. This is a complementarity of angle: there is only one set of phenomena here, the text; but to explain this we shift our angle as observers and set up a virtual entity "the linguistic system", which exists on the semiotic plane. Other complementarities are those of grammar and lexis, and speech and writing. Spoken and written language form a complementarity of state, like the liquid and solid states of a material substance; "the same" substance, but with different relations to the environment of space and time. Grammar and lexis form a complementarity of focus, with different roles in the total construal of experience (see Halliday, 2008).

5.4 Mixed criteria; compromise

Most of the time in setting up our categories we are faced with a mixed bag of criteria, which will typically not coincide and which, however we try to adjust them, will define only fuzzy sets with uncertain membership and boundaries. For example, in transitivity languages operate with some system of **types of process**, some repertory of doing and happening, sensing and saying, being and having. In English we can recognize three, or four, or six primary process types: material, mental & verbal, relational – where mental-&-verbal could be combined as "semiotic", there could be a "behavioural" category on the borderline of material and mental, and "existential " could be separated out from within the relational. There is no single right answer to the question "how many types of process are there?". But there are some powerful criteria for recognizing them as distinct, such as the following:

Only in mental process is there always a participant "+ consciousness" (the Senser)

Only material processes have "present-in-present" as unmarked present tense (the "present continuous")

Only mental processes come in reciprocal pairs (*I forget it/ it escapes me*)

Only in relational processes may the verb have no salience (no "stressed syllable")

Only semiotic processes can project (quote and report speech and thought)

In analysing discourse, there will always be cases where criteria conflict. The fruitful question to ask is not "which is right?", but "what are the consequences of interpreting this way or that?" Consider a clause with verb *indicate* or *imply* or *suggest*, such as *the result suggested a way out*, which could be relational (intensive/ identifying) or verbal. If you interpret as relational, you are locating it in the voice system in contrast with passive, and reading it as Token and Value, like *the result signalled a way out*. If you interpret as verbal, *the result* becomes a Sayer, as in *Smith suggested* . . .; and there could be an agnate projection like *the result suggested that there was a way out*. Looked at "from below", if the verb was (or could be) said without salience, as//the re/sult suggested a/way/out//, it will be relational. Seen "from above", if it occurs in a generalizing context, e.g. in science, this might suggest Token - Value; if in a particularizing one, e.g. in narrative, then perhaps verbal (cf. Halliday, 1976b).

When you engage with language, you are likely to shunt back and forth along the cline of instantiation, shifting perspective between the view from the text and the view from the system. (This is good exercise for the brain!)

6 Phonetics, semantics and context

This chapter has concentrated on the "formal" strata, those of lexicogrammar and phonology – often referred to as the "core" components of the linguistic system – because these are where the key theoretical concepts and descriptive methods of linguistics are most developed and where most of the work in SFL has been done.

What then of the other strata? – of semantics and phonetics, and the stratum of context theorizing what Firth called the "exterior relations" of language? Semantics and phonetics are the two "interface" strata of language, where language interacts with its environment: the ecosocial environment at one end (Lemke, 1993) and the physiological (and physical) environment at the other, both of course via the intermediary of the human brain. Phonetics has had a fairly independent evolution, latterly as "speech science", and while systemic phonology engages with it and depends on it (see e.g. Catford, 1977, 1985; Halliday & Greaves, 2008), there is no reason to proclaim a specifically systemic functional approach.

The need for – and challenge to – a systemic functional semantics came from three sources: (1) from stylistics, the linguistic study of literary texts; (2) from sociological linguistics as set out in the work of Basil Bernstein (1971, 1990), and (3) from computational linguistics especially text generation and parsing. Stylistics demanded ways of exploring, and explaining, all the levels of meaning in a literary work, especially that of symbolic articulation (Hasan, 1985b & d; Butt & Lukin, this volume). Bernstein's work demanded the explanation of different "coding orientations" as revealed in his research (see Hasan, 1996b and Hasan & Cloran, 1990, showing **semantic variation** by gender and social class in interaction between mothers and children). Computational linguistics demanded the theorizing of the "upper level" as a linguistic stratum in systemic relation with the wording (see Mann, 1984; Mann & Matthiessen, 1985; Matthiessen, 1987a, 1988b; Halliday & Matthiessen, 1999).

The problem for semantics is this. Since meanings are construed and enacted in the lexicogrammar, why do we build in semantics as a separate stratum? (Note that SFL never used "semantics" defined as the meanings of words. It has always been an overarching concept, including grammatical semantics as well as lexical semantics; cf. Halliday, 1970b). The reason is: because there are, in fact, two cycles of organization involved (characterized by Martin & Matthiessen, 1992, as "topological" and "typological"). Semantics is the transformation of the ecosocial environment into a meaning potential in terms of the topological domains of experience and social interaction. Lexicogrammar is the organization of these into linguistic form (grammar and lexis) in terms of metafunctionally related "typological" networks of grammatical and lexical features.

It is this "double articulation" within the content plane that makes possible the phenomenon of metaphor. Metaphor arises by deconstructing the congruent relation of wording to meaning and "cross-coupling" to a new alignment, in this way creating a new meaning which is the fusion of the meanings of both, in a process of **semantic junction**. For example, the word *motion* is **both** a process (the category meaning of "verb", which is the congruent wording of 'move') **and** an entity (the category meaning of its metaphorical wording as "noun"). Here the metaphor is grammatical – a junction of two grammatical classes; but the same semantic junction takes place in lexical metaphor (e.g. in *a sickle moon* the meaning of the word *sickle* is a junction of the meaning of the congruent wording *crescent* with that of *sickle* as a curving blade.

The Firthian project of bringing Malinowski's "context of situation" (but also, we would add, his "context of culture") into the compass of a linguistic theory has always been on the SFL agenda; see Hasan, 1985b & d, 1999b; Martin, 1992a, 1999; Butt & Wegener, 2007. Their researches have taken the notion of "system" up to the contextual stratum; and the structuring of the context in terms of field, tenor and mode helped to bring out the mechanisms whereby context **activates** the meanings and wordings of the content plane, and these, in turn, **construe** the features of the context (see Hasan, this volume).

The conceptual framework of SFL, and perhaps most critically the dimensions of realization and instantiation, have enabled scholars to explore semiotic

(Section 2.4)

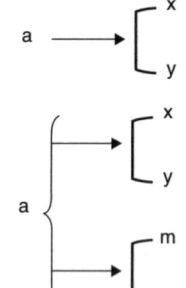

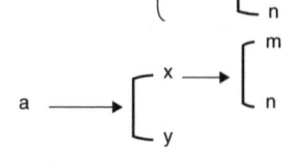

a ⟶ [x / y]   there is a system x/y with entry condition a
[if a, then either x or y]

a { [x / y], [m / n] }   there are two "simultaneous" systems x/y and m/n both having entry condition a
[if a, then both (i) either x or y and (ii) either m or n]

a ⟶ [x ⟶ [m / n], y]   there are two systems x/y and m/n, one dependent on the other; x/y has entry condition a and m/n has entry condition x
[if a, then either x or y; if x, then either m or n]

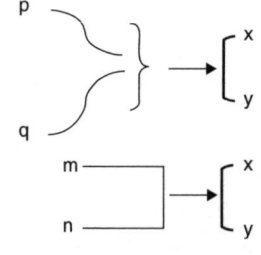

p, q } ⟶ [x / y]   there is a system x/y with conjunct entry condition p and q (note: p and q must be features from different systems, otherwise they could not cooccur)
[if both p and q, then either x or y]

m, n ⟶ [x / y]   there is a system x/y with disjunct entry condition either m or n
[if either m or n, or both, then either x or y]

a* ⟶ ∞ ⟶ x*   x is unmarked with respect to a [if a, then always x] (note: any paired symbol may occur, usually accompanied by "i...t" or "⟶...⟶" 'if ... then')

x*   x is unmarked with respect to all environments
[if any tangential feature, then always x]

Types of realization statement

insertion	+ X	[insert function X]
conflation	X / Y	[conflate function X with function Y]
expansion	X (P • Q)	[expand X to P plus Q, unordered]
ordering	X ^Z	[order Z after X] (note also # ^X 'put X first')
preselection	: w	[preselect feature w]
classification	: : z	[classify lexically as z] (where grammatical features have not yet been assigned)
lexification	= t	[lexify as t] (specify lexical item)

Note: names of systems are written in upper case, e.g. MOOD
names of features are written in lower case, e.g. indicative
names of functions are written with upper case initial, e.g. Subject
lexicogrammatical representations (wordings) are underlined/italic, e.g. *be*
semantic representations (meanings) take single quotes, e.g. 'be'

Systemic notation: summary of conventions

(Section 3.2)

rank \ metafunction [class]	ideational logical	ideational experiential	interpersonal	textual	(cohesive)
clause complexes (clause-)		TRANSITIVITY (process type)	MOOD MODALITY POLARITY	THEME CULMINATION VOICE	COHESIVE RELATIONS
phrase [prepositional] (phrase-)		MINOR TRANSITIVITY (circumstance type)	MINOR MOOD (adjunct type)	CONJUNCTION	
group [verbal] (group-)	INTERDEPENDENCY (parataxis/hypotaxis) & LOGICAL-SEMANTIC RELATION (expansion/projection) / TENSE	EVENT TYPE ASPECT (non-finite)	FINITENESS	VOICE DEICTICITY	REFERENCE ELLIPSIS/ SUBSTITUTION
[nominal]	MODIFICATION	THING TYPE CLASSIFICATION EPITHESIS QUALIFICATION	PERSON ATTITUDE	DETERMINATION	CONJUNCTION
[adverbial]	MODIFICATION	QUALITY (circumstance type)	COMMENT (adjunct type)	CONJUNCTION	
word (word-)	DERIVATION	(DENOTATION)	(CONNOTATION)		
	ACCENTUATION		KEY	INFORMATION	
information unit	simplexes				
info. unit complex	complexes				

A "function / rank matrix" for the grammar of English, where (i) rows show rank and primary class, (ii) columns show metafunction, and (iii) capitals show system(s) in each cell systems other than language in their relationship to the environment; see e.g. O'Toole, 1994; Butt & O'Toole, 2003; Kress & van Leeuwen, 1996. Experience in theorizing language by extending the descriptive methodology outwards, e.g. by extending networks from lexicogrammar to situation-specific and then to generalized semantics and then to context, has been critical in building up to a multimodal (or, better, "multisemiotic") conception of meaning (Halliday, 1973; Hasan, 1996b; Baldry & Thibault, 2006a; Martinec, 2005). The findings from these extensions of the field of action of SFL will in turn be immensely significant for its continuing evolution as an "appliable" theory (Matthiessen, this volume; Hasan, Matthiessen & Webster, eds, 2005, 2007, passim).

4

Language development

Clare Painter
University of New South Wales

Within SFL, the phenomenon typically referred to as 'acquisition' of the mother tongue is viewed as one in which children gradually create and transform their potential for meaning in the course of interacting with others in social contexts – a process not highlighted by the metaphor of acquisition. As Halliday (2004d:40) contends:

> 'There is still the view that the mother tongue is what the child is striving to "acquire" from the outset. In my view this conception is wide of the mark. What small children are doing is learning how to mean.'

Understanding this process of learning how to mean is central within SFL because it both illustrates and evidences key dimensions of the general theory, such as the stratificational and metafunctional organization of language, and the relation of text to both context and system; moreover it has provided a crucial underpinning for the SFL approach to developing a 'language based theory of learning' (Halliday 1993b), contributing insights relevant to a range of educational linguistic work. These various contributions of language development research will be clarified here by addressing three themes: first, the phases of language development proposed within the theory, secondly, the social dimensions of language development indicated by SFL research and finally the dynamic relation between learning language, learning through language and learning about language, long proposed by Halliday (1980) as three facets to the single process of developing one's mother tongue.

Language development data

The evidence for SFL theorising about language development rests primarily upon four longitudinal case studies of individual children developing English as their mother tongue in early childhood[1]. Each case study was undertaken by a parent-researcher who used frequent, regular notebook and/or audio recordings

Table 1 Major SFL case studies of the development of English as a mother tongue

Child subject	Age range	Focus of study	Most fully reported in
Nigel	6 months–$2^{1/2}$ years	ontogenesis of language	Halliday 1975a, 2003
Hal	9 months–$2^{1/2}$ years	ontogenesis of language	Painter 1984
Anna	9 months–$2^{1/2}$ years	ontogenesis of language	Torr 1997
Stephen	$2^{1/2}$–5 years	learning through language: language and cognitive development	Painter 1999a
Nick	5–15 years	ontogenesis of grammatical metaphor	Derewianka 1999, 2003

of the child's vocalisations, without attempting to test or manage the talk in any way, simply observing and/or participating in the conversations as they took place in the course of everyday life. These accounts are supplemented by a further parental case study of the ontogenetic development of 'grammatical metaphor' in English, based on both oral conversations and extensive samples of one child's writing at home and school. Names and ages of the children studied longitudinally and references to publications detailing the case studies are provided in Table 1. Despite the small number of individual children researched, the data base for SFL developmental linguistics is a very rich one in terms of the detail, continuity, authenticity and contextual range of the data and in terms of the availability of insider knowledge of co-text and context brought to be bear in its analysis – something long recognised as invaluable for the necessarily 'rich interpretation' (Brown 1973) of child language data. Using data from the first three case studies, the phases of language development will be outlined in the following section.

Language development: Phases in the process

Phase I: The protolanguage

The SFL account of the ontogenesis of language assumes that the story can be traced from birth, which is not to suggest that language itself in any form is an innate structure of the human brain. Rather, the claim is that from birth, an infant is a social being, linked with caregivers not only materially (in the need for food and warmth, etc) but semiotically – in enacting inborn propensities to attend to, and engage with communicating others (see further below). This position has been developed in recent years by Halliday's suggestion that the momentum of an infant's physical development in the material world may be correlated with its semiotic development in the first year of life. He argues, for example, that a baby's capacity to direct its action in the material world by reaching and grasping movements parallels its capacity to direct a cry so as to address another person, while the later ability to move independently and shift vantage point (via crawling) co-develops with the semiotic capacity to address another person in relation to some object or event in the environment by using a 'sign' (Halliday 2004a, 2004b).

An infant vocalisation counts as a sign when a recognisable meaning, such as 'I want' or 'that's interesting', is consistently coupled with a particular, but idiosyncratic, expression form, such as a vocalisation like 'ma' and/or a particular manual gesture. Such signs emerge at around 9 months of age to form a symbolic/communicative system that constitutes a 'proto' form of language – a groundbreaking suggestion when put forward in Halliday's (1975a) study of his son, Nigel, though evidence for the phenomenon can be found in many subsequent studies within and beyond SFL (See Blake 2000, Ch. 2). An infant's repertoire of signs is argued to be a proto form of language because it shares a number of features that render it a form of linguistic or semiotic communication, even though lacking others that are characteristic of a fully developed form of language (Halliday 1983, Painter 2005).

Infant signs are (proto)linguistic in that they develop to express small sets of opposed meanings: 'I want' implies, and may give rise to, a related meaning of 'I don't want' or 'I want right now'; 'that's interesting' may give rise to 'that's especially interesting' or 'that's an interesting noise'. Thus rather than being a simple inventory of signs, the meanings involved stand in opposition to one another, making each utterance an instantiation from an underlying 'system' of paradigmatic options, as with any language. A second feature of protolanguage is that its meanings can be interpreted as realising the various micro contexts of an infant's life, just as a more mature semiotic system functions to realise social contextual information. The four earliest relevant contexts, or microfunctions, are the instrumental ('I want'), the regulatory ('you do as I tell you'), the personal ('here I come' – reacting to the environment) and the interactional ('me and you').

Developments during the course of the nine months or so of the protolanguage phase are traced in the case studies by describing the child's meaning potential at six-weekly intervals, showing how the systems expand through the addition of more 'delicate' meaning choices and also additional functions: namely, the imaginative ('let's pretend'), the heuristic ('tell me') and finally the informative ('I'm telling you'). These latter two in fact only emerge as the language gradually changes character and shifts into the next phase of development. Figure 1 from Halliday (1984b, 2002–2007 volume 4: 241) exemplifies the kind of meanings made at a mid-point in the protolanguage phase. It can be seen that the description focuses on the meaning options and their realisations in sound rather than analysing oppositional relations within the sound system; thus far the SFL literature does not provide a detailed longitudinal case study of the ontogenetic development of English phonology.

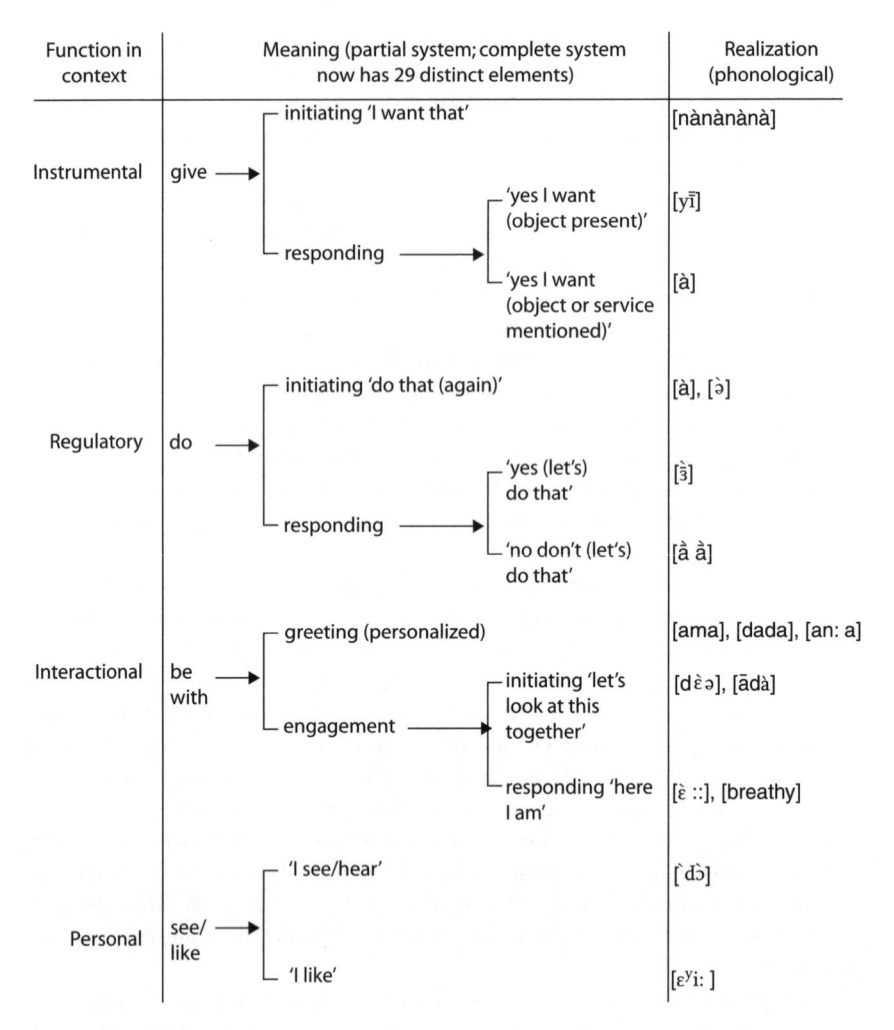

Function in context	Meaning (partial system; complete system now has 29 distinct elements)			Realization (phonological)
Instrumental	give	initiating 'I want that'		[nànànànà]
		responding	'yes I want (object present)'	[yī]
			'yes I want (object or service mentioned)'	[à]
Regulatory	do	initiating 'do that (again)'		[à], [ə̀]
		responding	'yes (let's) do that'	[з̄̀]
			'no don't (let's) do that'	[à̀ à̀]
Interactional	be with	greeting (personalized)		[ama], [dada], [an: a]
		engagement	initiating 'let's look at this together'	[dɛ̀ə], [ādà]
			responding 'here I am'	[ɛ̀ ::], [breathy]
Personal	see/like	'I see/hear'		[d̀ɔ̀]
		'I like'		[ɛʸi:]

FIGURE 1 Example protolanguage, middle (12 months) (Halliday 1984b, 2002–2007 volume 4: 241)

As can be seen from Figure 1, a protolanguage differs from a full language system in lacking any level of wording (i.e. lexico-grammar) to mediate between the meaning choice and the vocal expression form. That is, while every protolanguage meaning must be made manifest in a vocal and/or gestural form of expression in order to be addressed to another person, such expression-forms are not equivalent to lexical items (even when originating as imitations of mother tongue words). Protolinguistic meanings are holistic complexes, signifying a functional meaning (e.g. 'I want') in relation to some aspect of the environment (e.g. 'what I am looking at' or 'my toy bird') and protolanguage expressions realise the entirety of that meaning. Thus every new meaning needs a distinct expression form. There is no lexical level, where aspects of the environment can be categorised and referred to in relation to a range of different microfunctions.

Phase II: The transition

The child enters Phase II of language development when true lexical words begin to appear, usually at 16 to 18 months of age. At, or soon after this time, all three of the children studied discriminated two aspects of meaning and two aspects of expression form, allowing for combination and recombination of these. The meanings emerged as generalisations of protolanguage uses into two broader functions: that of acting on the world (via other people) and that of reflecting on and understanding the world. This is a distinction already latent in the protolanguage (see e.g. Halliday 2004a) but during the transition phase, it gets explicitly encoded by means of a phonological contrast. In the case of Nigel and Hal, non-falling tones signalled an active, or 'pragmatic,' mode that required a response from the addressee and falling tones signalled a reflective, or 'mathetic' mode, where the child's focus was on making sense of something. Thus for Nigel, *cat* with a rising tone would be a pragmatic demand, perhaps to be lifted to reach a cat, while *cat* with a falling tone would be a mathetic 'statement' or comment serving to classify the animal. In Anna's case the same distinction was signalled by a difference in voice quality rather than tone. Halliday (1978c) refers to these two modes as 'macrofunctions' since they are both larger (i.e. more general) than individual microfunctions and they differ in kind in being 'built into' the language in the form of the phonological contrast.

What emerges in the transition phase, then, is that the content or ideational meaning of the utterance is signalled by the articulation of the name, while its interpersonal or illocutionary meaning as a speech act (i.e. its status as a demand or comment) is signalled by intonation or voice quality. The significance of this is that for the first time, two strands of meaning – an ideational one relating to content or topic (e.g. cat vs dog) and an interpersonal one relating to speech function (e.g. demand vs comment) – can be separately notated in the utterance so that it is possible to mean two things simultaneously. These meanings do not combine in a synthetic, holistic way as with a protolinguistic sign, but by separable choices being mapped onto on another as shown in Figure 2. This uncoupling and recombining of associated variables is considered by Halliday (1993b) to be a key 'semogenic strategy' for expanding a meaning potential and occurs again later in relation to the systems of mood and key and also with the emergence of grammatical metaphor, discussed further below.

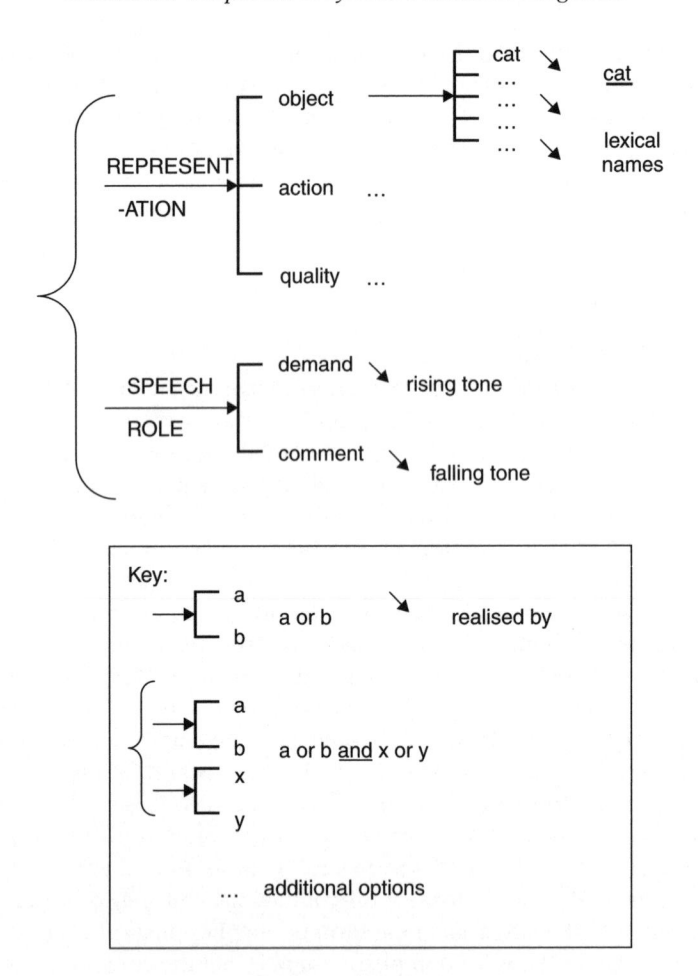

FIGURE 2 Transition with simultaneous systems

Despite the new potential for simultaneous strands of meaning, the early Phase II language of the children tended to maintain separate repertoires of vocabulary (and simple structures) for the different macrofunctions, so that both the vocabulary choice and the phonological realisation signalled the relevant macrofunction. In this respect the system is transitional between the protolanguage (where a sign is used exclusively within one microfunction) and the adult system (where any representational meaning can be freely combined with any illocutionary force). Gradually, however, this functional separation of the lexico-grammatical resources breaks down and each naming word or structure is available for use within either macrofunction, with the tone signalling simply whether the child's main focus is on representation or interaction. In due course, the two-way phonological distinction itself gives way so that, as with adult language, every utterance is equally a representation and a dialogic move.

Several interrelated developments observed over the course of Phase II in the languages of Nigel, Hal and Anna gradually effect this transition to fully-fledged language. An obvious one is that experience begins to be construed not simply through lexical choices but by means of grammatical constituent structure. Here there are interesting contrasts between the children studied, in that Nigel moved from single words to structures very early in the transition phase, and both he and Hal elaborated their grammatical resources principally in using language mathetically, for learning and making sense of experience (Halliday 1975a, Painter 1984). Anna on the other hand, who had to insert herself into conversations against the competition of an older sibling, tended to develop structures initially in using language within the pragmatic function (Oldenburg (Torr) 1986, 1990, Torr 1997).

While the development of constituent structures has always been a major focus in the study of child language, a milestone that has received almost no attention outside SFL is that of the emergence of the informative function. Summaries of the ontogeny of information from protolinguistic origins for Nigel, Hal and Anna can be found in Halliday (1984b, 2002–2007 volume 4: 247), Painter (1984:136) and Torr (1997:149–52) respectively. The development of the informative function involves the gradual appreciation by the child that linguistic exchange can be used not only to share current experience or to recall and re-share experiences that have been shared in actuality with the addressee, but can also be used to create an experience for someone who did not share it; in other words that it is possible to tell someone something they do not already know. The dawning realisation of this fundamental characteristic of language was marked grammatically in Nigel's language (Halliday 1975b) and more briefly and spasmodically via discourse structures in Hal's language during the second year of life (Painter 1984:207, 252, 1991:34–5).

This emergence of the informative function out of the mathetic function correspondingly involves changes within the pragmatic function, whereby utterances that demand a response must develop to include not simply demands for material responses (goods and services) but for verbal responses via information-seeking questions. Thus where early Phase II utterances are **either** mathetic, (construing experience but requiring no response), **or** pragmatic (demanding a response, initially a non-verbal one), Phase II utterances gradually abandon this distinction. In other words, by the end of the transition, every utterance is equally concerned with construing experience (via transitivity structures) and enacting a speech role of giving or demanding information or goods and services (via mood structures). The mapping of transitivity and mood structures onto one another in every instantiation of the language thus renders every utterance in effect **both** mathetic **and** pragmatic. Details of the development of the grammatical systems and structures of transitivity and mood in the speech of Hal and Anna are described in Painter (1984) and Torr (1997) respectively, while Nigel's development of structures is elaborated in Halliday (1975b, 2002–2007, volume 4, chapter 5) with the emerging systems of speech function and mood discussed in Halliday (1984b).

Managing the giving and exchanging of information and the associated grammatical realisations enables the child to engage in both more extended monologue and in true dialogue. These in turn require the child also to develop more sophisticated resources for organising text in respect of both context and co-text, via appropriate use of intonation patterns and other text-forming resources, such as anaphoric reference and logical linkers. These meaning resources build up a third layer of meaning – the textual metafunction – to be realised simultaneously with the ideational and the interpersonal, though this has not been as extensively documented and described in the SFL developmental literature. (See Halliday 1979a, Painter 1984:243–6, Torr 1997:190–1.)

Once the textual metafunction develops, the child's language is adult-like in being organised in terms of three simultaneous strands of meaning, the ideational (construing experience via transitivity choices and structures), the interpersonal (enacting dialogue via mood structures) and the textual (maintaining links to co-text and context via deixis, information structure, logical relations etc). The SFL description of the ontogenesis of language is thus primarily an account of how its metafunctional organization gradually develops out of the changing nature of a semiotic that at each point in development is functional for the child. Conversely, the developmental research provides evidence for the functional interpretation of the adult language provided by the general theory.

The account of ontogenesis offered by the case studies is also used by Halliday (1975a) to explain the nature of mature language as a three level system, comprising semantics, lexico-grammar and phonology. In these terms ontogenetic development is theorised as a move from a 'bi-stratal' protolanguage, comprising one level of content and one of expression, to a mature 'tri-statal' semiotic system, in which a level of lexico-grammar interposes between that of semantics and phonology. The case studies show not only the emergence of lexis and grammar out of a symbolic system without such a level of wording, but indicate that within the interpersonal metafunction at least, two levels of content may be required in the description by the end of the transition, since 'stratal tension' is in evidence from very early on. This is seen when a child's speech function choices have both 'congruent' and marked realisations in terms of grammatical mood, thus warranting a description of interpersonal meaning at two non-phonological strata. (See Painter 1984:214–8 for discussion and exemplification from Hal's language). This trajectory of development from a two to three level system as evidenced by the ontogenetic case studies has also provided a possible model for speculations concerning phylogenetic linguistic development in the human species (Matthiessen 2004) and for reflections on the evolution of consciousness (Halliday 2004a).

Phase III: Into language

As shown above, the focus in Hallidayan theorising about the phases of language ontogenesis has been on explaining the gradual development of a semiotic system organised on metafunctional and stratal lines, which, for the children studied, was in place by age 2 or 2 ½. However, language development continues well beyond this age of course. While it is not feasible to capture the development of an entire language much beyond this point, a number of more selective descriptions within Phase III have been produced since the late 1990s. On the one hand, these involve individual discourse-semantic or grammatical systems. For example, as well as the earlier-mentioned accounts of emerging transitivity, speech function and mood in the transition into Phase III, the case studies have provided details of the ontogenetic development of modality from age 2½ to 4 (Torr 1998), of attitude resources up to age 4 (Painter 2003a) and of causal and conditional relations within the clause and clause complex up to age 5 (Painter 1999a).

On the other hand, many other areas of linguistic growth have been brought into the picture in the process of explaining how a child's language develops as an instrument for learning. These are the focus of the case studies of Stephen and Nick (see Table 1) and will be taken up in the final section of this chapter. Before elaborating on this, however, the developmental story will be reconsidered with a focus on its interpersonal and social dimensions. This will serve to emphasise the SFL position that the nature of development cannot be viewed as some kind of flowering that occurs independently within the child, or through the child's autonomous explorations of the environment, but must be seen from its inception a profoundly social process.

Language development: A social process

The SFL account of language development is one that has always stressed the dialogic, interpersonal nature of the process from birth onwards (Halliday 1991b) and more recently the emotional character of the process has also been emphasised (Painter 2003a). In these respects, it chimes well with research from developmental psychology that demonstrates that infants from the earliest weeks of life can discriminate persons from objects (Trevarthen 1974), have an innate capacity for appreciating the 'like-me ness' of other persons (Melzoff and Moore 1998), can use facial and bodily gesture intentionally in a communicative context (Melzoff and Moore 1998) and within a few months of birth can engage in animated face-to-face interactions with a caregiver, characterised by a kind of synchrony of gazing, vocalising and kinesic behaviours (Trevarthen 1993, 1998). These behaviours are described within the literature in terms that suggest they function to achieve both an exchange of attention and a sharing of emotional state. With this in mind, Painter (2003a) reconsiders the early proto-language phase as a system of semioticised affect, prefiguring developments within the semantics of appraisal.

In explaining how language is learned, Halliday (1980) draws attention to the way a mother unconsciously 'tracks' the infant's growing linguistic system, enabling her initially to interpret the child's protolinguistic utterances effectively, even though naturally responding in her own language. At the same time, however, the adult is guiding the child towards the mother tongue right from these earliest interactions; filtering the child's meanings through a grid of adult relevance, so that, as Halliday points out:

"Even in Phase I the semantics of the mother tongue determines the meanings that the mother and others respond to, thus helping to shape the child's social reality." (1975c: 140, 2002–2007 volume 4: 301)

In recognising the guiding role of the adult, SF developmental linguistics has made connections with the Vygotskyan (1986:186–7) notion of the 'zone of proximal development' and made use of the related metaphor of 'scaffolding' put forward by Bruner and colleagues (e.g. Ninio and Bruner 1978) to describe the provision of adult 'supports' that are gradually dismantled over time as the learner gains mastery (Painter 1986, 1999a). A key aspect of this is the move from dialogic to monologic constructions in the child's developmental history. Halliday draws attention to this in Nigel's creation of narrative during the transition phase, showing how adults who had shared Nigel's experience were able to both track and guide the child's speech. One occasion is described where the adults' questions helped Nigel achieve a more elaborated version of his story that he could subsequently repeat as a monologue without assistance (Halliday 1975b, 2002–2007 volume 4: 186). Painter (1986, 1989) provides further examples of the co-construction of narrative, where the adult contributions assist with recall, sequencing, the grammatical construal of remembered experience and the inclusion of evaluative comment.

As well as assisting the child to build stories of personal experience, scaffolding has been shown to take the form of implicit adult guidance in providing justifications for refusals and requests (Painter 1986), in developing argument by challenging overgeneralisations (Painter 1996a, 1999a, 2004a), in guiding the child to privilege textual over observable experience (Painter 1996b, 1999a), and in the modelling of syllogistic reasoning (1996a, 1999a, 1999b). This last is seen in the following example, when Stephen was almost 5 years old, where the adult's final utterance pushes the child to reason from the information provided rather than expecting to be told a fact directly:

S: I keep thinking that the earth goes round the sun instead of the sun goes round the earth.
M: The earth does go round the sun!
S: [pleased] Oh! How come you can't feel it go round?
M: Yeah, it's funny that you can't feel it . . . [further talk omitted here]
S: Are the houses going round?
M: They're on the earth so they have to go round, don't they?
(Painter 1999a:305)

The claim by Vygotsky that 'what the child can do in cooperation today he can do alone tomorrow' (1986: 188) is amply illustrated in the scaffolding interactions found in the case studies, drawing attention to the relation between language as system (potential) and language as text (instance). This is a relation analogous to that between climate and weather (Halliday 1985a – third edition (revised by Matthiessen): 27), with the system being the linguistic 'climate' and inherently probabilistic in terms of the likelihood of any systemic option being manifested in texts. A text created on a particular occasion both reveals the system in place at that time, is an instance of that probabilistic system and also contributes to its change. The change may be simply shifting or maintaining the probabilities attached to any systemic choice, or – in the early years especially – may involve the incorporation of additional or more delicate options with a concomitant reorganisation of value relations.

It is because the child is a participant in the joint meaning-making during dialogue that the adult system can become indirectly more 'visible' to the learner. During conversation, the texts created instantiate choices from both the (child's) developing language and the (adult's) developed language, creating an instance that may go slightly beyond the child's current productive abilities based on his/her current system. Thus as Halliday (1993b: 105, 2002–2007 volume 4: 341) puts it, 'the effect of this dialectic of system and process is a kind of leapfrogging movement'; in other words, sometimes the child's system is ahead of the text being produced, as when using routinised utterances, while at other times the text is ahead of the system, as when a specific conversation enables a new move.

The affectively charged basis of infant communication and the nature of scaffolding interactions in which dialogue precedes monologue have been seen as two examples of the 'interpersonal gateway' suggested by Halliday (1993c), or the 'interpersonal first' principle in language ontogenesis (Painter 2004b). This principle holds that new developmental moves – even those ultimately most relevant to the ideational metafunction and the reflective interpretation of experience – are likely to be initiated within the interpersonal metafunction and/or within a dialogic context and/or in relation to emotionally charged content. Other examples of this principle from the case studies include the initial move into mother tongue words, the first instances of grammatical metaphor, the first occasions of information-giving, the first uses of mental process clauses and the early construals of causal and conditional relations (Painter 2004b). While all of these areas are crucial aspects of language for reflection, their ontogenetic origin is shown to lie within the interpersonal domain. And as Halliday (e.g. 1993b) notes, such new developments often take the form of a 'trailer' (or 'preview'), where the new move is tried out in a limited way (e.g. within some such interpersonal context) before being taken up in earnest.

While the dimension of instantiation is highly relevant to the dialogic basis of language learning, and the way language as a system changes (or maintains itself as the same) over time, it is the dimension of realisation that is crucial to a consideration of the social, rather than simply interpersonal, nature of language development (Halliday 1975c). This is because the text that instantiates the linguistic system is also a realisation of higher orders of meaning. As Halliday (1978b:124) explains:

> As a child learns language, he also learns through language. He interprets text not only as being specifically relevant to the context of situation but also as being generally relevant to the context of culture. It is the linguistic system that enables him to do this; since the sets of semantic options which are characteristic of the situation (the register) derive from generalized functional components of the semantic system, they also at the same time realise the higher order meanings that constitute the culture, and so the child's focus moves easily between microsemiotic and macrosemiotic environment.

The longitudinal case studies showing the emergence of the metafunctions are thus simultaneously an account of the child's construal and reconstrual of contexts for meaning. At the microfunctional stage, there are a number of distinct contexts for speech inferred by the researcher based on the child's apparent purposes for protolinguistic signs; at the early macrofunctional stage, the language itself is being organised on dichotomous lines, clarifying the fact that the child's construes each context as either active or reflective; by the end of the Transition, the metafunctional organization of the child's language construes each situational context as comprising three components (i.e. the register components of 'field', 'tenor' and 'mode'. (See Halliday 1975c, Painter 1991).

However, as Halliday points out above, it is not only the construal of the situation, but the construal of the culture instantiated by situations that is achieved in the social process of language development. Relevant here are studies into 'semantic variation' by Ruqaiya Hasan, showing the way in which caregiver-child interactions in the preschool years create subjectivities relevant to social class and gender (See e.g. Hasan 1992b, 2004b, Hasan and Cloran 1990). This research, drawing on Basil Bernstein's (1987) sociology, uses naturalistically collected audio taped data from everyday conversations between 24 Australian born mothers and their children. Quantitative analyses of the data demonstrate that different clusters of meaning choices are favoured by mothers in talking to their 3½ year old children depending on the social class positioning of the family and the gender of the child. The result is not that the children from different fractions of society learn different languages per se, but that they learn to make sense of things differently and to deploy their linguistic resources in subtly different ways.

For example, Cloran's (1989) analysis of the data suggests that through their talk, mothers unconsciously sensitise their female children to the realms of possibility and difference in point of view, while orienting their sons to the actuality of how things are and to factual knowledge. Similarly, children of the 'higher autonomy professions' create texts with their children that elaborate and make explicit the grounds for behaving and acting, while mothers of lower autonomy professions leave the principles and assumptions of everyday norms implicit in their interactions (Hasan 1992b). Since the focus of SFL semantic variation research is on cultural reproduction rather than language ontogenesis specifically, its data base is not designed to reveal linguistic development over time, but it does exemplify with quantitative analyses of the corpus what Schieffelin and Ochs (1986) refer to as 'language socialisation'; that is, the way cultural and subcultural ways of meaning are inevitably taken on in the process of learning the first language in early childhood. Within SFL this is entirely consonant with the general theory since "not only are the semantic options which make up the meaning potential **realised** explicitly in the lexicogrammar – they are also themselves **realizing** the higher-order meanings of the social semiotic." (Halliday 1975c: 129, 2002–2007 volume 4: 290)

Language development: Learning through language

While learning cultural and sub-cultural values through language in use is demonstrated in the semantic variation research discussed above, more strictly developmental work in learning through language has focussed on the child's building of everyday 'commonsense' knowledge in the early years and the subsequent linguistic demands of developing discipline based 'educational' knowledge during the school years (Halliday 1999, Painter 2007). In such an enterprise the lens is focussed on language in its function of construing, or making sense of, experience. This is the reflective mode of consciousness, present from the very beginning of the protolanguage (Halliday 1992d, 2004a), giving rise to the mathetic macrofunction during the transition and subsequently providing the impulse for continuing semiotic growth in the service of understanding experience. An account of this process can be seen as a linguistic take on cognitive development, contributing to a language-based theory of learning, since:

> The distinctive characteristic of human learning is that it is a process of making meaning – a semiotic process; and the prototypical form of human semiotic is language. Hence the ontogenesis of language is at the same time the ontogenesis of learning. (Halliday 1993b: 93, 2002–2007 volume 4: 327)

If this is recognised, what are usually referred to as cognitive strategies, such as comparing and contrasting, classifying, generalising and reasoning can be regarded as strategies for meaning, simultaneously manifested in language and providing a means to develop the language further.

This is the perspective adopted in Phillips' (1985) account of the role of comparing and contrasting in Nigel's language up to the age of 2½ years (summarised in Halliday 1999) and in Painter's (1999a) longitudinal study of Stephen's use of language from 2½ to 5 years. The latter study attends to language development in the service of learning in four key areas: the semiotic construal of things, of events, of semiosis itself and of cause-effect relations. These data demonstrate how new semantic challenges, such as grappling with superordination relations, determining the status of an instance of experience, establishing cause-effect relations, reconciling conflicting construals and trying to make sense of encounters with the printed word extend the language across a range of different discourse-semantic and grammatical systems. Such growth is argued to result in forms of text which are increasingly 'self-contextualised' and which in turn provide the impetus for further linguistic development (Painter 1996a, 1999b, 2007). Language development thus results from the interpersonal engagement with others discussed earlier, but always in the context of making sense of experience and building knowledge of the world.

Examples of linguistic developments that result from the cognitive challenges of the preschool years illustrate how learning language, learning through language and learning about language are a unified process (Halliday 1980). For example, in Stephen's language as a 2 and 3 year old, the development of 'context-free' classifying and defining clauses (*an X is a Y, X means Y*), the extension of causal links to provide criteria for categories (*that's a tiger because it's got stripes*), and the construal of generic categories like *babies* or *little boys* all assist in the building of lexical taxonomies and so allow the child to reflect on the meaning system itself (Painter 1996a, 2004a). Then over the course of the fourth and fifth years, the transfer of causal and conditional meaning (using *Why?/because* and *if.. then*) from interpersonal contexts such as bribes, threats and challenges to ideational contexts of reasoning, creates new forms of text in which hypothetical and syllogistic argument become possible, enabling reflection on a reality created by text rather than observation (Painter 1996a). Similarly, the explicit projection of the speech of others (e.g. *Kerry says ". . . "*) in order to reflect on the validity of different construals of experience; and the extension of the grammar of mental processes to consider sources of knowledge (*How do you know?*) and the perspectives of others (*he doesn't know*) all involve reflection on the nature and use of semiosis itself (Painter 1996b).

While many of these developments begin to prepare a child for the demands of learning through language in school (Painter 1999b), there are semantic challenges that cannot be entirely successfully met in the process of everyday conversations in the preschool years. These involve accessing abstract and grammatically metaphorical meanings on the one hand, and systematising disparate elements of knowledge on the other, achievements enabled largely by understanding the writing system and controlling written language forms (Painter 2007). Making sense of the writing system means coming to grips with abstract meanings, while systematising knowledge requires learning to access and create written forms of texts, which involve the phenomenon of 'grammatical metaphor' (see below). Because of this, Halliday (1993b) has argued that the overall trajectory of human semiotic development following the protolanguage is one from generalisation through abstractness to metaphor.

Generalisation occurs at the beginning of the transition phase with the advent of mother tongue words, which provide a means for classifying different instances of experience as the same through the use of a lexical names like *dog* or *jump*. More general categories like *animal* or *fruit* follow, and by age three categories begin to be generalised in expressions like *aeroplanes fly* (Painter 1999a). However it will be several years before a child can begin to construe abstract categories like 'truth', or 'courage' where the nouns do not construe a tangible entity. Halliday (1993b) has suggested that an interpersonal gateway to this may be the construal of attitudinal expressions, such as *that's not fair,* and Painter (2003b) argues that encounters with written symbol systems provide a strong impetus as the child tries to understand what written words *say* or how numbers relate. This is because, as Halliday (1993b: 109, 2002–2007 volume 4: 346) explains:

> Writing is learnt as a second-order symbolic system, with symbols standing for other symbols; hence the learner has to recognise two sets of abstract entities and also the abstract relation between them (for example, *word, letter, stand for, spell*).

The path of development from generalising to abstracting and then metaphor is exemplified in a paper by Painter, Derewianka and Torr (2007), based on data from all the case studies. This shows that while there are tentative moves made towards the construal of abstract categories during the preschool years, it is not until the child begins to grapple with disciplinary knowledge, that the final step of managing (ideational) grammatical metaphor is very gradually achieved. Such metaphor involves a 'skewing of the relationship between the levels of semantics and lexicogrammar' (Painter, Torr and Derewianka in press: 575), so that for example the unmarked realisation of a semantic 'figure' as a clause, as in *they decided,* may instead be realised as a nominal group, *their decision*, which then carries meanings both of a 'figure' and a 'thing' (Halliday 1985a – third edition (revised by Matthiessen)). Managing this inter-stratal play requires the child to deploy once again the semogenic strategy of uncoupling and recombining linked variables – a strategy used earlier as a means of entering the transition phases.

In the literature exploring the ontogenesis of grammatical metaphor, there are discussions focussing on the use of metaphor as a semiotic strategy from protolanguage to age 5 (Painter 2003b), on oral precursors of grammatical metaphor, often involving forms of linguistic play that encourage the unhinging of semantic and grammatical levels of the system (Derewianka 2003, Torr and Simpson 2003), and on the development of grammatical metaphor proper in the writing of one child, Nick, up to the age 15, based on analysis of a comprehensive corpus of his written texts in many different genres (Derewianka 2003). This study argues that transcategorisations, embeddings within the nominal group, 'faded' metaphors (such as *have a look* and *do a dance*) and the use of technical terms are all 'proto' forms of metaphor, some of which are present in Nick's spoken and written language from age 5 or 6. However, neither these nor examples of true grammatical metaphor (initially construing various kinds of meanings as 'things') are at all prominent in the child's writing until around age 9 years.

Since Derewianka (1999, 2003) discriminates many different forms of metaphor, the case study of Nick is able to show that different forms appear at different times and their use increases at different rates, aspects of development that are likely to depend partly on the educational contexts and the kinds of reading and writing the child is encouraged to engage with. Generally speaking, it would appear that the use of grammatical metaphor to assist in the construal of educational fields of knowledge like history and science by using 'technical' terms like *modernisation* or *extinction* occurs earlier than its textual use to structure the writing effectively by 'accumulat[ing] meanings "logogenetically"' (Painter, Derewianka and Torr 2007: 579). The latter development is needed to organise longer and more argumentative texts with appropriate thematic and information structures and does not appear strongly in the data until about age 14. Interestingly, in the conversations surrounding the production of his texts, Nick was evidently at times quite aware of the shifts he was making from his familiar oral forms of expression. This confirms the way achieving literacy at all levels involves a more conscious focus on language itself, demonstrating again the relation between learning language, learning **through** language and learning **about** language.

In summary, while there is still much to learn about language ontogenesis – for example about the development of phonological resources and those of the textual metafunction, about the growth of individual linguistic systems and about the nature and range of individual variation in all developments – the SFL literature in the area has particular value in respect of three broad contributions. On the one hand it affords insights into the nature of language as a stratified, metafunctional meaning resource realising 'higher' levels of social meaning in the process of instantiation as text, showing how it is possible for such a system to emerge from a much simpler kind of semiotic. At the same time, it demonstrates the fundamentally dialogic nature of its development, which both enables learning of the mother tongue and ensures that it simultaneously an apprenticeship into the culture. Finally, it provides a basis for building "a general theory of learning interpreted as 'learning through language' [which] should be grounded in whatever is known about 'learning language'" Halliday (1993b: 113, 2002–2007 volume 4: 351).

Note

[1] These data are supplemented by short term observation of a number of Chinese infants in the very early stages of language development (Qiu 1985) and by longitudinal data from five children of various ages between 1 and 6 years, used to investigate early forms of grammatical metaphor (Torr and Simpson 2003).

5

Language and other primate species

James D. Benson
York University

Paul J. Thibault
Agder University

Part 1: James D. Benson

Is language uniquely human? To ask this question is to enter a minefield of controversy, because it presupposes other equally fundamental questions: what is language and where did it come from? The answer from Hauser, Chomsky and Fitch (2002) is unambiguous. Humans do share communicative abilities with other species, but language, defined as a recursion mechanism (syntax) not found in other species, is unique to humans. Hauser et al dichotomize this distinction as Language in the Broad Sense (FLB) vs. Language in the Narrow Sense (FLN). Although this view has wide currency, given that many scientists working in disciplines other than linguistics are deeply interested in language, it is not surprising that it is not universally held. The two biennial conferences Evolution of Language, and Language Culture Mind attract an extraordinary range of disciplines: anthropology, archeology, artificial life, biology, comparative cognition, discourse analysis, ethology, genetics, neuroscience, paleontology, philosophy, primatology, psychology, mathematical modeling, semantics, semiotics, and social interaction. Research in even one of these domains, such as primatology, to take an obvious example, is extensive, but can only be hinted at here.

Animal communication, from bees to dogs, has long been studied, and is uncontroversial *qua* communication. Among primates, the calls of vervet monkeys are particularly well-known (Cheney and Seyfarth 1990). Vervets have three acoustically distinct vocalizations for three different kinds of predators which require three different kinds of escape routines: eagles, leopards, and snakes. As such, these vocalizations would qualify as part of FLB but not FLN. A less syntax *cum* recursion-oriented alternative to Hauser, Chomsky and Fitch is Deacon's (1997) concept of symbol. In Deacon's referential hierarchy of icon, index, and symbol, icons are recognitions, indices are correlations of indices, and symbols are relations between indices. For Deacon, monkey calls are indexical signs, not symbolic ones. Among the great apes, chimpanzee calls have been studied extensively, but are seen as expressions of emotional states. As such, they are indices, or part of FLB, not symbols, or part of FLN.

The bonobo Kanzi, however, is a strong challenge to the notion of language as an exclusively human phenomenon, since Kanzi learned to use a lexigram keyboard to communicate with humans without being explicitly taught or trained, just as human children do (Savage-Rumbaugh, Shanker and Taylor (1998). While Kanzi's foster mother Matata was being explicitly trained to use lexigrams without much success, the immature Kanzi succeeded in picking up the lexigrams on his own. As Deacon (1997: 126) observes: 'If the critical period effect is evidence of a language acquisition device, then why should an ape whose ancestor never spoke (and who himself can't speak) demonstrate a critical period for language learning? Kanzi's example throws a monkey wrench into the whole critical period argument as it applies to language acquisition in children'. Savage-Rumbaugh et al (1993) subsequently studied Kanzi's ability to carry out novel requests as compared with a two and a half year old human child, with the overall result that Kanzi had a 72% success rate vs. 66% for the child. The requests involved familiar words in novel combinations, such as 'Put the lemonade in the coke' vs. 'Put the coke in the lemonade'. For Deacon (1997: 124), Kanzi's success indicates that he has broken through the indexical barrier to symbolism. For Kanzi, like humans, the lexigrams remain indexical, but are related to each other symbolically, as they are for humans: 'He is now capable not only of communicating symbolically with a lexigram keyboard but has also demonstrated sophisticated comprehension of normal spoken English, including the ability to analyze a variety of grammatical constructions'.

In the field of Ape Language Research, skeptics abound. Bickerton (Calvin & Bickerton, 2000: 23-24), for example, disputes Deacon's 'suggestion that the rubicon between our species and others falls at the symbolic rather than syntactic level. In other words, it's words, not sentences, that dramatically distinguish our species from others.... In fact, as was apparent nearly two decades ago, the real rubicon, unpalatable though this may be to the philosophically minded, is syntax, not symbols'.

Nevertheless, Deacon's semiotic approach to language opens up interdisciplinary linkages in a way that FLN with its firewall between FLN and everything else does not. Consider, for example, Ellis' (2005) hierarchy of structure and causation that relates physics through the intermediate levels of particle physics, atomic physics, chemistry, biochemistry, cell biology, physiology, to symbolic systems afforded by language:

> multiple causality (interlevel as well as intralevel) is always operating in complex systems. Thus one can have top-down, bottom-up, and same level system 'explanations', all applicable simultaneously. Analysis explains the property of a system through the behavior of its component, lower-level parts. Systems

thinking, in contrast, tries to understand the properties of an interconnected complex whole, and explains the properties of an entity through its role in relation to higher levels in the system's structure.

Such a view is remarkably consistent with SFL explanations of language in terms of motivation (top-down), construal (bottom-up), and system networks (same level) operating simultaneously. In addition, such a view is consistent with explanations involving the very different SFL time-scales of logogenesis, ontogenesis, and phylogenesis. Indeed, such a view makes the boundary between FLB and FLN so permeable as to make it unnecessary, particularly in the light of the SFL metafunctional differentiation into ideational, interpersonal and textual, as well as making it unnecessary to fetishize recursion. From a primatological perspective, Taglialatela et al (2004) argue that Kanzi disproves the premise that 'a marked discontinuity exists between human language and the vocalization systems of all other animals'.

One entry into top-down explanations of bonobo-human interactions is through discourse. As Greenfield and Savage-Rumbaugh (1993) note: 'Up to now, the comparative study of communication and language in children and apes has focused almost exclusively on grammar and semantics. In this article, we focus instead on repetition and its pragmatic roles in communicative and conversational competence'. Discourse and the integration of discourse with activity on lower levels is the common thread which runs through all four chapters of Benson and Greaves (2005). The discourse move system proposed by Eggins and Slade (1997) is used throughout.

Chapter 1 provides evidence for the bonobo Kanzi's control of interpersonal discourse semantics in a complex negotiation with Sue Savage-Rumbaugh. By making his initial command ('GO OPEN GROUPROOM'), Kanzi assigned the complementary discourse role of compliance to Sue. In this particular negotiation, Kanzi used graphic symbols called lexigrams, rather than vocalizations, as his primary medium of communication.

Chapter 2 reinterprets the experimentation documented in Savage-Rumbaugh, *et al.* (1993) in terms of ideational lexicogrammar, and provides corroborative evidence for Kanzi having some degree of higher-order consciousness. Although discourse is not the focus of the discussion, the 660 novel requests that constituted the experiment nevertheless took place in a discourse context: the experimenter made a series of commands, and assigned Kanzi the complementary discourse role of compliance. Since compliance required that Kanzi perform actions, neither lexigrams nor vocalizations were at issue. Nevertheless, Kanzi's success rate depended on his ability to interpret lexicogrammatical structures.

Chapter 3, with a focus on the evolution of language, provides evidence for the bonobo Panbanisha's control of interpersonal discourse semantics in another complex negotiation with Sue Savage-Rumbaugh (based on Panbanisha's understanding of English lexicogrammar), where the difference between talking *about* Kanzi and talking *to* Kanzi is expressed by Panbanisha's timing and choice of vocalizations. In this case, Sue is asking questions, which assign Panbanisha the complementary role of answer, and Panbanisha's primary medium of expression is vocalization, with proximal vocalizations addressed to Sue, and distal vocalizations addressed to Kanzi in an adjoining location.

Chapter 4 addresses Kanzi's proximal vocalizations in greater detail, by considering whether or not a hearer can reasonably interpret Kanzi's vocalizations as a dialect of spoken English. A methodology is proposed for identifying Kanzi's vocalizations as allophones of English phonemes by making explicit the differing contributions to meaning-making made at all strata of language-in-context.

Part 2: Paul J. Thibault

The crucial issue in the perspective offered in Benson and Greaves (2005) perhaps lies in the ability of humans and bonobos to make use of cues and resources that jointly facilitate coordination of their respective actions and viewpoints. Rather than saying that bonobos and humans share a common code, it is more appropriate to say that there are sufficient convergences of move-types – initiating and responding – in their repeated interactions whatever the specific modality that is used so as to generate possibilities for action that both humans and bonobos can modify in response to the observed behaviour of each other in ways which converge on equilibria (Bullard 1994). Thus, similar linguistic utterances can elicit similar action responses in individuals of both species who have a shared learning history. It is in view of individuals' shared learning history that particular conventional relations are established between utterance-types of whatever modality and possibilities for action.

The lexigram fulfills this function in ways that show that linguistically mediated communication does not necessarily rest on recursive syntax as that which makes humans special with respect to other species. Thus, a fundamental property of language which many linguists have celebrated as the *sine qua non* of human intelligence and uniqueness may have less to do with this question than is often claimed. The pictorial mode of cueing that is characteristic of the lexigram shows that stable conventions for eliciting behavioural options have evolved in pan-human culture at the Language Research Center at Georgia State University and the Great Ape Trust of Iowa. These conventions enable the pictorial symbols of the lexigram to perform the function of cultural cueing *qua* culturally embedded and intentional mode of languaging. When humans and bonobos interact with each other and with their environment by means of the lexigram (among other things), the flow of their interaction is manifestly intentional and contentful. The interaction is organized in terms of the points of view of the participants. For this reason, it is necessarily situated and deictically and interpersonally grounded. It is grounded in the embodiments of the participants, the viewpoints this embodiment affords, and relevant features of the environment that are indexed.

Moreover, the selection of particular lexigram symbols in the interactional situations in which such selections are made clearly functionally presupposes that such selections are appropriate to the situation. This means that the given selection will make a contribution to the maintenance of both the situation and the individual's participation in it. Importantly, the selection also serves the function of the self-maintenance of the individual *qua* agent-in-interaction (Bickhard 2005: 206-207). The point is that such selections are normative: they can be right or wrong, good or bad, appropriate or inappropriate. This means that the selection of a lexigram symbol may (or may not) be supported by the environment in which it occurs. Kanzi may thus believe that someone has a surprise for him such that if he activates the "surprise" symbol on a given occasion, his presuppositions are shown to be true, whereas if no surprise is forthcoming, his presuppositions are interactively shown to be wrong. What we see here is what Bickhard refers to as "representational normativity" (2005: 207). The representational use of the given lexigram symbol does not therefore stand for or encode something external to it. Rather, the selection of a given symbol-in-interaction presupposes that the interactive-environmental situation is such that the choice of this sign in this situation will contribute to the agent's ongoing self-maintenance in the situation (Thibault 2005a, b). Without the digitalized recursive syntax that is seen as the hallmark of human language, we see that the pictorial forms of the lexigram function in remarkably similar ways. They mediate participants' ongoing attending to each other in interpersonally coordinated interaction and they provide discrete digital categorizations (banana, surprise, ball, M&M, etc.) to which both humans and bonobos in this environment orient and to which their intentions and thoughts are made to conform.

One thing seems pretty clear at this stage: pan-human culture has accumulated over several generations of bonobos without necessarily relying on recursive syntax as that on which the phase shift from social to cultural evolution is based (Thibault 2005c). The explanation therefore must be found elsewhere, rather than in recursive syntax *per se*. In saying this, I am not denying that recursive syntax does indeed play an important and distinctive role in the definition of human language. The question here is, rather, whether this role is in itself constitutive of something uniquely special about human culture and intelligence. Moreover, the theories of recursive syntax that have been used to defend this thesis have given primacy to the representational capacities that such a syntax bestowed on the human species and the evolutionary advantages that derive from this (Bickerton 1990; Pinker 1994). The digital categories that such a syntax makes possible and the very structure of its syntax are, in this view, hard wired in the human brain in ways that accordingly ascribe human uniqueness to special representational properties of the brain – properties which are furthermore directly expressed by the structure of human syntax.

One thing that is conspicuously absent in the individual-centered view sketched in the preceding paragraph are the ways in which organisms learn by attending to and modeling the outcomes – successful and unsuccessful – of both their own and others' attempts to learn. This is what human infants do with respect to more senior caregivers (Bråten 1998a, 2002; Halliday 1975a). This possibility depends on biological and cognitive convergences rather than the divergences between the observer and others in the situations within which they interact. For example, the discovery of mirror neurons in other species of primates and in humans leads to the question as to whether modes of co-participation in human-bonobo interaction are supported in both species by a neurosocial mirror neuron system that underpins and supports the capacity for interpersonal communion, empathic identification, and learning by altercentric participation in the interactions between the two species (Bråten 2007). This remains unexplored territory for no investigation has thus far been conducted on the brain processes of two individuals – human and bonobo – engaged in synchronous real-time interpersonally coordinated interaction.

With respect to the initial point made in the preceding paragraph about learning, let us think for a moment about the human infant. Take, for example, the case of a 16 month old infant on a walk with her father beside the lake near where they live. The infant says 'car' when she sees a car go by or 'flower' when she sees a flower on the side of the path, usually meaning also 'let's stop and pick it', or 'put' when she wants to put the flowers in her father's shirt pocket once they've been picked. These are things which infant and father do together on a regular basis. The infant has learned 'car', 'flower', 'put' and so on as a result of tracking her father's use of these terms over time and modeling the outcomes of his use of them as well as her own in their interactions. In this way, 'car' in these infant-father-world interactions gets conventionally associated with sightings of cars as they drive past us while out walking or with the need to be careful when crossing the street among other things in an ever widening circle of possibilities. What is important here is not some internalized and hard-wired representational capacity, but the ability of both infant and father to adopt an intentional stance towards each other (Dennett 1987; Cowley 2004). This is something that the infant has to learn of course.

In attributing the intentional stance to each other on the basis of their actions, including their vocalizations when people speak, we connect their actions to normative criteria. Such criteria help us to decide the best way in the circumstances to understand and respond to an action with respect to all the multiple competing possibilities that our brains generate. In this way, infant and father recognize that an utterance like 'car' is both intentionally sourced at a given agent's viewpoint and that the utterance is about something and that the speaker is attending to this something and probably seeking to coordinate her focus of attention with that of her interlocutor. The infant's uttering of 'car' therefore cues both interactants to jointly attend to the given phenomenon – e.g. a car passing by which catches the infant's attention. What Dennett calls the 'intentional stance' is a way of selecting from the range of competing brain processes all going on at the same time within the individual. Ascribing the intentional stance to someone's action is a way of making sense of what they do by selecting from all the multiple competing possibilities a version which is intelligible in the situation to hand. Language prompts people to adopt the intentional stance towards each other because language is itself a way of filtering the multiple possibilities going on in our brains and of connecting them to cultural norms. This can only rise through the emergence of norms which regulate interpersonally coordinated interaction between the interactants. The adopting of an 'intentional stance' by both participants in our example and the coordination of their respective stances in interpersonally coordinated interaction means that the two participants have the capacity to track and monitor their own and others' intentional stances.

The further point is that infant and father *qua* members of the human species are constituted by a cultural ecology and a cultural dynamics, not just a social dynamics. Social dynamics entail that agents possess capacities for (1) differential levels of cooperation that are sensitive to differences in individuals' learning histories; and (2) interpersonal coordination of their behaviours when faced with a plurality of potentially conflicting outcomes. Cultural dynamics, on the other hand, depend on the pooling and accumulation across generations of the constructive efforts of organisms in their environments such that the cultural landscape in which the interactions occur is, over time, altered. This further entails that the cognitive and semiotic resources of organisms are themselves transformed by their participation in cultural dynamics. How otherwise can the increasing behavioural, cognitive and semiotic variation of bonobos such as Kanzi and Panbanisha, who were co-reared with human in a hybrid pan-human cultural world, be explained? If, for example, Kanzi's enhanced representational capacities *qua* enhanced individual behavioural and cognitive variability rested on hardwired representational capacities based on a digital and recursive syntax, which in the case of the bonobo brain is clearly not the case, then it is difficult to explain from whence Kanzi's remarkable powers arose other than from within himself *per se*. This particular story is not terribly convincing because it rests on a viciously circular argument: recursive syntax and its representational capacities is what makes us humans special and we are so special because we have recursive syntax etc. This argument is caught in this trap because of its appeal to lower-scalar (biological) initiating conditions without taking into account higher-scalar boundary conditions (e.g. cultural ecology and dynamics).

Now, it is important at this point to stress that bonobos, like humans, are also social and cultural beings, as the ethological and biological evidence now clearly shows (Segerdahl *et al* 2005). Moreover, bonobos share enough neuroanatomical and genetic similarities with humans in spite of the differences so that we can say that both their forms of embodiment and the cognitive powers embedded in this embodiment in the form of their nervous systems make them sufficiently like humans in enough respects such that, given the convergence of interactive situations that have co-evolved in pan-human culture fostered by Sue Savage-Rumbaugh and colleagues at the two institutions mentioned above, bonobos and humans are able to learn from and to monitor each others' actions and behaviours in interpersonally coordinated interaction. This would therefore suggest that interpersonally coordinated interaction and associated conventions and norms play a key role in the explanation of enhanced cognitive and representational complexity in languaged bonobos.

Halliday (1985a) has characterized the interpersonal function of language in terms of the exchange of two 'commodities', viz. information and goods-&-services. This observation is germane to the discussion of Benson and Greaves (2005) above. The "interpersonal gateway" (Halliday 1993c; Thibault 2005d) into language is founded on the fine-grained interpersonal coordination of meanings and perspectives that takes place in discursive negotiation between individuals. However, the exchange of information and goods-&-services may not in fact be the most fundamental role of language in these processes of interpersonal coordination. Instead, the embeddedness of human and bonobo behaviour in interpersonally coordinated interaction is founded on a normative cultural dynamics of self- and other-tracking and monitoring that makes use of local theories of the self as virtual narrative entities that we co-construct through our interactions along our intertwined temporal trajectories (Thibault 2004a, 2004b). Interpersonally coordinated interaction is enmeshed in a web of stories that get told and are interwoven with the interactions that occur.

Harré (1983) points out that selves both account for and create interpretations of their own and others' actions at the same time that they try to fit their explanations and interpretations into a more global story in ways that are consistent with previously told and heard stories in a given interpersonal moral order. It is through the stories they tell that humans (and bonobos?) monitor and model their own and others' learning experiences. They are able to do so because the dynamics of interpersonal coordination that are afforded by language enables languaged beings to take up the intentional stance towards themselves and others in ways which are normatively grounded. In doing so, interpersonal coordination constrains individual brain dynamics to forms of languaging that entrain individuals and their internal dynamics to prevailing norms which prescribe limits on the forms of social behaviour and interaction that can be engaged in and narrated to others.

In pan-human culture and the forms of linguistically mediated interaction between the two species that have evolved there, the cultural environment is constituted of partly material objects and partly virtual ones (e.g. narrative selves, meanings). The participation of bonobos such as Kanzi and Panbanisha in the languaged environment of pan-human culture places new demands on the multiple competing dynamics of their brains (see above), viz. to make their own behaviour consistent, accountable and describable within the terms of a higher-scalar cultural dynamics of human language. That is why Panbanisha, when scolded by Sue for jumping on a dog in an episode I have analyzed elsewhere, can display something very close to what humans call shame (Thibault *et al* 2005). The interpersonal coordination of the behaviours and viewpoints of Sue and Panbanisha in this episode requires that Panbanisha look at and acknowledge her own transgression according to the categories and values of a normative cultural language (English) that reflects the viewpoints of others. It is in this way that bonobos like Panbanisha are able to participate in complex interpersonally coordinated interactions with humans such that her ability to recognize and interpret her wrongdoing from the perspective of the other and the language used makes her a competent participant in pan-homo cultural dynamics.

The further lesson I wish to draw here is that language dynamics mediate and entrain individual behaviours and perspectives to coordinated interaction formats that may implicate potentially very many individuals in different times and places. Bonobos like Kanzi and Panbanisha show that they can participate in and learn through such finely coordinated interaction dynamics. Moreover, the biological, cognitive, social and cultural convergences of individuals of the two species, in spite of the clear differences, indicate that such interpersonally coordinated and normatively driven interaction formats constitute scaffolds for the learning and individuating of the co-participating agents. Moreover, these interaction formats co-evolve with the agents themselves. On this analysis, humans and bonobos can achieve interpersonal coordination in the way described above because the language they have co-constructed in the situations in which they (humans and bonobos) co-participate embeds behaviour and viewpoints in higher-scalar language dynamics that are not confined within the skull of individuals, but are distributed across persons, places and times such that intentions, viewpoints and understandings are entrained to these dynamics and their associated norms. Pan-human language can emerge precisely because the environment of both species *qua* meaning-making agents is a cognitive-interactive environment that is created in their communication and which co-evolves with that communication.

6
Linguistic computing

Elke Teich
TU Darmstadt

1 Introduction

Linguistic work is unthinkable today without the support of computers. Tasks such as compiling samples of language and storing, searching and analysing these samples are much easier, quicker and more reliable to perform with the help of computation. Developing tools for the support of linguistic work is the domain of *Linguistic Computing*. Linguistic computing has something to offer for most linguistic research areas, including, for instance, language documentation/ description, grammatical analysis, speech analysis, discourse analysis, cross-lingual comparison (including the study of translations) and multi-semiotic analysis (text, sound, pictures). Linguistic computing is particularly relevant to branches of linguistics that have a serious interest in linguistic instances, since exploration and analysis of texts are facilitated. Also, employing computational tools often leads to a refinement of research methods and it can open up new perspectives on modelling language and theorizing about language (see a recent paper on machine learning and linguistic theory by Lappin and Shieber 2007).

By implication, computational tools are highly relevant for Systemic Functional Linguistics (SFL). First, SFL has an inherent interest in (the analysis of) naturally occurring text. While a well-trained linguistic eye can see a lot in *one* text, a computer is a much better instrument for dealing with (large) collections of texts. Second, some analysis tasks are practically impossible to carry out accurately without computational support, even just for one text. One such is lexical cohesion analysis (see e.g., Halliday and Hasan 1976; Hoey, 1991b; Teich and Fankhauser 2004). Finally, some central tenets of SFL theory can only be modelled out using computation. One such is the notion of language as a probabilistic system (Halliday 1991c; Nesbitt and Plum 1988). For a working model of language as a probabilistic system, i.e. one that could be used in applications such as natural language understanding or generation, a sound computational basis is crucial.

Systemic Functional Linguists can draw upon a range of existing tools supporting linguistic description, analysis and theory. In the remainder of this article, I will focus on analysis, presenting tools and techniques supporting the tasks typically arising when processing language samples (Section 2). I will then put linguistic computing in the context of neighbouring disciplines and give an outlook on future opportunities and challenges for SFL in relation to linguistic computing (Section 3). I will conclude with a collection of references to useful websites (Section 4).

2 Tools for linguistic work

There is not the one computational tool that caters for all the needs of a linguist. Most tools concentrate on a particular analysis task (syntactic analysis, discourse analysis etc), stratum (phonetics/phonology, lexico-grammar, semantics) or medium (text, audio, video). Some tools are in principle language-independent, but as a matter of fact the majority of them have been designed for well-studied languages, notably for English.

Since it is impossible to give a comprehensive overview here, I base this presentation on the processing steps that typically have to be performed when we want to analyse a set of linguistic data. No matter what the particular analysis interest is, the first job that needs to be done is *segmentation*, i.e. determining and marking the linguistic units that are to be analysed. Once segmentation is done, we want to *annotate* our data, i.e. add linguistic categories to the identified segments. Third, we typically want to *analyse* our data, i.e. explore it for patterns and interpret our findings. I will go through the possibilities of computational support for each of these in turn, explaining what segmentation, annotation and analysis involve and pointing out tools that support these steps, including some SFL-specific ones (Section 2.1). I will use English as the language of illustration, but will draw attention to issues of portability/applicability to other languages where appropriate. Also, I start from the assumption that the linguistic data we look at is text, that the text is available electronically in an open format (ASCII, html, XML) and that it is normalised. As a sample text I will use the extract in (1) below (taken from Halliday, 1985b: vii).

(1) *Writing and speaking are not just alternative ways of doing the same thing; rather, they are ways of doing different things.*

Finally, I will point out some tools for processing audio and video data, which is relevant for instance, for the analysis of speech, sign language and multi-semiotic discourse (Section 2.2).

2.1 Processing text: Segmentation, annotation, analysis

Segmentation. The first step when starting any analysis is to identify the units of analysis. In computational terms this is known as segmentation. Depending on the ultimate analysis goal, the segments of a text we are interested in could be words, clauses/sentences or elements of the logical structure of a text (e.g., stages in a generic structure). Automatic segmentation is not entirely trivial, but while the segmentation of a text into sentences operates fairly well just on the basis of strings of characters, segmentation of a text in terms of clauses, or sentences into clauses, requires prior syntactic analysis.

Two types of segmentation commonly performed and included in many computational tools are *sentence splitting* and *tokenization*. Sentence splitting, the process of identifying the sentences in a text, can be done using a heuristically-based approach on the basis of punctuation ("./;/!/?/:"). Among the punctuation marks, the full stop is the most ambiguous and other information sources have to be drawn upon (e.g., capitalised first character of the first word of a sentence). Sentence splitters do not work perfectly but achieve a reasonable accuracy. For a discussion see Grefenstette and Tapanainen (1994) or Manning and Schütze (1999:134-136). Tokenization is the process of identifying units at word level (including punctuation marks, abbreviations, acronyms, proper names, numbers etc.). There are various approaches for tokenization, but a lexicon is indispensable (see again Manning and Schütze 1999:124-130 for a discussion). Problems that have to be typically addressed by a tokenizer are contractions ("can't,") and multiword units ("of course", "$3.50"). Again, tokenization is not perfect, but achieves a level of accuracy good enough for the output to be suitable for further processing. The result of these two segmentation processes is a text explicitly marked up for its sentence boundaries and its tokens. See Figure 1 showing our example encoded in eXtensible Mark-up Language (XML).

Most modern concordance programs (e.g., Wordsmith (Scott 2004)) include a sentence splitter and a tokenizer, where sentences and tokens provide the basis for search as well as for deriving other secondary information about a text (or corpus), such as the number of sentences, average sentence length or type-token ratio (ratio of different vs. running items). From the representation shown in Figure 1 we can thus obtain the information that our text contains two sentences with 24 tokens (one with 14 tokens and one with 10 tokens) and 19 types.

Annotation. Once the units of analysis have been identified, we can proceed to annotate them. The boundaries between segmentation and annotation are not clear cut – both represent secondary data. However, annotation is what we typically associate with core linguistic analysis, whereas segmentation counts as pre-processing.

A fully automatic annotation with systemic functional categories is not possible at this stage, but there are (a) tools for automatic analysis of a number of

```
<sentence>                        <sentence>
  <token>Writing</token>            <token>rather</token>
  <token>and</token>                <token>,</token>
  <token>speaking</token>           <token>they</token>
  <token>are</token>                <token>are</token>
  <token>not</token>                <token>ways</token>
  <token>just</token>               <token>of</token>
  <token>alternative</token>        <token>doing</token>
  <token>ways</token>               <token>different</token>
  <token>of</token>                 <token>things</token>
  <token>doing</token>              <token>.</token>
  <token>the</token>              </sentence>
  <token>same</token>
  <token>things</token>
  <token> ; </token>
</sentence>
```

FIGURE 1 Result of sentence splitting and tokenization

non-SFL specific features, which can be very useful to have, and (b) tools that support manual SFL analysis. I will first discuss the possibilities of automatic annotation, again looking at word and sentence levels, and then proceed to discuss manual annotation, including SFL-specific tools.

At the word level, the most common kind of automatic annotation is part-of-speech (PoS) tagging. The two components of a PoS-tagger are the tagging procedure, which can be rule-based (e.g., Brill tagger (Brill 1995)) or statistically-based (e.g., TnT (Brants 2000), Tree Tagger (Schmid 1994)), and the tag set, which encodes the possible PoS for a language, often including selected grammatical categories (e.g., number) as well. Statistical taggers are in principle language-independent and can be trained for a particular language, if a tag set and a sample PoS-tagged corpus is available. For English, there are various tag sets, e.g., Penn Tree (Marcus et al. 1993), Susanne (Sampson 1995) or CLAWs (Garside and Smith 1997), as well as PoS-tagged corpora (e.g., BNC, Brown/LOB, Frown/FLOB). For a PoS-tagged output of our sample sentences using

```
<sentence>                                      <sentence>
  <token pos="VBG">Writing</token>                <token pos="RB">rather</token>
  <token pos="CC">and</token>                     <token pos=",">,</token>
  <token pos="VBG">speaking</token>               <token pos="PRP">they</token>
  <token pos="VBP">are</token>                    <token pos="VBP">are</token>
  <token pos="RB">not</token>                     <token pos="NNS">ways</token>
  <token pos="RB">just</token>                    <token pos="IN">of</token>
  <token pos="JJ">alternative</token>             <token pos="VBG">doing</token>
  <token pos="NNS">ways</token>                   <token pos="JJ">different</token>
  <token pos="IN">of</token>                      <token pos="NNS">things</token>
  <token pos="VBG">doing</token>                  <token pos=".">.</token>
  <token pos="DT">the</token>                   </sentence>
  <token pos="JJ">same</token>
  <token pos="NNS">things</token>
  <token pos=";">;</token>
</sentence>
```

FIGURE 2 Result of PoS-tagging (added to sentence and token mark-up)

the Penn Tree tag set see Figure 2, again encoded in XML. PoS-tagging achieves an accuracy of around 97% and thus counts as one of the most reliable kinds of linguistic processing.

On the basis of PoS-tags we can explore our text/corpus in many interesting ways, such as calculating lexical density (ratio of lexical words vs. function words), extracting instances of particular parts-of-speech or syntagmatic combinations of parts-of-speech, and analysing them further (e.g., collocation analysis or process type analysis).

Another type of annotation we may want to perform at word level is lemmatization, i.e., the explicit labelling of the citation form of a word (e.g., *thing* is the lemma of *thing, things*). If we deal with a highly inflecting language, it may be worthwhile to carry out a full-fledged morphological analysis. Depending on the analysis goal, annotation with morphological categories can be quite helpful (e.g., if we want to study the morpho-syntactic constraints of collocations in German). Lemmatization and morphological analysis are quite well understood and there exist automatic lemmatizers and morphological analysers for many languages.

At sentence level, annotation typically involves syntactic analysis. Syntactic parsers are available for both constituency and dependency structure and for quite a few languages. For a sample of a constituency analysis using the Stanford parser (Klein and Manning 2003) see Figure 3 (represented as a bracketed structure). Syntactic parsing will not return results as reliable as for instance, PoS tagging (see again the sample parse in Figure 3 which is questionable for the first sentence). If a high-quality syntactic annotation is the goal, an automatic analysis must be checked by linguists and corrected, if necessary. For inspection and editing of syntactic structure annotations some special tools are available (see e.g., Brants and Plaehn 2000). A linguistic data set annotated for syntactic structure is known as a tree bank. There are tree banks for a number of languages, including English (Penn Tree; Marcus et al. 1993), German (Tiger; Brants et al. 2002), Czech (Hajič et al. 2000) and Arabic (Maamouri et al. 2004).

A syntactic structure annotation can be quite useful also in the context of functional analysis, because we could try to derive particular functional categories from it, e.g., we could interpret a syntactic tree for Mood-Residue or Theme-Rheme. For a proposal in this direction see Honnibal 2004b.

There are many other types of annotation one may be interested in, notably explicit systemic functional annotation, such as lexico-grammatical annotation, cohesion, generic structure or appraisal. There are a few tools around that support manual annotation, ranging from specialised editors (e.g., MMAX (Müller and Strube 2001)) to tools geared to one particular type of analysis (e.g., RST-Tool (O'Donnell 2000)). For SFL, there is a small set of tools that support SFL-based analysis: UAM Corpus Tool, the successor of Systemic Coder (O'Donnell 1995), Systemics (O'Halloran and Judd 2002) and Macquarie University's SysAm (Wu 2000). I illustrate the functionality of these tools with UAM Corpus Tool.

UAM Corpus Tool is a set of tools for the support of manual systemic functional analysis. In principle, UAM Corpus Tool is language-independent, following Unicode for character encoding. UAM Corpus Tool supports the definition of annotation schemes in the form of system networks and the application of the defined schemes to a text/corpus. Segmentation of an input text can be carried out automatically for sentences and there is a simple tokenization. The latter is not stored explicitly, however. If any other unit is to be annotated, the text has to be manually segmented before starting the actual annotation. Since more often than not, what we want to do is clause analysis, we have to mark up clause boundaries manually first. As said before, automatic clause boundary detection is not trivial at all, since it requires a full-scale syntactic analysis. Also, we may want to chunk up a sentence differently depending on metafunction: for example, for theme analysis we may want to disregard embedded clauses but for process type analysis we want to include them. UAM Corpus Tool allows for different segmentations of one text, also above sentence level.

```
(ROOT
  (S
    (S
      (VP (VBG Writing)
          (CC and)
          (VBG speaking)))
    (VP (VBP are) (RB not)
      (NP
        (NP (RB just) (JJ alternative) (NNS ways))
        (PP (IN of)
          (S
            (VP (VBG doing)
              (NP (DT the) (JJ same) (NN thing)))))))
    (. ;)))

(ROOT
  (S
    (NP (PRP they))
    (VP (VBP are)
      (NP
        (NP (NNS ways))
        (PP (IN of)
          (S
            (VP (VBG doing)
              (NP (JJ different) (NNS things)))))))
    (. .)))
```

FIGURE 3 Result of parsing

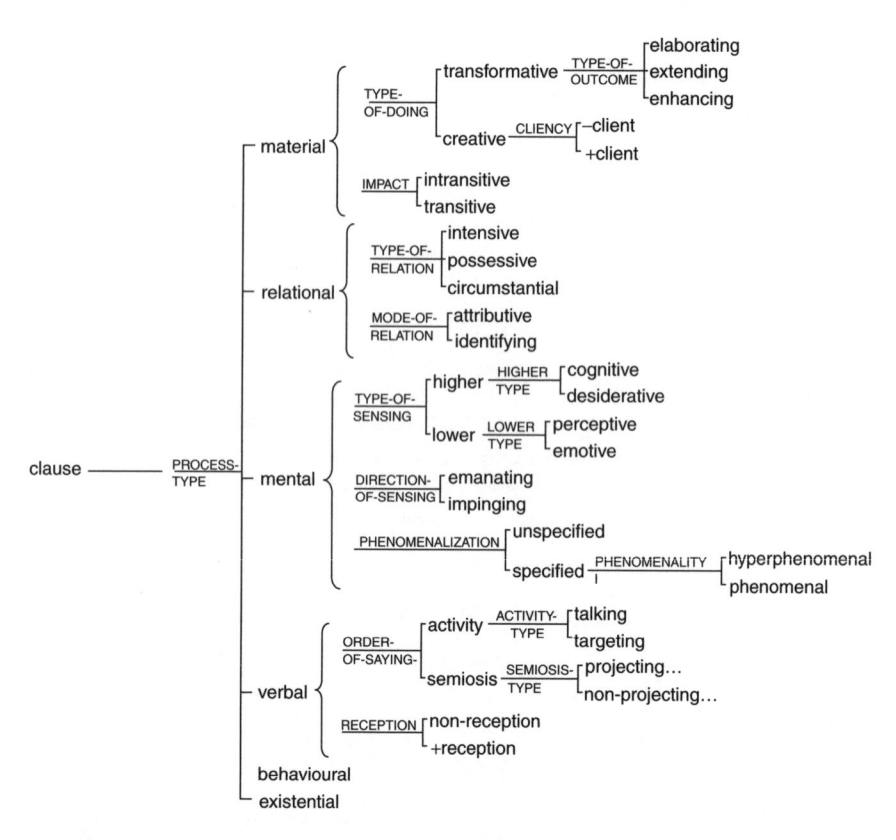

FIGURE 4 Annotation scheme for PROCESS TYPE

Once we have marked up the units of analysis, we can proceed to define an annotation scheme. For an example of such a scheme for PROCESS TYPE (English) see Figure 4.

Annotation then proceeds by choosing a feature path through the network for the unit that is being coded. The resulting annotation is stored as shown in Figure 5. This representation has a specific feature in that the annotated text segments are represented by their character offsets: 'start' denotes the first character of a segment (e.g., '1' in the first segment) and 'end' the last character ('75' in the first segment). This method of encoding annotations is known as stand-off annotation. It allows multiple segmentations of the same input as well as multiple encodings of the same or overlapping segments so that we can code for more than one metafunctional layer (e.g., PROCESS TYPE and THEME, as shown in Figure 5) or units of different strata (e.g., clause – intonation unit).

```
<segments>
 <segment start='1' end='75' features='process_type;relational'/>
 <segment start='76' end='124' features='process_type;relational'/>
</segments>


<segments>
 <segment start='1' end='75' features='theme;unmarked_theme'/>
 <segment start='76' end='124' features='theme;unmarked_theme'/>
</segments>
```

FIGURE 5   PROCESS TYPE and THEME annotations

On the basis of this representation we can explore the annotated text, asking, for instance, what the clauses with a relational process and an unmarked theme are. UAM Corpus Tool incorporates a search facility with which corresponding queries can be formulated and a concordance-like result is generated. For more details see O'Donnell (2007). While UAM Corpus Tool is a very comfortable tool for annotation of systemic features, annotation in terms of function structures is not (yet) explicitly supported. Also, it is not possible to import other kinds of annotation (e.g., PoS or syntactic annotations) in UAM Corpus Tool in the sense of building a true multi-layer corpus where the individual layers have been created by other tools (e.g., a tagger or a parser). This is the same for SysAm or Systemics. For a discussion of this problem see below. Current developments for UAM Corpus Tool include incorporating lexicons (e.g., of verbs and their process types) as well as using existing annotations as well as concordances so as to automise part of the annotation process.

Analysis. The key functionality needed for exploring an electronic text, raw or annotated, is *search*. The core function is the keyword-in-context (KWIC) search. KWIC searches return a *concordance*, i.e. a listing of a search term together with the contexts in which it appears. KWIC searches can be performed on strings, annotation elements, or combinations of strings and annotations. The most basic but very efficient kind of search is carried out using regular expressions. These are provided by, for instance, Wordsmith or the IMS Corpus Workbench (Christ 1994) with its search engine CQP. Figure 6 shows a CQP query searching for occurrences of nouns preceded by adjectives and the resulting concordance when applied to our sample text.

Search in UAM Corpus Tool works in a similar way, allowing the combination features from various annotation layers. For our sample text, a search for

```
[pos="JJ"][pos="NN.*"];

ing and speaking are not just alternative ways of doing the same
thing; rath
alternative ways of doing the same thing; rather, they are ways of
doin
ather, they are ways of doing different things. Writing evolves
when language
```

FIGURE 6 Regular expression search and resulting concordance

'relational' & 'unmarked theme' would return two hits (both clauses are relational and have an unmarked theme).

The problem with all SFL-specific tools is that there is no provision for importing annotations produced by other tools (e.g., a PoS tagger or a syntactic parser). In fact, this situation is quite typical of all kinds of scenarios of linguistic data analysis: most tools are purpose-specific and if we want to integrate their outputs, some additional programming has to be done. The answer to an increasing need for processing pipelines such as the one described here (segmentation – annotation – analysis) in computational linguistics is processing frameworks that support putting tools together to create a multiply annotated corpus. Such frameworks include UIMA, Gate (Cunnigham 2002) and AnnoLab (Eckart 2006, Eckart and Teich 2007). AnnoLab represents all data as XML records and specifically deals with integrating systemic functional annotations (as e.g., created with UAM Corpus Tool) with part-of-speech annotation or syntactic annotation (in principle any kind of annotation). This provides the opportunity of exploring constraints between different levels of linguistic organisation (e.g., phonology – grammar, syntactic structure – systemic features). When a full multi-layer functionality is not required, an alternative is to store annotations in a relational database and then use its methods of manipulating data records. SysAm, for instance, has chosen this option.

Search is the prerequisite for all other steps involved in analysis. Ultimately, linguists want to explore possible correlations between different types of annotation and/or decide whether any of the numerical results are significant or not. This is for instance crucial for register analysis, which needs to rely on statements about the distribution of linguistic features (see also Biber 1993). Standard concordance tools such as Wordsmith and UAM Corpus Tool have various options of creating frequency information including some simple descriptive statistics. For an example of a word frequency list of our sample text produced with Wordsmith see Figure 7.

If we want to carry out more sophisticated statistical analysis (clustering, factor analysis etc) however, we have to draw on statistics packages. One such

N	Word	Freq.	%
1	ARE	2	9,52
2	DOING	2	9,52
3	OF	2	9,52
4	WAYS	2	9,52
5	ALTERNATIVE	1	4,76
6	AND	1	4,76
7	DIFFERENT	1	4,76
8	JUST	1	4,76
9	NOT	1	4,76
10	RATHER	1	4,76
11	SAME	1	4,76
12	SPEAKING	1	4,76
13	THE	1	4,76
14	THEY	1	4,76
15	THING	1	4,76
16	THINGS	1	4,76
17	WRITING	1	4,76

FIGURE 7 Word frequency in sample text

non-commercial package is provided by the R Project for Statistical Computing (see e.g., Dalgaard 2002, Gries forthcoming).

2.2 Processing of multilingual text and other modes/modalities

The same types of processes – segmentation, annotation, analysis – also apply when analysing multilingual text (cross-lingually comparable text as well as translations). For parallel text-translation, there is the additional segmentation problem of determining the units of translation, known as text-translation alignment (see e.g., Kay and Röscheisen 1993). For aligned texts, there is a special kind of tool for exploration, the parallel concordance program (e.g., ParaConc (Barlow 2002)). For some examples of contrastive-linguistic, corpus-based research in relation to SFL see e.g., Teich (2003), Baumann et al. (2004), Lavid (2008), Hansen-Schirra et al. (2007).

Segmentation and annotation are also typical processing steps in the analysis of other modes and modalities. Depending on the type of signal, specialised processing techniques are called for.

For speech, there are tools supporting manual transcription of audio data and segmentation of the recorded signal (e.g., turns in a dialogue or intonation units). One such tool is Transcriber (Barras et al. 2001). Transcriber provides a graphical user interface for segmenting speech recordings, transcribing them, and labelling turns, topic changes etc. A similar functionality is offered by Shoebox (Shoebox 2008), which has been designed for field work and supports many language documentation tasks (e.g., interlinear glossing).

For phonetic and phonological analysis, there are some widely used tools supporting acoustic analysis on the basis of spectrograms and wave forms (e.g., Wavesurfer (Sjölander and Beskow 2000), PRAAT (Boersma and Weenink 1996)) as well as tools that support the creation, manipulation and analysis of speech databases (e.g., EMU (Cassidy and Harrington 2001)).

For multi-media data, there are some tools that support annotation and exploitation of multiple signals (video, audio, text), e.g., ELAN or Anvil (Kipp 2001). These tools can also be conveniently applied to the analysis of sign language (see e.g., Johnston 2004 on the creation of sign language corpora).

3 Context – recent developments – future prospects

Linguistic computing is computing in the service of linguistics. It is the complement to *literary computing*, which is computing in the service of literary studies. Together, the two form the core of *Computing in the Humanities*. Literary computing is primarily interested in creating sustainable digital records of literary texts and their properties, e.g., in the form of electronic editions. Some of this work is also relevant for linguistic computing, notably content and document encoding (see e.g., the Text Encoding Initiative (TEI)). Neighbouring disciplines are computational linguistics and corpus linguistics (in relation to SFL see O'Donnell and Bateman (2005), Wu (Chapter 7, this volume)).

Recent activities in linguistic computing include the representation of linguistic resources (such as tree banks, multi-layer corpora, lexical resources) and standards/best practices; see e.g., ISO, Ethnologue, Open Language Archives Community (OLAC), Linguistic Data Consortium (LDC). These activities are documented in workshops regularly organised around the central conferences in the field, e.g., the Language Resources and Evaluation Conference (LREC) organised by the European Language Resources Association (ELRA), as well as numerous community initiatives that provide e-science infrastructures. As more and more tools for linguistic data processing become available, providing such infrastructures becomes increasingly important, so that the collective knowledge of a community can be readily shared. The key issue here is to offer support for the creation of high-quality linguistic resources by providing stable reference points (such as high-quality annotated corpora/gold standards, annotation schemes, typical processing chains) as well as (automatic) quality checking of resources and guidelines for best practices.

There are many tools around that are potentially useful for systemic functional linguistic work, as this paper has attempted to show. However, in order to use these tools and appreciate their benefits, we have to be ready to reflect on some of our practices. This crucially involves a re-evaluation of linguistic analysis, both as process and as product. The process of analysis can be much better supported, if we share the products of analysis. In order to be able to share analysis products, we have to reach a basic agreement on how they are produced and computationally represented. This, in turn, requires a commitment to data – compare the language documentation and corpus linguistics communities, where analysis products have to pass a number of quality checks prior to distribution. A commitment to data will have positive repercussions on existing practices in the community in that analyses will become more accountable, can be stored in sustainable ways and are thus easily shared (cf. Bird and Simons 2003 for experiences in the area of language documentation). Also, promising new avenues for language modelling and theorizing will be opened, since computational methods of processing data offer interesting novel perspectives on both text and language (see e.g., Whitelaw et al. 2006, Teich and Fankhauser 2008). A recently formed, open initiative, the *Initiative for a Repository of SFL Resources* (IRSFL), seeks to pave the way for such developments. The goal of IRSFL is to create an e-science infrastructure for SFL by building up a multilingual text archive, collecting corpora of various languages, registers and genres as well as providing tools for linguistic data processing and working out guidelines for building up SFL-based resources and recommendations for best practices.

If we are convinced of the added value that computation brings to linguistics (see Martin, Chapter 9, this volume), then we have to realise that the technology offered by linguistic computing can only be used in meaningful ways if we make an appropriate investment. The development of computationally-supported methodologies needs to be based on a solid knowledge of language processing techniques. Linguistic computing therefore needs to be entered into our university teaching programs in the form of courses on linguistic data handling (compiling, encoding, maintaining and exploring data) as well as programming and more sophisticated data analysis, including statistics and text/data mining.

4 Collection of links

This section provides a collection of useful links for linguistic computing. All sites have been last visited in January 2008.

4.1 Starting points

Some good starting points to explore linguistic computing activities are the following websites.

- Summer Institute of Linguistics (SIL): http://www.sil.org/
- Linguistic Data Consortium (LDC): http://www.ldc.upenn.edu/annotation/
- Open Language Archives Community (OLAC): http://www.language-archives.org/
- Text Encoding Initiative (TEI): http://www.tei-c.org/index.xml
- Association for Computational Linguistics (ACL): http://www.aclweb.org/
- Linguist list: http://www.linguistlist.org/index.html
- IRSFL: http://www.hallidaycentre.cityu.edu.hk/sflrepository

A print resource for exploring the state-of-the-art in linguistic computing in relation to corpus linguistics is the *Handbook of Corpus Linguistics* (Lüdeling and Kytö, 2008).

4.2 Tools

The following is a list of links to the tools mentioned in this article.

- Annolab: www.annolab.org
- Anvil: http://www.anvil-software.de/
- ELAN: http://www.lat-mpi.eu/tools/elan/
- EMU: http://emu.sourceforge.net/
- Ethnologue: http://www.ethnologue.com/
- Gate: http://www.gate.ac.uk/
- Praat http://www.fon.hum.uva.nl/praat/
- R Project: http://www.r-project.org/
- Shoebox: http://www.sil.org/computing/shoebox/index.html
- SysAm: http://minerva.ling.mq.edu.au/
- TEI: http://www.tei-c.org/index.xml

Linguistic Computing 127

- Transcriber: http://trans.sourceforge.net/en/presentation.php
- UAM Corpus Tool: http://www.wagsoft.com/
- UIMA: http://incubator.apache.org/uima/
- Wavesurfer: http://www.speech.kth.se/wavesurfer/

4.3 Resources

The following is a list of resources that have been mentioned in this article.
Corpora

- BNC: http://www.natcorp.ox.ac.uk/
- Brown/LOB: http://icame.uib.no/
- Frown/FLOB: http://icame.uib.no/

Treebanks

- Penn Tree Bank: http://www.cis.upenn.edu/~treebank/
- Prague Dependency Tree Bank: http://ufal.mff.cuni.cz/pdt/index.html

7

Corpus-based research

Canzhong Wu
Macquarie University

1 Introduction

Systemic functional linguistics has a long tradition of using textual materials and corpus-based methodology for investigating language and language use. This dates back to the early stages of M.A.K. Halliday's work in 1949, when Halliday collected a corpus of natural text samples in Cantonese for studying the grammar of the dialects in the Pearl River Delta in southern China (see Halliday 1992e). Later in his PhD research (1959), he analysed a long Mandarin text in quantitative terms, showing the degree of association between different grammatical systems. In early 1960s, Halliday joined forces with John Sinclair to compile a corpus of spontaneous English conversation for studying grammar and lexis. This is also evident throughout the development of the SFL framework, not only in terms of numerous contributions by Halliday himself (e.g. 1992e; 2002; Halliday and James 1993) but also by other scholars (e.g. Nesbitt & Plum 1988; Hasan & Cloran 1990; Souter 1990; Tucker 1998; Matthiessen 1999).

The use of language corpora and corpus technology has particularly thrust into the spotlight in recent years in systemic functional linguistics. More and more systemic linguists (e.g., Pagano et al 2004; Halliday 1985a – third edition (revised by Matthiessen); Herke-Couchman 2006; Matthiessen 2006; Patpong 2006; Teruya 2006; Wu & Fang 2007) have started to take full advantage of available computer-readable textual data, and used them in a wide range of areas such as language description, discourse analysis, language acquisition, translation studies and natural language processing. It is conceivable that this trend will continue and intensify in the future with the wide availability of both spoken and written corpora and the increasing power of computational tools.

In this article, I first give an account of corpus linguistics, and locate the corpus along the cline of instantiation, and then describe the different roles of computational tools in corpus-based research. In particular, I illustrate the major features of SysConc, a concordance tool for doing automatic corpus analysis.

2 Corpus linguistics

Corpus linguistics is a study of textual instances in the context of use. It is a methodology for investigating language and language use and obtaining quantitative evidence through large quantities of naturally occurring texts.

2.1 What is corpus?

A corpus is a collection of texts that are selected and ordered according to a set of explicit criteria, including representativeness, balance and sampling. A corpus may be mono-generic, consisting of a single type of text, representing some variety of the language, e.g. weather reports and financial reports. It may also be multi-generic, representing multiple styles and genres. A multi-generic corpus may be representative of the whole language or just more or less of it according to the range of text types and their relative representation in the corpus. If the corpus seeks to represent a whole language, it has to be very big and the sampling well balanced in terms of text types, e.g. the Corpus of American English currently has 360 million words, equally divided into spoken, fiction, popular magazine, newspaper and academic. If the corpus seeks to serve as a reference corpus, it can be fairly small, e.g. the two classic small reference corpora, American Brown corpus and the British LOB (Lancaster-Oslo/Bergen) corpus, consist of just over one million words, in 500 samples of 2000 words each.

The size of the corpus relates very much to its purpose. For investigating certain uncommon lexical or grammatical phenomena, even very large corpora such as the Corpus of American English may not be sufficient: either the number of instances is too small to be statistically significant or there is no representation of them in the corpus. But for many other things, the corpus may be too big: there are too many instances, and one may need to use just a subset of the corpus or narrow down the search by supplying more contextual information of the search items.

Even though corpus-based methodology was used by field linguistics such as Boas (1940), it was only in late 1950s that Randolph Quirk started the first large-scale project "Survey of English Usage" to collect language data for empirical grammatical research, which laid a foundation for *A Comprehensive Grammar of the English Language* (Quirk et al 1985). This project was significant, and formed a reference point for future similar projects, but the data was not computerized at the time; the digitisation only took place in the mid 1980s when it evolved into Quirk and Greenbaum's subsequent project now known as the International Corpus of English (ICE).

The Brown Corpus was the first of the modern computer-readable corpora. It was named after Brown University, and was compiled by Nelson Francis and

Henry Kučera. It consists of one million words, in 500 American English texts printed in 1961, each containing 2000 words. The texts are classified into 15 categories as defined by the Library of Congress. The Lancaster-Oslo/Bergen corpus (LOB) consists of one million words of British English texts published in 1961, and has identical sample principles to the Brown corpus. The two corpora stand as the model for various others compiled in India (Hohlhapur, texts from 1978), New Zealand (Wellington, texts from 1986) and Australia (ACE, texts from 1986). Table 1 provides an overview of the composition of the ACE, Brown and LOB corpora.

As can be seen from the table below, these small sample reference corpora not only share a similar construction, but also contain only written/printed texts. In contrast, the ICE (International Corpus of English) corpora are a network of parallel corpora, each containing one million words of both written and spoken English texts, compiled in a dozen countries where English is either a first or second official language, such as ICE-AUS, a corpus of Australian English compiled at Macquarie University. Like other sample reference corpora, these corpora each have 500 samples of 2000 words.

With the increasing power and storage of computers and the wide availability of very large amounts of textual materials in electronic form, corpora have kept

Table 1 Composition of the ACE, Brown and LOB Corpora

	Text category	Number of texts		
		ACE	Brown	LOB
A	Press: reportage	44	44	44
B	Press: editorial	27	27	27
C	Press: reviews	17	17	17
D	Religion	17	17	17
E	Skills and hobbies	38	36	38
F	Popular lore	44	48	44
G	Belles lettres, biography, memoirs, etc.	44	75	77
H	Miscellaneous (government documents, etc.)	30	30	30
J	Learned (including science and technology)	80	80	80
K	General fiction	29	29	29
L	Mystery and detective fiction	15	24	24
M	Science fiction	7	6	6
N	Adventure and western fiction	8	29	29
P	Romance and love story	15	29	29
R	Humour	15	9	9
S	Historical fiction	22	-	-
W	Women's fiction	15	-	-
Total		500	500	500

on expanding in size and variety. Now the largest available corpus is the Bank of English, a collection of English texts, with 525 million words as of 2005 (see http://en.wikipedia.org/wiki/Bank_of_English). The majority of texts are British English, but there are also Australian and American: texts included. Undoubtedly, English has played a dominant role in the corpus, and will probably remain so in the near future, but this situation has started to change, and corpora in other languages have started to gather pace. According to Linguistic Data Consortium, there are currently 50,000 corpora accessible from its website (http://www.ldc.upenn.edu/), and a very significant number of corpora are in languages other than English, such as Spanish, German, Chinese and Japanese.

2.2 Locating the corpus

The cline of instantiation is a theoretical dimension in systemic functional linguistics for interpreting the relationship between potential, or system, and instance, or text: meaning potential is instantiated in text as instantialised potential (Nesbitt 1994: 54). Text and system are not two different phenomena of language; they are the same phenomenon of language seen from different observer perspectives: text is language seen from close up, and system is language seen from a distance (cf. Halliday 1991c & 1992e).

As observers of language, we can locate ourselves at any point along the cline of instantiation. The positioning of ourselves at a point along the cline of instantiation does not mean that we are constrained to that particular region. Rather, we have a degree of freedom to move around and draw on the resources along the way. We can investigate a text, and see how a particular linguistic system is instantiated in this particular text; we can also go beyond the single text, and look for recurrent patterns in sets of texts in order to characterize text types or the overall linguistic system, which is a typical methodology in corpus-based research.

The corpus is located at the instance end of the cline of instantiation, and it is a systematic collection of textual instances, so it is possible to move along the cline of instantiation from particular instances to make generalizations about sets of instances in terms of register, about sets of linguistic systems, or about the overall systemic potential. Figure 1 (adapted from Matthiessen, 1993: 273) shows how the cline of instantiation relates the systemic potential (overall system). By using a similar methodology, Matthiessen (2006) uses about 6500 analysed clauses in SysFan to draw up frequency profiles for some of the primary systems of clause (THEME, MOOD and TRANSITIVITY). Such work is very important not just because it is labour-intensive but also because it shows the power of the paradigmatic organization. As Halliday (2006: 213) puts it, it is an essential part for 'understanding and modelling the true complexity of a human language'.

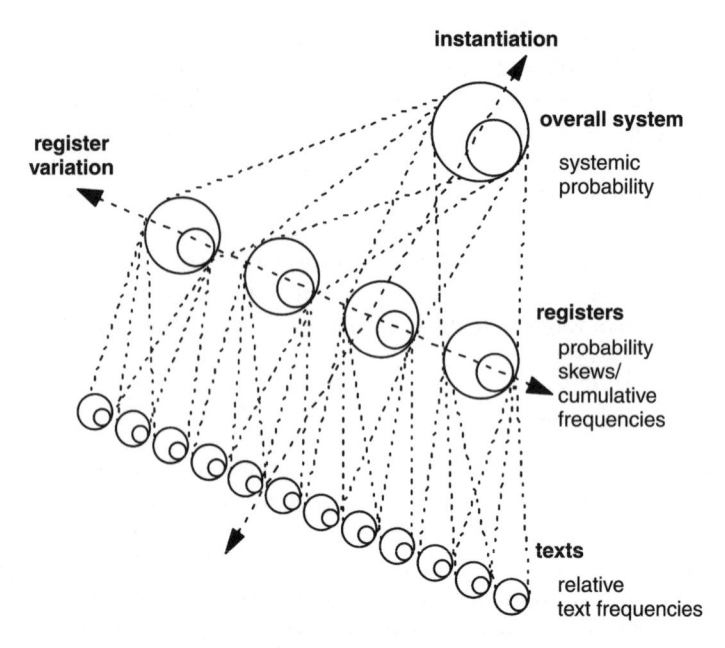

FIGURE 1 Instantiation and register variation

In contrast with Matthiessen, Halliday & James (1993) use a different strategy in their investigation of the system of POLARITY. Instead of relying on manual analysis, they extract their data from a corpus of 18 millions, and then analyse the extracted instances. Their research shows that the probability of 'negative' is around 0.1 whereas the probability of 'positive' is around 0.9, which is a reflection of the semantic markedness of the 'negative' term in the system of POLARITY.

2.3 Enhancing the corpus

Unlike earlier corpora, current corpora are significantly bigger and have more coverage. However, size and scope are not everything; they alone do not create extra meaning. For the corpora to meet the new demands from real-life language applications, they need to be enhanced and enriched with corpus encoding and annotation. This is not an easy task, and cannot possibly be achieved in a short term.

Realizing the challenges ahead, Bateman (2003) proposes three separate but interrelated steps: 1) changing existing corpora into marked up ones, 2) developing a standard for corpus annotation in XML (eXtensible Markup

Language), and 3) converting the marked up corpora into the standard. The first step is probably the most straightforward, and can in principle be implemented by individuals right away, while the last step does not seem to be a big problem once the second step is accomplished. The most crucial step is the second one: it is highly technical and complex. It not only involves the issue of how a corpus is annotated, but also requires different stakeholders to agree on a common standard for annotating corpora.

Fortunately, an initiative is now under way to address the e-science infrastructure for the member of the SFL community. This initiative, called IRSFL (Initiative for a Repository of SFL Resources), kicked off in 2007 and currently involves three universities: City University of Hong Kong, Macquarie University and Technische Universität, Darmstadt (see http://www.hallidaycentre.cityu.edu.hk/sflrepository/).

3 Computational tools for corpus-based research

Corpus-based research often involves analysing and interpreting large volumes of language data, and is typically carried out with the help of computational tools. This may involve collection of texts, production of frequency lists, annotation of corpora, extraction of lexical and grammatical patterns, analysis of data, and interpretation of findings; some of these can be fully automated but others demand more direct human involvement. Both types of analysis are important, and the key issue is how to strike a balance between the manual and automatic analysis, to integrate these processes into a unified system where computers and human users can do what they are most capable of doing. Some tasks such as pattern matching and frequency count can be automated by computers whereas other tasks that require high human intelligence must be done manually to achieve the best possible result.

3.1 Division of labour in linguistic analysis

Figure 2 shows the division of labour between manual text analysis and automated corpus analysis (cf. Wu 2000; Matthiessen 2006). In the figure, SysConc is located at the lexical end of delicacy within the graphological stratum (the bottom right corner of the diagram), and is one of tools that do simple pattern matching such as lexical or grammatical items as graphological strings. It is very useful for investigating word frequencies, word associations, and some morphological characteristics by producing concordances, frequency lists, collocational patterns. Since the tools located here do not involve any lexical or grammatical information, they are very constrained in their functionalities. However, since the information involved in the analysis is fairly simple, they can process large

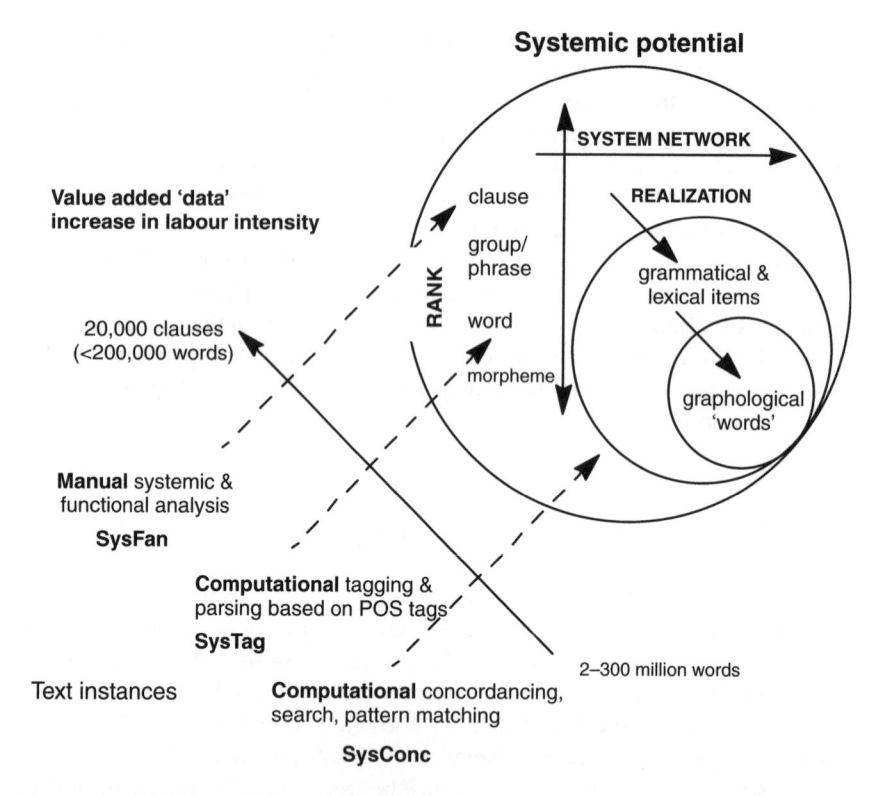

FIGURE 2 Division of labour in linguistic analysis

Diagram labels:
- Systemic potential
- SYSTEM NETWORK
- REALIZATION
- RANK: clause, group/phrase, word, morpheme
- grammatical & lexical items
- graphological 'words'
- Value added 'data' / increase in labour intensity
- 20,000 clauses (<200,000 words)
- Manual systemic & functional analysis — SysFan
- Computational tagging & parsing based on POS tags — SysTag
- Text instances
- Computational concordancing, search, pattern matching — SysConc
- 2–300 million words

volumes of text, e.g., of twenty millions words or more in a fully automatic fashion, though the texts may have to be chunked into smaller sections to be processed one by one.

SysFan is located at the other end of the scale, and is one of the tools that operate at the highest rank within the lexicogrammatical stratum – several steps away from the domain of SysConc and other similar tools. This is where tools may be located for doing systemic functional analysis of text. These tools are used to process large volumes of text to produce THEME, MOOD and TRANSITIVITY analyses of clauses and other systemic and functional analyses of other grammatical units. These analyses may be manual, semi-automatic or fully automatic depending on the amount of human intelligence involved, but the ultimate goal is to achieve fully automatic analysis of text at all levels.

The series of tools located in the middle region between SysFan and SysConc are also relevant to corpus-based research. As we move higher up, we are adding more value to the text: word-class tagging with taggers, grammatical annotation with parsers, and multi-dimensional and multi-functional analyses with manual analysers. However, the higher we move up, the less of the analysis can be automated. In the past few years, systemic functional parsers have been developed that can automate the analysis of texts, but they are restricted to small samples that may have to be adapted to fall within the parser's range (e.g., Kasper's FUG parser, 1988; O'Donnell's Coder, 1994). This is not surprising: linguistic parsing often involves very rich information (much richer than what current NLP systems can cope with, and certainly much richer than concordancing and pattern matching), and may include many steps of analysis. This is also one of the reasons why fully automatic analysis of large volumes of text has not yet become a reality. However, various attempts have been made towards partial parsing and tagging systems, and great results have been achieved within specific limited domains. For example, researchers have developed automatic word taggers and parsers producing class-based analyses rather than richer, functional analyses.

With the help of SysFan and SysConc, a two-pronged approach can be adopted to linguistic analysis. On the one hand, a small number of samples of text can be manually analysed by means of SysFan (say on the order of 200 to 2,000 clauses); on the other hand, the analysis can be checked and expanded for much larger number of samples using SysConc. At the most simplistic level, SysConc can be used to derive lexical information by producing lexical frequency lists from raw, tagged or annotated corpora.

3.2 Concordance tools for automated analysis

As the size of corpora has steadily increased in recent years, there has been a corresponding increase and improvement in concordance packages for analysing corpus data. They have become faster, more powerful and more user-friendly. In the earliest days of the COBUILD project, for instance, to generate static 'key word in context' (KWIC) concordances for each word in the 7.3 million-word corpus, the entire text database had to be sent off to an industrial-strength mainframe computer to get processed (Rundell 1996); nowadays concordances can even be obtained on the fly. Concordance programs which had been restricted to the large Unix-based machines have now become available to the ordinary PC users. In particular, many of the sophisticated systems which NLP researchers have used for developing probabilistic models of language are beginning to be feasible on today's desktop computers. Furthermore, concordance programs can now enable users to investigate and compare certain linguistic features of different languages by displaying simultaneously concordances from multilingual parallel corpora.

A concordance program is designed to facilitate the intensive study of linguistic phenomena in a natural and authentic context. It allows the user to search for lexical or grammatical items in a corpus, producing an exhaustive list of the search items with a short section of the context preceding and following each occurrence of the search item. Such a list is often called a concordance or a KWIC index.

Concordances have a wide range of applications, including the study of lexis and grammar, stylistic identification, collocational investigation, and so on, and they can be generated in either of two main ways (see Kennedy 1998). Firstly, the concordance program searches the text and finds each occurrence of each search item in a corpus, and makes a file containing each such occurrence with a predetermined amount of context. Secondly, a corpus is pre-processed by computer to index each word so that the concordance program can find all the occurrences of a search item instantly, and the size of the context can also easily be adjusted. The first approach is quite handy and efficient for a small-size corpus, but costly and impractical for a large-size corpus if we take into account the amount of time taken to produce the files and the amount of disk space needed. The second approach is more economical and more flexible, and thus more widely used.

In recent years a great number of concordance programs have been developed to facilitate the analysis of corpus data. Generally speaking, these tools have a lot of common functions, but they vary in one way or another. Many concordance tools are designed to investigate only one language at a time, e.g. IBM Concordance Browser (Kaye 1990), Conc (Thompson 1996), WordSmith (Scott 1996), but there are also some tools designed to process two or three languages at the same time. A bilingual concordancer like ParaConc (Barlow 1995), for example, allows the user to find and display all the instances of the search item in the source language, and at the same time show all the sentences in the second text that contain the meaning associated with the search item.

Concordance programs can be used for investigating word frequencies, collocations and morphological characteristics. With grammatically tagged corpora, they can also be used for examining the grammatical classes of words. However, most concordance programs are very constrained with respect to the kinds of analyses they can do, the type of output they can give, and even the size of the corpus they can process, making many linguistic research questions difficult, if not impossible, to address (Biber et al. 1998). One of the solutions is to take full advantage of a computer's capabilities and write our own programs. There are several obvious reasons for doing so, as described by Biber et al. (ibid.): (i) it allows the user to conduct analyses that are not possible with existing tools; (ii) it can ensure the accuracy and speed of many analyses; (iii) the output of the analysis can be tailored to the user's research needs; (iv) there is no limit to the size of the corpus that can be analysed. Besides these valuable points, there seems to be one more crucial one, i.e., a program of one's own is easier to extend and to incorporate into other programs, and this integration of different components will contribute to a more powerful and robust system or environment. SysConc is the product of this consideration.

4 SysConc: a tool for corpus investigation

SysConc is a concordance program (see http://minerva.ling.mq.edu.au/units/tools/), so it has most of the general features found in other concordance programs. It allows us to search for specific lexical items and collocational patterns and so on. However, at the same time it is rather different from other concordance programs. The differences are manifested at two "levels": theoretical and implementational. Theoretically, SysConc is geared towards systemic functional research, and is an integral part of the SysAm system; for instance, concordance analysis can be carried out according to the systemic types or some other hierarchical features, and the valid results can be fed into SysFan for manual analysis. Implementationally, SysConc, like other components of SysAm, was developed in Java, a powerful programming language built to be cross-platform and international. This can not only maintain SysConc's integrity, but also integrate SysConc with the other components of SysAm as well as other applications. In addition, the capabilities in Java such as networking and database access would certainly open new grounds for SysConc; for example, SysConc can be used to search the vast amount of information available on the web, or the annotated or analysed databases, to just name a few.

Figure 3 is part of the concordance lines of '*knowledge*' generated from ACE, with the first word to the right of the keyword sorted alphabetically, to show what follows the search item: there are altogether 127 instances in the one-million word corpus. This can then be examined in terms of KWIC statistics as shown in Figure 4: '*knowledge*' is preceded by '*the*' (16), '*of*' (15), '*general*' (5) and other word such as '*good*', '*traditional*', '*increasing*', '*no*', '*historical*', '*superficial*' etc.; it is followed by '*of*' (52), '*and*' (9), '*that*' (8), '*to*' (4) and '*about*' (3), etc.

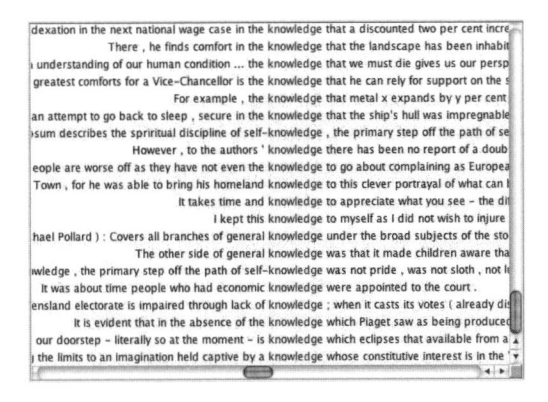

FIGURE 3 Concordances of '*knowledge*' from ACE

Left---			Left--			Left-		
Word	#		Word	#		Word	#	
the	7		of	11		the	16	
a	6		To	7		of	15	
to	5		in	5		general	5	
and	5		and	5		our	4	
who	2		have	4		a	4	
acquired	2		that	4		and	4	
secure	2		on	3		self	3	
there	2		a	3		his	3	
of	2		an	3		good	2	

Right+			Right++			Right+++		
Word	#		Word	#		Word	#	
of	52		the	22		to	4	
and	9		a	5		and	4	
that	8		it	4		of	3	
to	4		that	4		it	3	
about	3		and	4		is	3	
no	2		not	3		in	3	
which	2		we	2		language	2	
had	2		to	2		control	2	
was	2		mortality	2		other	2	

FIGURE 4 Collocational patterns of 'knowledge' in the corpus

The power of concordance programs lies in the availability of advanced search options they provide. In SysConc, the user can search for very sophisticated patterns in a single document, a set of open documents, documents located in the directory on the computer, or documents from the website via the Google search engine (see Figure 5), e.g. a single item like '*knowledge*' and '*knowledge of*', a set of items like '*knowledge that/which/of/in*' by using the option of Regular Expression, or a combination of items defined in a feature like 'Personal Pronouns'.

The search results can then be displayed in the form of concordance lines, and when demanded, a full context can be displayed at the left panel 'Context' (see Figure 6).

The beauty of using the 'Feature' search option is twofold. On the one hand, the search items are organized in a hierarchical way and stored on the computer. These items or part of them can be accessed any time in the future. On the other hand, these items and their occurrences mirror the structure of the 'Feature', as show in Figure 7, which gives us a very quick view of what is relatively more common: 'Third Person' (56.64%) and '*I*' (15.59%), for further investigation if necessary.

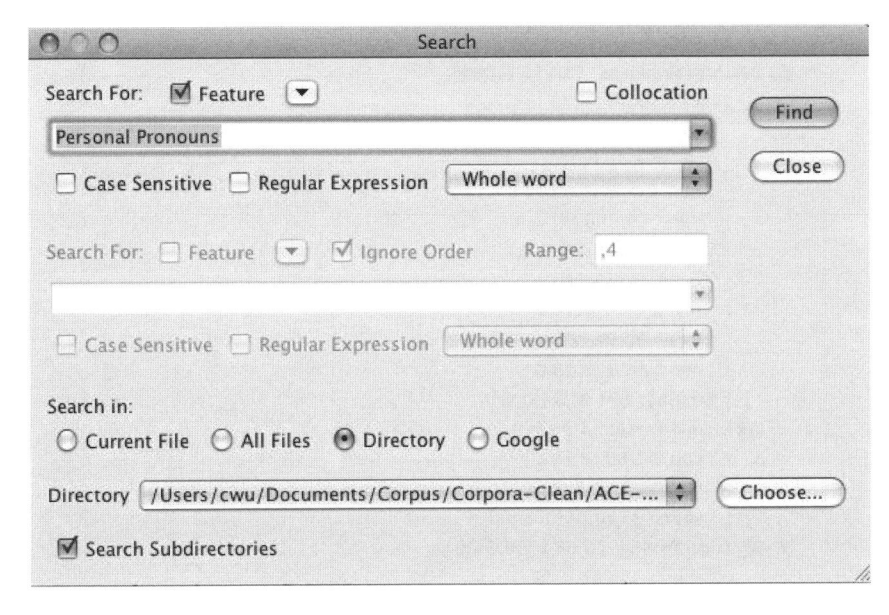

FIGURE 5   Search interface in SysConc

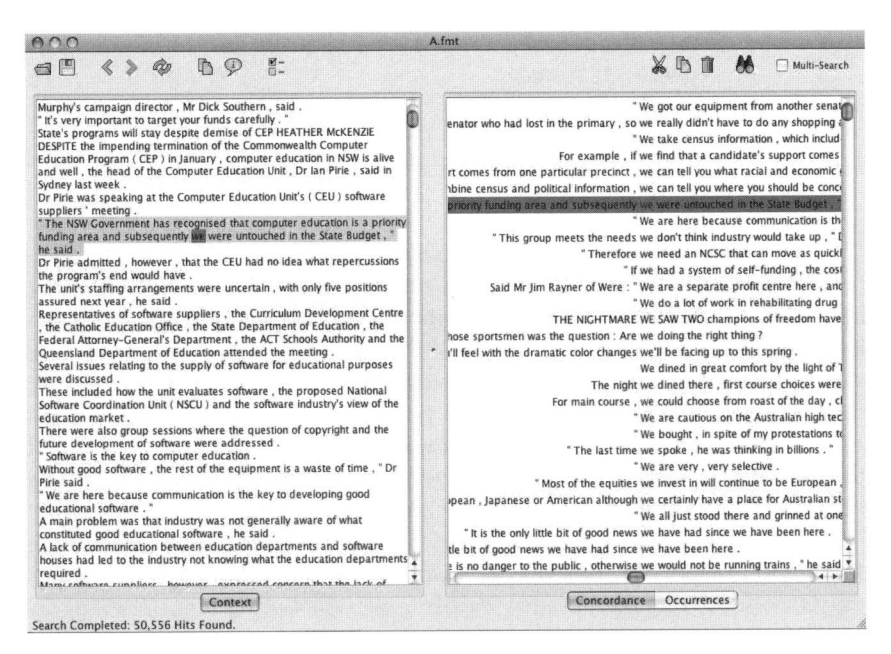

FIGURE 6   Search results of 'Personal Pronouns' from ACE

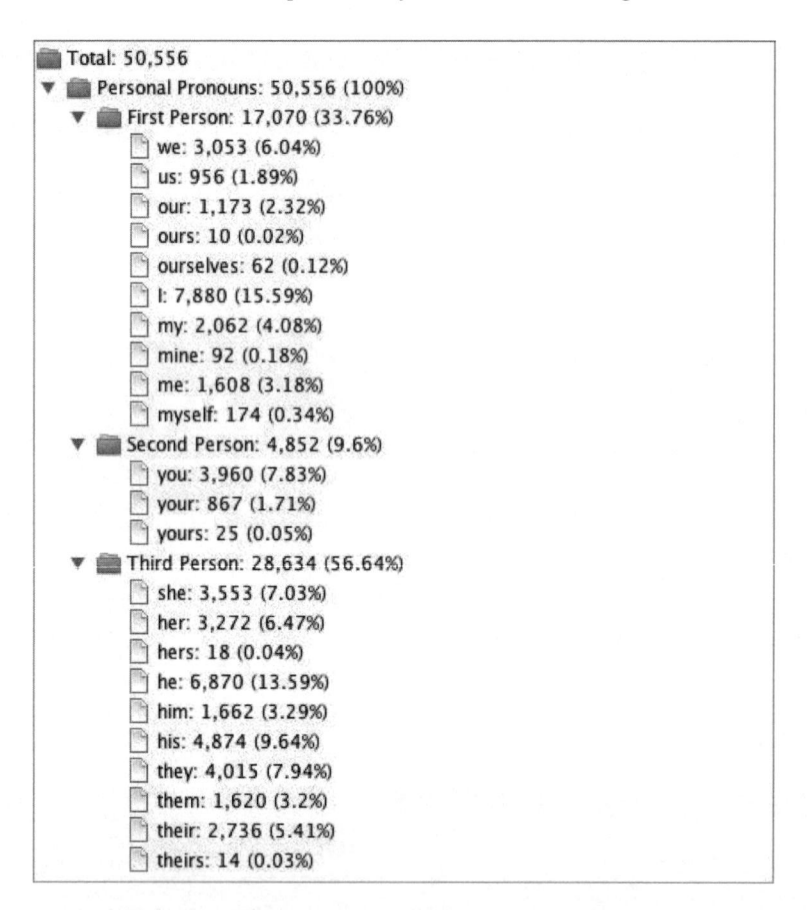

```
Total: 50,556
▼ Personal Pronouns: 50,556 (100%)
    ▼ First Person: 17,070 (33.76%)
        we: 3,053 (6.04%)
        us: 956 (1.89%)
        our: 1,173 (2.32%)
        ours: 10 (0.02%)
        ourselves: 62 (0.12%)
        I: 7,880 (15.59%)
        my: 2,062 (4.08%)
        mine: 92 (0.18%)
        me: 1,608 (3.18%)
        myself: 174 (0.34%)
    ▼ Second Person: 4,852 (9.6%)
        you: 3,960 (7.83%)
        your: 867 (1.71%)
        yours: 25 (0.05%)
    ▼ Third Person: 28,634 (56.64%)
        she: 3,553 (7.03%)
        her: 3,272 (6.47%)
        hers: 18 (0.04%)
        he: 6,870 (13.59%)
        him: 1,662 (3.29%)
        his: 4,874 (9.64%)
        they: 4,015 (7.94%)
        them: 1,620 (3.2%)
        their: 2,736 (5.41%)
        theirs: 14 (0.03%)
```

FIGURE 7 Relative frequencies of 'Personal Pronouns' in ACE

Corpora are useful only if we can extract information from them. The 'raw' corpora normally contain only texts in orthographic form; there is no other information such as word class, group/phrase and clause and so on. If a corpus is grammatically tagged, it will be much more useful. For example, by interrogating the tagged version of ACE, we could potentially extract all the passive clauses, which would otherwise not be possible with the non-tagged one. By searching for a combination of VBN (a word-class tag for past participle) and the passive voice indicators ('*be/ been/ being/ is/ am/ are/ were/ was*'), we are able to find 9945 instances in the corpus, as shown in Figure 8.

If we include '*get*' as another indicator for passive voice, we are able to get another 92 instances: *accused/ arrested/ asked/ automated/ baptised/ bored/ canalised/ caught/ confused/ destroyed/ divorced/ done/ engaged/ enrolled/ exchanged/ excited/ finished/ frightened/ frustrated/ fucked/ held up/ hit/ hooked/ hurt/ involved/ killed/*

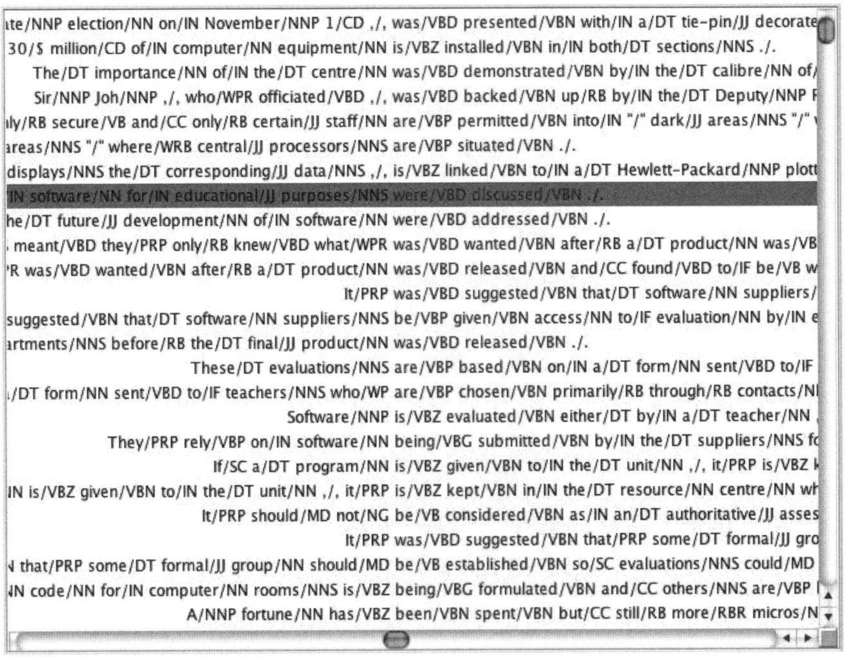

FIGURE 8 Part of concordances of the passive construction in ACE

knocked out/ labelled/ laced/ laid/ left/ lost/ married/ mixed up/ nicked/ offended/ overlooked/ paid/ passed on/ phoned/ quoted/ retrenched/ scratched/ slammed/ stuck/ stuffed/ sucked/ taken/ thought about/ thrown out/ tired/ told/ torn/ trapped/ treated/ used/ worn/ wrapped.

Undoubtedly, there would be some junk data in these instances, which need to be removed before the whole data are further processed in SysConc or fed into SysFan for manual analysis and interpreted in systemic functional terms, e.g. the systemic profiles of POLARITY and PROCESS TYPE within the passive clauses, the participant roles involved and so on.

5 Concluding remarks

Corpus-based research is a study of textual instances in the context of use, and is a very powerful approach for investigating language and language use. It has widely been used in a range of research contexts such as lexicography, language description, language teaching, translation and interpreting, and natural language processing.

The corpus is the central element in corpus-based research. In just over 30 years, the corpus has increased tremendously in both size and scope: the biggest corpus, the Bank of English, has now more than half a billion words, and much wider coverage than before. This provides a new means for accessing real language in unprecedented quantities, allowing us to investigate a wide variety of linguistic phenomena with improved reliability in authentic data. However, a corpus is just a corpus, and can never offer a full picture of the whole language, no matter how large it is.

The corpus is a true reflection of the language in use, but normally contains no more than orthographical information. As a result, it is relatively easier to extract lexical patterns from the corpus, but it is harder to retrieve information about the grammar. Apart from word boundaries and punctuations, the orthography does not typically provide information for indicating the structure of groups, phrases or clauses. In Chinese and some other Asian languages, it does not even give any indication of the structure of words. It is desirable that this kind of information be added to the corpus.

Corpus annotation tends to be very expensive and time-consuming, even with the help of sophisticated computational tools, like automatic taggers (systems for marking word classes or parts of speech) and parsers (systems for analysing the structure of higher units). But once the annotation is completed, the corpus becomes a more valuable resource than the original one, and thus allows a more reliable and more effective investigation of linguistic phenomena.

Corpus annotation is particularly important for systemic functional linguistics, where the language is viewed to be multi-dimensional and multi-functional. With the availability of the corpus fully annotated in systemic functional terms, we will be in a very good position to unravel the complexity of the language.

8
Clinical applications

Elizabeth Armstrong
Macquarie University

The investigation and treatment of communication disorders is a rapidly expanding field, covering both developmental and acquired speech and language disorders. These include such conditions as aphasia and dementia encountered in adults, and specific language and phonological developmental problems encountered in children. Exploration of disordered language is felt to potentially contribute to theories of normal language function, as well as provide the basis for treatment of disorders that can cause considerable disruption to an individual's life in terms of social, academic and vocational experiences and achievements.

For many years, intrapsychological models of language dominated in this endeavour, with clinical tests and treatments focused largely on the individual's ability to produce correct vocabulary and formally accurate sentences outside natural contexts. Linguistic 'skills' in such models include the ability to name objects and actions, complete sentences such as 'you eat with a..........,' and construct sentences given stimulus words to demonstrate syntactic knowledge. These skills are thought to be representative of the language skills of the individual, that are then 'used' in everyday discourse. A variety of standardized language tests have been developed over a number of years that assess an individual's language in this manner. Some of the frequently used tests for adult acquired disorders include the Boston Diagnostic Aphasia Examination (Goodglass, et al., 2000), the Western Aphasia Battery (Kertesz, 1982), the Psycholinguistic Assessments of Language Processing in Aphasia (PALPA) (Kay, et al., 1992), the Boston Naming Test (Kaplan, et al., 1983), and the Verb and Sentence Test (Bastiaanse, et al., 2002). For developmental disorders, tests include the Clinical Evaluation of Language Fundamentals (Semel, et al., 1995), the Boehm Test of Basic Concepts-3 (Boehm, 2000), the Test of Language Development-Primary-3rd edition (Hammill and Newcomer, 1997), and the Test of Auditory Comprehension of Language (Carrow, 1999).

While such models still predominate in fields such as speech pathology and neuropsychology, there is an increasing focus on social manifestations and ramifications of communication disorders (Byng & Duchan, 2005; Chapey et al., 2000). Discourse sampling has become an important clinical tool, although formal grammatical and 'information content' analyses of the discourse sample still predominate. For example, Saffran et al's (1989) analysis of aphasic discourse examines aspects such as the number of open and closed class words, nouns, determiners, verbs and pronouns used within the sample. Those analyses focusing more on 'content' (e.g. Doyle et al., 1998) examine *amount* of information conveyed, while semantic analysis (largely referential in nature) investigate '*word-finding difficulties*' (in terms of word categories ranging from general categories of proper and common nouns, to specific categories such as food, transport etc). Functional grammars, on the other hand, have more recently provided insights that are more consistent with a social focus on communication disorders. Systemic Functional Linguistics (SFL) (Halliday, 1985a – third edition (revised by Matthiessen)) in particular has been adopted by clinical researchers as a framework that provides insights into a speaker's use of linguistic resources across a range of contexts, and explicates both retained strengths as well as weaknesses in language function. In focusing on language in context, and focusing on discourse as the primary unit of communication, SFL broadens the scope for clinical researchers. Rather than focusing primarily on linguistic form, SFL frameworks enable researchers to explore language from SFL's well-established tripartite perspective i.e. the ideational, interpersonal and textual angles, hence addressing meaning from multiple perspectives and linking form to function.

Purpose of clinical analyses

Evaluation of an individual's language skills, when a communication difficulty has been reported, asks the following questions:

- What are the primary characteristics of the person's communication that are problematic e.g. what causes difficulty for other people in understanding the speaker's intention?
- What is the person able to do with language in terms of functions such as asking questions, making statements, describing things, participating in arguments, casual conversations, explaining things to other people, expressing opinions and feelings, writing emails?
- How are they able to do the above – what linguistic resources do they have?
- How are the above compromised – what linguistic resources are missing?
- What is the effect of contextual factors on the person's communication?
- How do communication partners converse with the person with the communication problem? Do they change their own typical pattern of communication? Do they facilitate or impede the other person's communication?

Such questions also relate to the broader theoretical questions that form the basis of research in the area:

- How do language and context interact? At what point of breakdown in the linguistic system does meaning become impossible to construe?
- How do the different language systems interact? Can one be impaired while another remains intact? What are the theoretical ramifications for this?

SFL Applications to date

In order to answer some of the above questions for both child (developmental) and adult (acquired) populations, a number of SFL analyses have been used. To date, studies have primarily reported analyses related to either one of the metafunctions or one stratum of language, rather than multi-stratal analyses. However, an important aspect of these studies has been the focus on discourse as the primary source of data. In order to demonstrate the applications of the various analyses, the headings below encompass applications to a variety of communication disorders, rather than focusing on the disorders individually. For a more detailed discussion of the different disorders, the reader is referred to a special issue of the journal Clinical Linguistics and Phonetics, 2005a (Vol. 19/3) that is devoted to SFL applications in this field.

Lexicogrammatical issues

Cohesion

As lexicogrammatical difficulties are often the most obvious manifestation of a communication disorder, these were some of the first aspects to be examined from a discourse perspective. Cohesion analysis (Halliday & Hasan, 1976) is probably the most frequently used SFL analysis in this field. It has been employed by several researchers in both adult and child language studies, in an effort to identify the nature of the lack of coherence often demonstrated in the discourse of individuals with communication difficulties. Cohesion breakdown has been documented in the discourse of individuals with aphasia (Ulatowska et al., 1980; Armstrong, 1987, 1991; Lemme, Hedberg, and Bottenberg, 1984; Nicholas, et al., 1985; Glosser and Deser, 1990), traumatic brain injury (Youse & Coelho, 2005; Ewing-Cobb, et al., 1998), dementia (Ripich and Terrell, 1988; Chenery and Murdoch, 1994; Lock and Armstrong, 1997), specific language difficulties evidenced in childhood (Liles, et al., 1995) and autism (Fine et al., 1994). Difficulties in all these groups include poor variety of lexical items and links throughout the text, excessive repetition, and the use of pronouns without clear referents. Treatment frameworks based on concepts of cohesion have been suggested by Armstrong (1991). These include working with the person on building identity and similarity chains throughout the text, rather than working on word retrieval out of context, and increasing lexical variety within these chains. Feedback to the person in order to facilitate better self monitoring of pronominal reference ambiguity has also been suggested.

Theme/Rheme

Textual meanings have also been explored in the use of theme/rheme patterns within the discourse of children with specific language difficulties in order to explore breakdown in continuity of texts in cases of Specific Language Impairment (SLI). Thomson (2000, 2003, 2005) compared the language of children with SLI with that of typically developing children. While some aspects of the analysis did not differentiate the groups, such as theme markedness, Thomson reported that children with SLI produced less multiple themes and demonstrated less linear thematic progression than the typically developing group, potentially contributing to their impoverished narratives. Thomson (2005) discusses the potential of theme analysis in further explicating the nature of narrative discourse for children with SLI, which had previously mainly been explored in terms of text structure and cohesion.

Clause complexes

As well as cohesion problems, pathological speakers also demonstrate difficulty creating logical relationships occurring between clauses. Examination of interclausal relationships in pathological discourse has been undertaken using clause complex analysis. In 1992, Armstrong reported on an aphasic speaker's patterns of clause complexes. This report and discussion was further developed with a longitudinal study of a further 3 individuals in 1997. Both studies found the aphasic speakers had great difficulty producing semantically clear clause complexes, and that this skill improved as the time post stroke increased. However, speakers demonstrated variation in their patterns of logical relations. One individual increased his use of elaboration over time, while another decreased usage. Two speakers increased their use of projection over time, while the other two showed no change in the projection-expansion ratio. Armstrong explored the effects of such changes on the texts produced, highlighting individual styles of discourse as well as the compensatory nature of some of the patterns seen. For example, a decrease in extension reflected the fact that the speaker was using a wider variety of relations to join clauses together, and conveying a greater variety of meanings, rather than simply adding pieces of information on in a consecutive fashion.

In 2002, Armstrong also explored non-brain-damaged speakers' use of clause complexes on a clinical recount task in order to examine the potential variations on such tasks in non-aphasic speakers – important for clinicians when attempting to judge whether brain-damaged speakers are 'within normal limits' or not as part of their diagnostic assessment of a client. In a study of 12 individuals, Armstrong again found great variability and concluded that it was possible to realize a recount in numerous ways in terms of logical relations. Some speakers produced a lot of elaboration, which provided much detail re participants and events, while others produced more enhancement, focusing on causal and temporal factors involved in the event being discussed.

Clause complex analysis has also been used to investigate the discourse of children diagnosed with Attention Deficit Hyperactivity Disorder (ADHD) (Mathers, 2005). While standardized language tests such as the CELF did not differentiate the group of children with ADHD from a normal control group, a measure of grammatical intricacy based on number of clauses entering into clause complexes did. This occurred particularly in relation to written rather than oral discourse. The children with ADHD scored significantly less on the grammatical intricacy measure than their typically developing counterparts. Such a finding correlated with anecdotal reports of children with ADHD having difficulty with written discourse. In addition, while typically developing children demonstrated differences between their oral and written discourse, the children with ADHD did not, the authors interpreting this finding as indicating a lack of sensitivity to genre on the part of the children with ADHD. While the authors acknowledged a limited sample size in this study, they interpreted their data as demonstrating that the children with ADHD "showed no adaptation to contextual change" (p. 223).

Transitivity

As noted above, clause level analysis has been undertaken in language pathology studies largely from a traditional formal grammar perspective. SFL's transitivity analysis provides a different perspective, in that it probes clause structures as they are used for different purposes, and different text types. Where formal grammars focus on meaning within the clause alone, SFL allows the analyst to examine verbs, for example, from a discourse perspective. Armstrong (2001), for example, probed the clause structure in the discourse of individuals with aphasia, exploring aphasic speakers' abilities to use different process types for appropriate genres. The study corroborated other studies of verb usage in fluent aphasia that had more recently acknowledged speakers' difficulties with verbs (previously thought to be only present in non-fluent aphasias). However, in describing different process types from a semantic perspective, the paper demonstrated that 'difficulty with verbs' does not necessarily best describe the disorder, but that different types are affected more than others e.g. some aphasic speakers used predominantly material processes, producing recounts that were largely factual in nature, with little description and few opinions/perspectives included. Armstrong (2005b) further addressed the use of mental and relational processes to convey opinions and feelings, finding that speakers with aphasia were less able to produce evaluations/opinions/feelings in their discourse than their non-brain-damaged counterparts.

Mortensen (1992) similarly investigated transitivity patterns in one individual with dementia. She reported restricted lexical variety in both nominal and verbal groups and at clause level. In addition, incomplete clauses, pronouns without referents, and repetition were common.

Modality

SFL has also been applied to fluency disorders. Spencer (2005) used the SFL framework to investigate interpersonal and textual features of the discourse of two individuals pre and post treatment for fluency disorders. Spencer noted that previous linguistic analyses of the language of individuals who stutter had utilized formal grammatical analyses, focusing on the word and sentence level. For example, many studies have focused on the "identification of where stuttering occurs and classifying the instances of breakdown according to their grammatical category and the position of the word in the sentence" (p. 191). In their 2005 study, Spencer et al. found increases in the use of modality markers in the discourse of two individuals after stuttering treatment. The authors interpreted this as in increased 'ability'/intention to prolong conversational exchanges. They also suggested that this increased usage "is indicative of acknowledgment of interpersonal relationships and the social structures governing appropriacy of language, including aspects of politeness. One of the speakers also increased his usage of continuative themes (e.g. *well, oh*, etc) following treatment. The authors suggested that such usage served to assist the speaker to embark on the 'propositional content of the message' and that they "may also serve to indicate to the listener that the speaker is considering the response rather than rushing in and hence have a positive effect on facilitating ongoing dialogue" (p. 199). While still preliminary, such analyses offer potential insights into the way motor speech problems can impact interpersonal communication, and the ways in which the discourse of speakers with such disorders can be impacted upon from a linguistic and general communicative perspective.

Mood and modality have also been explored in the TBI population. Togher & Hand (1998) focussed on the use of mood and modality in order to explore how these structures were realized in the discourse of individuals for whom lack of politeness in social interactions has often been noted to be problematic. They reported that the five individuals sampled were able to use different politeness markers, but were not always able to appropriately vary their use across contexts – in this case, across conversational partners of differing levels of familiarity and power balance (the person's mother, therapist, policeman, and bus-timetable call centre). In this case, the mood and modality analysis explicated features of the individuals' discourse which had previously only been described from a semantic or pragmatic viewpoint.

A focus on the semantic stratum

Exchange Structure and Generic Structure Potential

At the semantic stratum, interpersonal semantics has been examined in terms of exchange structure (Ventola, 1987) and generic structure potential (GSP) (Halliday and Hasan 1985) in a number of studies. Using both analyses, Togher et al. (1997) examined interactions between individuals who have suffered traumatic brain injury (TBI) and a variety of communication partners. Such individuals are known to have difficulty using language that is appropriate to the tenor of a situation. They demonstrate what are often termed 'inappropriate pragmatic behaviours' in conversations and as a result, often become socially isolated. Such behaviours include poor topic maintenance in a conversation, domination of the conversation, lack of politeness markers, and discussion of topics that are often irrelevant to the current situation. However, in their work, Togher et al. also found that communication partners interacted differently with their relative/friend with TBI than they did with individuals who did not have TBI, hence providing different communication options. For example, in a recorded telephone conversation with police (Togher et al., 1997), in which the person with the TBI was requesting his license back after a major accident, differences were found between this interaction and a similar one occurring with his brother, who was participating in the study as a non-brain-damaged control. The police officer tended to question the accuracy of the person with TBI's information giving more often, and was also less likely to follow up the person with TBI's contributions. In a practical follow-up to this study, Togher et al. (2004) conducted a training program for police to attempt to improve interactions with police and individuals with TBI. The training consisted of highlighting the generic structure of service encounters, focusing on breakdowns/differences in interactions with individuals with communication problems and ways to resolve these. Communicative changes in both the police and the individuals with TBI were noted after training. Examples of changes in the behaviour of the police officer included an improved establishment of the nature of the inquiry, and provision of clear answers. The individuals with TBI demonstrated less tangential speech and a greater proportion of the encounter devoted specifically to completing the 'transaction' rather than entering into irrelevant or unrelated talk. The authors concluded that the changes in the discourse of the individuals with TBI was a direct result of the changed communicative options and opportunities provided by the police officers.

Focusing more on the nature of the client/clinician interactions involving individuals with communication disorders, generic structure potential analysis and exchange analysis have also been used to explore the structure of speech pathology treatments. Ferguson and Elliott (2001) examined speech treatment sessions delivered by an experienced clinician and compared interactions with those of two student clinicians of varying experience. The purpose of the research was to explicate the nature of treatment sessions in terms of the types of communication opportunities that occurred, and how these were handled according to experience level. They analysed the moves within the interactions, coding each move according to a generic structural element, then examining sequences of elements. Results indicated that the GSP became more complex with experience. The least experienced student clinician conducted the therapy session in a straightforward linear pattern (moving from "establishing rapport, outlining therapy tasks, completing tasks, outlining the plans for the next session, reviewing the session as a whole, then leave taking" – p. 235). However the more experienced student demonstrated a more complex pattern, demonstrating recursion, where she not only described procedures before tasks, but also repeated them during tasks in order to keep the client focused. The interaction was even more complex when the experienced clinician was involved, demonstrating a "multiple and recursive pattern." This manifested itself in terms of the experienced clinician reviewing progress on each task throughout the session, introducing the next task and relating each task to future goals. In terms of exchange structure, the results reinforced previous findings regarding clinicians taking up limited roles within a session – primarily that of information giver rather than seeker, and service provider rather than seeker – consistent with the traditional role of 'therapist' in a medical model. The authors concluded that the analyses were particularly useful in highlighting the structure of therapeutic interactions and a potentially useful tool for "clinical education and reflective practice" (p. 242).

Speech functions

Examination of the system of speech functions has enabled further exploration of the kinds of interpersonal meanings that are able to be conveyed by individuals with communication disorders, and whether/how these meanings are compromised by such lexicogrammatical problems as encountered in aphasia. Conversations between people with aphasia and their communication partners have been analysed to this end. Initial studies indicated that primary speech functions are relatively well preserved in aphasia, although these are often realized by 'non-standard' grammatical forms (Ferguson, 1992). This finding has been corroborated by other 'pragmatic' analyses (e.g. Ahlsen, 2005; Avent, et al., 1998; Dronkers, et al., 1998; Holland, 1998). However, further analysis at the most delicate levels of the system network (Armstrong & Mortensen, 2006; Armstrong et al., 2006) has revealed restrictions in various speech functions for some aphasic speakers. For example, in one couple examined, the wife reported difficulty having a conversation with her aphasic husband. At a broad level of analysis, the husband was in fact able to fulfill the basic functions of initiating and responding (often where other pragmatic analyses cease). However, at a more delicate level, the husband showed a lack of rejoinders, preventing him from taking a very active part in the conversation. The wife tended to develop the conversation more. The husband rarely probed or challenged her statements, and rarely gave her the opportunity to respond to him in any way that might extend the conversation i.e. he gave his wife little chance for negotiation of meaning. It was the wife who predominantly structured the conversation.

Appraisal

Appraisal is another system that has proven to be of interest in the investigation of communication disorders. Sherratt (2007) has used appraisal analysis to investigate the emotive language of individuals following right hemisphere brain damage (RBD) after stroke. Such individuals are known to have 'pragmatic difficulties' in as much as they often present with flat affect (i.e. show little outward emotion) and often have difficulty conveying emotions to conversation partners. Sherratt reported less overall use of appraisal resources in a group of 7 males with right hemisphere damage, compared to 10 matched non-brain-damaged control speakers. The RBD group also graded their own emotions less and evaluated external phenomena more than the controls, rather than conveying their own feelings.

Following on the theme of emotive or 'evaluative' language, Armstrong & Ulatowska (2007a, 2007b) have documented the use of evaluative language by individuals with aphasia, with particular reference to their ability to express identity through such language. Using Labov's (1972a) and Martin's (2000a) categories of evaluative language, they have reported use of all types of evaluative language by speakers with aphasia, but again restricted variety of lexical items.

A further study of aphasic language in a group situation (Armstrong & Mortensen, 2007) highlighted the co-constructed nature of evaluation, particularly in the case of aphasia. The authors reported severely aphasic speakers still being able to participate in a conversation and give their opinions through either strongly reinforcing what others were saying (e.g. *exactly, yes yes yes*) or disagreeing, using the resource of graduation/amplification.

Such studies have moved clinical studies away from purely an 'information' focus on language. They acknowledge the fact that language is more than about conveying information – that speakers also provide their perspective on that information, and in so doing, express opinions, feelings and attitudes that are crucial to initiating and maintaining social relationships. As individuals with communication difficulties are often compromised in these endeavours, it is important to understand their retained strengths as well as their weaknesses in this regard. Such understanding is relevant to both attempting to address the kinds of language they need access to, via therapy, and also explaining to significant others how and why such aspects of communication are impaired.

Multistratal analysis

While several of the studies mentioned above have focused on particular systems from a specific perspective, several have also provided multistratal analysis. For example, Ferguson's 1992 study of speech functions in speakers with aphasia also examined lexicogrammatical realization, making the point that speech functions can be realized in non-standard ways by people with communication disorders. In their study of use of appraisal in aphasia, Armstrong & Mortensen (2007) explored the kinds of lexicogrammatical devices used to convey affect, appreciation and judgement.

One of the most detailed multistratal analyses of this population to date, however, is that of Mortensen (2003), which investigated written, rather than oral discourse. Similar to the investigation of oral discourse, written discourse in populations with communication problems has primarily been viewed from a formalist perspective. Common descriptions have included depiction of difficulties with motor planning or control, spelling, word retrieval and sentence formulation. Mortensen examined the written discourse of individuals with aphasia, cognitive language impairment (after traumatic brain injury), and non-brain-damaged control participants, writing two different types of text – a formal letter and a personal letter. Mortensen analysed the texts in terms of their global organization using generic structure potential analysis and semantic move analysis (Butt, 2000). Lexicogrammatical realizations of these meanings were examined through the systems of clause complexing and nominal group selection. All writers, those with and without brain damage, demonstrated the ability to adjust their language to meet the requirements of the two different text types – at both the semantic and lexicogrammatical strata. For example, obligatory elements of generic structure were present in all texts. Lexical density and grammatical intricacy also differentiated the two texts in all groups. However, other aspects differentiated the groups. For example, the individuals with aphasia demonstrated less use of optional elements of generic structure, and a decreased use of lexicogrammatical resources for both ideational and interpersonal meanings

Future directions

Future research in the area promises application to a wider variety of communication disorders. Following the work of Fine et al. (1994) in autism, for example, Bartlett et al. (2005) and De Villiers (2005) have proposed that the SFL framework may benefit exploration of Aspergers Syndrome (AS). Children with AS reportedly have good language skills, yet poor interpersonal skills (Paul, 2007). Bartlett et al maintain that the framework may enable the manifestation of these 'interpersonal issues' to be explicated from a linguistic perspective, which may shed further light on the nature of the interpersonal difficulties.

In providing a framework that offers the opportunity to explore contextual variation and a systematic linking between meaning and wording across a variety of contexts, SFL offers an exciting future in the field of communication disorders. The exploration of meaning in this area has been largely restricted to referential meaning to date, and the detailed tripartite system in the SFL model, encompassing interpersonal meanings in particular, promises to shed light on many of the social ramifications of communication disorders. These ramifications are often intuitively perceived, but are also often difficult to describe meaningfully and to explain. Hence, a linguistic model that is comprehensive from a grammatical perspective, but also includes contextual and even cultural parameters, enables researchers to examine everyday discourse of individuals with communication problems, and address both the communicative impairments and the strengths that constitute the individual's linguistic abilities.

9
Discourse studies

J. R. Martin
University of Sydney

1 Background

Systemic functional linguistics (hereafter SFL) has a long standing interest in discourse analysis, deriving historically from Firth's concern with meaning as function in context (e.g. 1957a) and Mitchell's canonical study of service encounters in a Libyan marketplace (1957). Halliday (e.g. 1967–1968) built a focus on discourse function into his grammar through his work on Theme/Rheme and (Given)/New structure; and his perspective on textual meaning beyond the clause (i.e. cohesion) is outlined in Halliday & Hasan 1976. Halliday 2002–2007 volume 2 brings together a useful collection of his work on text and discourse.

In addition Halliday's model of social context (e.g. Halliday 1978a on field, tenor and mode) stimulated SFL register studies around the world and led to the development of genre analysis, particularly in Australia (e.g. Hasan 1978, Martin 1985a). There are many SFL publications featuring discourse analysis, including Benson & Greaves 1985a, Benson et al. 1988, Steiner & Veltman 1988, Ventola 1991, Davies & Ravelli 1992, Ghadessy 1993a, Fries & Gregory 1995, Ghadessy 1995, Hasan & Fries 1995, Sanchez-Macarro & Carter 1998, Ghadessy 1999, Ventola 2000, Stainton & de Villiers 2001, Hasan et al. 2005, 2007; special issues of *Word* 1989 (40.1-2), *Language Sciences* (14.4) 1992 and *Cultural Dynamics* 1993 (6.1); and many issues of *Functions of Language*.

In section 2 below one reading of the theory informing this work will be outlined, based on Martin 1992a and Martin & Rose 2003. Subsequently in section 3 some recent developments and current trends in SFL discourse analysis will be reviewed.

2 Modelling discourse

Early work on cohesion was designed to move beyond the structural resources of grammar and consider discourse relations which transcend grammatical structure. Halliday (e.g. 1973a: 141) treated cohesion as involving non-structural relations beyond the sentence, within what he refers to as the textual metafunction (as opposed to ideational and interpersonal meaning). In Halliday & Hasan 1976 the inventory of cohesive resources was organised as . . .

- reference
- ellipsis
- substitution
- conjunction
- lexical cohesion

Gutwinski 1976: 57, a student of Gleason's, develops a closely related framework, including these resources (and in addition grammatical parallelism).

Reference refers to resources for referring to a participant or circumstantial element whose identity is recoverable. In English the relevant resources include demonstratives, the definite article, pronouns, comparatives and the phoric adverbs *here, there, now, then*. **Ellipsis** refers to resources for omitting a clause, or some part of a clause or group, in contexts where it can be assumed. In English conversation, rejoinders are often made dependent through omissions of this kind: *Did they win? - Yes, they did*. Some languages, including English, have in addition a set of place holders which can be used to signal the omission - e.g. *so* and *not* for clauses, *do* for verbal groups and *one* for nominal groups. This resource of place holders is referred to as **substitution**[1]. Reference, ellipsis and substitution involve small closed classes of items or gaps, and have accordingly been referred to as grammatical cohesion (e.g. Hasan 1968, Gutwinski 1976).

Also included as grammatical cohesion is the typically much larger inventory of connectors which link clauses in discourse, referred to as **conjunction**. For Halliday & Hasan 1976 this resource comprises linkers which connect sentences to each other, but excludes paratactic and hypotactic (coordinating and subordinating) linkers within sentences, which are considered structural by Halliday. Gutwinski, however, includes all connectors, whether or not they link clauses within or between sentences.

The complement of grammatical cohesion involves open system items, and so is referred to as **lexical cohesion**. Here the repetition of lexical items, synonymy or near synonymy (including hyponymy) and collocation are included. Collocation was Firth's term for expectancy relations between lexical items (e.g. the mutual predictability of *strong* and *tea*, but not *powerful* and *tea*).

The relationship between a cohesive item and the item it presupposed in a text is referred to as a **cohesive tie**. Gutwinski 1976 contrasts the different kinds of cohesive tie that predominate in writing by Hemingway and James, with Hemingway depending more on lexical cohesion than does James. Halliday & Hasan provide a detailed coding scheme for analysing cohesive ties, which takes into account the distance between a cohesive item and the item presupposed.

Later work concentrated on the semantics of these cohesive resources and their relation to discourse structure. Martin (e.g. 1992a) worked on reformulating the notion of cohesive ties as discourse semantic structure, inspired by the text oriented conception of semantics of the Hartford stratificationalists (Gleason 1968, Gutwinski 1976) with whom he studied in Toronto. In his stratified account, cohesion was reformulated as a set of discourse semantic systems at a more abstract level than lexicogrammar, with their own metafunctional organisation. Halliday's non-structural textual resources were thus reworked as semantic systems concerned with discourse structure, comprising . . .

- identification
- negotiation
- conjunction
- ideation

Identification is concerned with resources for tracking participants in discourse. This system subsumes earlier work on referential cohesion in a framework which considers both the ways in which participants are introduced into a text and kept track of once introduced. In addition the ways in which phoric items depend[2] on preceding or succeeding co-text, on assumed understandings or on other relevant phenomena (images, activity, sound etc.) are considered.

Negotiation is concerned with resources for exchanging information and goods & services in dialogue. This system subsumes some of the earlier work on ellipsis and substitution in a framework which considers the ways in which interlocutors initiate and respond in adjacency pairs. Drawing on research at Birmingham (e.g. Sinclair and Coulthard 1975) and Nottingham (e.g. Berry 1981), a framework for exchanges consisting of up to five moves was developed, alongside provision for additional tracking and challenging side-sequences (Ventola 1987). This work is closely related to studies in conversation analysis (CA), but with a stronger grammatical orientation (such as that canvassed in Ochs et al. 1996). Eggins & Slade 1997 introduce ongoing SFL research in this area, in relation to wider questions of discourse structure and social context (Coulthard 1992 updates the Birmingham based work).

Conjunction is concerned with resources for connecting messages, via addition, comparison, temporality, and causality. This system subsumes earlier work on linking between clauses in a framework which considers, in addition, the ways in which connections can be realised inside a clause through verbs, prepositions and nouns (e.g. *result in, because of, reason*). Drawing on Gleason 1968 a framework for analysing internal[3] (pragmatic/rhetorical) and external (semantic/propositional) conjunctive relations was proposed, including the possibility of connections realised simply by the contiguity of messages (i.e. links unmarked by an explicit connector).

Ideation is concerned with the semantics of lexical relations as they are deployed to construe[4] institutional activity. This system subsumes earlier work on lexical cohesion in a framework which considers the ways in which activity sequences and taxonomic relations (of classification and composition) organise the field of discourse (Benson & Greaves 1992). Drawing on Hasan 1985c, a framework for a more detailed account of lexical relations was proposed – including repetition, synonymy, hyponymy and meronymy; in addition, collocation was factored out into various kinds of 'nuclear' relation, involving elaboration, extension and enhancement (as developed by Halliday 1985a – second edition (1994) for the clause complex).

The result of these reformulations is a semantic stratum of text oriented resources dedicated to the analysis of cohesive relations as discourse structure. Once stratified with respect to lexicogrammar, these resources can be aligned with metafunctions in the following proportions:

- identification   textual meaning
- negotiation   interpersonal meaning
- conjunction   logical[5] meaning
- ideation   experiential meaning

Martin & Rose 2003 (2nd edition 2007) expand on these discourse semantic resources by including chapters on appraisal and periodicity. Appraisal complements negotiation by concentrating on interpersonal resources for evaluation, including systems of attitude, engagement and graduation. Attitude focuses on systems for construing affect, judgement and appreciation (roughly the lexically realised realms of emotion, ethics and aesthetics); engagement is concerned with the sourcing of attitude and acknowledgement of alternative voices (heteroglossia); and graduation covers force (intensification of inherently gradable meanings) and focus ('fuzzification' of inherently non-gradable categories). Work on this dimension of intersubjective meaning has refocused attention on prosodic realisation (across ideational boundaries) in various registers – history (Coffin 1997), narrative and literary criticism (Rothery & Stenglin 1997, 2000), news stories (White 1997), casual conversation, including humour and gossip and their implications for generation, ethnicity and gender (Eggins & Slade 1997) and popular science (Fuller 1998). For useful introductions to appraisal theory see Macken-Horarik & Martin 2003 and Martin & White 2005. Peter White's appraisal website is an important point of electronic access (www.grammatics.com/appraisal/index.html).

Periodicity develops suggestions by Pike (1982) and Halliday (in Thibault 1987) on information flow, inspired in particular by Fries' (1981) pioneering work on method of development and point. Ghadessy 1995 and Hasan & Fries 1995 include critical contributions in this area. Martin & Rose 2003 outline the way in which patterns of unmarked Theme selection in the clause establish a text's orientation to its field and the ways in which marked Themes and higher level hyper-Themes and macro-Themes package information into phases of discourse. Higher level Theme patterns are complemented, especially in writing, by hyper-New and macro-New functions which distill the point of preceding discourse.

For reasons of space, Martin & Rose 2003 do not elaborate Hasan's (1984, 1985c) work on cohesive harmony. Analysis of this kind concentrates on the ways in which cohesive ties (identity chains and lexical strings) interact with experiential meaning in grammar. For example, early on in Anthony Browne's children's story *Piggybook*, at group rank a 'nice' string and a 'house' string are repeatedly related through nominal group structure as Epithet to Thing: *nice house, nice garden, nice car, nice garage*. Similarly, at clause rank, a 'calling' string is related to a 'time of day' string as Process to Circumstance: *called every morning, called every morning, called every evening, called every evening*. Hasan defines interaction as taking place when two or more members of a string or chain relate in the same way to two or more members of another string or chain.

For Hasan, the purpose of cohesive harmony analysis is to provide a measure of the coherence of a text. She defines peripheral tokens as meanings in the text which do not participate in identity chains or lexical strings, relevant tokens as meanings which do so participate, and central tokens as relevant tokens which interact. She then suggests that:

- The lower the proportion of peripheral to relevant tokens, the more coherent a text is likely to be.
- The higher the proportion of central tokens to non-central ones (i.e. of interacting to non-interacting relevant tokens), the more coherent a text is likely to be.

She also raises the issue of breaks in the overall pattern of interaction in a text. These breaks may of course simply reflect the genre of a text as it moves from one stage to the next. As long as they are generically motivated, they will not be felt as disruptive. However it is likely that generically unmotivated breaks in string/chain interaction will affect coherence. Hasan's technology for measuring coherence has been taken up by a number of scholars; see especially Pappas 1985 on children's stories, Parsons 1990, 1991 on scientific texts, Cloran 1999a on pre-school mother-child interaction and Yang 1989 (cf. Hoey 1991a and Martin 1992a on nuclear relations for closely related approaches to cohesion and coherence[6]). To the extent that scholars are concerned that readers' feeling about the coherence of a text is something that needs to be quantified, cohesive harmony is an effective, though labour intensive tool.

This brings us the question of modelling social context in a functional theory which looks at what cohesion is realising alongside the ways in which it is realised. In SFL social context is modelled through register and genre theory. Following Halliday (e.g. 1978a) a natural relation is posited between the organisation of language and the organisation of social context, built up around the notion of kinds of meaning (Matthiessen 1993). Interpersonal meaning is

Table 1 Types of meaning in relation to social context

	'reality construal'	contextual variable
INTERPERSONAL	social reality	tenor
IDEATIONAL (logical, experiential)	'natural' reality	field
TEXTUAL	semiotic reality	mode

related to the enactment of social relations (social reality) – tenor; ideational meaning is related to the construction of institutional activity ('naturalised reality') – field; and textual meaning is related to information flow across media (semiotic reality) – mode. A summary of these correlations between types of meaning and register variables is outlined in Table 1.

Following Martin 1992a, field is concerned with systems of activity, including descriptions of the participants, process and circumstances these activities involve. For illustrative work see Halliday & Martin 1993, Martin & Veel 1998. Tenor is concerned with social relations, as these are enacted through the dimensions of power and solidarity. For foundational work on tenor see Poynton 1985. Mode is concerned with semiotic distance, as this is affected by the various channels of communication through which we undertake activity (field) and simultaneously enact social relations (tenor). For exemplary work on differences between speech and writing, see Halliday 1985b.

In Martin 1992a, an additional level of context, above and beyond tenor, field and mode has been deployed – referred to as genre. This level is concerned with systems of social processes, where the principles for relating social processes to each other have to do with texture – the ways in which field, mode and tenor variables are phased together in a text. In Australian educational linguistics, genres have been defined as staged, goal-oriented social processes (Martin 1999), a definition which flags the way in which most genres take more than a single phase to unfold, the sense of frustration or incompletion that is felt when phases don't unfold as expected or planned, and the fact that genres are addressed (i.e. formulated with readers and listeners in mind), whether or not the intended audience is immediately present to respond. In these terms, as a level of context, genre represents the system of staged goal-oriented social processes through which social subjects in a given culture live their lives. An overview of this stratified model of context is presented in Figure 1; this image includes Lemke's (e.g. 1995) notion of metaredundancy, whereby more abstract levels are interpreted as patterns of less abstract ones – thus register is a pattern of linguistic choices, and genre a pattern of register choices (i.e. a pattern of a pattern of texture). For further discussion see Christie & Martin 1997, Eggins 1994, Eggins & Martin 1997, Martin 1992a, 2001a, Ventola 1987, Martn & Rose 2008.

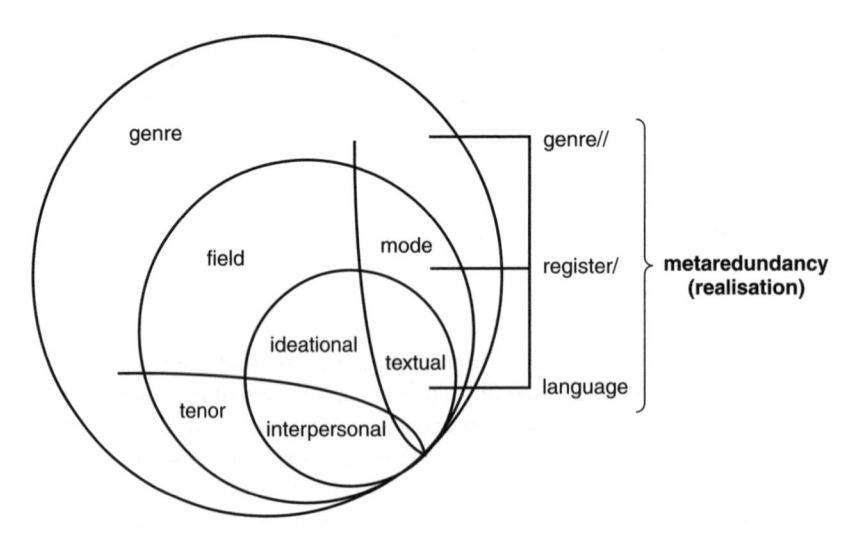

FIGURE 1 Metafunctions in relation to register and genre

3 More recent developments

Throughout the 90s SFL discourse analysis developed along several parameters, including relevant aspects of phonology and grammar. Higher levels of phonological anlaysis, pushing well beyond the tone group as far as rhythm is concerned, are pursued in van Leeuwen 1992 and Martinec 2000a. In grammar, research expanded across languages and language families, including relevant work on textual meaning. Caffarel et al. 2004 includes chapters on French, German, Telegu, Chinese, Japanese, Vietnamese, Tagalog and Pitjantjatjara – each with an emphasis on showing how the various grammars operate in discourse. The papers in Steiner & Yallop 2001 explore the implications of functional descriptions of this kind for translation and multilingual text production. For English one significant trend has been the development of computer assisted analysis programs which facilitate the coding of large quantities of text for SFL grammar and discourse features – including O'Halloran & Judd 2002; Matthiessen & Wu's SysAm (minerva.ling.mq.edu.au/Resources/AnalysisTools/Tools.htm); O'Donnell's Systemic Coder (www.wagsoft.com/Coder/index.html); and Webster's Functional Grammar Processor (e.g. Webster 1995, Webster & Kit 1995). These tools are making it possible to undertake large scale semantic analyses with a view to quantitative interpretation and have given new impetus to longstanding SFL interests in corpus based research (Plum & Cowling 1987, Nesbitt & Plum 1988, Halliday 1991c, 1992e, 1993b, Halliday & James 1993, Matthiessen 1999). This work on automated discourse analysis is complemented by work on synthesis, for example the text generation research introduced in Matthiessen & Bateman 1991, Bateman et al. 1999 and Teich 1999.

At the level of discourse semantics, some of the most important developments have to do with interpersonal meaning. Eggins & Slade 1997 present a rich model of speech function, especially designed for analysing initiating moves and responses in casual conversation. This has be insightfully applied to human/bonobo interaction (Benson et al. 2002). Hasan and her colleagues (Hasan 1996a) have developed a finely tuned set of semantic networks designed for the study of adult/child interaction in home and school. These have been instrumental in exploring Bernstein's theories of language and socialisation (e.g. 1996), especially in relation to gender and social class, and represent the most important linguistically informed body of research into semantic styles and their implications for education (see especially Cloran 1989, 1999a, 1999b, Hasan 1990, 1991, 1992a, Hasan & Cloran 1990, Williams 1995, 1996, 2000, 2001). Hasan 1995a and Halliday 1995b insightfully review the implications of close textual analysis for Bernstein's work, and deal incisively with populist misunderstandings; Cloran 2000 provides an accessible introduction to semantic networks and their deployment in the study of socio-semantic variation.

Ideational semantics is elaborated in Halliday & Matthiessen 1999, who are particularly concerned with establishing a semiotic perspective on what is generally viewed as cognition. Their project includes work on what they call sequences which is relevant to conjunction. Matthiessen 2002b explores Rhetorical Structure Theory (RST) from the perspective of this research, continuing a dialogue between SFL conjunction analysis and RST (Mann et al. 1992) which began in the 80s (Martin 1992a: 249-264; Stuart-Smith 2007). For relevant work on causation in Dutch see Degand 2001. From the perspective of discourse analysis what has been slow to emerge is an understanding of different kinds of expectancy relations linking clauses across registers. Temporal sequencing and causal reasoning tend to be foregrounded over tropes of other kinds – description, classification, composition, comparison, critique, review, stirring, coaxing, serving and so on; research is urgently required in these areas.

As far as participant identification is concerned the main developments have come from language typology through consideration of the ways in which nominal group resources interact with Theme, and in some languages with conjunction (the so-called 'subject-switching' systems found in Papua and Australia). These issues are explored in Caffarel et al. 2004 in relation to Martin 1993. Textual meaning has also been investigated in relation to information flow in general across languages (Hasan & Fries 1995, Lavid 1997, Downing & Lavid 1998) and in relation to layers of Theme and New in English discourse (Halliday & Martin 1993, Ghadessy 1995). Halliday's work on grammatical metaphor as a resource for packaging meaning has been instrumental in this area of inquiry (Halliday 1998a, Halliday & Matthiessen 1999, Simon-Vandenbergen et al. 2003).

This raises the question of higher level units in discourse which has been explored in various ways. The work of Gregory and his colleagues on phasal analysis (Gregory 1995, 2002; Stainton & de Villiers 2001), takes into account a full metafunctional spectrum of meaning (ideational, interpersonal and textual) in order to determine phases and transitions in discourse. Cloran's work on rhetorical units (RU) on the other hand is more selective in its parameters, having been designed to focus on the register variable of mode (Cloran 1994, 1995, 1999a, 1999b, 2000; Cloran et al. 2007). She looks in particular at the context dependency of the participant functioning as Subject in a clause and at the tense of that clause's verb (the 'deixis' of the clause in other words) and on this basis sets up classes of RU ranging from those positioning language as ancillary to the task in hand to those in which language constitutes the social activity. The interdependencies among RUs are explored through her concept of embedding, and used to investigate parent/child interaction in the home as part of Hasan's language and socialisation project outlined above.

The relation of all three of these perspectives on units of discourse to work on genre structure is an important issue which has not been resolved. Certainly the conversational data that Gregory and his colleagues and Cloran are investigating is not the kind that has generally attracted genre analysts (see however Eggins & Slade 1997), presumably because of the difficulty in recognising clear stages of the kind found in the analysis of narrative, exposition, service encounters, appointment making or classroom discourse. As a result the issue of generalising discourse units across registers remains a pressing one in SFL informed discourse analysis (cf. Taboada 2000, 2001; Martin & Rose 2008).

As far as register analysis is concerned there has been significant work in tenor, mode and field. The main tenor initiative draws on appraisal analysis to explore solidarity, as exemplified in Eggins & Slade's 1997 who analyse the face work done through casual conversations involving family members, friends and co-workers. The outstanding mode initiative is multi-modal discourse analysis, inspired by the work of O'Toole 1994 and Kress & van Leeuwen 1996 on images (see also van Leeuwen & Jewitt 2001). Martinec 1998, 2000b, 2000c, 2001 extends this work to the modality of action, and van Leewuen 1999 to the modality of music and sound. These tools have encouraged SFL discourse analysts to consider the ways in which language negotiates meaning in cooperation with other semiotic systems (Baldry 1999, Baldry & Thibault 2006b, Eggins & Iedema 1997, Iedema 2001, O'Halloran 1999a, 2004, Kress & van Leeuwen 2001, Royce & Bowcher 2006, Unsworth 2001, Ventola et al. 2004) and to focus on some of the new kinds of discourse evolving in the print and electronic media (Caple 2008, in press, Knox 2007, 2008, in press, Knox and Patpong 2008, Lemke 1998, Veel 1998).

Research into field has explored several kinds of school and workplace discourse. Work on institutionalised learning includes - mathematics (O'Halloran

1999a, 1999b, 2000, 2005, Veel 1999), science (Halliday & Martin 1993, Martin & Veel 1998, Unsworth 1998, Halliday 2004b), geography (Wignell et al 1990, van Leeuwen & Humphrey 1996, Martin 2001b), history (Coffin 1997, 2006, Veel & Coffin 1996, Martin 2001c, Martin & Wodak 2003) English (Martin 1996a, Rothery & Stenglin 1997, 2000), English for Academic purposes (Ventola 1998, 1999, Ventola & Mauranen 1995, Lewin et al. 2001, Ravelli & Ellis 2004), social science (Wignell 2007) and knowledge structure (Christie & Martin 2007). Work on workplace communication includes: administration (Iedema 1997a, 1998, 2000, 2003, Iedema & Degeling 2001, Iedema & Scheeres 2003), science & technology (Rose et al. 1992, Rose 1997, 1998, White 1998), speech disorders (Armstrong 1987, 1992, Fine et al. 1989, Fine 1994, 1995, 2006, Oram et al. 1999, Ovadia & Fine 1995), medicine (Jordens et al 2001), law (Iedema 1993, 1995, Gibbons 2003) and museums and galleries (Ferguson et al 1995, Martin & Stenglin 2006, Ravelli 1996, 1998, 2006). For innovative work on SFL in relation to counselling discourse, see Muntigl 2004.

The range of this research has had a number of implications for genre analysis, including analysis of their structure and intertextual relations with one another. Work on administrative directives (Iedema 1997a, Martin 1998) and print media news stories (Iedema 1997b, White 1997) for example revealed genres that are best characterized as having a nucleus/satellite structure (as opposed to a more traditional part/whole beginning, middle and end organisation) – a kind of orbital structure with an obligatory core stage and optional elaborating stages that are not strictly sequenced. Martin 1996b follows up the implications of this for experiential structures in general, analogizing from genre structure back to grammar. Across fields, the problem of longer texts arose and attempts were made to model these as series of smaller genres drawing on Halliday's 1985a – second edition (1994) categories of expansion (elaboration, extension and enhahcement). This serial perspective on macro-genres as genre complexes is introduced in Martin 2001b (see also Iedema 2000, Jordens et al. 2001) and further developed in Christie 2002 for classroom discourse (see also Martin & Rose 2008).

Another important dimension of genre analysis across fields has to do with mapping relationships among genres from both typological and topological perspectives. Using paradigms and system networks to model valeur, narrative and factual genres are explored typologically in Martin 2001a, Martin & Plum 1997; this kind of analysis depends on categorical distinctions. The notion of genres as more gradient semantic regions is explored topologically in Rose 1997, 1998, Veel 1997, Martin 2001b, 2001c and Martin & Rose 2008 for a range of factual genres from science, geography and history. The relation of work on macro-genres and genre topology to the question of 'genre mixing' is discussed in Martin 2001b. Martin & Rose 2008 consolidates work in this tradition. For SFL work on genre in relation to other approaches see Hyon 1996, Hyland 2002.

4 Connections

Obviously in a survey of this kind I have had to be selective. One of the most obvious extensions would be to the work of present and past staff and students at the University of Birmingham. Fortunately this work is ably surveyed in Coulthard 1992, 1994 and Caldas-Coulthard & Coulthard 1996. Of these colleagues special mention should be made of Michael Hoey, who has developed the Hatfield Polytechnic strain of discourse analysis inspired by Eugene Winter (Hoey 1991a, 2001, Scott & Thompson 2000). In America, the clearest links are with west coast functionalism, especially Fox 1987 since she brings several discourse semantic regions (CA, RST and participant identification) to bear on the 'grammar' of text development. Some further connections are explored in Martin & Rose in 2003.

The strength of SFL work on discourse probably lies in its relatively well developed descriptions of genre and functional grammar, and the adaptability of SFL modelling across modalities (to image, music and action for example). This grounds research firmly in the materiality of both global and local perspectives on meaning (Bednarek & Martin in press). The challenge for future work lies in filling in the middle ground between text and clause through intensive corpus based work on discourse semantics and register (Bednarek 2006, 2008). The success of this enterprise depends on the development of relevant software to both enhance and supplant manual analysis. I expect this technology to affect our conception of language and attendant semiotic systems as radically as the invention of writing and the tape recorder have shaped our discipline in the past, since we'll be able to manage large-scale socio-semantic analyses of data for the first time.

Annotated references

Martin 1992a outlines the reading of SFL discourse analysis assumed here. Martin & Rose 2003 provide an accessible introduction to this work, focusing mainly on writing; Eggins & Slade 1997 complement this with a focus on spoken discourse. Halliday & Martin 1993, Christie & Martin 1997 and Martin & Veel 1998 illustrate this kind of analysis across a range of fields. Unsworth 2000 is designed for prospective researchers who want to take up these tools. Hasan 1996a surveys her pioneering work on cohesion, genre, semantic networks and the relation of language to social context. Hasan et al. 2005, 2007 include several articles surveying past and current SFL research on discourse and social context.

Notes

[1] Ellipsis and substitution are sometimes treated as a single resource (e.g. Halliday 1985a – second edition [1994]). From the perspective of English, ellipsis is

substitution by zero; more generally, looking across languages, it might be better to think of substitution as ellipsis (signalled) by something.
2. For definitions of 'phora' terms (e.g. anaphora, cataphora, endophora, exophora, homophora) see Martin 1992a.
3. The terms internal and external are from Halliday and Hasan 1976; van Dijk (e.g. 1977) opposes pragmatic to semantic relations. The contrast is between *He came, because I just saw him* (internal = 'why I'm saying he came') and *He came because I saw him and told him to* (external = 'why he came').
4. I use the term 'construe' to place emphasis on the role texts play in making meaning (knowledge if you will) and thus constructing social context (reality if you must); cf. Halliday & Matthiessen 1999.
5. In SFL the ideational metafunction includes two subcomponents, the experiential and the logical; experiential meaning is associated with orbital structure (mononuclear), and logical meaning with serial structure (multinuclear); Martin 1996b).
6. Fries 1992 discusses the influence of cohesive harmony on the interpretation of words, demonstrating the dialectic between global and local features in the texturing of discourse.

10

The place of context in a systemic functional model

Ruqaiya Hasan
Macquarie University

> ... 'context of situation' is best viewed as a suitable schematic construct to apply to language events ... it is a group of related categories at a different level from grammatical categories but rather of the same abstract nature.
>
> [*J R Firth: 1957b:182*]

1 Introduction

Some fifty years ago, any mention of the term CONTEXT was in effect an identifier of the kind of linguistics one professed. Today the situation is reversed: except for one or two restricted models, the word is currency in the discipline of linguistics. This does not mean, though, that meaningful dialogue between different models is now free of problems: despite a substratum of some commonly accepted meanings, the term continues to have different value in different linguistic models[1]. This chapter will be concerned primarily with an examination of the category of context in Halliday's systemic functional linguistics (henceforth, SFL),[2] where the concept has played a crucial role throughout the development of SFL from general linguistics to scale and category to system and structure to the model's present position as a systemic functional theory whose aim is to offer a scientific description of the nature and function of language. Inherited from Malinowski (1923, 1935) via Firth (1957b) at the general linguistics stage, context has been greatly elaborated since Halliday first used it in his early writings (1959; 1961)[3]. Perhaps the most decisive step was taken in Halliday, McIntosh and Strevens (1964), where the 'scientific study of language' was said to depend on an understanding of 'how language works' in the social processes of life. The authors theorized context of situation in terms of MODE OF DISCOURSE, FIELD OF DISCOURSE, and STYLE OF DISCOURSE – the last of which, following Gregory's (1967) suggestion, was later labelled 'TENOR OF

DISCOURSE'; the authors related these contextual parameters to a kind of language variety, which they called REGISTER.

What was remarkable about this theory of context was not the abstraction of these three parameters from the referential domain of the word 'context' in its 'ordinary' usage[4] – some abstraction of this kind had already been made by Firth (1957b). Rather, *The users and uses of language* (1964: 75–94), the section of Halliday *et al* most relevant to this discussion, was remarkable for its methodical establishment of the relationship of what Austin (1962) called 'words and vocables' or Firth, 'bits and pieces of language' to each contextual parameter and for an explicit indication of their place in the ecology of text in context, suggesting that distinct varieties of text could be recognized by reference to variation in language use correlating with variation in values of these parameters. Equally clear was the implication that the authors' perspective on the context of culture and of situation is founded primarily on the centrality of discourse, i.e., on the process of 'language as text', a principle that holds true to this day: the SFL description of context has been overwhelmingly socio*linguistic* rather than socio*semiotic*[5] or socio*logical*. Partial accounts of some of the developments following upon Halliday *et al* (1964) may be found in (Butt 2001; Butt and Wegener 2007; Cloran 1994; Halliday 1973b; Halliday and Hasan 1976; 1985; Hasan 1985c; 1985d; 1995b; Martin 1999; Matthiessen 1993; 2007a). The aim of this chapter is to explore two major issues: (i) the place of context in the theoretical framework of SFL, and (ii) its descriptions in relation to the linguistic analysis of the uses of language.

2 The place of context in scientific linguistics

According to my understanding of SFL, the acceptance of linguistics as a scientific study of language implies that such a study will be comprehensive: not only will it offer a coherent and viable account of 'the architecture of language' as system (Matthiessen 2007a), but also the offered account will have the potential of making sense when confronted with the social practices whereby language is maintained – including both its phylogenetic and ontogenetic development (Painter, this volume) as well as language change, including both synchronic variation and diachronic change.

2.1 Context and the system and process of language

Context as a theoretical category is crucial to any coherent account of all the above aspects of the study of language, though its origins lie in its contribution to a principled study of PAROLE. *Contra* Saussure, when examined with reference to its context, parole provides irrefutable evidence of its orderliness.

A large number of studies[6] of naturally occurring discourse establishes beyond doubt that the well regulated nature of parole depends not on the whims of a single individual – Saussurean '*sujet parlant*' nor the Chomskyan 'ideal native speaker' – but on the exchanges of meaning between *ordinary* speakers as participants in some concerted social activity.

This finding should have put both language use and context centre stage in linguistics, but the dominance of the idea that 'linguistics proper' has to be concerned solely with *langue*, or worse still, with competence,[7] has led formalistic linguists to believe that in the words of Leech (1974: 80) they have 'a justification for ignoring as far as possible the study of context where it interferes with the study of competence'. One severe problem with this conception of 'linguistics proper' was to deny it the possibility of explaining coherently either synchronic variation or diachronic change, making the so-called 'linguistics proper' a rather undesirable framework for the comprehensive scientific study of language (Labov 1972b). It seems quite clear that for such an account of language, linguistics needs to take as its object of enquiry both the system and the process of language as had been suggested by Halliday *et al* (1964; 1971b) – in fact, we can claim quite confidently that there can be no comprehensive scientific linguistics without parole, and no study of parole without context: a viable linguistics needs to incorporate both. And indeed soon after Halliday *et al* (1964), the category of context, which had since Firth 1957b (appeared) as something of a surrogate for semantics, became recognized in SFL as a stratum in its own right in the theoretical linguistic framework.[8] Clearly, the integration of some category into a theory is not a magical single step affair: a category grows into an element of the theory as the understanding of its nature and function grows; and the justification for its integration lies in the work it does (Butt and Wegener 2007) – the explanatory and descriptive power it generates for the theory. Figure 1 presents a view of Halliday's integration of the categories of parole and context into SFL.

2.2 The relationship of language and context

Figure 1 displays four categories, and two relations, one on the vertical axis, called REALIZATION, the other on the horizontal, called INSTANTIATION. The four categories can be organized into two distinct sets by reference to each relation. Thus, set (1) consists of the members (a) CONTEXT OF CULTURE and (b) LANGUAGE AS SYSTEM (see the left column). Set (2) consists of the members (a) CONTEXT OF SITUATION and (b) LANGUAGE AS TEXT (the right column). The two members of each pair are related to each other realizationally, so that 1a is to 1b as 2a is to 2b. These same four categories can be re-classed by reference to the relation of instantiation: set (3) shown along the top line of the rectangle consists of the two members, (a) CONTEXT OF CULTURE, and (b) context of

```
                          instantiation
              SYSTEM  ◄─────────────────────►  INSTANCE

CONTEXT      context of  ◄─────────────────►  context of
              culture                          situation

                         (cultural           (situation
                          domain)              type)
 realization

                         (register)          (text type)

LANGUAGE    language as  ◄─────────────────►  language as
              system                            text
```

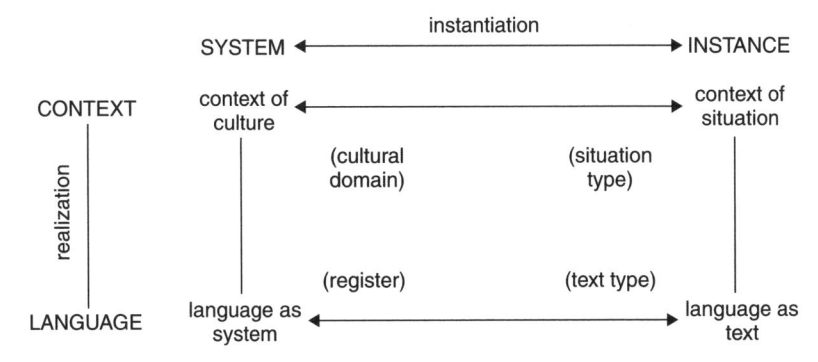

Note: Culture instantiated in situation, as system instantiated in text.
　　　Culture realized in/construed by language; same relation as that holding between linguistic strata (semantics: lexicogrammar: phonology: phonetics).
　　　Cultural domain and register are 'sub-systems': likeness viewed from 'system' end.
　　　Situation type and text type are 'instance types': likeness viewed from 'instance' end.

FIGURE 1 Language and context: system and instance (Halliday 1991d, 2002–2007 volume 9: 275)[9]

situation, while set (4) shown along the bottom line of the rectangle consists of (a) LANGUAGE AS SYSTEM, and (b) LANGUAGE AS TEXT. The two members of each pair are related by instantiation, so that 3a is to 3b as 4a is to 4b. Thus each category enters directly into two relations, and also indirectly into some relation with the remaining other category. To understand the significance of this dense pattern of relationships it is necessary to understand the meaning of instantiation and realization, and what is implied by this mode of integration for the 'architecture of language' according to SFL.

Instantiation is the relationship between a potential and its instance, so in set 3, context of culture is the potential, i.e. the system, while context of situation is an instance of that potential. Halliday (1988b; 1992d; 1993c; 2008) points out that instance and system are not two distinct kinds of phenomena: they are in fact the same thing viewed from different time depths. Instance is what is immediate and experienced; system is the ultimate point of the theorization of what is experienced and imaginable by extrapolation. System thus takes shape through the distillation of the relations among the significant properties of instances: the system of culture is not simply an inventory of all its situations; it is an organization of the possible features of all possible situations in all their possible permutations, where 'possible' means socially recognizable – something that the acculturated can interpret, act on and in, and evaluate[10]; in addition, both system and instance are sensitive to perturbations in each other's properties. What this means is that anything new entering the system of culture will enter only through variation in the properties associated with some context of situation, i.e., cultures change through human social practices. The same observations apply, *mutatis mutandis*, to the categories of set 4, i.e., language system in relation to its instance, language as text. One reason 'linguistics proper' is unable to account for language maintenance and language change is its banishment of language use; this logically prevents it from recognizing any category comparable to that of instantiation. If systemic change and innovation depend on language use, then in such models language system cannot claim access to the resources of parole, which is where texts manifest their properties maintaining the existing patterns and innovating new ones. There exists a dialectic between language system and language use: the system furnishes resources towards the formation and interpretation of the process, and the process furnishes resources towards the system's maintenance, innovation, and change.

The realization relationship is inherently semiotic: its roots lie in the nature of the sign itself, which being a union of CONTENT and EXPRESSION (Hjelmslev 1961) is necessarily stratified. The concept of realization refers to that relation whereby the stratified phenomena are calibrated permitting language in use to be subjectively experienced as a seamless flow where meaning, wording and sound work together (Halliday 1992d; Hasan 1995b; in press; Matthiessen 1995b; 2007a; Butt 2008). SFL recognizes five strata: context is the 'highest' stratum in the theory, and it is language external. The remaining four strata are language internal: SEMANTICS and LEXICOGRAMMAR are the elaboration of what Hjelmslev called content, and PHONOLOGY and PHONETICS, that of expression. The most important to the present discussion are the first three strata in the theory, viz., context, semantics and lexicogrammar: the functioning of realization[11] across these strata is critically different from that across the last two. At these three higher strata – context, meaning and wording – realization functions as a dialectic: looking from above, contextual choices ACTIVATE semantic choices activate the lexicogrammatical ones; looking from below lexicogrammatical choices CONSTRUE semantic choices construe contextual ones (Hasan, Cloran, Williams and Lukin 2007; Hasan, in press). To put it simply, to explain why anyone says anything one must appeal to the context which exerts pressure on the speaker's choice of meaning; and to explain why these patterns of wordings appear rather than any other, one must appeal to the meanings which, being relevant to the context, activated those wordings: semantics is thus an interface between context and linguistic form.[12] This activation-construal dialectic does not extend to the strata below lexicogrammar: one may claim that lexicogrammar activates phonological choices, but it would be clearly wrong to claim that phonological choices construe lexicogrammatical choices: they simply signal them, which is in keeping with their status as an aspect of expression; the status of the category of wording which is signalled by the sound is known by reference to its relation to other categories at the level of lexicogrammar, as is evident from examples such as *a whiting couldn't possibly be singing*.

2.3 Context, language system and linguistic theory

The implications of this mode of integrating context of situation and parole into the linguistic theory are substantial. Briefly, the recognition of the instantiation relation opens a legitimate avenue for the description of practices that contribute to language maintenance, the two faces of which in a living language are stability and change, regularity and variation.[13] SFL anticipated Weinreich, Labov and Herzog (1968), in recognizing systemic variation as an inherent attribute of language system (Halliday *et al.* 1964). Thus one face of language maintenance is presented in language use as an overwhelming endorsement of systemic regularities, and the other, as selective departures from them. These departures do not simply take the shape of replacement of this signal by that as usually documented in diachronic phonetic changes: very much more important are the phenomena we might describe as 'expansion' or development. Two processes significant for language development are (i) 'semo-genesis' (Halliday 1992d; 1995c) and (ii) variation be it 'user based' i.e., dialectal or 'use based', i.e. diatypic. Context is pivotal to the study of both kinds of variation: it is the locus of variant occurrences, and speakers are located by reference to context within their social world. At the same time, being an instance of culture, it carries the potential of tracing the work that varieties of a language do in the maintenance and change of cultural patterns of life. The pay off for the integration of context thus allows an opening into the valuable field of the sociology of language as a natural step in the theory.

Seen in this light, register variation gains a central position both in the life of a language and that of the speaker as well as her speech community. Based on the range of social processes in which the individual participates, her register repertoire is a significant indicator of her SOCIAL POSITIONING (Bernstein 1990) and her social positioning is at least partly a function of her register repertoire (Hasan 1999a; in press): register repertoire is in fact a cog in the social wheel of what Bourdieu (1990) used to call 'structured structuring structures'. It follows that what is true of the individual, is also true of the speech community, whose socio-political positioning vis a vis other communities is indicated by a comparison of their respective register repertoires, as even a cursory enquiry into the current political situation of the world will quickly show: it is not an accident that international/world languages have always been languages of powerful speech communities, certain segments of which logically participate in considerably wider range of social processes. While the potential for development is identical across the languages of the world, their actual state of development can and does vary: communities with less developed languages[14] are also communities with fewer material resources.

The varieties of language begin life as acts of parole, but through the working of instantiation and realization, they eventually end up enriching the system of language. Nowhere is this more obvious than in the functional character of language. Since the early 1970's Halliday (e. g. 1970b; 1971b) has drawn attention to the fact that the contexts of language use leave their indelible impression on the inner structure of language: the structure of language is as it becomes in meeting the demands its speakers make on it, the functions it is made to serve in their life. Simplifying, in SFL, the arguments for the recognition of the metafunctions rest on what is revealed by the analysis of language use in natural context. In this examination, the tripartite structure of the context of situation is significant; it emphasizes the nature of talk as a form of social action. The parameters are in fact the three most obvious aspects of linguistic action. Thus field of discourse refers to the nature of social action, apropos of which language is being used. Tenor of discourse refers to the nature of social relationship amongst those involved with the action – not which specific individual, but how the individuals are socially positioned vis a vis each other, since this is what will impinge on the production and reception of the messages. Mode of discourse refers to the mode of contact for the actors in the discourse event, since clearly the nature of the message will be different for a co-actor in absentia compared with that for the co-present interactant. As the last comment shows, the nature of the message changes as the values of the contextual parameter change: this is what it means to claim that language in use suits itself to the speaker's socio-semantic needs.

It follows that given a substantial quantity of naturally occurring use of language in context, and given a viable method of analysing this data, the question can be meaningfully raised: is there any specialization of meanings in relation to the three different contextual parameters? It would clearly be impossible to give an answer in terms of specific meanings of lexemes or syntagmatic structures: the former is too sensitive to variation in contextual values; the latter, very much less so. But if the question is answered in terms of classes of meanings, and if paradigmatic analysis provides a viable ground for the classification of those meanings – as it does in SFL – then the answer to the question may be given in a meaningful way. Figure 2 is borrowed from Halliday (1973c, 2002–2007 volume 3: 353); it is a schematic representation of the results of one such finding.

As the legend in Figure 2 shows, the first column represents raw data of text as language in use, the second represents the situation types relevant to some specific group of texts – the instances of text types/registers: from each bundling of texts in some situation type radiate three lines representing each of the three vectors of tenor, mode and field in that order. The formal resources of worded meanings that realize the features of each vector have been identified by specific labels in Figure 2: tenor is associated with INTERPERSONAL worded meanings, mode with TEXTUAL and field, with IDEATIONAL ones. These are the labels Halliday uses for the three metafunctions of language recognized in SFL.

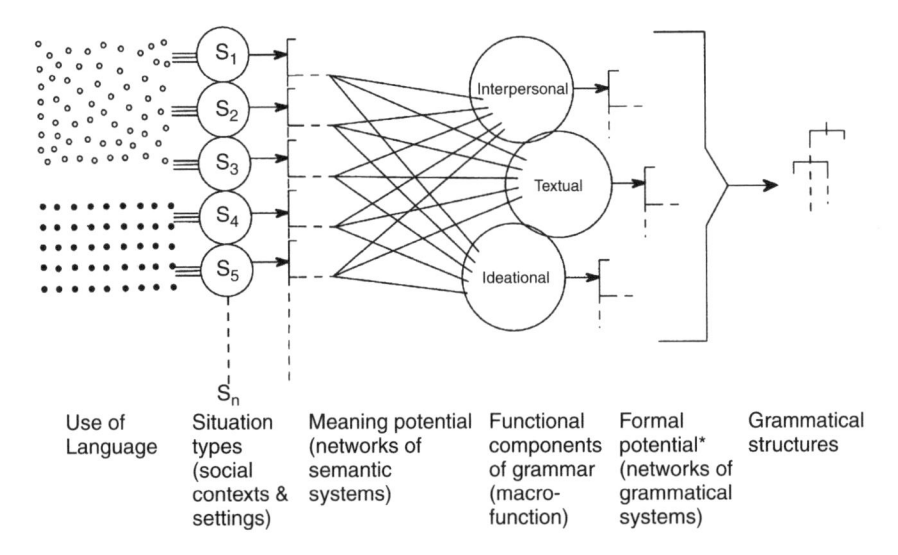

FIGURE 2 language use, situation types, and metafunctional specialization of linguistic form

The remaining columns in the Figure represent the paradigmatic resources of the language system at the stratum of meanings and wordings, which the hearer encounters as syntagmatic structures: the latter are represented in the form which, in the 70's, was overwhelmingly employed to represent such structure.

This analysis cast a new light on the work being done in the 1970's in the description of lexicogrammar: it became obvious that, seen in a paradigmatic perspective, the lexicogrammar that construes interpersonal meanings forms itself into a complex of system networks, options within which are closely related to each other by dependency and simultaneity – these are the systems of MOOD, MODALITY, PRIMARY TENSE, EVALUATION and GENERAL QUANTIFICATION. By contrast, the lexicogrammar which construes textual meanings organizes itself into another complex of system networks, options of which are similarly closely related to each other by dependency and simultaneity within the complex but show relatively fewer relations to other complexes – the systems in question are such as those of THEME, INFORMATION FOCUS, PHORICITY and KEY. The same is true *mutatis mutandis* regarding the ideational lexicogrammatical resources, which are called upon for the construal of ideational meanings – such as those of TRANSITIVITY, REFERENCE, EXPANSION, PROJECTION, and TENSE. Halliday has suggested that this characteristic organization of the semantic and lexicogrammatical resources, whose internal organization is shaped in response to each of the three contextual vectors, can be interpreted as a validation of the hypothesis (see also Halliday 1979b) that (i) the form of human language is necessarily functional, and (ii) that this functionality of form has arisen in response to the evolution of human language as a resource for acting semiotically in social contexts. Functionality in language thus resonates primarily throughout the strata of context, semantics and lexicogrammar; albeit, traces of functionality are found also at the stratum of phonology where segmental phonology is overwhelmingly ideational, while the prosodic is overwhelmingly interpersonal and/or textual. All said, the metafunctional resonance is clearest at the higher three levels which, as pointed out earlier, enter into realizational dialectic. This appears reasonable since the postulate of functionality in language does depend to a large extent on the dialectic of realizational relations linking context, meaning and wording mutually. Before leaving this discussion, it should be added that here, as also in the preceding paragraphs, the focus has been on the analysis of situated language use, but what the analysis has revealed is the way in which parole in context contributes to the shaping of the resources of the system. As Halliday (1971b, 2002–2007 volume 10: 62. italics original.) says

> The image of language as having a 'pure' form (*langue*) that becomes contaminated in the process of being translated into speech (*parole*) is of little value . . . We do not want a boundary between language and speech at all, or between pairs such as langue and parole, or competence and performance—unless these are reduced to mere synonyms of 'can do' and 'does'.

2.4 An appliable theory for the study of language in its social context

This section has attempted to provide an account of the space that Figure 1 opens up for the exploration of the category of context: it has presented what Dawkins (2006) might describe as 'mutually buttressed evidence' in favour of the SFL modelling of language and the need to integrate context and parole in linguistic theory; without this inclusion a comprehensive scientific description of language is not feasible. The integration is critical to the conceptualization of functionality in language, and makes possible a coherent description of not only the inner structure of language – its semantic and lexicogrammatical organization – but also of the system's maintenance and development: diachronic change is an important aspect of these processes. Language development is supported by the relations of realization and instantiation which link language and society, system and instance: they allow an evidence based account of ontological development, and help us understand the significance of patterns of language development in the community, especially their relevance to the community's social positioning vis a vis others. The cogenetic relation between language and society is in fact the foundation of a viable discipline of sociolinguistics, which needs not only naturally occurring data; it needs also the appropriate theoretical apparatus for perceptive interpretation (Hasan, in press). The appliability of linguistics depends on this open-ended view of language and society, system and instance, semiosis as social practice. Formalistic linguists have sometimes deridingly described SFL as 'applied linguistics': an alternative view is that the explanatory and successful application of linguistics to a wide range of social practices demonstrates the probity of the theory's modelling of language. Just as the exploration of space would have been impossible without a good modeling of the earth in its physical context, so also successful applications of linguistics would be impossible without a good modeling of language in its social context.

3 Describing context in textual processes

This section attempts to discuss issues in the description of context in SFL: how is context described, with what implications for understanding its nature, and, for expanding its potential for application to discourse analysis. According to SFL, there exist two possible perspectives for the description of context, which can be identified by reference to figure 1: the description may be from the point of view of instance, or from that of system. The former is concerned with what is going on here-and-now as language is being used on some specific occasion; the latter, with a description of context in any case of language use whatsoever, i.e. with the potential of context. A good deal of ink and energy were deployed in SFL in the 1980's in praising the former, and downgrading the other as incapable of describing instances (Martin 1985b). With hindsight, it seems clear that both perspectives have to work together: to demand only the dynamic perspective is to say by analogy that the lexicogrammar – which after all is a description of the system – is incapable of describing the linguistic patterns in the instance, the text; further, it is to deny, by implication, the possibility of a theoretical basis for discourse analysis (Hasan 1995b). In the event, the dynamic approach did not remain truly as dynamic as first mooted; and the synoptic was never entirely as synoptic as was implied. In actual practice, in the work of all SFL scholars, the description of context has *always* straddled the two perspectives. The reason for this inheres in the system-instance relation: an orderly description is a step toward 'system-ization'; and linguistics is about orderly descriptions. The dual perspective has been beneficial to the study of context: it has, in a manner of speaking, enabled the description to be 'tested' by patterns in large scale studies of instances, thus contributing to the understanding of both system and instance.

3.1 Concept 'relevant context'

Both Firth and Halliday began with the system perspective and – one might say – moved too quickly to the instance – a necessary step, perhaps, because that's where the immediately visible pay-off is. Firth explicitly built in the attribute of 'relevance' thus implying that there was somewhere in the environment something that might not be relevant. His categories for context description were worded as follows (Firth 1957: 182; emphasis added):

A. the *relevant* features of the participants: persons and personalities.
   (i) the verbal action of the participants.
   (ii) the non-verbal action of the participants.
B. the *relevant* objects.
C. the effect of the verbal action.

However, it was not clear how relevance was to be established: relevant for whom or to what. Halliday *et al* (1964) clarified this issue by suggesting that their vectors of field, mode and tenor are relevant by virtue of the fact that they would always leave a 'trace' in the text: what is relevant in the context of situation would be illuminated by the language of the text. In both cases, parameters of context were offered as 'abstractions' from situation; but the relationship of the contextual parameters to what there was in the situation remained shrouded in mystery.

These uncertainties – and many others – were foregrounded for me in the late 1960's, when I was faced with a mass of running prose, which represented transcribed stories produced in the oral mode by children for one of the research projects conducted by Bernstein's Sociological Research Unit[15]. The children had responded to a request to tell a bed time story to 'this teddy bear' about 'this sailor, this boy, this girl, and this dog'. What was one to describe as the relevant features of the context? who were the relevant participants? What could be anticipated about the children's language use if one took the requesting researcher and the responding child as the relevant interactants? Were the sailor, the boy etc relevant participants/objects? If not what were they doing in the children's stories? How was it to be established that the children had really told stories? Was everything they said part of one story? What intersubjectively objective recognition criteria could one offer for the resolution of any of these issues to those research assistants who were to actually help in the analysis of the data?

In Malinowski's ethnographic descriptions (1935) narrative function and its dual context had been highlighted: the fact that the language of the story 'referred to' a separate context – one, an imaginary one of the story itself, and another one relating to the actual process of telling the story to someone. With hindsight, I recognize that the solution to some of my research problems was achieved by putting together Malinowski and Halliday *et al*. The latter implied that 'context' refers to selective phenomena in the total speech environment; and the traces of these selective phenomena are found in text as language instance. The former suggested the simultaneous operation of two contexts, which though related were yet distinct. It appeared reasonable to suggest

(Hasan 1973c) that the IMMEDIATE CONTEXT of discourse has two aspects, viz., a MATERIAL SITUATIONAL SETTING (MSS) and a RELEVANT CONTEXT. I referred to the material situational setting as a 'dormant' force. Elements of this dormant force enjoy the possibility of impinging on the ongoing parole (discussion below). By contrast, relevant context refers to that frame of consistency which is illuminated by the language of the text.

This conceptualization of relevant context immediately raises certain issues: (i) are the elements of a relevant context referred to by the language of the text always materially present in the speaker's speech environment? The answer is 'no': for example we do produce written instructions, where the address is physically absent – so, how should the theory interpret the everyday word 'environment' or 'situation'? (ii) if relevant context is recognized only by reference to 'the text', then what are the recognition criteria for the boundaries of a text? Unless we know what source of evidence is, we can hardly use it to recognize that which is made evident by the source; and (iii) what exactly is going on when two distinct relevant contexts are operating simultaneously, as in children's story telling data? Are the two contexts related? And if so, how? The first two issues are briefly addressed below;[16] for the last issue see Hasan (1971; 1985a; 1999b), Halliday (1977b).

3.2 Relevant context and material environment

Hasan (1973c) and Halliday and Hasan (1976) had suggested that a register is known by the meanings that are at risk in it: a register is what meanings in text are supposed to instantiate.[17] If relevant context is that which is based on the interpretation of the language of the text, then, clearly, it is something 'made by (worded) meanings', which is to say that it is a SEMIOTIC CONSTRUCT. It is this semiotic construct that is being abstracted from other elements of the situation and it need not consist merely of those elements of the material situation, that may be present here and now as the process of text is occurring. The tripartite structure consisting of field, tenor and mode is assigned to this semiotic abstraction: it cannot sensibly be assigned to 'the material situational setting', which consists simply of material objects, person(s) – but not personalities, which always form part of the relevant context – and their attributes. The language of a text may or may not contain any traces of these situational existents – whether it will do so depends on other features of the relevant context. If traces of elements of the material situational setting are encapsulated in the text, then such tracing semantic elements become part of the relevant context.[18] So the elements of the material situational setting are a 'dormant force' precisely in this manner: they are capable of impinging on a certain class of relevant contexts – though 'conditions apply'! for this to happen[19]. If and when they do impinge, they might lead to change(s) in the context: these changes are primarily relevant to the production of sub-texts, i.e. they are in some way connected to the text already in progress; or they function as an independent, parallel text, which in the end acts as an interruption of the text already in progress (Cloran 1999a; Hasan 1999b),[20] though there are registers where the global structure of the text moves via what might be called 'associative movement', as for example in informal conversations between friends, where 'one thing leads on to another'.

3.3 Relevant context

The clarification of the relationship between material situational setting and relevant context proves helpful in providing an orderly way of describing the 'unexpected', encountered under certain conditions. It can also be used to suggest a viable classification of relevant contexts: relevant contexts may be

(i) capable of being perturbed by their material situational setting, informal conversation being a quintessential example; or
(ii) not subject to such perturbation – except in serious emergency – the production of verbal art, or the presentation of speech at a Convocation being quintessential examples.

Taking language in use as verbal action in service of some social activity, the three parameters place a grid on the space occupied by its relevant context: the space may be seen as exhaustively describable in terms of the three parameters called field, tenor and mode of discourse, on which the description of relevant context depends.

Relevant contexts differ from each other by virtue of the values of the three named parameters. Each parameter is, in effect, treated as a reservoir of 'values'. From this perspective, the make up of a specific relevant context consists of all the values 'selected' in each of the three parameters that 'apply' to the text responsive to the context: such a set of values specific to a relevant context has been referred to as a CONTEXTUAL CONFIGURATION (Hasan 1978) (acronym CC). An indicative account of some values ascribed to each in SFL is provided below.

3.4 Relevant context and contextual configuration

Beginning with field, which concerns the nature of social ACTION, we might think of the many different actions we undertake using language, such as shopping, teaching, telling a bed time story; playing a board game; giving someone a bath; attending to a patient; making appointment for consultation; supervising a child eating food, and so on. Clearly, there are an enormous number of actions, any of which could be unfolding: the only condition for the linguist's interest is that the action must necessarily involve some use of language. The GOAL or PURPOSE of action is quite often mentioned in the CC. Here too one might elaborate on the kind of goal as, say, visible/invisible: for example, when giving a bath, the mothers talk to their children: describing the context of such talk we might note that the visible goal is to engage/entertain the child; however, a number of such verbal actions over time lead to 'socializing' the child in a particular way of being, doing and saying, and this could be treated as an invisible goal. Parents are often aware of this happening. The recognition of goal/purpose as separate from the action itself often poses problems: for example could you be engaged in pedagogic action of lecturing with the goal of exchanging commodities? As work on discourse analysis continued, higher level generalizations were also made, e.g., 'service encounter' which could be instantiated by buying food, or stamps, or tickets for a trip etc.; or, say, 'pedagogic action' which would 'cover' teaching, revision, discussion, testing and what not.

Tenor, concerned with social RELATION, lent itself to descriptions of ROLE. Thus such roles as mother-child; teacher-young pupil; lecturer-adult student; customer-vendor, doctor-patient; friend-friend were used as implying a certain kind of relationship between the interactants. Contact with Bernstein's work brought further details such as ASCRIBED roles and ACHIEVED roles; further, SOCIAL STATUS was introduced though selectively to handle symmetrical/asymmetrical discourses: examples of values would be PEER or HIERARCHIC; in some cases the vector of hierarchy was further elaborated. DEGREES OF FORMALITY have also been used as an attribute of relation. SOCIAL DISTANCE, introduced in SFL early (Hasan 1973c), attempted to capture the interactive biography of the specific interactants, as this acted on agentive and semiotic roles. The character of their interactive biography – how often they have interacted; how many different kinds of social processes they have participated in together; and what social status they carry vis a vis each other – all are essential to how the interactants are likely to relate to each other.

Mode of discourse, concerning CONTACT, was seen as a two part affair: MEDIUM and CHANNEL. The values of channel refer to how 'the said' was to be accessed. Two obvious values were AURAL or VISUAL. Medium referred to what 'language was doing', and the early examples consisted of such values as SPOKEN, WRITTEN; DIALOGUE, MONOLOGUE; WRITTEN-AS-IF-SPOKEN; (e.g. in drama; novel etc) WRITTEN-TO-BE-READ-ALOUD, such as sermon; EXTEMPORE e.g. informal conversation or PREPARED e.g., a paper presented at a conference; ANCILLARY language used as an instrument for assisting material action e.g. directing arrangement of furniture in a room, or CONSTITUTIVE. (e.g., seminar discussion or writing a paper, where the activity is primarily conducted by languaging). Clearly, 'what language is doing' was an informal description and as such, was subject to one's interpretation. In time, mode began to include labels of genres e.g., discussion, moral fable, humour, and so on.

What is interesting in the above description is its vagueness, the absence of 'checkable' criteria, and the reliance on 'common sense'. It is as if, other than

Table 1 A partial account of an imaginary contextual configuration

VARIABLES	VALUES OF THE VARIABLES
Field	professional consultation: medical; application for appointment ...
Tenor	client: patient-as-applicant and agent for consultant: receptionist; maxim social distance ...
Mode	aural channel: minus visual contact; telephone conversation; spoken medium ...

the context's tripartite division, its description has no underlying regularities, and no reasoned framework to work with: the assumption seems to have been that being acculturated persons the linguists would know what they were talking about, just as one might assume that native speakers 'know' the grammar of the clauses they are producing and comprehending. So faced with a text already there, the SFL linguists have largely been doing what any ordinary speaker of language would do, i.e., construing from the language of the text what the text is all about – who was doing what to/with whom and why, when and where. And conversely, when it came to predicting an example of the relevant context for an *imaginary* language use – a text not yet there – one did the same, supposedly, in reverse. As an example of the description of such an imaginary context, consider Hasan (1978:231) summarised in Table 1:[21]

The account in Table 1 is highly selective, guided solely by the imaginary text I wished to analyse. In this description of relevant context, the only items that have the status of a theoretical category are those in the left column. They alone have 'the same abstract nature' as the 'grammatical categories' (see Firth quoted p. 166); the others are intuitive, based on (the memory of) experiences. I am not implying that such descriptions are *ipso facto* incorrect; or that partial descriptions are unacceptable: simply that such descriptions are not based in any consciously and carefully prepared framework for what, for want of an established term, one might call CONTEXTUALIZATION. What has been attempted so far by way of contextualization is a common sense account: if the same conventions were applied to 'doing the description of a clause', by analogy a description *without* grammatics, then the linguist would be reduced to simply identifying the 'doer', the 'doing' the 'when', the 'how' etc. by way of 'doing transitivity'. Naturally systemic linguists would not approve of this practice – and they do not, when it is used, as often, in some educational sites.

There is much in this situation to cause discomfort. More recently efforts have been made to find perhaps better alternatives. The following section is a brief exploration of what is involved in such an effort.

3.5 Is a systemic description of the contextual configuration possible?

Given the discussion of Figure 1, it is tautological to say that linguistic descriptions are made from a system perspective. For example, the lexicogrammar in SFL is unquestionably a grammar of the language seen from the system perspective.²² When it comes to describing the grammar of an instance, this same lexicogrammar functions largely adequately as a resource.²³ This is not surprising: system and instance are not two totally different kinds of phenomena, and the very effort to move towards an orderly description is a move toward the system perspective (Hasan 1995b; Halliday 1999). It is also to be noted that, although the distinction between grammatics and grammar is valuable, grammatics, if it is to account for how hearers understand and how speakers say, must strive to a state of close iconicity to grammar. The same has been taken to be true *mutatis mutandis* for the other strata in the theory – there is however one exception and that exception is the level of context: SFL linguists have in general treated context description qualitatively differently from description at other strata, for example, that of lexicogrammar.

There are two possible reasons for this: first, perhaps there is no agreement with Firth's (1957b:182) suggestion that 'context of situation' is best viewed as a . . . schematic construct to apply to language events . . . it is a group of related categories at a different level from grammatical categories but rather of the same abstract nature'. Although no one has so far explicitly disputed the Firthian claim, there have been suggestions that discourse analysis is indeed a very different kind of thing from doing grammar (Martin 1985b). However, no proof has been forthcoming that context is more different from meaning than meaning is from grammar, or grammar from phonology. The second reason for the reluctance to create a systematic framework might lie in a feeling that as an instance of the system of culture, the description of context of situation is probably better provided by sociology or anthropology. Certainly this is the object of enquiry for those two fields, and they do describe them but not from the perspective of language. SFL, on the other hand, does attempt to describe instances of registers, which it defines by relation to relevant context. And since a register's structure potential is the realization of its contextual configuration, it seems important to be able to provide a theorized framework for the description of the prime mover in the shaping of the discourse. It is important to remember also that although relevant context may in specifiable cases be linked through reference to phenomena located in the material situation, it is itself a semiotic construal, and as such it should be within the descriptive orbit of linguistics. Relevant context refers to a semiotically mediated universe; and it is one important function of SFL as a social semiotic theory of language to throw light on this construct. As it is, there are hardly any system networks in SFL concerning contextualization. In fact, partial contextualization system networks comparable to the lexicogrammatical ones are in a nascent stage; so far only three such have appeared in print (Cloran 1987; Hasan 1999b; Bowcher 2007)²⁴; the most exhaustive set of contextualization system networks remains in mimeo form (Butt, 2003). These contextualization systems have the distinction that instead of taxonomising realized meanings, they actually systemize the realization-activating contextual features and attempt to relate context to wording via meaning which acts as the interface between the two. In so doing they are building on similar efforts by Halliday in Halliday and Hasan (1985: 34ff; and elsewhere). There have also existed partial system networks with reference to the features of the contexts of some specific genres (Martin 1992a; Ventola 1987). To actually create a substantial contextualization system network of all three parameters with realization statements that reach lexicogrammatical choices via the semantic ones is a huge enterprise requiring a lifetime of work: what I want to do here is to give some example that might indicate (i) that a paradigmatic description of the relevant context is possible; and (ii) that its options can be shown to be realizationally related to lexicogrammatical choices via semantics.

3.5.1 The point of origin for contextualization system network

The set of contextualization system networks is as represented in Figure 3a. The point of origin is relevant context: this is what the contextualization system networks are meant to describe. This allows entry into three simultaneous system networks, relating to the three parameters already mentioned, and additionally, a fourth system, called ITERATION which allow a recursive set of choices leading to context and text (=con/text) conjunction such that the integrity of the original alpha-context is maintained; the vector will also account for con/text disjunction, where either a parallel or interrupting discourse occurs (for illustration see Hasan 1999b).

3.5.2 Field of discourse

The first parameter in Figure 3a refers to the field of discourse. Figure 3c is one tentative display of the vectors and their primary systems which pertain to the FIELD OF DISCOURSE; it is in effect a revision of some parts of field system

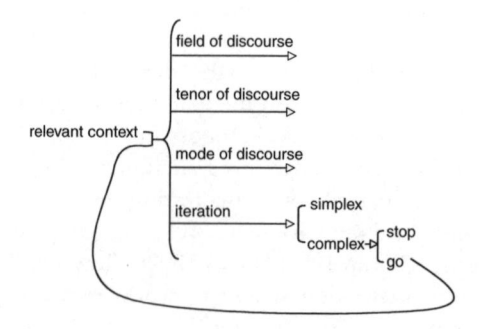

FIGURE 3a Parameters of systemic options in relevant context

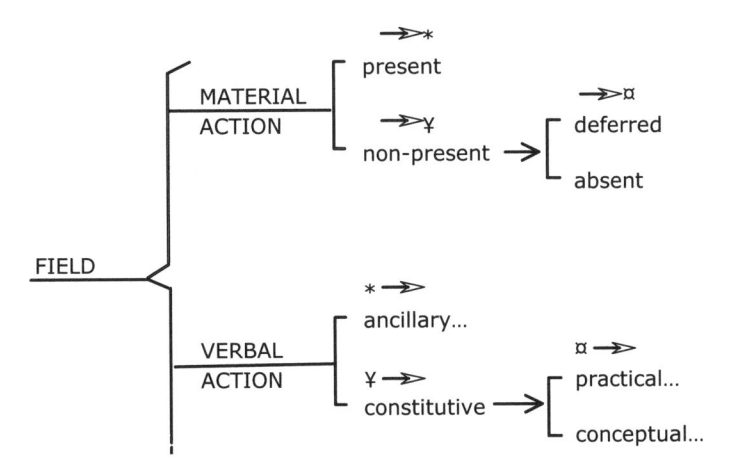

The Place of Context in a Systemic Functional Model 183

FIGURE 3b Primary systems of FIELD MK 1: (from Hasan 1999b: 279)

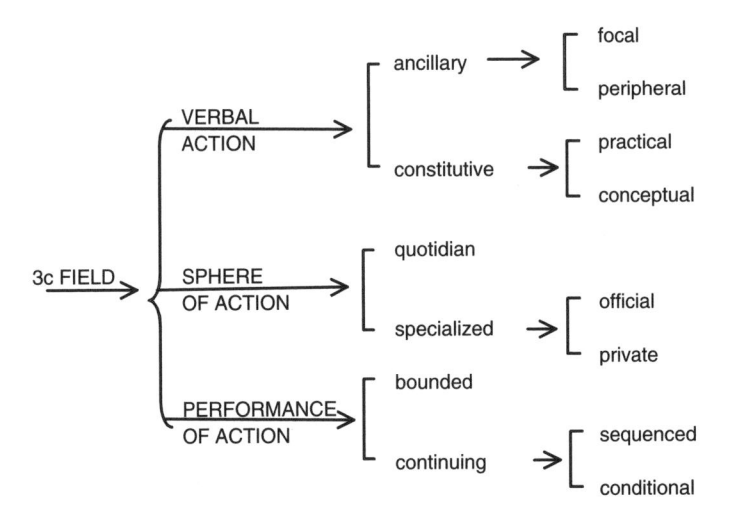

FIGURE 3c Primary systems of FIELD MK 2: a tentative suggestion

in Hasan (1999b: 279), referred to here as 'FIELD MK1', which is reproduced as Figure 3b. As will be noted field-mk1 puts material action and verbal action on par as two vectors. This makes it necessary to build in a large number of constraints on the possible combinations of choices from these two vectors. As pointed out by Halliday,[25] this is less than desirable.

Figure 3c presents a tentative system network for field, called here FIELD MK-2. In this figure, only the vector of VERBAL ACTION is brought into the network; the second vector is called SPHERE OF ACTION; the primary options of which are shown as SPECIALIZED and QUOTIDIAN. The third field vector is PERFORMANCE OF ACTION, with options BOUNDED or CONTINUING; the latter allows entry into a more delicate system SEQUENCED and CONDITIONAL. Time and space will not allow any detailed discussion, but a brief word on each of the field vectors of choice.

For the linguist the importance of material action is subsidiary to the verbal one: a non-verbal/material action becomes relevant only if it is encapsulated in the field of discourse by linguistic realization. The primary options in VERBAL ACTION remain as ANCILLARY or CONSTITUTIVE as shown in Figure 3b above. If verbal action is ancillary, the prediction would be that reference to some elements of the material situation is mandatory; these must include speaker, addressee, and the processes in which they are engaged while using language. If verbal action is constitutive, material action may or may not be present in the MSS; if it is present, its traces may be found in language use; however, there will be no direct reference to it except as interruption of some kind. Figure 3c shows ancillary and constitutive verbal action as mutually exclusive, and so they are, in general; there are, however, occasions of language use where quite regularly, ancillary verbal action will occur sporadically in the midst of overwhelmingly constitutive verbal action: consider for example, a classroom presentation of information where the teacher may say things such as 'take a look at this map' or 'find page 16 in your book'. These sayings contribute to the ongoing activity, and the issue that one faces is what importance to attach to such sporadic 'shifts': at what point does it become necessary to say that the context has changed. This issue has been discussed sporadically in SFL literature.

The primary options of SPHERE of action are called specialized or quotidian. This systemic contrast makes a distinction between such actions as cooking, bed-making, bathing the child, buying a bus ticket, shopping for food and so on, which are all quotidian actions, and specialized actions which typically entrain participation by 'trained' personnel. They tend to be institutionalized, which implies that such actions are culturally expected to keep to a certain routine. The variation in the degree of specialization is reflected in the option official v. private. The former are more ritualized e.g. court proceedings; medical procedures, police interrogations; by contrast, actions in the private sphere will have a relatively relaxed routine within a framework of fixed expectations: consider for example the daily national news, the TV interview, the newspaper feature articles, and so on. Together with the options that depend on conceptual constitutive verbal action, they will account for a large number of actions for which we use language. The third field system is called PERFORMANCE: its primary options are shown as bounded v continuing. A bounded action will by default complete in one spatio-temporally located interaction, for example shopping for fruit, bathing the child, getting the child a snack and so. By contrast, continuing performance of action will call for intermittent actions, each of which requires a distinct spatio-temporal location; for example, buying a car or a house is a different kind of action from that of buying vegetables; it will require different occasions for different so called 'stages' of activity, and some stages may occur recursively each on a different spatio-temporal site; the culmination of such separate but related actions will lead to a final state of accomplishment. The continuing action could be either sequenced as in buying cars or conditional as for example, a certain repeated effort and physical presence of the pupil form a condition for entry into final test; the revision action in the classroom presupposes that earlier an action of presentation of concepts/information has occurred.

The problem in constructing a system network of this kind is to keep in mind on the one hand the large variety of instances of language use, and on the other, the need to specify which contextual options will 'go with which other', what dependency and simultaneity relations there might exist among the various social practices in a community. For example, how realistic is it to say that verbal action in court proceedings could be ancillary? In other words much thinking has to be done to successfully describe the possible combinations and permutations of these features.

This last point is worth making: at no point could one have made the kind of objection to any feature entered in Hasan's (1978) contextual configuration in table 1. In fact disagreement with anyone's description of context presented nonsystemically is possible only if we have the language use in front of us and there is disagreement on the referential value of some linguistic pattern. Systemizing the possible relevant features of context makes the claims explicit, puts the relevant environment 'on line' and raises the options to the conscious level as an object under description. Thus the description can become a focus of discussion, and objections can be made as they were with regard to the description represented in field mk-1 (see Figure 3b). For such discussion, a text does not have to be present; simply the calibration of the options will point to problems if there are any. Naturally the problems are recognized on the basis of acculturation; if the analyst is not familiar with the context of culture, the nature of the situation will not be familiar either. Much more elaborate field networks with several realization statements will be found in Hasan (1999b) and in Butt (2003). For work such as this to proceed, discussions such as for example Bowcher's (2007) are essential. I would be so bold as to add that, incomplete and defective as the 1999b field network is, it is not any worse than the MOOD system networks drawn in the early 1960's SFL. It was the continued use and discussion of the network that led to today's versions.

3.6 Contextual configuration and text structure

The role of relevant context and particularly of the contextual configuration is central to the analysis of text in Halliday's SFL (Halliday 1977b; 1985, and elsewhere). Hasan (1973c) had already argued that the frequency of lexical and grammatical categories might not be helpful in the recognition of a register; attention to the patterns of meaning prove more useful in this enterprise. Based on further research Hasan (1978; 1979; 1985 etc) later argued that recognition of a register depends on the range of possible structural shapes of texts that are seen in the community as instances of that particular register. Any text has one ACTUAL GLOBAL STRUCTURE (AGS) or what the formalists called schematic structure (Schank & Abelson 1977); but any one register enjoys a range of AGS, such that they have certain distinctive patterns in common. It is this distinctive pattern that is contained within a GENERAL STRUCTURE POTENTIAL (GSP). Discussion of how the selection of contextual features will result in the alteration of the AGS is found in Hasan (1978; 1979; 1985). She also suggested two different kinds of elements of GSP; (i) the OBLIGATORY elements that are always to be found in any complete instance of a register; and (ii) the OPTIONAL ones which realize contextual features that are not central to the definition of that specific register, and might in fact be responsive to some element of the MSS; in addition, the elements may have a FIXED order in sequence or they may be MOBILE within limits (Hasan 1984b). The critical register-identifying part consists of obligatory elements and their order in sequence, while the optional elements and optionality of order in structure is indicative of the range of variation within one register.

No two texts belonging to the same register are expected to be exactly alike – a feature that many scholars have commented on. When do the differences between two texts become such that they have to be seen as instantiating distinct registers? The onset of systemic description of contextualization, and conscious search for the relation of those features to the semantic level, suggests that the contextual features most relevant to the GSP – the recognition criterion for some specific register – are options that have primary to mid degree of delicacy. As we move further to the right end of the network, the options lose this power; instead they become critical to the texture of the text, emphasizing its unique instantial nature. Putting it simply, the register of two texts will not be different if in one case the speaker is buying potatoes in a retail store and breakfast cereal from another such store: but with potatoes weight and quality count and must be specified, whereas with breakfast cereal the default situation is to look for brand names and package size. It is elements of meaning such as these that will enter into texture, creating some kind of cohesive harmony pattern which will be unique to each text, though generalizations can be made about the text on the basis of the cohesive harmony patterns. However, attempts to decide on a common-sense basis, the purchase of which objects will form part of the same CC, thus predicting which register the CC pertains to, are likely to prove a futile exercise. It is not the object itself but the density of contextual relations that surrounds the object that will determine the matter. There is from a common sense point of view much in common between buying a blouse and a length of some fabric, but an examination of the GSP of the two will most probably put them in different categories.

4 Concluding remarks

This chapter has perhaps contained more questions than answers. Certainly I am aware that the systemic description of context did not receive the kind of attention it deserves. There is no CC simply consisting of field: all three parametric choices must be seen together. Another important issue is the ways in which two or more context might combine – i.e., context conjunction – or they might form two or more distinct contexts within an interaction that is taking place between the same interlocuters in the same spatio-temporal location, i.e. disjunction of relevant contexts: is such conjunction and disjunction of context 'un-describable' from the system perspective? The arguments about the relationship of language and context and of system and instance suggest to me that this is not the case. In fact such descriptions have been provided for a long time (Goffman 1974; Cross 1979; Cloran 1994; 1999a; Hasan 1995b; 1999b). Some of the most interesting areas of study are how and when an ongoing text and its context can be subverted? Cloran (1982) in her research involving a range of different contexts demonstrated that it is in fact very difficult to achieve such change with an established context. In view of this, the reputed changes of conversational discourse stand in need of very close attention from the point of view of the relevant context. Is there a register change here or is there simply a con/textual serialization?

Notes

[1] This is also true of what Fawcett (1999) calls 'dialects of SFL', which explains the indefinite article in the title.
[2] The other two prominent models of context in SFL are those of Martin (1985b, 1992a) and Fawcett (1980; 1999); both are appreciably different from Halliday's theory of context. It goes without saying that the interpretation of the theory is mine. Readers might compare other authors' interpretations of both, e.g., Matthiessen 1995b; 2007a; Martin 1992a; 1999, and Fawcett 1999.
[3] As is well known, Halliday 1961 is the foundation of the Scale and Category model.
[4] Before Malinowski's appropriation of the term to refer to the cultural-situational phenomena in semiotic environments, 'context' had referred to 'environment' in general or to the linguistic environment in a text, i.e., to today's 'co-text'.
[5] The situation is changing with interest in multimodality; see for example Bowcher (2007).

⁶ Even within the limits of SFL, this literature is too extensive to be referenced here in the traditional form in a publication of this scope. Beginning with scattered observations by Firth (1957b), followed by Mitchell (1957), and a large scale study by Huddleston, Hudson, Winter and Henrici (1968), and Halliday and Hasan (1976), text analysis really took off after Halliday (1977b) and Hasan (1978). By now a large number of scholars have made valuable contributions. Any bibliography of SFL publications will indicate very clearly the outstanding names in the field.

⁷ Saussure had offered only two reasons for the elevation of langue as the only legitimate concern of 'linguistics proper': (i) that parole needs langue to achieve the desired effects; and (ii) that the study of parole is unfeasible due to its irregular nature. He undermined the strength of the first in granting that ultimately langue has its origin in parole; the second reason loses its force once context is integrated into linguistic theory. The autonomy of Chomsky's competence from everything social (at least in its initial appearance) makes the exclusion of performance from linguistics qualitatively different: it is impossible to support or refute the hypotheses about competence, since the scope of the concept has never been clear enough to be debated in any detail.

⁸ The reader is invited to compare the figure representing 'the complete framework of levels for linguistic description' in Halliday et al (1964:18) with later figures which show context, semantics, lexicogrammar and phonology as linguistic strata.

⁹ The first version of this figure was in Halliday 1991d; the second version in Ghadessy ed. (reprinted 2007) is the most explicit.

¹⁰ I am not implying that such comprehensive description of any system is currently available in any approach, simply that the cultural and semiotic systems must be inclusive rather than exclusive, allowing for variation and change, characteristics that pertain to both language and culture systems.

¹¹ I have often commented (e.g., in my presentation to EESFLW, Gorizia 2006, and elsewhere) that realization is one of the hardest working concepts in SFL; it has been used for interstratal relations; also for the relation between system and structure; and of course as an interstratal relation it is both a dialectic, as at the higher three levels strata, and works as 'true' content expression where phonetics and phonology in relation to the content strata are concerned.

¹² For the concept of meta-redundancy, see (Lemke 1985; 1992d).

¹³ Although Marie Smith Jones, the last speaker of Eyak, died barely a month ago (Guardian Weekly, 8/2/08 P28-9), her language actually died with the death of her sister in the early 1990s, because that is when the avenues were closed for the language system to develop and to change.

¹⁴ The idea of 'less developed languages' has been anathema to linguistics, but this reaction is not based on careful thinking. To say that a language, such as English, was less developed in ancient times than it is today is not to imply that it lacked the potential to develop. In fact, so long as we do not think that the system of language is hardwired in the brain, we allow it the possibility of growth and decline.

¹⁵ These stories have been discussed in Hasan 1984a and 1984b, as well as in Hasan 1973a, b mimeo.

¹⁶ The account of the developments described were brought about by a large number of colleagues; important amongst these to me was the work of Halliday, my

immediate research students such as Butt, Cloran, Cross, Bowcher, Armstrong, and a wider community of colleagues such as Kress, Martin and those led by Michael Gregory in Toronto. My own work has foregrounded the role of meaning/semantics in identifying register varieties and in the realization of contextual features, as is evident from my attempts (Hasan 1973c; 1980; 1984b; 1985b; 1995b etc).

[17] The term 'genre' was borrowed into SFL from Bakhtin by Martin (1985b and thereafter). Genre had been consciously avoided because like the term 'style' it carried connotations from its use in literary studies that did not fit the concept of register (hence also Bakhtin's modification by 'speech' in the term he used 'speech genre'). Genres in literary studies were innocent of Firthian-Hallidayan conceptualization of context; they were recognized purely by the global arrangement of their form. There was no reasoning for linking a literary genre and its instance, except literary conventions.

[18] We do not have adequate language of description for the relations I am describing here. Reference being experiential is particulate; it will concern elements of material situational setting, but the latter is capable of impinging in a non-referential way. Try helping your child solve a mathematical problem while engaged in cooking a complex dish – there will be hesitations, pauses, repetitions because the material situation is 'dividing' speaker attention. The language of the text might then bear traces of MSS, without there being any reference to any specific element of the MSS.

[19] These were listed in Hasan 1980, and were validated in an empirical research (Cloran 1982).

[20] Martin had begun referring to these as 'genre combination'; there are some obvious problems in this nomenclature (Hasan 1999b); I have preferred 'con/text integration/disjunction'.

[21] Many examples may be found, for example, in Vol 2 of Halliday's collected works.

[22] Attempts to produce consistent 'dynamic' i.e. instance based or pro-spective descriptive frameworks have typically fizzled out. The concept of pro-spective grammar was introduced by John Sinclair; for an example see (Ravelli 1995).

[23] Certainly there are problems especially in oral language use e.g. the *ums* and *ers*, the incomplete clause, the mid-clause changes in structure, the unmotivated repetitions, and sometimes an innovative pattern; but these have not been found to militate against either comprehension or analysis.

[24] Strictly speaking, Bowcher offers valuable critique of Hasan 1999b and attempts to extend that field network to cover multimodal phenomena; I am informed that Butt (mimeo) is being 'trialled' by researchers at Macquarie.

[25] I thank Michael Halliday who pointed out in a personal discussion that on the level of grammar or semantics this representation of constraint for choices across two simultaneous vectors would be considered 'ill-formed'. The issue is not simple and calls for a detailed discussion; but 3b offers field-mk2 as an attempt to correct this situation by exploring the possibility of building in material action through realization. A strong justification for this would be that material action is itself not in 'field': what is in field is reference to or traces of material action in the language of the text. Nonetheless it is important to say that the modifications built in 3c raise other serious problems. The problem is under investigation by a group of researchers at Macquarie University.

11

Stylistic analysis: construing aesthetic organisation

David G. Butt and Annabelle Lukin
Macquarie University

Introduction

The central task of stylistic analysis is to elucidate a form of organisation in text under investigation. This form of organisation exists over and above the organisation which we can discern at a number of levels in anything made in language. In fact, stylistic analysis focuses on the higher order of organisation which 'recruits' aspects of conventional linguistic patterning to a **transcendent** semantic enterprise — a pattern of meaning which is realised by consistencies in those conventional choices 'lower down', and which is therefore **immanent** in the texture undergoing analysis. Yet this pattern is in no way accounted for by the sum of meaningful arrangements in the units displayed in the lower levels of linguistic realization. Hence, we can legitimately apply 'transcendent' in that the higher organisation both motivates and bestows a new value on the **ensemble of relations** across a text. Yet the pattern is also immanent since it is to be 'read off' from the very texture of the artefact, that is from the multiplicity of choices taken up in the construction of its linguistic form. Literary texts offer the clearest cases of this higher order of organisation, this extra level of **"symbolic articulation"** (Hasan, 1971). For in literature, more is required of writers and readers — they do more 'work' in creating and transforming **semantic potential**. This 'work' is exemplified and elaborated below. The experience of war and training for war are used to test our claims of a higher order organization, even when demotic, idiomatic expressions supply much of the 'recruited' linguistic material of the analysed texts. Studies of the poets W. H. Auden (1907 – 1973) and Bruce Dawe (1930–) illustrate the organization at issue and the way argument and evidence may be built up through a process of **reciprocal delimitation** (a dialectic of semantic enquiry).

A related form of higher order organisation may be evident in many genres of text, at least to some degree. In non-literary texts, such organization is one basis for what we make of the consistency of purpose in a text — the **goal**

orientation expressed through texture (a term used by Hasan in elaborating parameters of context and register, see e.g. Hasan 1999b). Generalisations about the purpose of an interaction, establishing the actual form of transaction being enacted, are rarely resolved by the explicit declarations of speakers and writers. For instance, it is important to consider purpose against different temporal horizons: e.g. parents may encourage their children into sports for many reasons, from immediate exercise to the long term goals of adjusting to team work and of accepting defeats graciously. But the 'goals' or 'motivations' of particular parents are *not* merely there for the enquirer or even for the parent.

In other cases, consistencies of motif and of organisational structures in discourse can reflect the legal requirements of a register — the form its professional roles must take to be counted as professional. Other evidence of tendentiousness in the semantics may express the ideology (the agenda) of a given institution (as in the diminution of a political figure by a particular newspaper). The discourse of patient and psychiatrist supplies an interesting case: in many instances a consultation can have the design of 'conversation' in a novel or play, with every aspect of the exchange echoing and qualifying the elements in 'play' between the two agonists. And there is 'art' in such an exchange, as in the articulation of speeches and writings which move us to action, or to the experience of strong emotion. But this 'art' is best classified as the Greeks would have: as "**techne**" (Roochnik, 1996).

In verbal art, the metaphysical implications of the higher consistency, and the intensity of the organising relations, suggest that we are dealing with a phenomenon of another category, one with temporal and cultural horizons quite unlimited by immediate conditions. Russian formalists Shklovsky, Zirmunskij, Jakobson and Tynyanov, as well as the narratologist Propp, tried to capture these, and other characteristics of verbal art, by emphasising the goal directed, aesthetic orientation of verbal art. Their characterisations varied in their teleological implications, but brought out a contrast with language that was driven causally in an automatized fashion by day to day circumstances (Steiner, 1984: see 12 entries under 'teleology' in index). By this opposition between **teleology** and **causation**, we take them to be attending to the way the texture of verbal art appears like a response to a goal which is only available to us when the final form of the work gives full realization to the semantic relations which delimit its semantic potential. At least we can think of the 'end' or 'goal' of the work being a provisional theme for particular readings at a specific cultural time. Verbal art is an emergent activity — its central theses seem to have drawn the wording to the relations necessary for its ultimate articulation. A causal text is driven directly in the context of situation; or that is the convenient, heuristic divide. But we should keep an open mind on this division between registerial 'techne' and verbal 'art': often people speak in day to day matters 'sub specie aeternitate', with the nobility of Antigone arguing the case for her brother's burial against the King of Thebes; and it is clear that many works of art have been, initially, responses to specific quotidian conditions. Art must be seen for its power for changing immediate conditions by changing how people experience the meaning of the moment — the moment as fulfilment in time (kairos) rather than just as time passing (chronos). As tyrants know, art has a profound agency which is enacted daily through the lives of artists, through habits of meaning and artistry which are inherently subversive. In this way, Auden's line (in "On the Death of W.B. Yeats") needs to be itself re-evaluated: "For poetry makes nothing happen . . ." Whether we focus on the new cultivation of love by the Roman poet Ovid, which drew the ire of the Emperor Augustus in his late drive for moral austerity, or on the personal poetries of Akhmatova and Pasternak during Stalin's communisation of Russia, or even on the music of Shostakovitch, which, while saying nothing in words, did not declare to Russians that they were living in the 'best of times', tyrants know things begin to happen in poetry and arts (more widely). Verbal art releases something so mercurial that it cannot be regathered once introduced into the channels of public exchange (See conclusion below).

The special character of linguistically based stylistics, and, therefore, the achievement by which it may be distinguished from other traditions of interpretative practice, is its argument for **motivated selection**. The case has to be explicit and sufficient to be confirmed by a 'court' of linguistics. In such a heuristic domain — a 'court' judging linguistic consistencies — it is remarkable how broadly the participating 'jurists' can be selected. The crucial criterion for linguistic claims is simply the identification of options in language — the **unconscious patterning** of semiotic choices. The only point of necessary consensus in order to conduct business is that choices exist for language users, and that these choices have semantic consequences. We can see from the traditional position of linguistic enquiry that the linguist's concern for paradigms attests to this consensus. And, while folk reports on grammatical relations are often worse than useless, most people can usefully explain the semantic differences of one arrangement in a text by comparison with alternative versions (thereby providing some reliability for inferences concerning **unconscious design**, whether artistic, forensic, ritual or casual).

Motivated selection

When considered from the point of view of argument and evidence, claims of motivated selection are based on a consistency of choice which cannot be reasonably explained away as random. Cultural and even personal motivations, for the artist as well as for the analyst, must be considerations when setting out into an inquiry, given that some problem has brought the analyst to the textual cruces of the investigation. It is likely that the cultural parameters that drew us to the textual enquiry (including the selection of the texts) will suggest to us the need to prioritize certain textual dimensions as being of greater relevance to our investigation on probabilistic grounds, i.e. probabilities in the system of language; and probabilities drawn from previous analyses. In the second stage of stylistic analysis, we are trying to throw a light under the organisation of the linguistic choices. While such elucidation can never be totally cut off from the cultural issues which brought the text into discussion (and should never be), our method is an attempt to see the text against the language as system, in order to clarify its value as instance. This formulation sounds paradoxical; but it begins in a **figure and ground metaphor** — uniqueness of the instance is the specific way it draws upon the background field of possibilities. Here, using Halliday's central concept of "**meaning potential**", we can think of the "figure" (a traditional word in rhetoric and semantics for the 'shape' of a meaning) in the terms of contemporary work in systems theory. The meaning potential is a "**phase space**": a domain of possible, semantic activity. The individual text utilises the possibilities of the 'space' as an ensemble of actual realizations. Such realizations can be in keeping with the probabilities of take up across the phase space (what is typically selected), or they may be variously **marked** or contrastive with respect to the history of transactions with that phase space. There are, in fact, various histories involved at this point: choice may be marked or unmarked for the language, for the register, for a dialect, or for the given text. We do our best, then, (through the use of corpora, and through other forms of reference) to establish benchmarks for a language, for a register, for a dialect, and for an idiolect. We are trying to establish a profile of the way meaning potential is taken up in a particular use or instance of text. In the terms of systems theory and the notion of phase space, we are working out a unique "**phase portrait**" (Cohen and Stewart, 1994: 199ff).

Like two other concepts central to our argument here — the **"systemo-functional" view of text** (see Steiner, 1984: 99ff), and the notion of "**dominant**" (a term originally from Christiansen, see ibid: 105ff) — the idea of "motivated selection" was earliest developed by Russian linguists famously (but disparagingly) described as "Formalists" (see O'Toole, 2001: 163-173 for a succinct survey of modern Russian literary theory; see also O'Toole and Shukman, *Russian Poetics in Translation, vols 1–8);* Steiner 1984; Striedter 1989; on the use of Russian and Czech literary theory by some systemic functional linguists, see Lukin and Webster 2005). In this brief discussion, we will mention only Tynyanov (1978) and Jakobson (1978, 1987), and the latter only in his European phases, in Moscow and in Prague. For the most balanced integration of Russian literary theories with linguistic functionalism and narratology, see O'Toole's study of Russian short stories (1982) and his various articles in literary stylistics. Motivated selection can be applied to any consistency of meaning when we think of meaning in the terms of the British linguistic tradition (specifically the legacy of J.R. Firth as elaborated by Halliday, see Butt 2001), namely: that meaning is a function of all the levels of language working together (as realization), not just the domain of a single, abstracted level of 'semantics'. The contrast with American generative traditions can hardly be overemphasised.

Claims concerning motivated selection in no way depend upon, or equate with, any idea of conscious intention with respect to language choices. It does not exclude the possibility of consciously applied design, or technique; but, as with certain choices in spoken or written registers generally, instances of conscious choice are like (merely) the (oddity of a) meniscus over the top of a child's glass of water — an oddity which indicates some care in the pouring and which demands some attentiveness in the response of the drinker. But we are socialised into the fundamental, meaning bearing contrasts of our languages. They are learnt context by living context, in 'processual frames', probable units of our incipient futures. They are of a piece then with our sense of living, and share something with the deep organic habits of breathing (of which we can become conscious and to which, for particular purposes, we can apply training and technique). Our "fashions of speaking" (Whorf 1956) are metonymic with respect to our patterns of living: there is a hanging together which provides a basis for expectation, for the probabilities, with respect to that inclination to a future. The metonymy between conditions of living and patterns of language is the basis of our dynamic, semiotic activity.

Three central questions

How then do we marshal evidence for this higher order thematic organisation, which constitutes, in Hasan's (1971, 1985b) terms: "the deepest level of meaning in the text", or the central "**thesis**" to which the patternings in a text contribute? The Hasan-Halliday approach sets out from 3 questions, 3 logically ordered, interpretive issues:

1. What does the text mean?
2. How does it mean what it does? and
3. Why is it valued as it is?

These questions provide a cycle of hermeneutic method by which an investigation can be refined (or revised) at many different levels of analysis — cultural, semantic, lexicogrammatical, phonological, cross modal (viz. graphological, filmic) — and the passage of interpretive inference can be kept in sight with the steps of reasoning themselves becoming part of the hermeneutic outcome. Their visibility certainly assists in the persuasiveness of the analysis.

The central concepts of stylistics, along with those steps of reasoning — methods of interpretative inference — were demonstrated in work by Halliday and by Hasan as far back as the early 1960s (1964b; Hasan 1964). What we find is the essential role of stylistics as comparison and of the quantitative basis of reasoning even of small quantities which bring out a relation, or proportion which has a clear thematic relevance. In Yeats's "Leda and the Swan" a "cline of verbness/verbality" (Halliday 1964b, 2002–2007 volume 2: 12) shows how, by comparison with various prose extracts, the organization of the poem shifts verbs away from the canonical role of finite predicator in an α ('free') clause. The thematic relevance emerges as the de-verbized items are set against deixis and specification in the nominal groups of the poem. The motivated nature of the findings is underwritten when we are told that a similar proportion could be found in an extract on plutonium in the New Scientist (ibid). This confirms the 'strangeness' of the textual arrangements, even though any of the individual structures of the poem could not be judged deviant. The role of 'norms', the importance of seeing norms in terms of register, and the fact that powerful (numerical) argument can be achieved through small scales of enquiry, are all set out in this early study. The key is a clarity of argument based on functions and structures of language as 'system'.

Hasan's doctoral thesis took the issues of comparison and genre into new territory in her comparative study of style in two novels. Included in the unpublished thesis is a sketch of a functional grammar which is a necessary tool for stylistics enquiry. This work prepares the way for a set of papers in the late 1960's, early 1970's in which the "place of stylistics" in the study of verbal art (e.g. 1968, 1971, 1975) is elaborated in a theory which encompasses the core issues of stylistics today.

First of all, Hasan distances her work from the stylistic fashion of the time (late 60s), namely: the preoccupation with Chomskyan "grammaticality" and the writing of rules for the syntactic 'violations' of textual eccentricities (viz. like those of Cummings or of Dylan Thomas). In her pursuit of "sensicality", the organization for which she argues is (as always in Hallidayan linguistics) relatedness of meaning. By moving between the conditions of the text as 'instance' and the background of the language as 'system', Hasan demonstrates the "consistency of foregrounding". It is this consistency which accounts for a number of dimensions of our experience of verbal art:

1. the sense we can have of a unity;
2. our experience of a deeper level of thematic organization which needs to be distinguished from the subject matter, and which constitutes a kind of "thesis" in the work;
3. and our recognition of a semantic uniqueness in the work — what sets the text off from other texts in the culture (and hence defines what would be lost if the text itself were lost to the speech community).

Our 3 questions, set out above, on meaning, method and value have been addressed: whatever the subject matter, whatever the 'states of events' reported, the defining character of verbal art is in the way such 'states of affairs' are organised to achieve a thematic purpose. This level of organization is referred to by Hasan as 'symbolic articulation'. In such a way, any of the linguistic patterns of a text constitute the verbal relations recruited to the strategy of "symbolic articulation". The deepest level of meaning is realized in symbolic articulation, which is realized by verbalization (i.e. the utilization of patterns in semantics, lexicogrammar, phonology and the 'inner' context of a work). This layering explains why Hasan speaks of verbal art as a "patterning of patterns". It is *not*, however, a case of connotative semiotics (after Hjelmslev) since all the systems are phenomena of language, not some other system utilizing language.

A demonstration of Hasan's approach, which is carefully scaffolded for those working their way into stylistics and its modes of argument, can be found in her analysis of Anne Sexton's poem "Old" (Hasan, 1988). This study encompasses not only an investigation of the language of the poem 'in the round', it positions the poem against critical evaluations which show what is at risk when critics do not have to provide a linguistic warrant for their appraisals.

Halliday's 1971a language study of Golding's novel *The Inheritors* puts the concepts and methods of linguistic stylistics in a new light and on a remarkable scale. The notion of norm has 3 relevant meanings in the study: there is the norm of the first 216 pages of the book, by contrast with the probabilities exhibited by English more widely (as 'system'); there is a brief transitional stage; and there is a norm for the final section of the novel (16 pages) by contrast with the earlier pages. The final section 'restores' the norms of the system, but, in so doing, draws a strong contrast with the earlier sections of the work. The transitivity patterns, which are the basis of comparison in the study, demonstrate Golding's ability to utilise (albeit unconsciously) the quotidian resources of the language in the creation of a contrast between world views — how the world is construed in terms of processes and agents by old stone age and then by new stone age peoples. The strangeness of the first 200 pages recedes as familiar probabilities of participants and process are re-established for the reader. Halliday makes plain what can be involved in the linguistic construction of reality.

In addition to the European contributors already cited, Michael Gregory was at the centre of a number of North American specialists in functional linguistics, including Peter Fries, Michael Cummings, Jim Benson and Bill Greaves. These linguists combined the linguistic and literary work from the Firthian tradition with their own interactions with developments in the U.S. and Canada. Michael Gregory's work was multi-faceted, but organised around the importance of displaying variation in meaning. As with the publications of Halliday and Hasan, Gregory's commitment to meaning was not diverted by Chomskyan rhetoric, and his studies of poetry and drama remain as benchmarks for other practitioners (see e.g. Gregory 1974, 1978, 1981). Also, like his British colleagues, Gregory's focus on variation led him to extend the tools of textlinguistics and situational descriptions (Gregory and Carroll 1978, Gregory and Malcolm 1981). The concept of a "phase", for example, was a particularly useful concept which enabled analysts to capture the complexity of subtle shifts in the semantic 'tides' or 'rhythms' of a work. A late paper (in Fries et al, 2002) sets out this concept and its ramifications for discourse analysis (literary and interactional). Fries's career has both extended the tradition of his father's linguistics (his father was Charles Fries, 1887–1967) and brought SFL work into American forums. Peter Fries has specialised in the abstract textual function, the resources for text 'flow'. These have been examined across genres, including the prose of Henry James (e.g. Fries, 2003). Cummings, Benson and Greaves have pursued a linguistic/stylistic programme (see e.g. Cummings and Simmons, 1983) which has encompassed historical studies (e.g. from Old English; from Milton), collaborations with primate research centres, and exchanges with linguists from congruent American theories. The strongest connection with contemporary U.S. theory has been with the Stratificationists, led by Sydney Lamb. Both Halliday's social modelling and Lamb's cognitive model are underpinned by the potential of "realization systems" (hence, stratification), and both are represented by networks of choice (a tool that assists stylistics in way that "deviation" and "rules" do not).

Developments in SFL stylistics could be organised around a number of dimensions: 1. By the core concepts, including the contact between the Halliday-Hasan methods and other traditions (Prague School and Russian Formalism); 2. By relations with other stylistic sub-disciplines (viz. narratology); 3. By genres (poems, plays, novels, short stories and other valued texts); 4. By authors ('canonical' or not); 5. By significant SFL anthologies; 6. By the linguistic systems that are most crucial to the argument on textual organization and uniqueness (viz. those crucial to claims of a 'dominant' in a work or suite of texts); 7. By engagement with criticism and its domains of contestation (e.g. ideology; deconstruction; Post Colonialism; semiotic distance); and 8. By stylistics which interacts with other modalities of semiotic expression (including the development of theory for bringing out isomorphisms and homologies between verbal art and plastic arts).

1. Halliday's study of Priestley's play *An Inspector Calls* (1982/2002) draws on the Russian Formalist concept of automatized and de-automatized choice, showing how the unremarkable background of modality and modulation is foregrounded so that the microsemiotic tensions of our taken for granted world provide the central thematic meanings of the play. Connections with the stylistics of L.M.O'Toole and with Russian and Czech theorists are explored below. **By bringing out the cognate theories of distinct functionalist traditions in stylistics, it becomes easier to appreciate the degree to which the conceptual tools of stylistics have been refined and tested across a wide front of cultures and eras. Such tools are not subjective or peripheral by comparison with the wider claims of linguistics to scientific method.**

2. Studies by O'Toole and by Paul Thibault exemplify in particular the SFL engagement with narratology and Post Modernism. O'Toole's 1982 study of the Russian short story juxtaposes the abstractions of Barthes (for example) with traditional, Aristotelian notions to achieve greater refraction between perspectives.

Thibault's specialisations include detailed work on Nabokov (1984, 1991), on Saussure (1997), and on the signifying body and brain (2004a). A similar breadth of engagement is exemplified by Robin Melrose (1996), whose work on post modernism encompasses both literary and scientific argumentation.

3, 4 & 5. The wide coverage of literary genres and canonical and lesser known writers is on display in a number of key anthologies. These include Birch and O'Toole (1988), Carter (1982), Toolan (1992), and Miller and Turci (2007). A point that needs to be emphasised, however, is the way that style has also been analysed across a number of genres of non literary culture (eg. in Halliday 2002–2007 volume 2 and Toolan, 1992) and even of scientific value. The study of Darwin's *The Origin of Species* by Halliday is an instance with special relevance to Halliday's own approach to science (see Butt 2005). Inversely, in a re-evaluation of critical comments on Tennyson's "In Memoriam", Halliday argues, on the basis of choices taken up, and those relinquished, that Tennyson expressed an active openness to the Darwinian revolution around him, not a reactionary nostalgia. If Darwin prepared for his scientific argument artfully, Tennyson composed his verbal art mindful of science. The argument of the study takes us on to the next dimension.

6. Typically in the relational thinking required by stylistics, it is the ensemble effect of patterns of choice from a number of systems which creates the "semantic drift" (Butt 1983). Such "patterns of patterns" are laid bare in Hasan's treatment of "The Widower in the Country" by Les Murray (Hasan, 1985b). Nevertheless, it is often clear that one or other metafunctional orientation or major system is dominant in its contribution to what is most distinctive in a text's organisation. In Halliday's work on *The Origin of Species*, it is the textual resources which are the focus of attention, specifically the way in which they prepare for the reader's reception of the word "evolution" as the final word of the final sentence of the work.

7. Hasan's writings on ideology and semiotic distance have a direct relevance to textual interpretation of all kinds, including literary-aesthetic. They establish the distance between creation and reception, and they supply co-ordinates for construing the background from culture to context to lexicogrammar.

Such concepts are essential in the contexts of World English and its many literatures. The unique working relationship between the Singaporean poet Edwin Thumboo and the American linguist Jonathan Webster (based in Asia since the early 1980s) continues to generate stylistic analyses which illuminate the subtleties of a poetry which draws on strong 'local' connections as well as internationalist perspectives — Malay, Christian, Post-colonial, institutional, historical, and personal. In the analysis of Thumboo's "David", Webster brings out the semantic relevance of triplets of dependency in the clause complexing, such complexing being a resource not sufficiently considered in most analyses. This is a significant example of how reasoning proceeds in stylistics, from the broadest, latent systems in towards a 'gestalt' of the semantic controls being exercised by the poet (Webster 2001; see also Webster's study of foregrounding, 1998).

8. The metafunctional principle, the role of strata, and the rankscale (of constituency), as well as the representation of choices through networks, all have provided the transdisciplinary tools needed for analogical thinking across different semiotic modalities. Halliday's notion of "meaning potential" is the organising principle; and mapping the potential through systemic options in different modalities has produced a clarity about the contrasts, as well as some homologies, between verbal art and other forms of artistry.

Setting out from the lexicogrammar

While the meaning engendered by text is a function of all its levels of patterning, in this discussion we will attempt to illustrate stylistic concepts by prioritising the level of form, of lexicogrammar. The cultural theme of warfare and preparing for war, constitutes the domain which brought the problems for stylistic analysis to us. And this domain turns out to be propitious in a number of ways: for instance, in showing how the most prejudicial, ugly idioms of community speech can still be recruited to a form of organization both artistic and existentially novel (viz. seeing in a new light, as "for the first time": T.S. Eliot, 'Little Gidding' from *The Four Quartets*).

The analyst's statements about lexicogrammar are an index of how the discussion of meaning will be anchored. Our main method in this paper will be to build our statements of meaning out from lexicogrammatical analysis. Our point of departure here is the view that lexicogrammar does not 'represent' the meaning but contributes to (or makes) meaning by its very form. Such 'poiesis' is a consequence of: 1) the clause internal relations, which are relatively explicit due to the hard work of grammarians over 2500 years, and 2) cross clausal relations. SFL linguists have worked assiduously on aspects of these relations — contextual modelling, cohesion, rhetorical structures, appraisal theory, generic structures, narratology — the cumulative effects of which are yet to be laid out in a new synthesis of rhetoric and contemporary understanding of grammatical functions. The cross clausal effects, as well as certain clause internal **reactances** in grammar, need to be considered systemically — in relation to the level of context, the active frames of our socialisation, as mentioned above. Viewed in such a way, we can see a tumult of **semiotic currents**, an **implicate order** which supplies the waves, whorls and vortices which carry us along as we make our acts of meaning. Such **complexity** and **self organization** are now being confronted by a linguistics with **multi-dimensional modelling**, extensive corpora, and a willingness to pursue complex configurations of meaning across different modalities or channels.

How, then, does one proceed? How, in particular, do we conduct a semantic enquiry and deliver on the claims implicit in stylistic analysis, namely: the (qualified) objectivity; the systematicity; the criterion of relevance in all our involved analysis; the evidence of motivated selection; the arguments against randomness in the textual phenomenon we invoke; and the problem of exclusion? A brief note should be offered on this last point — what is meant by "exclusion". If we can use a theory and its method to obtain equal evidence for contradictory points of view, we have to say that the theory (and its methods) are "too powerful", namely, they do not sufficiently define an outcome. They do not reject any interpretation as wrong or (more realistic in textual matters) of being highly improbable. What we aim to achieve in stylistic analysis is to carry the reader to shared findings, conclusions which have the character of inexorability when looked at from the perspective of linguistic reasoning. As in a courtroom, the forms of counter claims and arguments, in particular those that have themselves a claim to reasonableness, need to be anticipated and addressed along the way in analysis.

The examples we present below are truncated in relation to working through alternative proposals, and even in relation to the many other lines of analysis which can be brought to bear in support of the conclusions drawn here on thematic organisation. What we do achieve, in a short span, are progressive steps which reveal a higher order of textual consistency (ie. higher than any linguistic unit other than 'text'), and which are checkable. Inspection can move directly to rejection, if the semantic consequences of the combined patternings revealed are not convincing. What we can show in the texts is what Hasan focuses upon in her stylistic method: "**consistency of foregrounding**" (see e.g. Hasan, 1964, 1968, 1985b). For Halliday, our findings are an exemplification of the diverse resources by which particular meanings can be given "**prominence**". Prominence may be achieved by either fulfilling a textual consistency or by breaking with it (viz. Halliday, 1971a).

Setting out by dividing a text into clauses is a limited strategy: it is limited by practical considerations (like the length of the text; the time you have to devote to the analysis); and it is limited as theory (viz. one may ask: "Isn't there a more direct way in to the meaning than through the grammar?"). The initial problems — the practical — can be addressed by "**principled selection**". For the analysis of a very long text, one must argue one's way down from generic elements to a crucial sampling of the texture (especially a sampling which involves text internal comparisons, as in Halliday 1971a). The principle of selection can be argued out on the basis of issues which brought you to the text, whether artistic or socio-political or otherwise. Relational databases have changed the temporal horizon of the researcher — analysed data can be built up over years, re-configured in seconds, and re-visited for new comparisons and interpretation. At this point, we can see a basis for claiming that stylistic analysis is discourse analysis conducted under a more specific brief, namely in the pursuit of an account of **aesthetic organisation**.

The theoretical issue of starting in the grammar is also to be seen from the perspective of general linguistic theory. The units on a grammatical rankscale are themselves the realizations of semantic patterns and, by comparison with, say, tropes, rhetorical strategies, rhetorical structures, semantic primes, and semantic components, the grammatical units are relatively uncontroversial amongst linguists. This is to say that, even when linguists disagree about such units (or even about rank-scale), specialists (and non-specialists) have few problems reading these differing definitions across theories and across eras (even going back to classical notions). The grammar — the lexicogrammar — provides a core of practice against which findings can be calibrated and checked, even up and down on the other levels of linguistic order (ie. context, semantics, phonology/phonetics).

Furthermore, since most grammatical arrangements cannot be consciously monitored by their speakers or hearers, there is an opportunity to display covert consistencies in a text when one can check how the grammar has been fashioned to the kinds of purpose reviewed at the beginning of this discussion. The clause is *not* a limitation in approaching a verbal text: it is a semantic and methodological strategy for anchoring the enquiry and its evidence. By enabling a cross calibration of efforts across practitioners, the variation which does arise in analysis and interpretation can be displayed less equivocally; that is, more reliably. Claims of variation in expression or reception have only the weight of opinion if this form of calibration is not implemented.

In the following selective moves of analysis, we demonstrate the approach with a synoptic directness which, we admit, does not reflect the more exploratory experience of the analysis that went into interpreting each poem. But, it is a close reflection of what emerges as soon as one adopts a systematic analysis of the choices taken up metafunction by metafunction. The steps for example 1 involve a setting out of ideational meanings — the experiential analysis of the clauses and a diagram of their logical relations. These two perspectives on the text, along with the construal of the semantic consequences of the choices, already make a strong case for "motivated selection". Both studies of child language development and enquiry into primate evolution indicate that interpersonal meanings are likely to be dominant and prior in the histories of language (i.e. personal and cultural); and, certainly, forms of evidence from interpersonal and textual systems give the interpretations here greater consistency. In example two, the argument hangs by the interpersonal impact of choices in the text, set out against the patterns in cohesion and transitivity selections.

Journey to a War

Auden's Sonnet XII can be analysed into 17 units, most of which are unequivocally a clause (see Table 1; "Nanking, Dachau" we might regard as a minor clause, one not selecting for any element of mood). Looked at from the point

Table 1 Sonnet XII from W.H Auden's "In Time of War", in Auden and Isherwood (1973). Roman numerals indicate line number. Hindu-Arabic numerals indicate clause numbers

i.	[1] Here war is harmless like a monument:
ii.	[2] A telephone is talking to a man;
iii.	[3] Flags on a map declare [4] that troops were sent;
iv.	[5] A boy brings milk in bowls. [6] There is a plan
v.	For living men in terror of their lives,
vi.	[7] Who thirst at nine [8] who were to thirst at noon,
vii.	[9] Who can be lost [10] and are, [11] who miss their wives
viii.	[12] And, unlike an idea, can die too soon.
ix.	[13] Yet ideas can be true, [14] although men die:
x.	[15] For we have seen a myriad faces
xi.	Ecstatic from one lie,
xii.	[16] And maps can really point to places
xiii.	Where life is evil now.
xiv.	[17] Nanking, Dachau.

of view of taxis (see Figure 1), one section of the sonnet creates interpretive difficulties: whether to treat "There is a plan [for living men in terror of their lives]" as an embedded expansion of the nominal head word "plan" and, following this, whether to treat the relative clauses 7, 8, 9, 10, 11, 12 (which are marked off by commas, i.e. the punctuation of non-defining relative clauses) as part of the embedding, given that they qualify "men" (which is within the embedding).

Whether we choose to represent the relations of clauses 7-12 as qualifying within an embedding or as outside the embedding, the semantic consequences are alike. Both hypotaxis and embedding 'mean' something similar in this context; and, in combination with the findings of transitivity analysis (below), they contribute to a "**semantic drift**" (Butt, 1983) which is in evidence from an extraordinary diversity of lexicogrammatical choices. Clausal elements can be raised or diminished through the various grammatical relations accorded them. They achieve a **semantic weight** through their nuclear status, their dominance, and their priority or **textual visibility.** Any element allocated to a hypotactic or embedded clause has already been 'diminished' semantically.

One effective task (which is easily achieved in analysing a short text, though not difficult with long pieces) is to track the allocation of Subject, Theme and Actor/Agent across the text. This establishes how these nuclear roles are presented in the ensemble of the metafunctions, how they are behaving polyphonically (see Halliday on polyphony, e.g. Halliday 1981b, and Pound's use of fugal structures (Davis, 1984)). In this poem, in fact, the Actor/Agent role almost

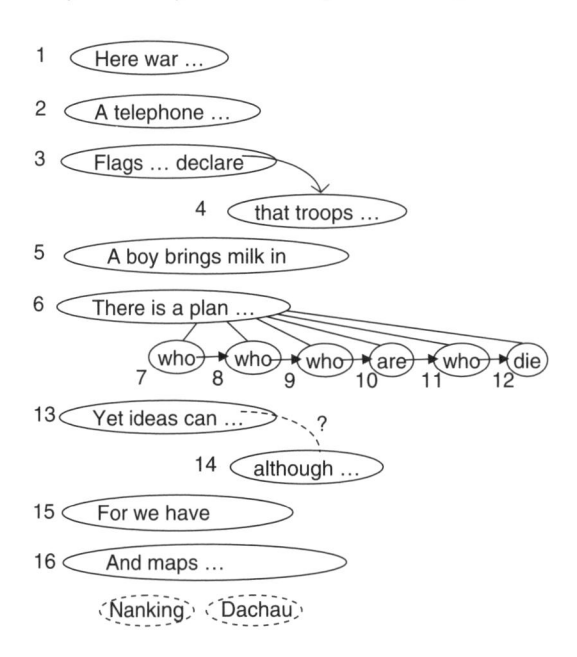

FIGURE 1 Clausal taxis in Auden's Sonnet XII

immediately emerges as 'strangely' bestowed by the poet: there is a clear signal of the alienating device discussed by Viktor Shklovsky (1990 [Ch1, in 1925], first published in 1917) as "making strange".

The central participants of the 17 clauses are immediately displayed when we consider the 2 tables which set out the relational process clauses (semantically, clauses of 'being') from the verbal, material, and behavioural processes (for the purposes here, listed as kinds of 'doing'; see Table 2 and Table 3). If we then seek the role of human agency amongst the 'doing' (including the borderline "can be lost" and "are"), we find a semantic split. If we take just two simple notions, such as the choice in participant role (allocated between adult and child), and the difference between acting on something and suffering a process as grammatical 'patient', we can display the consistent control being exerted on the encoding of choice (Figure 2). A more technical way of displaying the same result iconically would be to show which aspects of a lexicogrammatical network were taken up, and those avoided.

The only fully transitive relation with human Actor/Agent is clause 5: the reference to the boy. All other humans suffer experiences which do not involve a distinctive agency (as with middle voice behavioural processes: thirst, die) or which have the implication of a distant, removed, unspecifiable agent (viz. agentless passive: "troops were sent"). This excludes the reference to the author's

Table 2 'Being' clauses in Auden's "Sonnet XII"

cl. no.	clause
1	Here war <u>is</u> harmless like a monument
6	There <u>is</u> a plan for living men in terror of their lives
9	Who <u>can be</u> lost …
10	and … <u>are</u> …
13	Yet ideas <u>can be</u> true
16	[[where life <u>is</u> evil now]]

Table 3 'Doing' clauses in Auden's "Sonnet XII"

cl. no.	clauses
2	A telephone <u>is talking</u> to a man
3	Flags on a map <u>declare</u>
4	that troops <u>were sent</u>
5	A boy <u>brings</u> milk in bowls
7	who <u>thirst</u> at nine
8	who <u>were to thirst</u> at noon
11	who <u>miss</u> their wives
12	And, unlike an idea, <u>can die</u> too soon
14	although men <u>die</u>
15	For we <u>have seen</u> a myriad faces ecstatic with one lie
16	And maps <u>can</u> really <u>point</u> to places [[where life is evil now]]

point of view (and ours, as readers) in clause 15 (lines 10-11). The Phenomenon ("a myriad faces . . .") that "we have seen" only extends the states of being of humans, not their domains of agency. Only clause 2 amongst the 9 clauses of quadrant 4 is a principal clause (not subordinated or embedded). Overlaying Subject and Theme analyses gives inflection to the weird effects of this war poem — the static, non-human, abstract character of what most of us might assume is a fury of events. The intaglio of interpersonal, textual and ideational choices (especially of transitivity and taxis, as set out briefly here) can be summarised in the following paragraph.

The language of the poem realizes a control that the poet has exercised over the consistency of meanings which are foregrounded — all expressions of an (adult) human effecting a decision or affecting a material event are suppressed. Even the grammatical roles of ordinary soldiers suffering experiences as (grammatical) 'patients' are subordinated or downranked by their appearance in qualifying and embedded clauses. The unifying purport of all the arrangements (whether you are inclined or disinclined to thematic statements!) is that humans

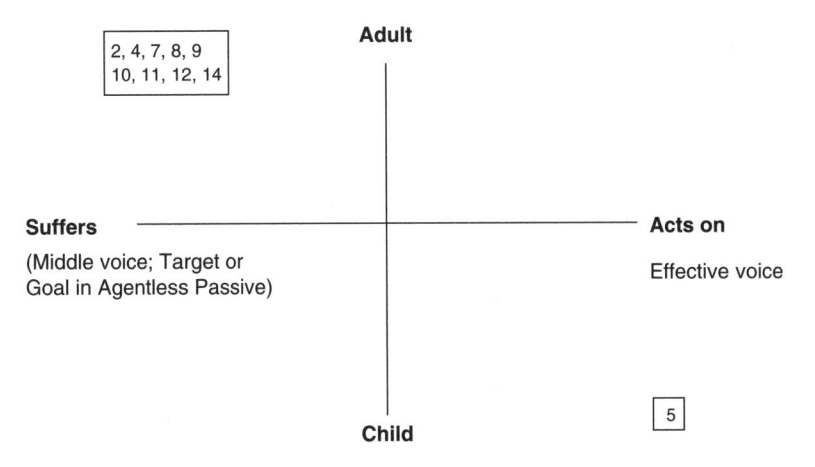

```
                    Adult
    ┌──────────┐    │
    │2, 4, 7, 8, 9│  │
    │10, 11, 12, 14│ │
    └──────────┘    │
                    │
Suffers ────────────┼──────────── Acts on
                    │
(Middle voice; Target or          Effective voice
Goal in Agentless Passive)
                    │
                    │
                    │              ┌─┐
                    │              │5│
                    │              └─┘
                  Child
```

FIGURE 2 Participant type versus agency in Auden's Sonnet XII; numbers indicate clause numbers

are not potent or agentive in the war being described. There is no evidence of control and human intelligence in the experience of 'battle'. Rather, the existential "There is a plan" grammatically dominates the "for living men in terror of the lives, who thirst/thirst . . . can be lost . . . are . . . miss their wives . . . die too soon". Certainly "troops were sent"; but the agency (implicit) is projected from the verb "declare", with the -er role (sayer) taken by "Flags on a map (declare that troops were sent.)". The human agent which is prominent in a main clause, and more prominent because of the counterpoint to the gathering non-human agency, is the boy in line 5: "A boy brings milk in bowls". Here the semantic dissonance of a "boy" and "milk" amidst war lend a further inflection to the absurdity expressed through the grammar, with humans carried along with the inexorability of the tumult of events. The clause also reminds us of the rationale for treating the lexis and the grammar together in lexicogrammar, and how the ranks of form *are* scales of a semantic ensemble.

'Byt': the aesthetic organization of the ordinary

A common challenge to our argument about "consistency of foregrounding" is that works of art are not as unified in their meanings as the notions of "consistency" and "organization" imply. The many voices of a work — the polyphonies of Joyce and Dostoevsky, for example — are indicative of a heterogeneity of textures and design. At first glance, this objection looks plausible, or even undeniable. As the scale of a work increases, and as the subject matter incorporates multiple personae in numerous narratological complexities, the patterning in a text is difficult to track and difficult to encompass in one 'thesis'. And, possibly, with some works, such seeking after consistency can be inimical for the interpretive potential. Again, this is a domain in which one might keep an open mind, awaiting demonstrations rather than theoretical commitments on behalf of authorial design, or, on the other hand, in favour of reader response (as if a polarity existed).

Four dimensions of the issue to keep in mind are:

i. Works cited as polyphonic and heterogenous are often those that have undergone the longest periods of authorial gestation and design (typically selection and organization).
ii. The linguistic and generic resources most responsible for the uniqueness of the work — what constitutes the "dominant", and sometimes what can be regarded as the "**deformation**" of our thematic expectations — can be usefully thought of as realizing the higher level organising principle referred to at the outset of this discussion (the transcendent/immanent paradox).
iii. The work itself, realizing particular strategies of semantic control, provides new co-ordinates in the meaning potential of the culture, and, therefore, eludes plausible, even provisional, summarizing theses. (This is the basis of the work's cultural value).
iv. Heterogeneity is typically related to letting more of the world 'into' the work, more intrusions of "ordinary life" (an unsatisfactory rendering of the Russian term "**byt**". See e.g Steiner, 1984: 121ff.)

Certainly there is the fact that we can have strong and elaborate notions of an author's **style** — to the point where one might prepare for writing by training in the styles of others (Joseph Brodsky is a modern case of this classical method, i.e. a case in which this strategy has been placed on record). Such experience of a definite style attests to the "motivated selection" in the verbal art.

But, whether we can bring out the **latent patterning** (Butt, 1988) of such semantic experiences, our experiences as readers depend on the tools, the time, and the theory which we bring to bear on the implicate orders of text; our experiences depend on how far we take the attack on randomness across the higher order, cross textual relations of discourse. In discourse, every choice is connected, just by different orders and degrees of relevance. In verbal art, there are more degrees of order amongst relations which, for most of us in our text making, cannot be recruited to any consistency of semantic purpose. Through 'poiesis', we can see even the quotidian take on an artistic value by being brought into a consistency of organization. The principle of organization can recruit even the profane, the pathological, and the abhorrent, with the discovery involved through such organizations supervening against the cultural negativity of "byt".

Bruce Dawe is renowned for foregrounding and experimentation with Australian vernacular in his poetry. He is a "poet of the spoken voice" (Goodwin, 1986: 220), and this feature, together with his popularity, has lead many critics to question the 'literariness' of his work (e.g Goodwin, 1986, Kuch, 1995, Law, 1979, Martin, 1979, Wallace-Crabbe, 1976, among others). This following poem, first published in 1971 in *Condolences of the Season*, allows us to continue our investigation of aesthetic responses to the contexts of war. What is contrastive here with respect to the sonnet of Auden is that the individuated point of view of a privileged 'caste' (the 'foreign' Oxbridge observer in China in 1938) is not the source of subject matter. As in Browning's well known "My Last Duchess", we are presented with a monologue of a mind out of balance, but an imbalance legitimated by institutions (aristocratic in Browning's poem; military and the misanthropy of an underclass in Dawe).

This poem is a relentless racist and sexist barrage from a drill sergeant, and is reminiscent of Patton's famous speech to the Third Army on the eve of the Allied invasion of France, July 5th 1944 [http://www.pattonhq.com/speech.html]. Patton is reported to have told his nephew: "You can't run an army without profanity; and it has to be eloquent profanity. An army without profanity couldn't fight it's way out of a piss-soaked paper bag." In the Oscar winning portrayal of the general released in 1970, the general's characteristic profanity was censored. [For a contrasting portrayal of a drill sergeant, see Henry Reed's "Naming of Parts", analysed from a stylistic perspective in O'Toole 1988].

In arguing that this poem displays aesthetic organisation, it is useful to cite the term **skaz**, from the Russian word meaning "to tell, relate". The term was adopted by the Russian Formalists to refer to a literary work characterised by the style of the narrator's speech. Thus it is "the orientation, of a special literary-artistic kind, towards the narrative-type of oral monologue; it is the artistic imitation of monologic speech, incorporating narrative plot, and, as it were, constructed as if it were being immediately uttered" (Vinogradov, cited in O'Toole and Shukman, 1977: 26). Vinogradov notes "The writer draws after him a chain of other people's linguistic consciousness, a suite of narrators" (ibid: 19). Dawe served for nine years in the Royal Australian Air Force, and has said of this poem: "I didn't invent the metaphors. They come hot from the lips of the drill instructors we had at Rathmines when I was doing my recruit training in the air force" (http://www.australianbiography.gov.au/dawe/interview4.html, accessed February 20th, 2008).

The image we get of the drill sergeant is an impression created over and beyond the lexis and metaphor. For instance, when the clause to line relation is considered (see Table 4) we can see one basis for the staccato effects. While one long clause (19) extends from lines 11-16, most other clauses are short enough to share a line with at least one other. Five lines of the poem have 3 or more clauses. We can further elaborate this picture when we turn to an analysis of the

Table 4 Bruce Dawe's 'Weapons Training'. Roman numerals indicate line number. Hindu-Arabic numerals indicate clause numbers

	Weapons Training
i.	[1]And when I say eyes right [2]I want [3]to hear
ii.	those eyeballs click and the gentle pitter-patter
iii.	of falling dandruff [4]you there what's the matter
iv.	[5]why are you looking at me [6]are you a queer?
v.	[7]look to your front [8]if you had one more brain
vi.	[9]it'd be lonely [10]what are you laughing at
vii.	[11]you in the back row with the unsightly fat
viii.	between your elephant ears [12] open that drain
ix.	you call a mind [13]and listen [14]remember first
x.	the cockpit drill [15]when you go down [16]be sure
xi.	[17]the old crown-jewels are safely tucked away [18]what could be more
xii.	distressing than to hold off with a burst
xiii.	from your trusty weapon a mob of little yellows
xiv.	only to find back home because of your position
xv.	your chances of turning the key in the ignition
xvi.	considerably reduced? [19]allright now suppose
xvii.	for the sake of argument [20]you've got
xviii.	a number-one blockage [21]and a brand-new pack
xix.	of Charlies are coming at you [22]you can smell their rotten fish-sauce breath hot on the back
xx.	of your stupid neck [23]allright now what
xxi.	are you going to do about it? [24]that's right [25]grab [26]and check
xxii.	the magazine man [27]it's not a woman's tit
xxiii.	[28]worse luck [29]or you'd be set [30]too late you nit
xxiv.	[31]they're on you [32]and your tripes are round your neck
xxv.	[33]you've copped the bloody lot [34]just like I said
xxvi.	[35]and you know [36]what you are? [37]you're dead dead dead

interpersonal features, specifically modality and mood. The poem has only two instances of modality ("could" and "can" in clauses 18, 22), both of ability. There is no modality around probability or obligation, indicating that in the giving of information and demanding of goods and services the business at hand is non-negotiable.

While the single speaker brings out his addressees in his talk, none of their voices is heard. When mood and speech function are considered (see analysis in Table 5 and summary of analysis in Table 6) we find the sergeant's discourse involves questions, statements and commands, and that statements and commands predominate. The statements cluster towards the later part of the poem, and construct for the trainees a deadly roleplay in which they are ultimately

Table 5 Process type, mood and speech function analysis (Weapons Training)

	Clause	Process type	Mood	Speech function
1	when I say eyes right	verbal	-	-
2	I want	mental	declarative	command
3	to hear [[those eyeballs click]] and the gentle pitter-patter of falling dandruff	mental	-	-
4	you there what's the matter	relational (*)	interrogative	question
5	why are you looking at me	behavioural	interrogative	question
6	are you a queer?	relational	interrogative	question
7	look to your front	behavioural	imperative	command
8	if you had one more brain	relational (*)	-	-
9	it'd be lonely	relational	declarative	statement
10	what are you laughing at	behavioural	interrogative	statement/command?
11	you in the back row with the unsightly fat between your elephant ears	-	-	-
12	open that drain [[you call a mind]]	material (*)	imperative	command
13	and listen	behavioural	imperative	command
14	remember first the cockpit drill	mental	imperative	command
15	when you go down	material	-	-
16	be sure	mental	imperative	command
17	the old crown-jewels are safely tucked away	material	-	-
18	what could be more distressing than [[to hold off with a burst from your trusty weapon a mob of little yellows ‖ only to find back home because of your position [[your chances of turning the key in the ignition considerably reduced?]]]]	relational (*)	interrogative	statement
19	allright now suppose for the safe of argument	mental	imperative	command
20	you've got a number-one blockage	relational	-	-

(*Continued*)

Table 5 Cont'd

	Clause	Process type	Mood	Speech function
21	and a brand-new pack of Charlies are coming at you	material	declarative	statement
22	you can smell their rotten fish-sauce breath hot on the back of your stupid neck	behavioural	declarative	statement
23	allright now what are you going to do about it?	material	interrogative	question
24	that's right	-	-	-
25	grab	material	imperative	command
26	and check the magazine man	*mental*	*imperative*	*command*
27	it's not a woman's tit	relational	declarative	statement
28	worse luck	-	-	-
29	or you'd be set	relational	declarative	statement
30	too late you nit	relational	declarative	statement
31	they're on you	relational	declarative	statement
32	your tripes are round your neck	relational	declarative	statement
33	and you've copped the bloody lot	relational	declarative	statement
34	just like I said	verbal	-	-
35	and you know	mental	interrogative	statement
36	what you are?	relational	-	-
37	you're dead dead dead	relational	declarative	statement

Table 6 Mood and speech function analysis (Weapons Training)

mood		speech function	
declarative	10	statement	11
interrogative	7	question	4
imperative	8	command	10

'dead dead dead'. The commands are predominantly expressed via the imperative form. The questions might be considered rhetorical; if they were to be answered, one can easily construct the most likely answer (*Are you a queer? No sir.*). With the exception of the question at clause 23, the questions aim to humiliate.

From an experiential point of view, the sergeant's discourse has an unexpected preoccupation with mental experience: the drill is not based around action. The cohesion analysis is set out in Table 7 (we have included only chains, i.e. meanings with more than one token), and the single most dominant chain is the one around mental experience. There are seven mental processes (see Table 8); but we must note that the five behavioural processes are oriented to mental experience, and that in a further four clauses (4, 8, 12, 18) we find either the Range or Medium is a mental organ (drain, in "open that drain you call a mind") or a feeling ("what could be more distressing..."). In total then, nearly half of the process types construe mental experience. Not only does the material process type represent a small proportion of the total clauses, none of these processes enters into cohesion chains; so no field around material action is built up in the poem. This is the kind of semantic consistency which falls outside of the net of clause analysis (narrowly defined); but which relies on clause analysis, in order to provide evidence of the semantic 'consequences' of choice.

What Dawe appears to be foregrounding, then, is the regulation of mental experience as central to the training of these recruits. In the process of becoming a soldier, as portrayed in Dawe's poem, it is the soldier's mind that is the focus for the drill sergeant, rather than the body. This preoccupation is expressed on a number of levels: the previous paragraph summarises the experiential and textual expressions of this preoccupation. When the findings from the interpersonal and experiential analysis are brought together, our case for claiming that the poem is about the regulation of mind is even clearer: eight of the nine commands are commands over mental experience or behaviour.

Configurations of meaning: conditions of living

Stylistic analysis is defined by its concern for the semantic consequences of linguistic patterns; but it can never be just an analysis of language in a written

Table 7 Cohesion analysis (Weapons Training)

title	weapons	training				
1		say	eyes	right		
2			want			
3			eyeballs			
			hear			
4			matter	there	be	
5			looking		be	
6					be	queer
7			look	front		
8			brain		have	
9			brain		be	
10			lonely			
			laughing	back		
11			unsightly	between		
			ears			
12		call	mind			
13			listen			
14	drill		remember	down		
15						
16			(sure)			
17						cockpit
						crown jewels

Stylistic Analysis: Construing Aesthetic Organisation 213

line													
18	weapon								mob	chances			breath
19		argument	distressing find	home	be	yellows	have	(key)					
20			suppose	position				(ignition)					
21						Charlies					neck	rotten	
22			smell	back		their			pack				
23			stupid										
24													
25	magazine		check		be								
26	magazine							tit					
27					be					luck			
28			nit(wit)	on						set			
29				round	be	they					neck		
30								tripes					
31		said					copped						
32			know	know	be								
33					be							dead	
34												dead	
												dead	

Table 8 Process type summary (Weapons Training)

process type	number	
material	open, go, tuck away, come, do, grab	6
behavioural	look x2, laugh, listen, smell	5
mental	want, hear, be sure, remember, suppose, check, know	7
verbal	say	2
relational	be (11), have (2), cop (1)	14

text or in an individual situation or performance. For this reason, students of linguistics can find the process of stylistic analysis doubly challenging: it soon becomes clear that analysis demands more than the accurate application of linguistic tools. Textual organisation is metonymic with respect to complex cultural configurations which may be, or may not be, explicitly encoded elsewhere in the culture. One has to relate the linguistic analysis to such configurations of lived experience, to the problems of the "**speech fellowship**" living the experience (Firth discussed in Butt 2001: 1809).

This demand on analysts follows from a fundamental distinction, about verbal art, emphasised by the Prague School figure Mukařovský (1977: 9). Verbal art contrasts with other forms of aesthetic activity in that the raw material of verbal art already has the intricate symbolic values (and "valeurs", de Saussure 1978 [1916]: 112ff) of a natural language. Verbal art has been produced by at least two cycles of semantic realizations (see Hasan's representation of symbolic articulation, in Hasan 1971, 1985b). It is as if a sculptor's wood or stone could be read off for the whole history of human cultural evolution; as if the grain or granulations were a code from human prehistory (think here of the deep historical roots of our exchange/mood systems) up to the current act of reading in its ephemeral context. Furthermore, imagine that this implicate order of meanings in wood and stone had then undergone a transformation of purpose — combining craft, culture and change — into a signifier constantly renegotiating its signified with every new reading, with every social configuration supplying new conditions under which a reading takes place.

An axis of relevance has to be established, then, around which analysis and its findings are organised. There may be many dimensions of relevance. But such relevance has to be argued for, and this can be extremely difficult with verbal art, given the two **cycles of semiosis**, the uniqueness of relations across the text, the deeply implicit nature of the themes, and the indirectness of realization between genre, meaning and texture. Verbal art is confined by no single purpose or immediate outcome in the socio-material order of the linguistic community. But it acts on that order. There is an aspect of art, directly related to our estimation of its uniqueness (of expression), which is a catalyst for new states of being and acting — it can create a new contrast between habitual practices of action and conventions of symbolic representation. Again, it was Mukařovský who stressed the way the art drew attention to its own symbolic nature (1977: 68–71; and see the example of Lawrence's "There was no Time, only Space", in Butt 2007: 88ff).

The experience of the world is de-naturalised by this process of noticing, and changing, the symbolic patterns we previously regarded as pre-symbolic in their meaning. There are patterns we take to be so veridical that they are in fact 'nature', or a pre-linguistic demand on the way sense would need to be achieved, the way truth would have to be represented! Against any "cliché" of experience (see Shklovsky 1917: 11–13, as cited in O'Toole and Shukman, 1977: 35; and Stevens 1990 [1957]: 204) a work of verbal art, no matter how conservative in its declared subject matter, cannot help but force its readers into a radical reaction. In the first instance, as suggested above, a text that 'works on us' (albeit in varied ways) brings us closer to noticing the role of symbolic structures in our lives, namely, the power such structures have in directing our experience, even the most apparently determined of our perceptual experiences: vision; hearing; sensations of touch (See Shklovsky on "making strange", in O'Toole and Shukman, 1977: 35). Once we can venture past that first 'notification' of symbols mediating in our moment to moment construals of a world, we have been radicalised irrevocably. No version of the world, no cultural arrangement, no symbolic pattern is beyond reproach, re-evaluation and re-negotiation. From the vastness of space and time to the human roles of family members, our whole psycho-social fabric becomes not just a work in progress but a weave that requires unravellings and new techniques of spinning, for new degrees of plausibility — new images, new practical fictions for measuring out our worlds, for making our futures.

12
Resources and courses

Mick O'Donnell
Universidad Autónoma de Madrid

This chapter provides details of resources for those practicing Systemic Functional Linguistics (SFL), and where to get more information, both in terms of online information sources, and universities where you can study SFL. Subsections include:

1. SFL Information Sites
2. SFL Discussion Lists
3. SFL Bibliographies
4. Electronic & Hardcopy Archives
5. Publishers of SFL Books
6. SFL Friendly Journals
7. SFL Conferences and Summer Schools
8. SFL Seminar Series
9. Associations
10. Systemic Software
11. Courses in SFL
12. Distance Learning

SFL Information Sites

Various websites offer information on various aspects of SFL. Most of the current chapter is available under the ISFLA Systemic Information site (see below):

- *ISFLA Systemic Information site: http://www.isfla.org/Systemics/*
  Comprehensive range of information on all aspects of SFL.
- *ASFLA*: http://www.asfla.org.au/
  The website for the Australian SFL Association offers information about the association itself, and upcoming Australian meetings.

- *Systemic Modelling Group*: http://minerva.ling.mq.edu.au/home.htm
  The website for Christian Matthiessen's group at Macquarie University. The site contains a great deal of information, some out of date. See particularly the Glossary of Systemic terms and their language coding software.
- *Nordic Systemic Website:* http://www.sdu.dk/Om_SDU/Institutter_centre/Isk_sprog_og_kommunikation/Forskning/Forskningsprojekter/Nordisk_SFL.aspx
  An SFL site for the Nordic SFL community.
- *Systemic Functional Room*: http://www2.ocn.ne.jp/%7Eyamanobo
  A Japan-focused SFL information site. Interesting browsing. Includes the JASFL pages (Japanese SFL Association), which provides details of the association, upcoming meetings, publications in Japan, the JASFL journal, etc.
- *LanguageRA*: http://www.languagera.org/
  An SFL site for the Chinese SFL community.
- *SFL New Researchers Network*: http://www.univ-brest.fr/erla/systudy-sfl/
  This site offers information for young researchers in SFL (mainly those doing a Ph.D.), providing links to information sites, resources, and a few interesting articles addressed at new postgraduates. Also information for joining the systudy-sfl discussion list, oriented at new researchers.

Some websites for linguistic descriptions related to SFL:

- *Appraisal Homepage*: http://www.grammatics.com/appraisal/
  Full description of Appraisal theory, and how to join the appraisal discussion list.
- *Critical Discourse Theory*: http://www.discourses.org/
  Teun van Dijk's "Discourse and Society" site.
- *Functional Grammar*: http://www.functionalgrammar.com/
  Information site for Simon Dik's Functional Grammar.
- *Rhetorical Structure Theory* (RST): http://www.sfu.ca/rst
  Information on all aspects of RST, and how to join the RST mailing list.

SFL Discussion Lists

Below are listed the email discussion groups for SFL and related issues. The website given for each entry describes how to join.

- **Sysfling**: http://www.isfla.org/Systemics/Contact/Sysfling.html
  The international discussion group for SFL.
- **Sys-func**: http://listserv.uts.edu.au/mailman/listinfo/sys-func
  A (primarily) Australian-based Systemic discussion group.
- **Systudy-sfl**: http://www.univ-brest.fr/erla/systudy-sfl/
  A discussion list for (mainly) Doctoral students studying SFL.
- **SFL_Education**: http://groups.yahoo.com/group/sfl_education/
  A discussion listserv for educationalists interested in SFL

- **Appraisal Analysis**: http://www.grammatics.com/appraisal/
  A discussion list for those interested in Appraisal Theory.
- **gsfemportugues**: http://br.groups.yahoo.com/group/gsfemportugues/
  An SFL discussion list in Portuguese.
- **JASFL**: http://www2.ocn.ne.jp/~yamanobo/JASFL/jasfl_e_group.html
  A email list used for distribution of announcements of conferences and newsletters in Japan.

SFL Bibliographies

The main listing of SFL publications (articles and books) is available from: http://www.fb10.uni-bremen.de/anglistik/langpro/bibliographies/extract-search.html.

The ISFLA site includes a page listing various bibliographical resources for SFL, see: http://www.isfla.org/Systemics/Print/index.html. This page includes:

- a comprehensive bibliography of Halliday's works;
- a comprehensive bibliography of Jim Martin's works, with links to PDFs;
- a listing of published SFL books;
- links to other SFL bibliographies.

This site also provides some topicalised bibliographies, including:

- *Computational treatments of SFL*;
- *Early Childhood Language and Literacy Development*;
- *SFL treatments of Chinese*;
- *Logogenesis*;

Noboru Yamaguchi provides various bibliographic resources, see: http://www2.ocn.ne.jp/~yamanobo/systemic_bibliography/bibliography.html

Electronic & Hardcopy Archives

The ISFLA Paper and Thesis Archive is an electronic archive of articles and doctoral theses in SFL. Recently, 60 of Jim Martin's articles were added, in PDF format. See: http://www.isfla.org/Systemics/Print/index.html

Geoff Thompson at Liverpool University maintains an archive of SFL articles (on paper). A catalogue will soon be available, and copies of articles will be available by post. The archive was collected by Martin Davies, previously at Stirling University, Scotland, and moved to Liverpool on his retirement.

Liverpool also holds copies of the Nottingham Occasional papers and Nottingham Monographs. The list of available publications and an order form is available from: http://www.isfla.org/Systemics/Print/NottinghamOrderForm1.doc

Publishers of SFL Books

If you are interested in publishing a book in SFL, the following publishers are most relevant:

- **Continuum**: Currently the largest publisher of SFL books. Contact Gurdeep Mattu (gmattu@continuumbooks.com) with your book proposal.
- **Equinox**: Also a major publisher of SFL books. Contact Janet Joyce (jjoyce@equinoxpub.com) with your book proposal.
- **Benjamins**: Contact Paul Peranteau (paul@benjamins.com).
- **Peter Lang**: Their *Linguistic Insights* series have carried some SFL-oriented publications. Contact Maurizio Gotti (maurizio.gotti@unibg.it) to discuss a proposal.

SFL Friendly Journals

The following journals are frequent publishers of SFL-related articles:

- **Functions of Language**: (Benjamins, 2 issues per year). The most SFL oriented of the published journals. See: http://www.benjamins.com/cgi-bin/t_seriesview.cgi?series=FOL
- **English for Specific Purposes**: (Elsevier, 1 issue per year). Strongly SFL. See: http://www.sciencedirect.com/science/journal/08894906
- **Journal of English for Academic Purposes**: (Elsevier, 4 issues a year). See: http://www.elsevier.com/wps/find/journaldescription.cws_home/622440/description
- **Journal of Applied Linguistics** (Equinox, 2 issues a year). Aims at advancing research and practice in Applied Linguistics as a principled and *interdisciplinary* endeavour. See: http://www.equinoxjournals.com/ojs/index.php/JAL
- **Social Semiotics**: (Routledge, 4 issues a year). Papers related to semiotics. See: http://www.tandf.co.uk/journals/journal.asp?issn=1035-0330
- **Critical Discourse Studies**: (Routledge, 3 issues a year). A central journal for CDA. Friendly to SFL work. See: http://www.tandf.co.uk/journals/journal.asp?issn=1740-5904
- **Journal of Literary Semantics**: (de Gruyter, 2 issues a year). Papers on the application of linguistics to literary texts. See: http://www.degruyter.de/journals/jls/detailEn.cfm

- **Text & Talk**: (de Gruyter, 6 issues a year). Focus on Language, discourse, and communication studies. See: http://www.degruyter.de/journals/text/detailEn.cfm
- **Language in Contrast**: (Benjamins, 2 issues a year). Accepts papers in contrastive linguistics. See: http://www.benjamins.com/cgi-bin/t_seriesview.cgi?series=LiC
- **Japanese Journal of Systemic Functional Linguistics**: (Journal of the Japan Association of Systemic Functional Linguistics). See: http://www2.ocn.ne.jp/%7Eyamanobo/JASFL/jasfl_op.html
- **DELTA**: A Linguistics Journal published in Brazil. Leila Barbara is the Editor. Papers are accepted in Portuguese and English. Contact: delta@lael.pucsp.br

SFL Conferences and Summer Schools

Details of conferences and institutes are available from the ISFLA site, giving both a chronological listing of up and coming meetings relevant to SFL, and also a listing of conferences for each of the SFL associations:
   http://www.isfla.org/Systemics/Conferences/index.html
The major SFL meetings are:

- **International Systemic-Functional Congress** (ISFC): location rotates between Europe, Americas, Australia and Asia in a 4 year cycle with occasional variation.
- **European Systemic-Functional Linguistics Conference and Workshop**: held annually in European locations. Contact the current president of ESFLA (see 'Associations') if you are interested in hosting.
- **Australian SFL Conference**: meets every year except when the international meeting is in Australia.
- **Chinese Association of Functional Linguistics**: holds an SFL conference every second year, alternating with an SFL-oriented Discourse Analysis meeting,
- **JASFL Meetings**: The Japanese Association of SFL generally hold two meetings a year, Spring and Autumn.
- **North America**: NASFLA: usually holds a special meeting within other North American linguistics meetings (such as LACUS). See their website for details: http://www.yorku.ca/cummings/nasfla/
- **Latin America**: The Latin American Association of SFL holds meetings roughly every two years, in locations ranging from Mexico to Argentina.
- **LACUS**: The Linguistics Association of Canada and the United States holds an annual meeting, which is very friendly to SFL.

There are also a number of SFL-oriented one-off meetings on particular topics each year, on topics such as "Language, Mind, Brain", Multimodality, World Englishes, etc. See the ISFLA conference page for details.

SFL Seminar Series

A number of weekly or monthly seminar series exist, each session being a talk on a SFL-related topic:

Australia

- **Sydney University Friday SFL Research Seminar**. Location: University of Sydney. Time: 4.00 – 5.30pm, every Friday during semester (except for holidays). Contact: Susan Hood (sue.hood@uts.edu.au).

Austria

- **Austrian SFL discussion group**: The Austrian SFL discussion group holds meetings every semester on the 3rd Friday of every 2nd month. Location: Salzburg, Austria. Contact: Peter Muntigl (peter.muntigl@sbg.ac.at) for details on the time, place and topic of future meetings.

Associations

- **ISFLA** *International SFL Association*:
  Website: http://www.isfla.org/
- **ASFLA** Australian SFL Association
  Website: http://www.asfla.org.au/
- **NASFLA** North American SFL Association
  Website: http://www.yorku.ca/cummings/nasfla/
- **ALSFAL** Asociación de Lingüística Sistémico-Funcional de América Latina (Associação de Linguistica Sistemico-Funcional da América Latina)
  Website: http://www.pucsp.br/isfc/alsfal/
- **ESFLA** European SFL Association
  Website: http://www.esfla.org
- **Nordisk SFL** Nordic Society for Systemic Functional Linguistics
  Website: http://www.sdu.dk/Om_SDU/Institutter_centre/Isk_sprog_og_kommunikation/Forskning/Forskningsprojekter/Nordisk_SFL.aspx

- **JASFL**   Japanese Association of SFL
  Website: http://www2.ocn.ne.jp/%7Eyamanobo/jasfl.html
- **CAFL**   Chinese Association of Functional Linguistics
  Website: http://www.languagera.org
- **AFLSF**   Association Francaise de la Linguistique Systemique Fonctionelle
  Website: http://www.univ-brest.fr/erla/aflsf
- **SYSFLAN**   Systemic Functional Linguistics Association of Nigeria
  Website: http://www.isfla.org/Systemics/Associations/SYSFLAN.html
- **SFLA of India**   Systemic Functional Linguistics Association of India
  Website: http://www.isfla.org/Systemics/Associations/SFLAI.html

Systemic Software

Systemic Annotation Software: There is currently no software available which allows *automatic* analysis using SFL. However, several programs help users to annotate texts according to a Systemic framework. The purpose of such annotation is twofold: firstly, annotating real texts is a good way for students to learn the descriptive categories, as the instances in the text will test their abilities to apply the description. Secondly, an annotated corpus of texts can be used as the basis for statistical studies of texts, for publication purposes. Some systems are described below:

- **Systemics** (Kay O'Halloran and Kevin Judd): This software comes with built-in interfaces to analyse a text in terms of a pre-defined Systemic model of language, including generic structure, clause complexes, and clause structure (clause, group and word). Another interface allows mark-up of reference chains and lexical relations. While the 'grammars' are provided, they can also be modified by the user if required. This tool is limited to analysing single texts, and does not produce statistics. It is thus useful for students learning SFL (or teachers teaching it).
  Platform: Windows, Macintosh, Linux.
  Cost: Roughly US $45
  Website: http://courses.nus.edu.sg/course/ellkoh/Overview.html
- **SysFan** (Canzhong Wu and Christian Matthiessen): SysFan is similar to Systemics, in that it comes with pre-loaded model of language, and the usual user just analyses text according to that model (although experts can change the model). The tool starts off with a segmentation interface, where the user

segments their text into sentences. The user can then open each sentence in another interface, where they further divide the sentence into component clauses, and can assign clause complex structure to these clauses (both structurally, as in relations of α β, 1, 2, 3, etc., and also paradigmatically in terms of the features, e.g., *hypotactic:projection:idea*. The tool then allows each clause to be analysed into Transitivity, Mood and Theme structures (both structurally and paradigmatically). SysFan allows the user to view various profiles over the text, such as what types of processes make up the text, and which participant types they use.
Platform: Windows, MacOS X
Cost: Free.
Website: http://minerva.ling.mq.edu.au/units/tools/

- **UAM CorpusTool** (Mick O'Donnell): CorpusTool takes a different approach to the tools above. While *Systemics* and *SysFan* are oriented towards allowing students to analyse text with standard SFL, CorpusTool is a tool for performing linguistic studies of text (it is more oriented towards the doctoral student than to the beginner). Intentionally, the system does not come with a preloaded language model, but requires the user to specify a coding model of their design, suited to the language phenomena they are exploring. The user specifies multiple layers of analysis (e.g., Document, Sentence, Clause, Group, etc.) and annotates each text at that layer (a 'project' can contain any number of texts). Once the corpus is annotated, the user can search for instances in the corpus, even across layers (e.g., *passive-clause in english*; *finite-clause containing pronoun:subject*). Concordance searching is also possible, using parts of speech. The tool provides a number of statistical reports on the corpus, for instance, contrastive statistics between two subsets, lexical density reports, etc.
  Platform: Windows, MacOS X, Linux
  Cost: Free.
  Website: http://www.wagsoft.com/CorpusTool/index.html

- **RSTTool** (Mick O'Donnell): a tool designed specifically for analysis of texts in terms of Rhetorical Structure Theory (RST).
  Platform: Windows, Linux/Unix.
  Cost: Free.
  Website: http://www.wagsoft.com/RSTTool/index.html

- **MCA** (Anthony Baldry): The *Multimodal Corpus Analysis System* (MCA) allows you to construct a corpus of video or audio files and annotate it in various ways, and then retrieve documents (or parts of) which match a search query.
  Platform: Web-based.
  Website: http://mca.unipv.it/

Software for Drawing System networks: Some tools exist to facilitate the drawing of system networks, which can then be exported into Word documents, or web page formats. Systemic Coder (http://www.wagsoft.com/Coder/) allows graphical editing of system networks, which can then be copy/pasted into Word, or saved in a large number of image formats. UAM CorpusTool (see above) allows graphical editing also, and supports copy/paste as well as save to PDF format.

Other Systemic Software and Resources: Apart from the above, the following systems and resources are valuable:

- **KPML** (John Bateman): a sentence generation system using Systemic Grammar. The system is given a semantic level specification of a sentence and generates corresponding sentence, via a lexico-grammatical structure. See: http://www.fb10.uni-bremen.de/anglistik/langpro/kpml/README.html
- **KPML Grammars** (for various languages): See: http://www.fb10.uni-bremen.de/anglistik/langpro/kpml/genbank/generation-bank.html
- **SysConc** (Canzhong Wu): A Concordancer. See: http://minerva.ling.mq.edu.au/units/tools/
- **The Process Type Database** (Amy Neale): An extensive Excel database of clauses classified by their process type (using Fawcett's classification). Around 5400 verb senses included. See: http://www.itri.bton.ac.uk/%7EAmy.Neale/
- **Glossary of Systemic Terms** (Christian Matthiessen): A comprehensive listing of terms used in SFL and what they mean. See: http://minerva.ling.mq.edu.au/resource/VirtuallLibrary/Glossary/sysglossary.htm

Courses in SFL

Below we list some of the primary centres around the world for studying SFL. For more details and other sites, see:
http://www.isfla.org/Systemics/Courses/index.html

AUSTRALIA

To gain an in-depth education in SFL, the best location by far is currently the Department of Linguistics, *Macquarie University*, Sydney. A large number of SFL courses are offered at all levels, undergraduate and postgraduate, in particular by David Butt. Doctoral courses can also be completed in distance learning mode from overseas. For more information, see: http://www.ling.mq.edu.au/

SFL as we know it today was largely developed by M.A.K. Halliday in the Linguistics Department, *University of Sydney*. Since his retirement, there has been less concentration of SFL taught there. However, Jim Martin continues to teach SFL, teaching three undergraduate courses in functional grammar, discourse semantics, and media discourse. He also offers a masters course on register and genre. See: http://www.arts.usyd.edu.au/departs/linguistics/

The English Department at the *University of New South Wales* offers several SFL-oriented courses, taught by Louise Ravelli and Gillian Fuller. See: http://empa.arts.unsw.edu.au/

For those interested in education, The Faculty of Education, *University of Technology, Sydney* (UTS) offers a range of courses with an SFL orientation (http://www.uts.edu.au/fac/edu/).

In Adelaide, South Australia, *Lexis Education* (http://www.lexised.com) is a company with close ties to education. They offer various professional development courses for teachers in the area of language and literacy, with a focus on ESL. The content is very much in line with genre-based literacy. John Polias and Brian Dare are directors of the company.

EAST AND SOUTH EAST ASIA

China: SFL abounds in China, mainly in the English or Foreign Languages departments. Nearly always courses are at the Masters or Doctoral level. One exception is the English Department at Sun Yat-Sen University, where Huang Guowen and others teach an undergraduate course, as well as four Masters level SFL courses, and one Doctoral level.

In Beijing, *Peking University, Tsinghua University* and *Beijing Normal University* are three of the main sites for studying SFL within their Masters and Doctoral programs. Beijing Normal University has established the Centre of Systemic-Functional Linguistics headed by Peng Xuanwei.

In Shanghai, the main centres for SFL are *Fudan University* and *Shanghai Jiaotong University*.

Other centres throughout China are *Ocean University*, Qingdao, under Prof. Zhang Delu; *Xiamen University*, under Prof. Yang Xinzhang; and *Suzhou University*.

Hong Kong: The Department of Chinese, Translation and Linguistics at *City University of Hong Kong* offers courses which are SFL-centred or SFL-oriented. Jonathan Webster, the head of department, is also director of the Halliday Centre, which is a research centre into matters related to SFL, offering frequent seminars.

Christian Matthiessen, previously at Macquarie University, Sydney, heads the Department of English at *The Hong Kong Polytechnic University*. His colleagues in the Department already offer an established programme of courses in SFL, especially in the contexts of ELT, corpus studies and professional communication.

Japan: Terry Royce teaches SFL and multimodality as part of his discourse analysis course in the MA Program at Teachers College, *Columbia University*.

Singapore: The Department of English Language & Literature at the *National University of Singapore* offers courses in SFL and multimodal analysis. Kay O'Halloran runs the Multimodal Analysis Lab, a university-level research centre specialising in systemic functional approaches to multimodal analysis, and scholarships are available for doctoral students.

EUROPE

Denmark: The Institute of Language and Communication in the *University of Southern Denmark* is a centre of SFL teaching and research, with eight faculty with an interest in SFL, including Uwe Helm Petersen and Thomas Andersen. Classes are given in English, Danish and German.

France: The Department of English at the *Université de Bretagne Occidentale*, offers some English courses, and David Banks is available to supervise doctoral students.

Germany: John Bateman in the English Department at *University of Bremen* teaches courses with SFL orientation. Given his central role in computational linguistics, this would also be an ideal place for a Ph.D. in computational linguistics.

The Department of Applied Linguistics, Translating and Interpreting at the *Saarland University* is another centre for SFL in Germany. A team led by Erich Steiner teach and research in linguistic issues of translation. A strong research presence makes this a good place to study, particularly if you are interested in translation or computational linguistics.

At the *Technische Universität Darmstadt*, Elke Teich and others teach English Linguistics and Computational Linguistics from an SFL standpoint, and have strong interests in representational issues in SFL.

Italy: The English Language Studies Program at the *University of Bolognia* offers extensive undergraduate training in SFL, including courses such as "Introducing Functional Grammar" and "Exploring Functional Grammar".

For those interested in studying multimodality in an SFL framework, alternatives include *Trieste University* (Chris Taylor) and *Pavia University* (Anthony Baldry).

Spain: Largely due to the teaching of Angela Downing in Madrid, Spain has a strong SFL presence in the English Departments of many universities. Angela Downing has retired, but the *Universidad Complutense de Madrid* still has a strong SFL orientation, with many SFL-influenced courses. See: http://www.ucm.es/info/fingl/

Close by, the English Department at the *Universidad Autónoma de Madrid* is also strongly systemic, with 6 teaching staff who are Systemicists by training. Most of the linguistic courses in the undergraduate degree are SFL influenced. For doctoral studies, staff have expertise in ESL, contrastive studies, critical discourse, etc. See: http://www.uam.es/departamentos/filoyletras/filoinglesa/

UK: SFL started in the UK. Most of the first generation who studied under Halliday while he was in Edinburgh or London have retired; however, a new generation are taking their places.

At *Liverpool University*, the School of English is a major centre of SFL in the UK. Geoff Thompson is one of the leaders of the new generation of SFL, and he and others offer various courses with SFL content, particularly at the MA level. Michael Hoey also teaches in the department, a major figure in discourse studies. There is also a strong emphasis on Corpus Linguistics, represented by Mike Scott (developer of WordSmith) and Michaela Mahlberg.

The Department of English at *Birmingham University* is another major centre, represented by Michael Toolan, Susan Hunston, and others. Many of the courses have an SFL orientation. Corpus Linguistics is strong here.

The Centre for Language and Communication, in the Department of English, Communication and Philosophy at *Cardiff University* was until recently the home of prominent Systemicists, Robin Fawcett and Gordon Tucker (both retired), Lise Fontaine and Tom Bartlett continue to teach SFL courses.

MIDDLE EAST

Israel: Jonathan Fine at *Bar-Ilan University* has researched extensively into the relationship between language and psychiatric disorders, based on Systemic theory. He is available to supervise dissertations in this area, and teaches one undergraduate course in the area.

AMERICAS

Canada: The English Department at *Glendon Campus, York University* was one of the major centres of SFL in the world. In the 1960s, Michael Gregory became head of department, and was soon joined by Jim Benson, Michael Cummings and Bill Greaves. Gregory is now retired and the others are teaching one SFL course per year. However, between them they trained a new generation of Systemicists, who are teaching around Canada, including Elissa Asp (Department of English, *Saint Mary's University*, Halifax), Glenn Stillar (*University of Waterloo*), and Lynne Young (*Carleton University*, Ontario).

On the western side of the country, SFL has a strong presence in Vancouver. At the *University of British Columbia*, prominent Educationalist Geoff Williams is Head of the Department of Language & Literacy Education. Jessica deVilliers is in the English department, and teaches several SFL-influenced courses. At *Simon Fraser University*, Maite Taboada teaches a discourse analysis course.

United States: Because of the dominance of Chomskyan linguistics in the States, SFL has been slow to penetrate here. However, interest is growing. The School of Education at the *University of Michigan* runs an undergraduate program which is SFL in orientation (courses by Mary J. Schleppegrell and Jay Lemke). There are also a number of graduate students applying SFL.

At *UC Davis*, Cecilia Colombi teaches SFL courses within the Spanish department, at undergraduate and graduate levels.

Heidi Byrnes in the German Department at *Georgetown University* has been pushing the Genre-based literacy approach in a U.S. context, and teaches Language Education.

Brazil: A team at the *Catholic University of Sao Paulo*, lead by Leila Barbara teach a number of SFL courses, at least one or two per semester at Graduate level. SFL sometimes enters undergraduate courses as part of Linguistic Theory.

Distance Learning

Various courses in SFL can be taken in distance mode. In Australia, Macquarie University offers

- **Macquarie University** (Sydney, Australia): The Linguistics Department Macquarie offers 16 postgraduate degrees (both MA and Ph.D.) in distance mode, including programs in applied linguistics, communication in professions and organisations, speech and language processing and TESOL. Currently, over 400 students are taking these courses in over 30 countries.
- **University of Sydney** (Australia): The Department of Linguistics offers an "offshore" Master of Applied Functional Linguistics for off-shore delivery at Sun Yat-Sen University in Guangzhou, China. This includes 2 courses by Jim Martin, teaching Functional grammar and Discourse Semantics.
- **Open University** (UK): The Open University offers distance teaching at both undergraduate and postgraduate levels, with degrees in Applied Linguistics, English Language and Literature, and Modern Language Studies. The SFL courses can also be taken as part of a diploma or as free standing modules. All courses are available in European Union countries and Switzerland, and the MA courses (with electronic tutoring) are available globally. For more information, see:
http://www.isfla.org/Systemics/Courses/UK.html#ou

Web-based SFL Courses

Christian Matthiessen has taught various SFL summer schools and institutes. The web-pages resulting from these courses contain valuable learning resources. See:

http://web.mac.com/cmatthie/iWeb/SMMG_resources/SMMG_Courses.html

Keywords

1 Theory
2 Architecture
3 System$_1$
4 System$_2$
5 Structure (/ system)
6 Structure (/ syntagm)
7 Realization
8 Rank; rank scale
9 Semiotic & semantic
10 Semogenesis
11 Context
12 Cohesion
13 Expression
14 Acoustics
15 Complexity
16 Metaphor
17 Variation; register & genre
18 Text & discourse
19 Communication disorders
20 Corpus
21 Computational linguistics
22 Base
23 Probability
24 Function

Theory

A scientific theory is a system of interrelated concepts designed to describe and explain a particular class of phenomena, to which it connects by (some combination of) deductive and inductive reasoning (sometimes referred to as "abduction"). The reach of a theory may be a general domain (like language) or any specialized region within it (like phonology or language disorders); from the theory are derived (i) methods of analysis and description and (ii) hypotheses – predictions about what holds true, and which may or may not turn out right. The theory includes a metalanguage whose terms are mutually defining (the metalanguage may employ words in daily use, but if so these are not constrained by their everyday senses and definitions).

A theory of language describes the "architecture" of language, setting up parameters, or dimensions, which together seek to explain how language works. These theoretical categories are features of language as such, and therefore valid for all human languages; they are distinct from the categories used in description, which are set up for each language and so enable languages to be compared and typologized. The scope of a description may be particular (to one language), comparative (across two or more languages) or typological (setting up systemic and structural "types" of any component of language).

The theory of language is called "linguistics". On this analogy, writers in SFL often use "grammatics" for theory of grammar, to avoid the ambiguity in the word "grammar" which is commonly used both for the phenomenon itself and for the study of that phenomenon.

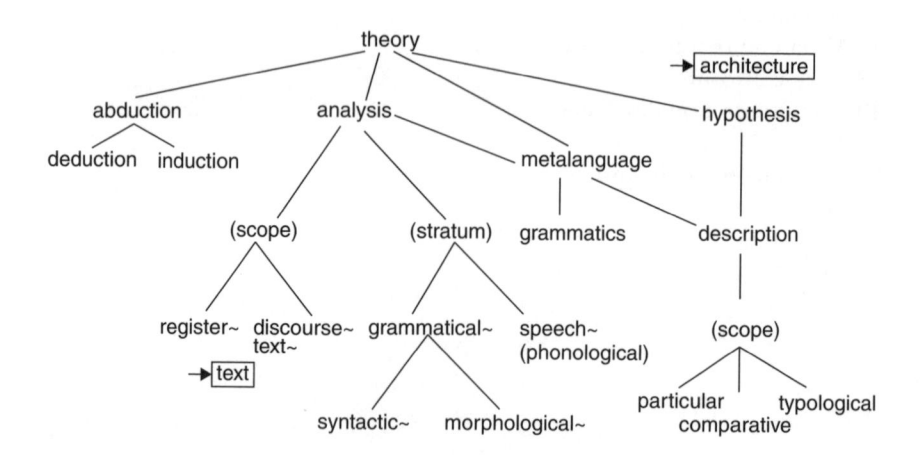

```
                              theory
                             /  |  \                    →│architecture│
            abduction    analysis               ─── hypothesis
           /        \      / | \
      deduction  induction /  |  \── metalanguage
                          /   |    
                      (scope) (stratum)  grammatics    description
                       / \     / \                        |
               register~ discourse~ grammatical~ speech~  (scope)
                         text~       / \     (phonological) / \
                        →│text│    /   \                particular  typological
                              syntactic~ morphological~   comparative
```

Architecture

In SFL language is described, or "modelled", in terms of several dimensions, or parameters, which taken together define the "architecture" of language. These are (i) the hierarchy of strata (context, semantics, lexicogrammar, phonology, phonetics; related by realization); (ii) the hierarchy of rank (e.g. clause, phrase/group, word, morpheme; related by composition); (iii) the cline of instantiation (system to instance); (iv) the cline of delicacy (least delicate to most delicate, or grossest to finest); (v) the opposition of axis (paradigmatic and syntagmatic); (vi) the organization by metafunction (ideational (experiential, logical), interpersonal, textual).

Different applications of linguistics demand attention to many different aspects and features of language. Multidimensional modelling is a way of managing the complexity of language so that particular problems can be identified and strategies devised for observing happenings, analysing data, and interpreting the relevant findings.

Descriptive work, particular or comparative, typically involves "shunting": shifting perspective by moving "up and down", or "along", one or other of these dimensions. Shunting along the cline of instantiation means shifting the perspective between system and text; on the principle of "abduction", the move from system to text can be validated against the findings of text analysis, and the analysis by matching up with the description of the system.

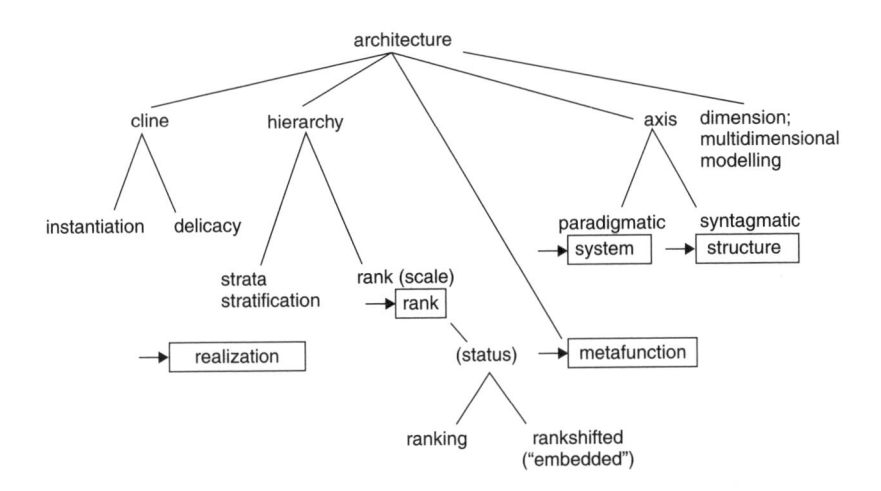

System₁

System (in the sense of system₁) is the organizing concept for modelling paradigmatic relations in language. A paradigm is a set of forms which share a common environment, like the set of English finite verbal operators *can/ could/ may/ might/ shall/ should/ will/ would/ must/ ought/ need/ dare*. Underlying these are several systems of contrasting features ("terms"), such as VALUE: high (*must...*) / median (*will...*) / low (*may...*); ORIENTATION: subjective (*must...*) / objective (*certainly...*), and others, together making up the system network of MODALITY; and also features from the system network of TENSE.

Each system in grammar and phonology has its point of origin at a particular structural rank. A set of related systems is modelled as a system network; the systems are related to each other by simultaneity and dependence along the scale of delicacy. Each system has an entry condition (its location in the network), a small set of mutually exclusive terms (many are binary, but this is not a necessity), together with the realization of each term in the linguistic structure.

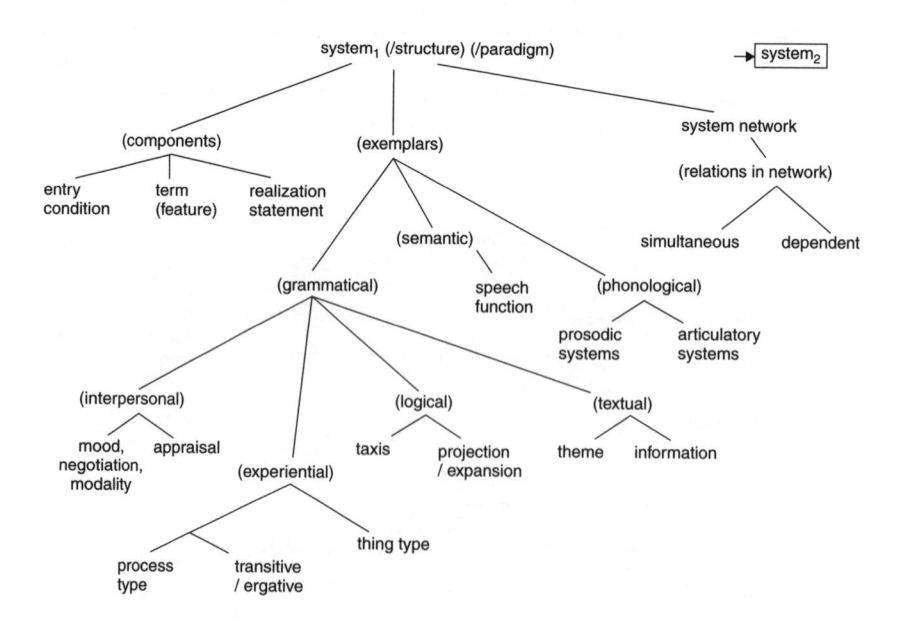

System$_2$

The term "system" is extended to be applied to language as a whole (the linguistic system), in the opposition (language as) system / (language as) text. System$_2$ and text are related by instantiation: the text is the observable instance of the underlying systemic potential.

In this sense, system relates to general systems theory. Language can be characterized as a complex dynamic system, one that persists through constant change in interaction with its (eco-social) environment. It belongs to the class of semiotic systems (systems of meaning), in contrast with systems of other kinds, physical, biological and social.

System$_1$ and system$_2$ are in fact the same concept, though operating on a different scale. In both cases the system is the (representation of the) potential that inheres in a given set of phenomena. These systems have all evolved; evolved systems contrast, in turn, with designed systems, which have been brought into being to explain (and sometimes to control) some realm of human experience. A scientific theory is a designed system of this kind.

Usually, "system" is used to cover system-&-process: the system, together with the processes that derive from (or "realize") it in real or virtual time.

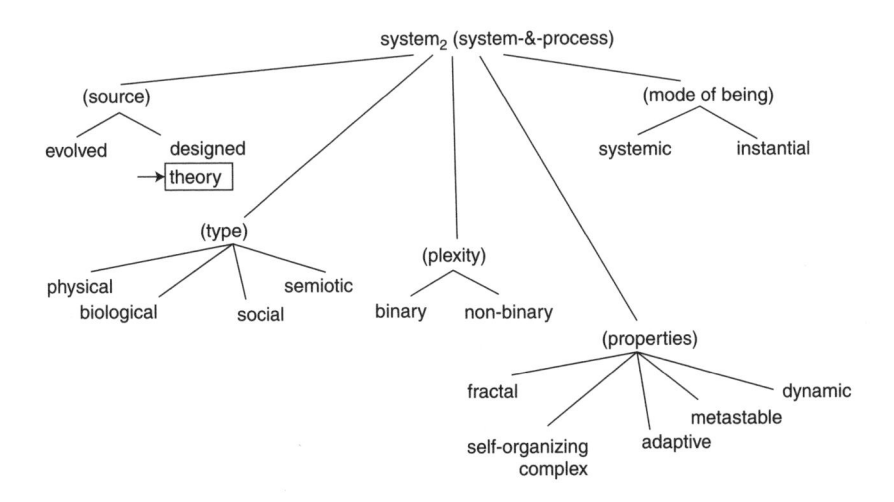

```
                        system₂ (system-&-process)
        ┌──────────────┬──────┬──────┬──────────────┐
    (source)                                   (mode of being)
    ┌─────┴─────┐                              ┌────┴────┐
  evolved   designed                       systemic  instantial
              →│theory│
              (type)              (plexity)
        ┌──────┼──────┐          ┌────┴────┐
     physical      semiotic    binary   non-binary
        biological  social                    │
                                         (properties)
                                    ┌────┬────┼────┬────┐
                                 fractal            dynamic
                                                metastable
                                  self-organizing  adaptive
                                     complex
```

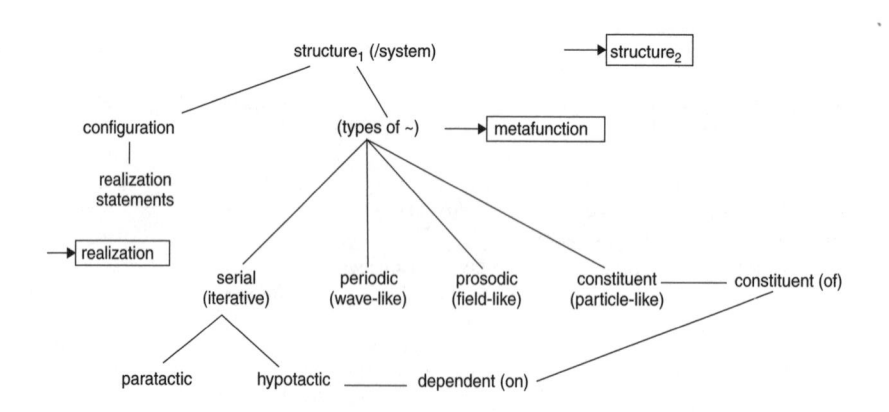

Structure (/ system)

Structure is the organizing concept for modelling syntagmatic relations in language, in contrast to system, which models paradigmatic relations (see "System"). Each rank in grammar and phonology is the locus of structural configurations, each of which is specified in the realization statements associated with the systemic features.

Structural configurations have traditionally been represented in constituency (part/whole) terms; but not all structures are formed of clearly defined parts. This varies with the metafunction: experiential ones typically are, but interpersonal structures tend to be prosodic, with unclear boundaries, while textual ones tend to be periodic, creating an ebb and flow of discursive prominence. But since these configurations get integrated into a linear syntagm, they can all be (and conventionally have been) reduced to a constituency model.

Logical structures are serial in nature, formed by building up a unit "complex" (such as a clause complex) as a sequence in which each pair (each "nexus") is related either paratactically (with the two having equal status) or hypotactically (with one dependent on the other). Dependency, where clause *b* is dependent on clause *a*, is distinct from constituency, in which (as happens in rank shift) clause *b* is a constituent of clause *a* (see "Rank; rank scale").

Structure (/ syntagm)

A syntagm is a string of classes, in grammar or phonology, such as (grammatical) nominal group + verbal group + prepositional phrase, as in the clause *the sun was shining on the sea*. Underlying this string are several structures, deriving from different metafunctions; these are represented as configurations of elements, such as (i) Actor • Process • Location (experiential), (ii) Theme • Rheme (textual), (iii) Subject • Finite • Predicator • Adjunct (interpersonal). The functional labels show the part played by each element in the configurations as a whole; they do not specify the sequence in which they occur. The same principle applies in logical structures, where the structural elements are those of the (paratactic or hypotactic) nexus, such as Dominant • Dependent (system of taxis), Projecting • Projected, or (e.g.) Effect • Cause (system of logical semantic relations).

In phonology a syntagm of strong syllable + weak syllable(s) may realize a structure of Ictus • Remiss in the foot; a syntagm of consonant + vowel + consonant may realize a structure of Onset • Rhyme in the syllable.

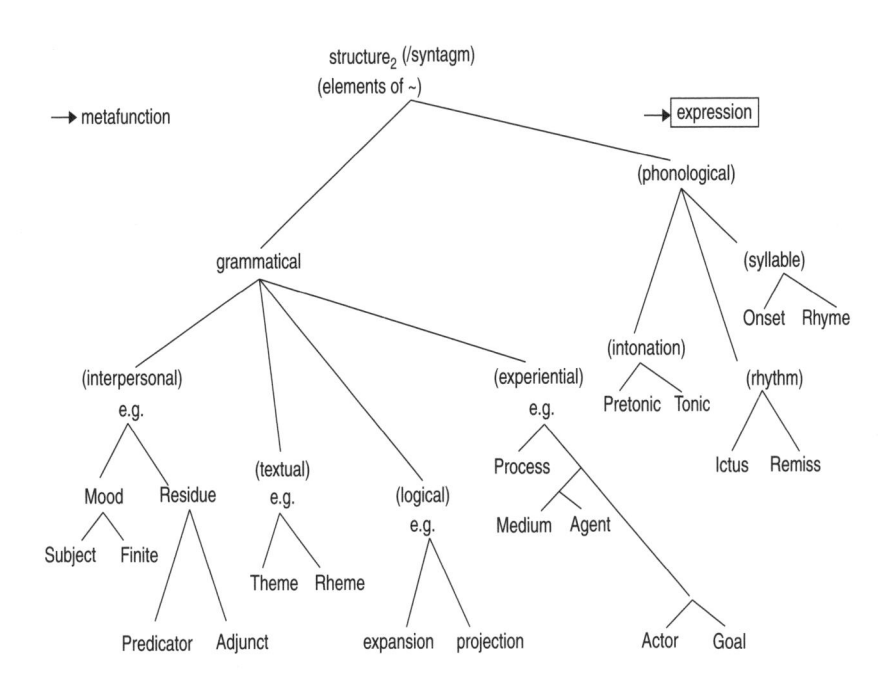

Realization

Realization is the general name for the relation among the strata of a semiotic system (including language). In SFL theory, the strata form a hierarchy (context / semantics / lexicogrammar / phonology / phonetics) such that each stratum is said to "be realized by" the one below, and to "realize" the one above. In a realizational system, the relation between strata is one of token and value (or "signifier" and "signified"), as opposed to a causal system, in which the relation is one of cause and effect.

Sometimes, following Hjelmslev, semantics and lexicogrammar are grouped together as the "content plane", phonology and phonetics as the "expression plane". The nature of the realization relation can be made more specific by saying that the context "activates" the strata of content, while the content strata "construe" the context, with "realize" referring particularly to the relation between content and expression.

By a further step, when we focus on the relation between semantics and lexicogrammar (within the content plane), we see a difference according to the metafunction. Ideationally, the term "construe" is appropriate – the lexicogrammar construes the semantics and, through this, the context (the lexicogrammar as "construal of experience"). But interpersonally, the role of the content strata is more active; they "enact" our personal and social relationships (lexicogrammar as "enactment of the social process"). Sometimes the third member of the triad is picked out by saying that, textually, the lexicogrammar "creates" or "presents" the patterns of discourse.

The term "realization" is also used intrastratally, to refer to the relation between system (systemic feature) and structure, e.g. "passive in material process clause realized by the conflation of Goal / Subject", and between structure and syntagm, e.g. "Subject realized by nominal group". In the context of text generation, these constitute intermediate links in the realizational chain.

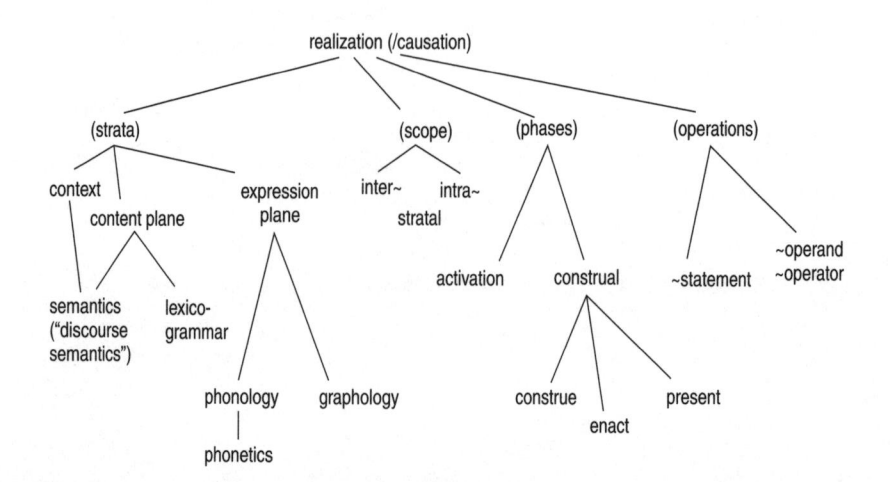

Rank; rank scale

Structure in lexicogrammar and in phonology is modelled in SFL as a scale of rank: a hierarchy in which a unit of any rank consists of one or more units of rank next below: a tone unit of one or more feet, a group of one or more words, and so on.

The reason for modelling structure this way (rather than as an indefinite number of "immediate constituents") is systemic: each rank is the point of origin for a particular system or set of systems.

A typical rank scale for these two strata is shown in the figure; this gives a good account of English and many other languages.

Each unit may, in principle, be expanded into a unit complex (clause complex, group complex & c.) having the same value in structure as the simple unit. Some larger units in grammar may be "rankshifted", embedded inside the structure of another unit of the same rank as, or of lower rank than, themselves; a "ranking" unit is one which has not undergone such rank shift.

Semantic structure may be modelled in various ways: either as specific (to one metafunction, or to one register or genre) or as generalized to all; with orientation either to the context or to the lexicogrammar; with or without a clearly defined concept of rank.

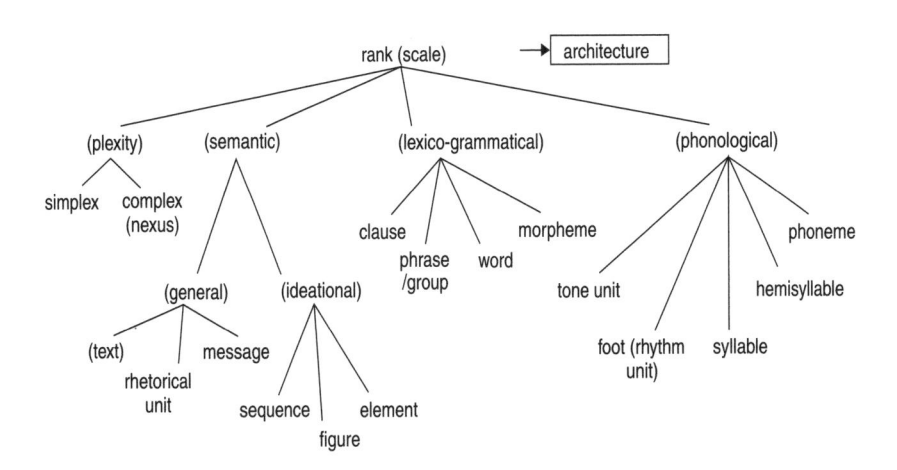

Semiotic & semantic

Semiotic means 'having to do with meaning ("semiosis")'. A semiotic system is any system of meaning; it constrasts with a material system, or system of matter. Semantic means 'having to do with meaning in language'; hence the semantic stratum – the stratum specifically concerned with the organization of meaning in language.

Semiotic systems other than language include (i) systems evolved by other species, like the Bonobo, and (ii) other human systems: systems of signs, such as maps, figures, diagrams; images of all kind; visual arts; music – any set of phenomena that functions as a system of meanings. A multimodal text is one that combines language with one or more other semiotic modalities.

A "semogenic" system is one which creates meaning. Language is a semiotic of this type; so are the visual and musical arts; but not, for example, a system of signs like traffic lights, which is semiotic but not semogenic.

Both semantic and semiotic are used to refer to changes in meaning ("semantic drift", "semiotic current") and to meaning modelled in topological terms ("semantic space", "semiotic dimension"). A meaning that is topologically defined is said to have a semiotic address.

The term "meaning potential" refers to the total reach of a semiotic system. Applied to language it usually refers to language as a whole; where "potential" is being used as specific to one stratum, "wording potential", "sounding potential", there "meaning potential" refers just to the stratum of semantics.

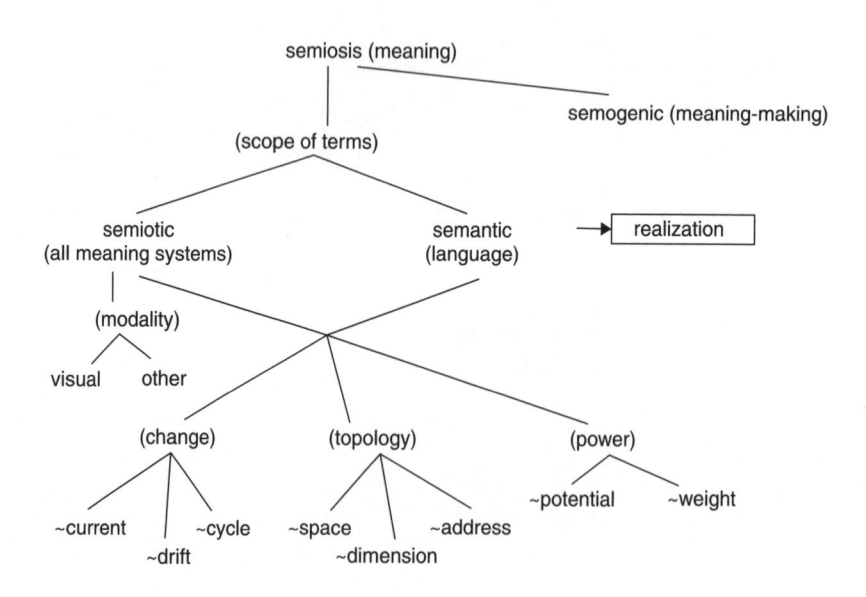

Semogenesis

The growth of meaning follows three trajectories through time. (1) The growth of the system of language is a process of evolution, with constant change in interaction with the eco-social environment. (2) The growth of the speaker is a process of development, with growth, maturation and decay through infancy, childhood, adulthood, senility and death. (3) The growth of the text is a process of "individuation", the unfolding of a particular instance of spoken or written discourse.

Within (2), the child proceeds through phases, beginning with protolanguage (phase of primary consciousness; meaning not yet referential); then a transition (emergence of stratal organization, with lexicogrammar and phonology); then the mother tongue (phase of higher-order consciousness; meaning based on reference).

The scope of referential meaning, in turn, expands through three stages: first generalization (naming classes of phenomena), then abstractness (construing abstract referents), and then metaphor (reconstruing by cross-coupling between semantics and lexicogrammar).

Adult language incorporates all phases and stages of its history, from protolinguistic interjections onwards.

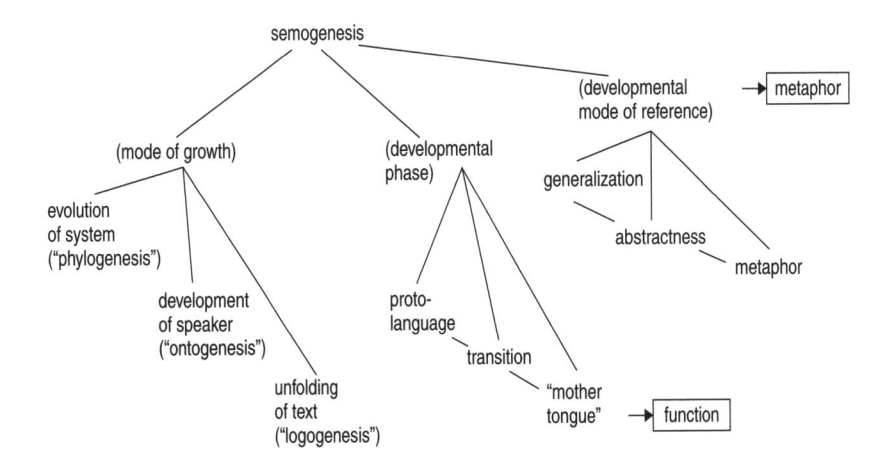

Context

The context is the extralinguistic environment in which language operates, as spoken or written discourse. In SFL, context is modelled as a stratum in the linguistic hierarchy, "above" (i.e. realized by) the stratum of semantics.

The "context of situation" is the environment of the text. It is described in terms of the three variables of field of discourse, tenor of discourse and mode of discourse: what's going on – the domain of the social action; who are taking part – the social positioning of the interactants; and how the text is involved – the mode of contact for the actors in the discourse event. The "immediate" context is distinguished into the "material situational setting", which is the concrete environment of the instance, and the "relevant" context, the features of which determine the "contextual configuration". This is an abstract construct relating the instance to the underlying potential of the system.

The "context of culture" is the environment of the linguistic system. The situation is thus being interpreted as the instantiation of the culture, analogous to the text as instantiation of the language system. In the perspective from the "system" end, we can recognize sub-cultural constructs: the institutions and domains of action of the culture. These provide the context for sub-systems in the language, the functional varieties that we recognize as contextually activated registers and genres.

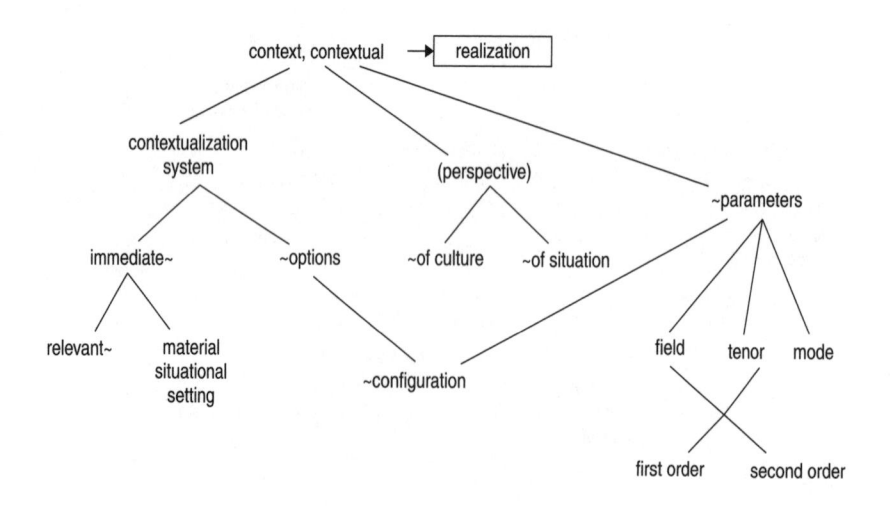

Cohesion

Cohesion is the semantic force, or rather the set of semantic forces, which hold a text together beyond the reach of grammatical structure.

The resources which create cohesion are partly grammatical and partly lexical. The grammatical resources are reference, ellipsis (including substitution) and conjunction. The lexical resources are the taxonomic relations (synonymy / antonymy, hyponymy, meronymy) and collocation. Each instance of cohesion in a text is called a "cohesive tie".

Cohesive harmony is the deployment of cohesive resources in a text such as to create patterns of ideational or interpersonal continuity; for example, where two parties in a referential chain maintain a particular set of relations in transitivity over a sustained sequence of clauses. It is cohesive harmony that gives "texture" to a text, particularly where such patterns of continuity overlap.

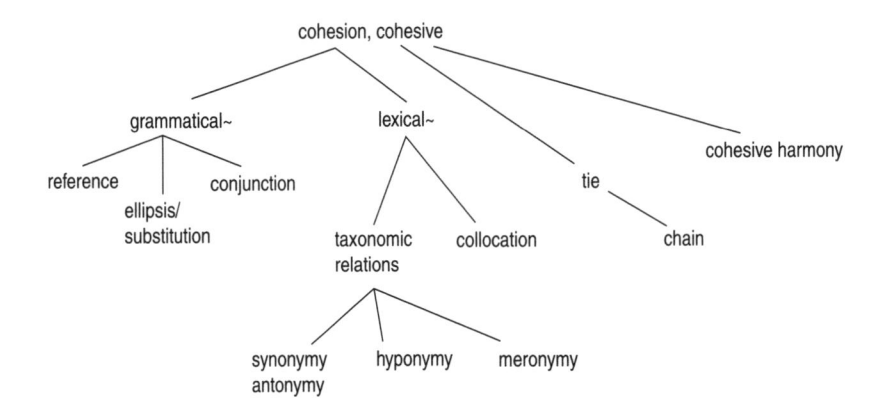

Expression

The resource for the expression plane in language is the human body, with the organs of speech and hearing, of motor control and of seeing, operating under the direction of the brain. The body in this context is referred to as the "signifying body".

The organs of speech are those of articulation and prosody, together with the airstream mechanisms, pulmonic and glottalic. These phonetic resources are systemized by the phonology into the sound patterns of each particular language.

The dynamic potential of the body is also brought into service in the paralinguistic patterns of gaze, gesture and other bodily movement, which are ancillary to speaking and listening.

The written mode of expression ("graphology") involves the body in producing written symbols by some means or other, manual or mechanical, and receiving them through saccadic movements of the eyes.

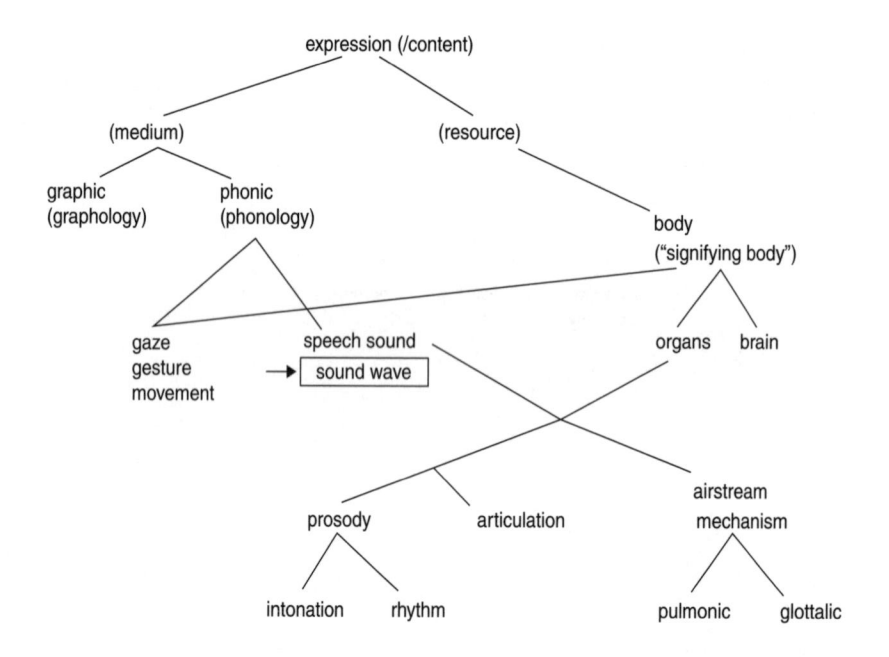

Acoustics

Acoustic analysis is the analysis of sound waves; in the context of linguistics, this means sound waves produced in speech. The wave form in displayed visually in a spectrogram; this shows the frequency, amplitude and duration of any selected stretch of the speech signal over some period in real time.

These features are what are perceived by the listener as pitch, loudness and length, including the rhythmic pulse that provides the underlying "beat" of the language. The relation between the acoustic parameters and the listener's perception is highly complex, especially in relation to the prosodic features of intonation and rhythm.

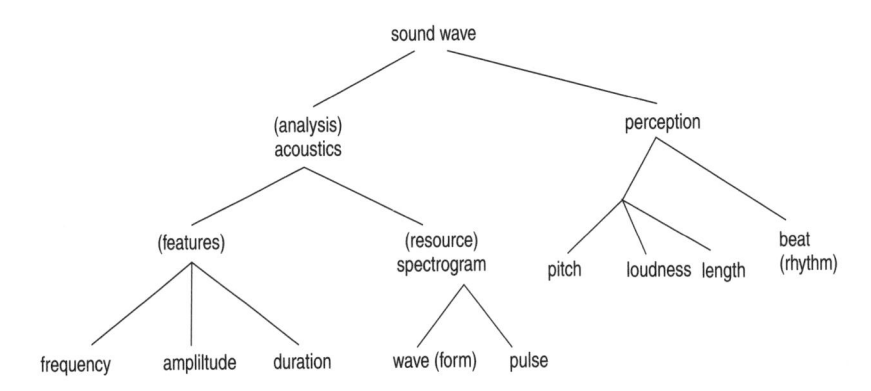

```
                        sound wave
                       /          \
              (analysis)          perception
              acoustics            /  |  \  \
              /        \          /   |   \   beat
        (features)  (resource)  pitch loudness length (rhythm)
        / | \      spectrogram
       /  |  \       /    \
frequency amplitude duration wave (form) pulse
```

Complexity

Complexity in language takes various forms, which have evolved as language itself evolved, in construing human experience and enacting social relationships that themselves were becoming increasingly complex. Linguistic categories tend to be:

- indeterminate, or "fuzzy" (e.g. classes with a hard core and fuzzy edges)
- continuous ("clines") rather than discrete (e.g. lexis and grammar)
- multivalent, with ambiguities (this or that) and blends (this and that)
- hidden ("cryptotypic"), with latent patterning and "implicate order" (e.g. symbolic articulation in literary texts)
- fractal, reappearing at several levels and locations
- quantitative, based on probability rather than certainty
- complementary (e.g. complexity as density in lexis, intricacy in grammar)

Other strategies include systems of marking (unmarked (or "default") / marked) coupling (congruent / metaphorical), prominence (backgrounded / foregrounded).

These have evolved as language's way of managing the complexity of the human condition, with what is called "unconscious design". The categories themselves are "ineffable" (they cannot be exhaustively identified or defined in language). Each language (or language area) has its characteristic ways of meaning, or "semantic style", deriving from the particular assemblage in which these resources are deployed.

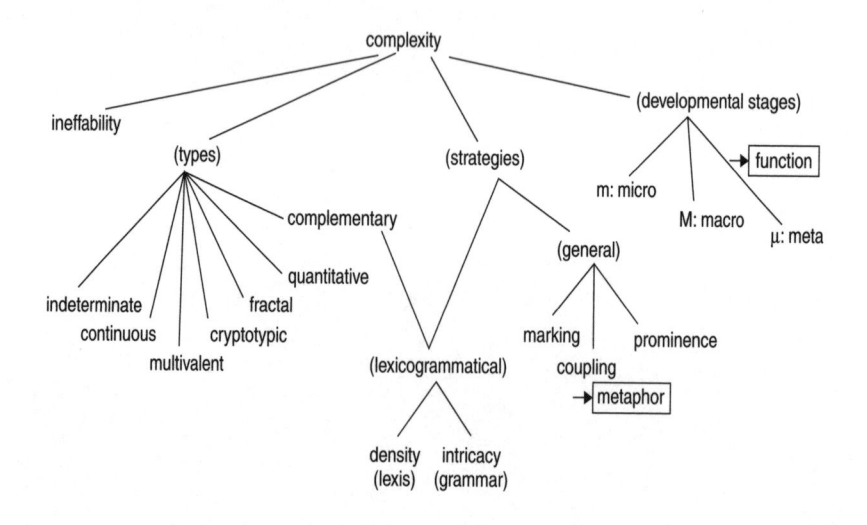

Metaphor

Metaphor is a cross-coupling between the semantics and the lexicogrammar, whereby a meaning that is congruently expressed by wording *a* is expressed instead by wording *b*. In rhetoric and stylistics, "metaphor" is restricted to lexical metaphor, where *a* and *b* are lexical items. In SFL this is extended to include grammatical metaphor, where *a* and *b* are grammatical classes and/or ranks, e.g. (congruent) *farms produce(d) wheat*, (metaphorical) *farm wheat production*. Grammatical metaphor features in both ideational and interpersonal metafunctions.

When children develop language, they first master congruent forms of wording, and only later move on to the metaphorical. The three critical steps are (i) generalization (from "proper" to "common"); (ii) abstractness (from concrete to abstract); (iii) metaphor (from congruent to metaphorical). Full control of metaphorical modes of meaning is only attained in adolescence.

Metaphor involves semantic junction, whereby new meanings are construed from the combination of *a* and *b*; e.g. *production* is both a process (from the congruent form *produce*) and an entity (from its metaphorical form as a noun) – in other words, it is a virtual entity, which "exists" as an abstract tool for thinking with.

Grammatical metaphors typically occur in "syndromes"; e.g. *decreased grain production leads to the possibility of food shortages*, where every element has undergone a metaphoric shift; compare the more congruent version *less grain is being produced, so food may become scarce*. This clustering of interdependent features is what produces the characteristic style of a contemporary written text.

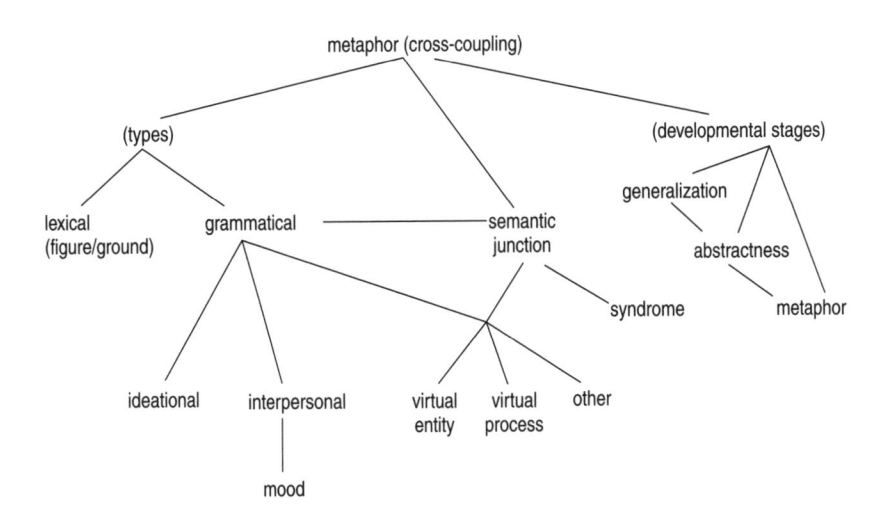

Variation; register & genre

Language changes over time (diachronic variation). Language also varies at any one time (synchronically), in two ways: according to the user (dialectal variation) or according to the use (functional, or diatypic, variation). This functional variation takes the form of different registers and genres.

A register is a text type seen from the "system" end, as a functionally motivated subsystem within a language that is characterized by a "general (or "generalized") structure potential and by distinctive (usually quantitative) patterns of selection within the lexicogrammar and semantics. The register range (or "repertoire") is the total register variation known to a given individual or community.

A genre is a higher-level grouping of texts having the same compositional structure ("generic structure"), corresponding to rhetorical categories of procedural, expository, narrative and so on. The structure is specified in terms of a sequence of elements each having a distinct function with respect to the whole and each characterized by particular lexicogrammatical features. Compositional concepts such as "phase-&-transition", "main point" and "method of development" are understood in explicit linguistic terms through the methods of discourse analysis.

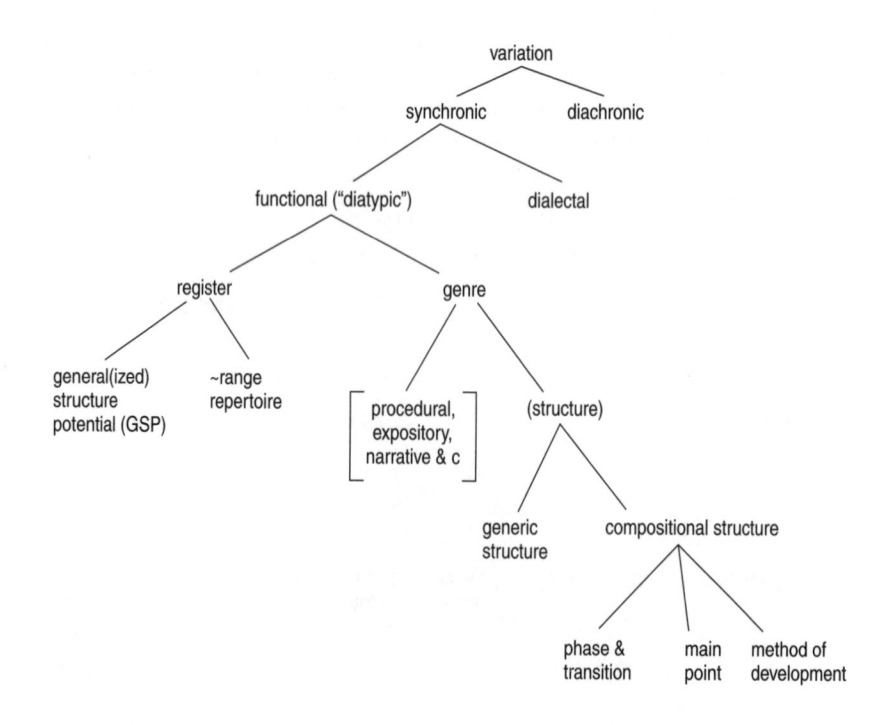

Text and discourse

These two terms refer to the same thing, but with a difference of emphasis. Discourse is text that is being viewed in its sociocultural context, while text is discourse that is being viewed as a process of language. "Text analysis" and "discourse analysis" suggest somewhat different priorities, although the two are often used interchangeably.

Multimodal (or "multisemiotic") discourse is text which uses some other semiotic modality or modalities as well as language. Such texts draw on a range of multimodal resources, and call for special modes of transcription and analysis.

Hypertext is text which is assembled in computational form, typically in various formats and modalities; it contains multiple sources of information on some given topic or issue, and is designed to be accessed and "mined" from many angles and along many lines of enquiry.

Intertextuality refers to the dependence of one text upon others, where in order to understand the full import of the text you need to be aware of its semiotic "history" – the (often hidden) dialogue it is engaging in with another text or texts, or even with a whole discursive tradition.

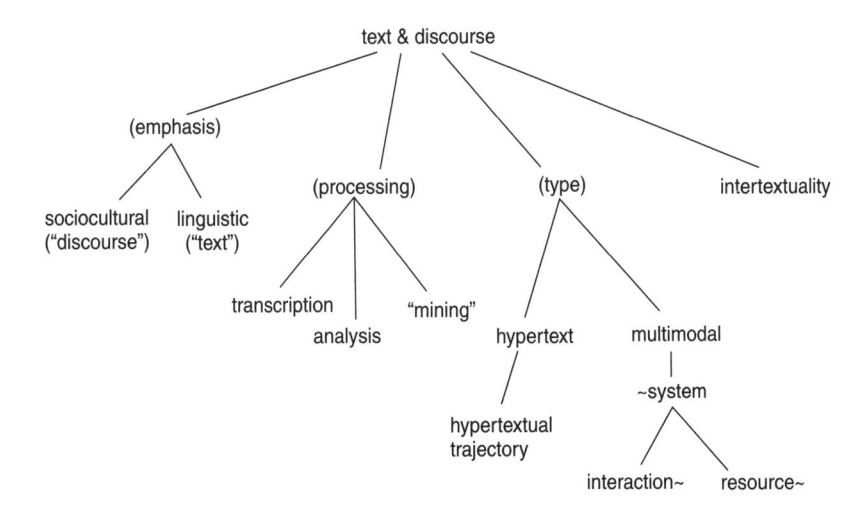

```
                          text & discourse
              ┌──────────────┬──────┬────────────────┐
         (emphasis)      (processing) (type)      intertextuality
          ╱    ╲           ╱    ╲     ╱   ╲
   sociocultural linguistic       ╱    ╲  hypertext multimodal
   ("discourse") ("text")  transcription "mining"       │
                                analysis              ~system
                                         ╱            ╱    ╲
                                hypertextual    interaction~  resource~
                                 trajectory
```

Communication disorders

Communication disorders are classified stratally, as "speech disorders" (phonetic) and "language disorders" (lexicogrammatical / semantic); and by their origin, as developmental or acquired. SFL has been shown to be an effective tool in the analysis of language disorders, both developmental (autism, Asperger's syndrome, ADHD (attention deficit hyperactivity disorder)) and acquired (aphasia, dementia, cognitive impairment from traumatic brain injury).

Researchers using SFL emphasize the subject's participation in social interaction rather than their performance in decontextualized tests of particular features. Discourse samples are analysed in terms of effectiveness as meaning and wording, with all metafunctions taken into account; features studied include cohesion, clause complexing, Theme – Rheme, appraisal, modality, transitivity; exchange structure, speech function, and GSP (generalized structure potential).

The linguistic analysis provides a basis for treatment of the disorder, and at the same time sheds light on the normal functioning of language.

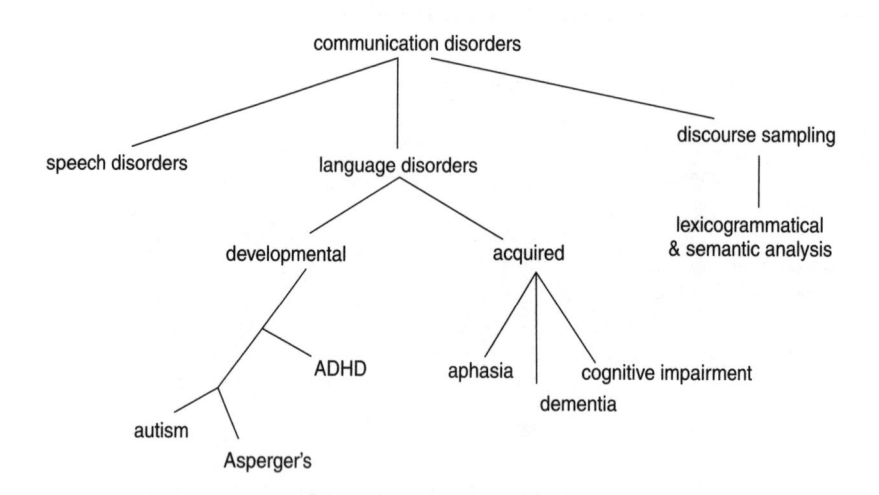

Corpus

A corpus is an extensive body of text assembled for use in linguistic research. Modern corpora are assembled and processed by computer. The text may be stored in the computer, or it may be interrogated for certain specific features and then discarded; in either case, as it is compiled it will usually be annotated in some way in order to record the sources of the text and other details such as registers and contexts.

Parallel corpora contain pairs or sets of texts which are in some way matched; for example, translations, or specimens of the same genre in different languages or dialects. A multi-layer(ed) corpus will contain a number of different modes of representation, which may include the output of both computational processing, such as parsing, and manual analysis and notation.

The usual format for implementing a search procedure is a concordance, which displays all (or selected) occurrences of a given word or lemma, together with their immediate environment in the text.

A corpus is usually compiled according to a specific principle, for example covering a range of registers, or literary genres, or historical periods. In this it contrasts with a text archive, which is built up opportunistically as suitable material becomes available.

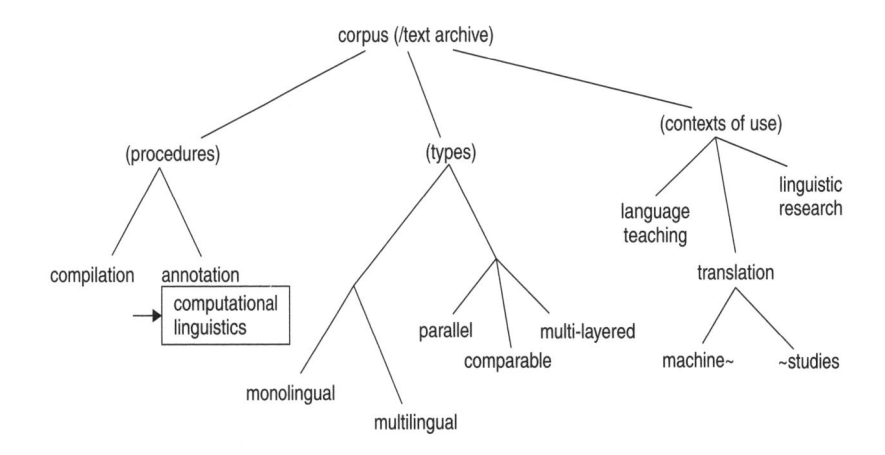

Computational linguistics

Natural Language Processing by computer (NLP) includes generation and understanding of text; and also machine learning, whereby the system builds up its own resources for these tasks. Linguistic computing is that field of NLP that is designed as an instrument for linguists.

Linguistic computing makes use of a "data base": a monolingual or multilingual text base, with perhaps additional data from multimedia sources.

Text processing consists in (i) segmenting, (ii) annotating and (iii) analysing the text. (i) Segmentation involves "sentence splitting", marking off written sentences and their parts; and "tokenizing", determining which words are instances of the same lexical item (tokens of the same type), and perhaps also calculating the mean ratio of items to occurrences. (ii) Annotation involves "tagging", assigning words to word classes ("parts of speech") using a limited set of specified tags; "lemmatizing", identifying the headword, or "lemma", covering a given set of variants; and "parsing", assigning syntactic structures, conventionally in the form of a tree. A tree bank is an ordered inventory of tree structures from a parsed data set, used for training and testing parsers and as a resource for further parsing. (iii) Analysis includes any form of linguistic analysis, beginning with searching and concordancing relevant instances from the text.

A computational tool for the linguist may take the form of a work bench, which provides resources for encoding, annotating and organizing large quantities of text. This can be accessed via different entry points, and automatic processing can be combined with manual operations of analysis and interpretation.

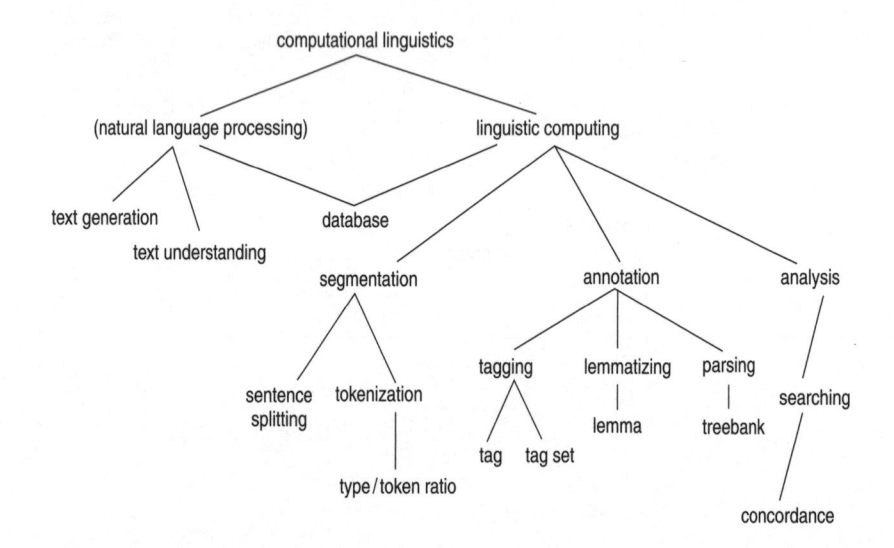

Base

The "base" in text generation is the repository of information that is stored so as to be drawn on by the system in operation.

In SFL this is modelled as a meaning base (or "semiotic base") to be organized on metafunctional lines. It will thus consist of three components: an ideation base, an interaction base and a text base.

Each of these, and therefore the base as a whole, is located within the system of language. In this it constrasts with the "knowledge base" of other text generation systems (deriving from the artificial intelligence model) which is located outside language, as an independent construct given in its own terms.

The term "data base" (now usually written as one word) is familiar in reference to any collection of structured data; in linguistic computing it will normally refer to language data – text in normalized form, with or without annotation; sometimes including multimedia discourse. A spoken data base is a database of spoken text, in audio form with transcription, and again possibly also annotation. A relational database is a data base of stored annotations (e.g. syntactic structure or word class) for use in data manipulation.

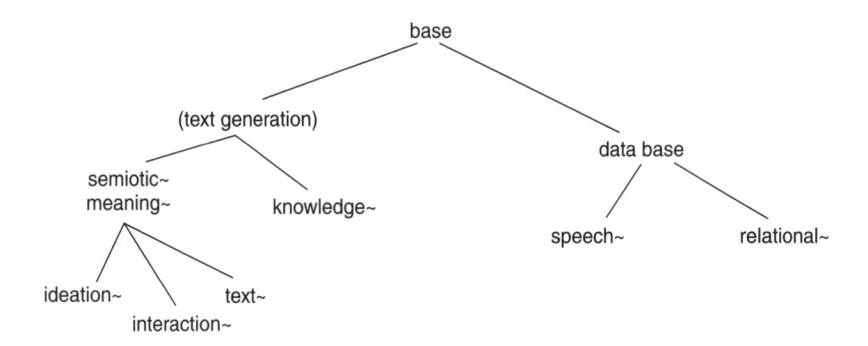

```
                            base
                    ╱                  ╲
            (text generation)        data base
             ╱        ╲              ╱        ╲
      semiotic~                  speech~       relational~
      meaning~     knowledge~
       ╱    ╲
  ideation~  text~
       interaction~
```

Probability

Systems in grammar and phonology have inherent probabilities associated with each of their terms; these can be derived from the study of frequencies in a large-scale corpus, although techniques for doing this automatically are still some way off. Such work as has been done suggests that, in grammar, primary systems (those of the greatest generality) tend towards one of two probability profiles: either the terms are roughly equal, or they are skew by about one order of magnitude. This is stated for binary systems, but the pattern can be extrapolated to systems with a greater number of terms.

Global probabilities are those pertaining to the language as a whole, in all contexts and registers. Local probabilities are those that are particular to one subsystem or text type, or even to one body of text. Difference in the frequency patterns of primary systems ("resetting of probabilities") is perhaps the main feature that distinguishes different registers of a language. Questions of probability may arise in clinical, developmental, educational and forensic linguistics, and are now increasingly seen as being central to computational operations with language.

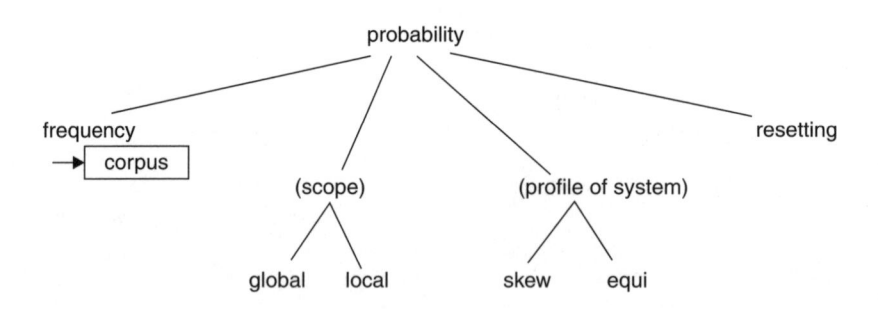

Function

From its beginnings in infancy human language is organized along functional lines. The protolanguage develops, in the first year of life, around a small number of "microfunctions", such as instrumental (getting goods-&-services), regulatory (ordering people about), personal (like and dislike, interest), interactional (being together); these are the uses to which the infant can put its emerging semiotic resources.

As the child moves into the mother tongue, these are generalized into a simple opposition of two "macrofunctions", pragmatic (language to act with) and mathetic (language to learn with); this works as a strategy for transiting to the abstract "metafunctions" which form the dominant motif in the organization of the adult language.

The metafunctions are (i) ideational, comprising both experiential and logical – language in the construal of experience; (ii) interpersonal – language in the enactment of human relationships; (iii) textual – language in the creation of discourse, which is an enabling function with respect to the other two.

"Function" is used in a distinct, through related, sense to refer to the elements of structure in grammar and phonology. A "functional grammar" is functional in both these senses.

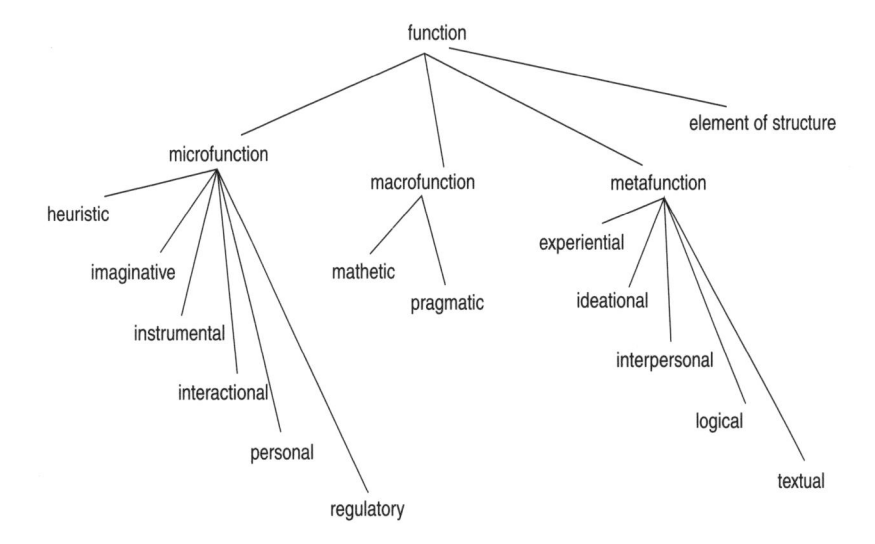

References

Aarts, J. and Meijis, W. (eds) (1990) *Theory and Practice in Corpus Linguistics.* Amsterdam: Rodopi.

Abercrombie, D. (1964) Syllable quantity and enclitics in English. In D. Abercrombie et al. (eds), *In Honour of Daniel Jones.* London: Longmans. Reprinted in D. Abercrombie (1965) *Studies in Phonetics and Linguistics.* London: Oxford University Press (Language and Language Learning 10).

Ahlsen, E. (2005) Argumentation with restricted linguistic ability: performing a role play with aphasia or in a second language. *Clinical Linguistics and Phonetics* 19(5): 433–51.

Aijmer, K. and Altenberg, B. (eds) (1991) *English Corpus Linguistics: Studies in Honour of Jan Svartvik.* London: Longman.

Armstrong, E. M. (1987) Cohesive harmony in aphasic discourse and its significance in listener perception of coherence. In R. H. Brookshire (ed.).

Armstrong, E. M. (1991) The potential of cohesion analysis in the analysis and treatment of aphasic discourse. *Clinical Linguistics and Phonetics* 5(1): 39–51.

Armstrong, E. M. (1992) Clause complex relations in aphasic discourse: a longitudinal case study. *Journal of Neurolinguistics* 7(4): 261–75.

Armstrong, E. M. (1997) *A Grammatical Analysis of Aphasic Discourse: Changes in Meaning-making over Time.* Unpublished Ph.D. Thesis. Macquarie University, Sydney.

Armstrong, E. M. (2001) Connecting lexical patterns of verb usage with discourse meanings in aphasia. *Aphasiology* 15: 1029–46.

Armstrong, E. M. (2005a) Language disorder: a functional linguistic perspective. *Clinical Linguistics and Phonetics* 19(3): 137–53.

Armstrong, E. M. (2005b) Expressing opinions and feelings in aphasia: linguistic options. *Aphasiology* 19(3/5): 285–96.

Armstrong, E. M. and Mortensen, L. (2006) Everyday talk: its role in assessment and treatment for individuals with aphasia. *Brain Injury* 7(3): 175–89.

Armstrong, E. M. and Mortensen, L. (2007) Expressing opinions and feelings in an aphasia group setting. Paper presented at *Speech Pathology Association of Australia National Conference, Sydney, May 27–31, 2007.*

Armstrong, E. M. and Ulatowska, H. K. (2007a) Stroke stories: conveying emotive experiences in aphasia. In M. Ball and J. S. Damico (eds), *Clinical Aphasiology: Future Directions – A Festschrift for Chris Code.* Hove: Psychology Press.

Armstrong, E. M. and Ulatowska, H. K. (2007b) Stroke stories: the aphasia experience. *Aphasiology* 21: 763–74.

Armstrong, E. M., Ferguson, A., Mortensen, L. and Togher, L. (2005) Acquired language disorders: some functional insights. In R. Hasan, C. M. I. M. Matthiessen and J. J. Webster (eds): 383–412.

Armstrong, E. M., Mortensen, L., Byng, S., McVicker, S. and Pound, C. (2006) Communicating in aphasia group therapy. Paper presented at *Speech Pathology Association of Australia National Conference, Fremantle, May.*

Asp, E. and de Villiers, J. (Forthcoming) *When Language Breaks Down: Analysing Discourse in Clinical Contexts.* Cambridge: Cambridge University Press.

Auden, W. H. and Isherwood, C. (1939) *Journey to a War.* New York: Random House. Reprinted in (1973) London: Faber and Faber. Reprinted (1990) New York: Paragon House.

Austin, J. L. (1962) *How to Do Things with Words.* Oxford: Clarendon Press. 2nd edn, ed. J. O. Urmson and M. Sbisà, 1975.

Avent, J. R., Wertz, R. T. and Auther, L. L. (1998) Relationship between language impairment and pragmatic function in aphasic adults. *Journal of Neurolinguistics* 11(1–2): 207–21.

Baldry, A. (ed.) (1999) *Multimodality and Multimediality in the Distance Learning Age.* Campo Basso: Lampo.

Baldry, A. and Thibault, P. J. (2006a) Multimodal corpus linguistics. In G. Thompson and S. Hunston (eds)

Baldry, A. and Thibault, P. J. (2006b) *Multimodal Transcription and Text Analysis.* London: Equinox.

Barlow, M. (1995) *A Guide to ParaConc.* Available: http://www.ruf.rice.edu/~barlow/pc.html, May 20, 2000.

Barlow, M. (2002) ParaConc: concordance software for multilingual parallel corpora. *Proceedings of the Workshop on Language Resources for Translation Work and Research, LREC 2002, Las Palmas, Spain.*

Barras, C., Geoffrois, E., Wu, Z. and Liberman, M. (2001) Transcriber: development and use of a tool for assisting speech corpora production source. *Speech Communication* 33(1–2): 5–22.

Bartlett, S., Armstrong, E. M. and Roberts, J. (2005) Linguistic resources of individuals with Asperger Syndrome. *Clinical Linguistics and Phonetics* 19(3): 203–13.

Bastiaanse, R., Edwards, S. and Rispens, J. (2002) *Verb and Sentence Test.* Oxford: Harcourt Assessment.

Bateman, J. A. (1989) Dynamic systemic-functional grammar: a new frontier. *Systems, Structures and Discourse: Selected Papers from the Fifteenth International Systemic Congress (Word 40.1–2).*

Bateman, J. A. (2003) Functional linguistics and human language technology: new opportunities – or has SFL missed the boat?. Paper presented at *ISFC30, Lucknow, India, December 12, 2003.*

Bateman, J. A. (2008) *Multimodality and Genre: A Foundation for the Systematic Analysis of Multimodal Documents.* London and New York: Palgrave Macmillan.

Bateman, J. A., Matthiessen, C. M. I. M. and Zeng, L. (1999) Multilingual language generation for multilingual software: a functional linguistic approach. *Applied Artificial Intelligence: An International Journal* 13(6): 607–39.

Baumann, S., Brinckmann, C., Hansen-Schirra, S., Kruijff, G., Kruijff-Korbayová, I., Neumann, S. and Teich, E. (2004) Multi-dimensional annotation of linguistic corpora for investigating information structure. *Proceedings of Frontiers in Corpus Annotation Workshop, HLT-NAACL 2004, Boston, Massachusetts.*

Baumgartner, P. and Payr, S. (eds) (1995) *Speaking Minds: Interviews with Twenty Eminent Cognitive Scientists.* Princeton, NJ: Princeton University Press.

Benson, J. D. and Greaves, W. S. (eds) (1985a) *Systemic Perspectives on Discourse Vol. 1: Selected Theoretical Papers from the 9th International Systemic Workshop* (1982, Toronto). Norwood, NJ: Ablex (Series of Advances in Discourse Processes Vol. 15).

Benson, J. D. and Greaves, W. S. (eds) (1985b) *Systemic Perspectives on Discourse, Vol. 2: Selected Applied Papers from the 9th International Systemic Workshop* (1982, Toronto). Norwood NJ: Ablex (Series of Advances in Discourse Processes Vol. 16).

Benson, J. D. and Greaves, W. S. (1992) Collocation and field of discourse. In W. C. Mann and S. A. Thompson (eds): 397–409.

Benson, J. D. and Greaves, W. S. (eds) (2005) *Functional Dimensions of Ape-Human Discourse.* London and Oakville, CT: Equinox.

Benson, J. D., Cummings, M. J. and Greaves, W. S. (eds) (1988) *Linguistics in a Systemic Perspective.* Amsterdam: Benjamins.

Benson, J. D., Fries, P., Greaves, W. S., Iwamoto, K., Savage-Rumbaugh, S. and Taglialatela, J. (2002) Confrontation and support in bonobo-human discourse. *Functions of Language* 9: 1–38.

Bernstein, B. (1971) *Class, Codes and Control Vol. 1: Theoretical Studies towards a Sociology of Language.* London: Routledge and Kegan Paul (Primary Socialization, Language and Education).

Bernstein, B. (1987) Social class, codes and communication. In U. Ammon, N. Dittmar and K. J. Mattheier (eds), *An International Handbook of the Science of Language and Society Vol. 1.* Berlin and New York: De Guyter.

Bernstein, B. (1990) *Class, Codes and Control Vol. 4: The Structuring of Pedagogic Discourse.* London and New York: Routledge

Bernstein, B. (1996) *Pedagogy, Symbolic Control and Identity: Theory, Research, Critique.* London: Taylor and Francis (Critical perspectives on Literacy and Education). Revised edn, Lanham, Boulder, New York and London: Rowman and Littlefield, 2000.

Berry, M. (1981) Systemic linguistics and discourse analysis: a multi-layered approach to exchange structure. In M. Coulthard and M. Montgomery (eds): 120–45.

Biber, D. (1993) The multi-dimensional approach to linguistic analyses of genre variation: an overview of methodology and findings. *Computers and the Humanities* 26: 331–45.

Biber, D. and Finegan, E. (1989) Drift and evolution of English style: a history of three genres. *Language* 65: 489–517.

Biber, D. and Finegan, E. (1991) On the exploitation of computerized corpora in variation studies. In K. Aijmer and B. Altenberg (eds): 204–20.

Biber, D., Conrad, S. and Reppen, R. (1998) *Corpus Linguistics: Investigating Language Structure and Use.* Cambridge: Cambridge University Press.

Biber, D., Johanson, S., Leech, G., Conrad, S. and Finnegan, E. (1999) *The Longman Grammar of Spoken and Written English.* London: Longman.

Bickerton, D. (1990) *Language and Species*. Chicago: University of Chicago Press.
Bickhard, M. H. (2005) Consciousness and reflective consciousness. *Philosophical Psychology* 18(2): 205–18.
Birch, D. and O'Toole, L. M. (eds) (1988) *Functions of Style*. London: Pinter.
Bird, S. and Simons, G. (2003) Seven dimensions of portability for language documentation and description. *Language* 79: 557–82.
Blake, J. (2000) *Routes to Child Language: Evolutionary and Developmental Precursors*. Cambridge: Cambridge University Press.
Boas, F. (1940) *Race, Language and Culture*. New York: Macmillan.
Bod, R., Hay, J. and Jannedy, S. (eds) (2003) *Probabilistic Linguistics*. Cambridge, Mass: MIT Press.
Boehm, A. E. (2000) *Boehm Test of Basic Concepts*. 3rd edn, Oxford: Harcourt Assessment.
Boersma, P. and Weenink, D. (1996) PRAAT, a system for doing phonetics by computer, version 3.4. *Institute of Phonetic Sciences of the University of Amsterdam, Report 132*.
Bowcher, W. L. (2001) *Play-by-play Talk on Radio: An Enquiry into Some Relations between Language and Context*. Ph.D. thesis. University of Liverpool.
Bowcher, W. L. (2007) Field and multimodal texts. In R. Hasan, C. M. I. M. Matthiessen and J. J. Webster (eds): 619–46.
Brants, S., Dipper, S., Hansen, S., Lezius, W. and Smith, G. (2002) The TIGER Treebank. *Proceedings of the Workshop on Treebanks and Linguistic Theories (TLT)*, Sozopol, Bulgaria.
Brants, T. (2000) TnT - A Statistical Part-of-Speech Tagger. *Proceedings of the Sixth Applied Natural Language Processing Conference ANLP-2000*, Seattle, WA.
Brants, T. and Plaehn, O. (2000) Interactive Corpus Annotation. *Proceedings of the 2nd International Conference on Language Resources and Evaluation (LREC 2000)*, Athens, Greece.
Bråten, S. (1998a) Intersubjective communion and understanding: development and perturbation. In S. Bråten (ed.): 372–82.
Bråten, S. (ed.) (1998b) *Intersubjective Communication and Emotion in Early Ontogeny*. Cambridge and Paris: Cambridge University Press and Editions de la Maison des Sciences de l'Homme.
Bråten, S. (2002) Altercentric perception by infants and adults in dialogue: Ego's virtual participation in Alter's complementary act. In M. I. Stamenov and V. Gallese (eds), *Mirror Neurons and the Evolution of Brain and Language*. Amsterdam and Philadelphia: John Benjamins. 273–94.
Bråten, S (ed.) (2007) *On Being Moved: From Mirror Neurons to Empathy*. Amsterdam and Philadelphia: John Benjamins. (Advances in Consciousness Research).
Brill, E. (1995) Transformation-based error-driven learning and natural language processing: a case study in part-of-speech tagging. *Computational Linguistics* 21(4): 543–65.
Brookshire, R. H. (ed.) (1984). *Clinical Aphasiology: Conference Proceedings*. Minneapolis, MN: BRK Publishers.
Brown, R. (1973) *A First Language*. London: Allen and Unwin.
Browne, A. (1989) *Piggybook*. London: Little Mammoth.

Bullard, J. (1994) Learning equilibria. *Journal of Economic Theory* 64: 468–85.
Burns, A., Kim, M. and Matthiessen, C. M. I. M. (In Press) Doctoral work in translation studies as an interdisciplinary mutual learning process: how a translator, teacher educator, and linguistic typologist worked together. *The Interpreter and Translator Trainer*.
Butt, D. G. (1983) Semantic 'drift' in verbal art. *Australian Review of Applied Linguistics* 6(1): 38–48.
Butt, D. G. (1988) Randomness, order and the latent patterning of text. In D. Birch and L. M. O'Toole (eds).
Butt, D. G. (1999/2004) *Parameters of Context*. Sydney: Macquarie University Department of Linguistics (mimeo).
Butt, D. G. (2000) Semantic cycles: structure statements at the level of meaning. In D. G. Butt and C. M. I. M. Matthiessen (eds), *The Meaning Potential of Language: Mapping Meaning Systemically*. Mimeo. Department of Linguistics, Macquarie University. 228–33.
Butt, D. G. (2001) Firth, Halliday and the development of systemic functional theory. In S. Auroux, E. F. K. Koerner, H.-J. Niederehe and K. Versteegh (eds), *History of the Language Sciences: An International Handbook on the Evolution of the Study of Language from the Beginnings to the Present*. Berlin and New York: Walter de Gruyter. 1806–38.
Butt, D. G. (2003) *Parameters of Context: On Establishing the Similarities and Differences between Social processes*. Macquarie University: Centre for Language in Social Life. Mimeo.
Butt, D. G. (2005) Method and imagination in Halliday's science of linguistics. In R. Hasan, C. M. I. M. Matthiessen and J. J. Webster (eds): 81–116.
Butt, D. G. (2007) Thought experiments in verbal art: examples from modernism. In D. R. Miller and M. Turci (eds): 68–96.
Butt, D. G. (2008) The robustness of realizational systems. In J. J. Webster (ed.): 59–83.
Butt, D. G. and O'Toole, L. M. (2003) Transactions between matter and meaning: a functional theory for the science of text. In M. Amano (ed.) *Creation and Practical Use of Language Texts* Proceedings of the Second International Conference Studies for the Integrated Text Science, 21st Century Centre of Excellence Program International Conference Series No. 2: Nagoya: Nagoya University. 1–23.
Butt, D. G. and Wegener, R. (2007) The work of concepts: context and metafunction in the systemic functional model. In R. Hasan, C. M. I. M. Matthiessen and J. J. Webster (eds): 589–618.
Butt, D. G., Fahey, R. and Henderson-Brooks, C. (2003) Outer and inner weathers. In R. Meares and P. Nolan (eds), *The Self in Conversation Vol. 2*. Sydney: Australia and New Zealand Association of Psychotherapy.
Byng, S. and Duchan, J. (2005) Social model philosophies and principles: their applications to therapies for aphasia. *Aphasiology* 19(10/11): 906–22.
Byrnes, H. (ed.) (2006) *Advanced Instructed Language Learning: The Complementary Contribution of Halliday and Vygotsky*. London and New York: Continuum.
Byrnes, H. (ed.) (In Press) *Instructed Foreign Language Acquisition as Meaning-making: A Systemic Functional Approach*. (Special issue of *Linguistics and Education*).

Caffarel, A., Martin, J. R. and Matthiessen, C. M. I. M. (eds) (2004) *Language Typology: A Functional Perspective*. Amsterdam: Benjamins (Current Issues in Linguistic Theory).

Caldas-Coulthard, C. and Coulthard, M. (eds) (1996) *Text and Practices: Readings in Critical Discourse Analysis*. London: Routledge.

Calvin, W. H. and Bickerton, D. (2000) *Lingua Ex Machina: Reconciling Darwin and Chomsky with the Human Brain*. Cambridge, MA and London: MIT Press.

Candlin, C. (ed.) (2002) *Theory and Practice of Professional Discourse*. Hong Kong: CUHK Press.

Caple, H. (2008) Intermodal relations in image nuclear news stories. In L. Unsworth (ed.): 125–38.

Caple, H. (In Press) What you see and what you get: the evolving role of news photographs in an Australian broadsheet. In V. Rupar (ed.), *Journalism and Meaning-making: Reading the Newspaper*. Kresskill, NJ: Hampton Press.

Carrow, E. (1999) *Test of Auditory Comprehension of Language*. Bloomington, MN: Pearson Education.

Carter, R. (ed.) (1982) *Language and Literature: An Introductory Reader in Stylistics*. London and Boston: Allen and Unwin.

Cassidy, S. and Harrington, J. (2001) Multi-level annotation in the Emu speech database management system. *Speech Communication* 33: 61–77.

Catford, J. C. (1965) *A Linguistic Theory of Translation*. London: Oxford University Press.

Catford, J. C. (1977) *Fundamental Problems in Phonetic*. Bloomington, Indiana: Indiana University Press.

Catford, J. C. (1985) "Rest" and "open transition" in a systemic phonology of English. In J. D. Benson and W. S. Greaves (eds) (1985b).

Chapey, R., Duchan, J. F., Elman, R. J., Garcia, L. J., Kagan, A., Lyon, J. and Simmons Mackie, N. (2000) Life Participation Approach to Aphasia: A Statement of Values for the Future. ASHA Leader 5(3): 4–6.

Chatman, S. (ed.) (1971) *Literary Style: A Symposium*. London: Oxford University Press.

Chenery, H. and Murdoch, B. E. (1994) The production of narrative discourse in response to animations in persons with dementia of the Alzheimer's type: preliminary findings. *Aphasiology* 8: 159–71.

Cheney, D. L. and Seyfarth, R. M. (1990) *How Monkeys See the World: Inside the Mind of Another Species*. Chicago: University of Chicago Press.

Christ, O. (1994) A modular and flexible architecture for an integrated corpus query system. *Proceedings of the 3rd Conference on Computational Lexicography and Text Research (COMPLEX), Budapest, 1994*.

Christie, F. (ed.) (1992) *Literacy in Social Processes* (Papers from the Inaugural Australian Systemic Functional Linguistics Conference, Deakin University, January 1990). Darwin: Centre for Studies of Language in Education.

Christie, F. (1997) Curriculum macrogenres as forms of initiation into a culture. In F. Christie and J. R. Martin (eds): 134–60.

Christie, F. (ed.) (1999) *Pedagogy and the Shaping of Consciousness: Linguistic and Social Processes*. London: Cassell (Open Linguistics Series).

Christie, F. (2002) *Classroom Discourse Analysis*. London: Continuum.

Christie, F. and Macken-Horarik, M. (2007) Building verticality in subject English. In F. Christie and J. R. Martin (eds): 156–83.
Christie, F. and Martin, J. R. (eds) (1997) *Genre and Institutions: Social Processes in the Workplace and School.* London: Pinter (Open Linguistics Series).
Christie, F. and Martin, J. R. (eds) (2007) *Language, Knowledge and Pedagogy: Functional Linguistics and Sociological Perspectives.* London and New York: Continuum.
Christie, F. and Unsworth, L. (2005) Developing dimensions of an educational linguistics. In R. Hasan, C. M. I. M. Matthiessen and J. J. Webster (eds): 217–50.
Cloran, C. (1982) *The Role of Conversation in Negotiating New Contexts.* Unpublished BA Honours Dissertation. Sydney: Linguistics, Macquarie University.
Cloran, C. (1987) Negotiating new contexts in conversation. *Occasional Papers in Systemic Linguistics* 1: 85–110.
Cloran, C. (1989) Learning through language: the social construction of gender. In R. Hasan and J. R. Martin (eds): 361–403.
Cloran, C. (1994) *Rhetorical Units and Decontextualisation: An Enquiry into Some Relations of Context, Meaning and Grammar.* Nottingham: School of English Studies, Nottingham University (Monographs in Systemic Linguistics 6).
Cloran, C. (1995) Defining and relating text segments: Subject and Theme in discourse. In R. Hasan and P. H. Fries (eds): 361–403.
Cloran, C. (1999a) Context, material situation and text. In M. Ghadessy (ed.): 177–217.
Cloran, C. (1999b) Contexts for learning. In F. Christie (ed.): 31–65.
Cloran, C. (2000) Socio-semantic variation: different wordings, different meanings. In L. Unsworth (ed.): 152–83.
Cloran, C., Stuart-Smith, V. and Young, L. (2007) Models of discourse. In R. Hasan, C. M. I. M. Matthiessen and J. J. Webster (eds): 647–70.
Coffin, C. (1997) Constructing and giving value to the past: an investigation into secondary school history. In F. Christie and J. R. Martin (eds): 196–230.
Coffin, C. (2006) *Historical Discourse: the Language of Time, Cause and Evaluation.* London: Continuum.
Cohen, J. and Stewart, I. (1994) *The Collapse of Chaos: Discovering Simplicity in a Complex World.* London: Penguin.
Copeland, J. E. and Davis, P. W. (eds) *The Seventh LACUS Forum.* Columbia, South Carolina: Hornbeam Press.
Coulthard, M. (2004) Author identification, idiolect and linguistic uniqueness. *Applied Linguistics* 25(4): 431–47.
Coulthard, M. (ed.) (1992) *Advances in Spoken Discourse Analysis.* London: Routledge.
Coulthard, M. (ed.) (1994) *Advances in Written Text Analysis.* London: Routledge and Kegan Paul.
Coulthard, M. and Montgomery, M. (eds) (2001) *Studies in Discourse Analysis.* London: Routledge and Kegan Paul.
Cowley, S. J. (2004) Contextualizing bodies: how human responsiveness constrains distributed cognition. *Language Sciences* 26(6): 565–91.

Cranny-Francis, A. and Martin, J. R. (1992) Contratextuality: the poetics of subversion. In F. Christie (ed.): 285–344.
Cranny-Francis, A. and Martin, J. R. (1994) In/visible education: class, gender and pedagogy in Educating Rita and Dead Poets Society. *Interpretations: Journal of the English Teachers Association of W.A.* 27(1): 28–57.
Cross, M. (1979) *Just Pretend You're the Shopkeeper: The Structure of Children's Cooperative Imaginative Role Play.* Unpublished BA Honours Dissertation. Sydney: Macquarie University, Linguistics Department.
Cummings, M. and Simmons, R. (1983) *The Language of Literature: A Stylistic Introduction to the Study of Literature.* Oxford: Pergamon.
Cunningham, H. (2002) GATE - A general architecture for text engineering. *Computers and the Humanities* 36: 223–54.
Dalgaard, P. (2002) *Introductory Statistics with R.* Berlin and New York: Springer.
Davidse, K. (1992) Transitivity/ergativity: the Janus-headed grammar of actions and events. In D. Martin and L. J. Ravelli (eds), *Advances in Systemic Linguistics: Recent Theory and Practice.* London: Frances Pinter.
Davidse, K. (1999) *Categories of Experiential Grammar.* Nottingham: University of Nottingham Department of English Studies (Monographs in Systemic Linguistics).
Davies, M. and Ravelli, L. J. (eds) (1992) *Advances in Systemic Linguistics: Recent Theory and Practice.* London: Pinter.
Davis, K. (1984) *Fugue and Fresco: Structures in Pound's Cantos.* Maine: The National Poetry Foundation, University of Maine.
Dawe, B. (1971) *Condolences of the Season: Selected Poems of Bruce Dawe.* Melbourne: Chesire.
Dawkins, R. (2006) *The God Delusion.* London: Bantam Press.
de Saussure, F. (1978 [1916]) *Course in General Linguistics.* Edited by C. Bally and A. Sechehaye in collaboration with A. Riedlinger. Glasgow: Fontana/Collins.
de Villiers, J. (2005) Discourse Analysis in Autism Spectrum Disorder. *Linguistics and the Human Sciences* 1(1): 245–60.
Deacon, T. (1997) *The Symbolic Species: The Co-evolution of Language and the Human Brain.* London: Allen Lane (The Penguin Press).
Degand, L. (2001) *Form and Function of Causation: A Theoretical and Empirical Investigation of Causal Constructions in Dutch.* Peeters: Leuven, Paris, Sterling (Studies op het gebied van de Nederlandse taalkunde 5).
Dennett, D. C. (1987) *The Intentional Stance.* Cambridge, Mass.: The MIT Press.
Derewianka, B. (1999) *Language Development in the Transition from Childhood to Adolescence: The Role of Grammatical Metaphor.* Unpublished Ph.D. Thesis. Macquarie University.
Derewianka, B. (2003) Grammatical metaphor in the transition to adolescence. In A.-M. Simon-Vandenbergen, M. Taverniers and L. J. Ravelli (eds): 185–219.
Dixon, R. M. W. (1997) *The Rise and Fall of Languages.* Cambridge: Cambridge University Press.
Djonov, E. (2007) Website hierarchy and the interaction between content organization, webpage and navigation design: A systemic functional hypermedia discourse analysis perspective. *Information Design Journal* 15(2): 144–62.

Donaldson, M. (1978) *Children's Minds*. Glasgow: Fontana/Collins.

Downing, A. and Lavid, J. (1998) Information progression strategies in administrative forms: a cross linguistic study. In A. Sánchez-Macarro and R. Carter (eds): 99–116.

Doyle, P. J., McNeil, M. R., Park, G., Goda, A., Rubenstein, E., Spencer, K., Carroll, B., Lustig, A. and Szwarc, L. (1998) Linguistic validation of four parallel forms of a story retelling procedure. *Aphasiology* 14(5/6): 537–49.

Dronkers, N. F., Ludy, C. A., and Redfern, B. B. (1998) Pragmatics in the absence of verbal language: descriptions of a severe aphasic and a language deprived adult. *Journal of Neurolinguistics* 11(1–2): 179–90.

Eckart, R. (2006) Towards a modular data model for multi-layer annotated corpora. In *Proceedings of the 21st International Conference on Computational Linguistics (COLING) and the 44th Annual Meeting of the Association for computational Linguistics (ACL), Main Conference Poster Sessions, Sydney, Australia.*

Eckart, R. and Teich, E. (2007) An XML-based data model for flexible representation and query of linguistically interpreted corpora. In G. Rehm, A. Witt and L. Lemnitzer (eds), *Data Structures for Linguistic Resources and Applications – Proceedings of the Meeting of Gesellschaft für Linguistische Datenverarbeitung (GLDV) 07*. Narr, Tübingen. 327–36.

Eggins, S. (1994) *An Introduction to Systemic Functional Linguistics*. London: Pinter.

Eggins, S. and Iedema, R. (1997) Difference without diversity: the semantics of women's magazines. In R. Wodak (ed.), *Gender and Discourse*. Thousand Oaks, Calif.: Sage. 165–96.

Eggins, S. and Martin, J. R. (1997) Genres and registers of discourse. In T. A. van Dijk (ed.), *Discourse as Structure and Process*. London: Sage (Discourse Studies: a multidisciplinary introduction, Vol. 1). 230–56.

Eggins, S. and Slade, D. (1997) *Analysing Casual Conversation*. London: Cassell. Republished in (2005). London: Equinox.

Ellis, G. F. R. (2005) Physics and the real world. *Physics Today* 58(7): 49–54.

Ellis, J. (1966) *Towards a General Comparative Linguistics*. The Hague: Mouton.

Ellis, J. (1987) Some "dia-categories". In R. Steele and T. Threadgold (eds): 81–94.

Elmenoufy, A. (1969) *A Study of the Role of Intonation in the Grammar of English*. Ph.D. thesis. University of London.

Ewing-Cobb, L., Brookshire, B., Scott, M. A. and Fletcher, J. (1998) Children's narratives following traumatic brain injury: linguistic structure, cohesion, and thematic recall. *Brain and Language* 61: 395–419.

Fang, Y. (1993) A contrastive study of Theme and Rheme in English and Chinese. In K. Hao, H. Bluhme and R. Li (eds), *Proceedings of the International Conference on Texts and Language Research, March 29–31, 1989*. Xi'an: Xi'an Jiaotong University Press.

Fang, Y., McDonald, E. and Cheng, M. (1995) On Theme in Chinese: from clause to discourse. In R. Hasan and P. H. Fries (eds): 235–74.

Fawcett, R. P. (1980) *Cognitive Linguistics and Social Interaction*. Exeter and Heidelberg: University of Exeter and Julius Groos.

Fawcett, R. P. (1997) Invitation to systemic functional linguistics: the Cardiff Grammar as an extension and simplification of Halliday's systemic functional grammar. *Helicon* 22.

Fawcett, R. P. (2000) *A Theory of Syntax for Systemic Functional Linguistics*. Amsterdam and Philadelphia: John Benjamins.

Ferguson, A. (1992) Interpersonal aspects of aphasic communication. *Journal of Neurolinguistics* 7(4): 277–94.

Ferguson, A. and Elliot, N. (2001) Analysing aphasia treatment sessions. *Clinical Linguistics and Phonetics* 15(3): 229–43.

Ferguson, L., MacLulich, C. and Ravelli, L. J. (1995) *Meanings and Messages: Language Guidelines for Museum Exhibitions*. Sydney: Australian Museum.

Fine, J. (1994) *How Language Works: Cohesion in Normal and Nonstandard Communication*. Norwood, NJ: Ablex.

Fine, J. (1995) Towards understanding and studying cohesion in schizophrenic speech. *Applied Psycholinguistics* 16: 25–41.

Fine, J. (2006) *Language in Psychiatry: A Handbook of Clinical Practice*. London: Equinox.

Fine, J., Bartolucci, G. and Szatmari, P. (1989) Textual systems: their use in creation and miscalculation of social reality. *Word* 40(1–2): 65–80.

Fine, J., Bartolucci, G., Szatmari, P. and Ginsberg, G. (1994) Cohesive discourse in pervasive developmental disorders. *Journal of Autism and Developmental Disorders* 24: 315–29.

Firth, J. R. (1957a) A synopsis of linguistic theory, 1930–1955. In J. R. Firth et al.

Firth, J. R. (1957b) *Papers in Linguistics 1934–1951*. London: Oxford University Press.

Firth, J. R. et al. (1957) *Studies in Linguistic Analysis*. Oxford: Basil Blackwell (Special Volume of the Philological Society).

Forey, G. and Lockwood, J. (2007) "I'd love to put someone in jail for this": an initial investigation of English in the business processing outsourcing (BPO) industry. *English for Specific Purposes* 26: 308–26.

Fowler, R., Hodge, B., Kress, G. and Trew, T. (1979) *Language and Control*. London: Routledge and Kegan Paul.

Fox, B. A. (1987) *Discourse Structure and Anaphora: Written and Conversational English*. Cambridge: Cambridge University Press (Cambridge Studies in Linguistics 48).

Francis, W. N. (1982) Problems of assembling and computerizing large corpora. In S. Johansson (ed.), *Computer Corpora in English Language Research*. Bergen: Norwegian Computing Centre for the Humanities. 7–24.

Fries, P. H. (1981) On the status of theme in English: arguments from discourse. *Forum Linguisticum* 6(1): 1–38. Republished in J. S. Petöfi and E. Sözer (eds) (1983) *Micro and Macro Connexity of Texts*. Hamburg: Helmut Buske Verlag (Papers in Textlinguistics 45). 116–52.

Fries, P. H. (2002) Theme and New in written advertising. In G.W. Huang and Z.Y. Wang (eds): 56–72.

Fries, P. H. (2003) The presentation of reality in James and Hemingway. In M. R. Wise and R. Brend (eds), *Language and Life*. Amsterdam: John Benjamins. 297–316.

Fries, P. H. and Gregory, M. (eds) (1995) *Discourse in Society: Systemic Functional Perspectives*. Norwood, NJ: Ablex (Advances in Discourse Processes Vol. L: Meaning and Choices in Language - Studies for Michael Halliday).

Fries, P. H., Cummings, M., et al. (eds) (2002) *Relations and Functions within and around Language*. London and New York: Continuum.

Fuller, G. (1998) Cultivating science: negotiating discourse in the popular texts of Stephen Jay Gould. In J. R. Martin and R. Veel (eds): 35–62.

Garside, R. and Smith, N. (1997) A hybrid grammatical tagger: CLAWS4. In R. Garside, G. Leech and A. McEnery (eds) *Corpus Annotation: Linguistic Information from Computer Text Corpora*. London: Longman. 102–21.

Garvin, P. (1985) Types of grammatical relations. In R. A. Hall and Jr. Columbia (eds) *The Eleventh LACUS Forum*. South Carolina: Hornbeam Press. 55–72.

Ghadessy, M. (ed.) (1993a) *Register Analysis: Theory and Practice*. London and New York: Pinter.

Ghadessy, M. (1993b) On the nature of written business communication. In M. Ghadessy (ed.) (1993a): 149–64.

Ghadessy, M. (ed.) (1995) *Thematic Development in English Texts*. London: Pinter (Open Linguistics Series).

Ghadessy, M. (ed.) (1999) *Text and Context in Functional Linguistics*. Amsterdam: Benjamins (CILT Series IV).

Gibbons, J. (2003) *Forensic Linguistics*. Oxford: Blackwell (Language in Society series).

Gibbons, P. (2002) *Scaffolding Language, Scaffolding Learning: Working with ESL Children in the Elementary Mainstream Classroom*. Portsmouth, NH: Heinemann.

Gleason, H. A. Jr. (1968) Contrastive analysis in discourse structure. *Monograph Series on Languages and Linguistics 21* (Georgetown University Institute of Languages and Linguistics). Reprinted in A. Makkai and D. Lockwood: 258–76.

Glosser, G. and Deser T. (1990) Patterns of discourse production among neurological patients with fluent language disorders. *Brain and Language* 40: 67-88.

Goffman, E. (1974) *Frame Analysis*. Harmondsworth: Penguin Books.

Goodglass, H., Kaplan, E. and Barresi, B. (2000) *The Boston Diagnostic Aphasia Examination – 3*. 3rd edn, Oxford: Harcourt Assessment.

Goodwin, K. L. (1986) *A History of Australian Literature*. Basingstoke: Macmillan.

Greaves, W. S. (2007) Intonation in systemic linguistics. In R. Hasan, C. M. I. M. Matthiessen and J. J. Webster (eds): 979–1025.

Greenfield, P. and Savage-Rumbaugh, S. (1993) *Journal of Child Language* 20: 1–26.

Grefenstette, G. and Tapanainen, P. (1994) What is a word, what is a sentence? Problems of tokenization. *Proceedings of the 3rd Conference on Computational Lexicography and Text Research (COMPLEX), Budapest, 1994.*

Gregory, M. (1967) Aspects of varieties differentiation. *Journal of Linguistics* 3: 177–98.

Gregory, M. (1974) A theory for stylistics exemplified: Donne's 'Holy Sonnet XIV'. *Language and Style* 8(2): 108–18.

Gregory, M. (1978) Marvell's 'To His Coy Mistress': the poem as a linguistic and social event. *Poetics* 7(4): 351–62.

Gregory, M. (1981) Linguistics and theatre: Hamlet's voice: aspects of text formation and cohesion in a soliliquoy. *Linguistics and the Humanities Conference, University of Texas, Arlington*. Reprinted in *Forum Linguisticum* 7(2): 107–22, 1982.

Gregory, M. (1995) *Before and Towards Communication Linguistics: Essays by Michael Gregory and Associates*. Edited by J. S. Cha. Seoul: Sookmyng Women's University.

Gregory, M. (2002) Phasal analysis within communication linguistics: two contrastive discourses. In P. Fries, M. Cummings, D. Lockwood and W. Sprueill (eds), *Relations and Functions in Language and Discourse*. London: Continuum. 316–45.

Gregory, M. and Carroll, S. (1978) *Language and Situation: Language Varieties and Their Social Contexts*. London: Routledge and Kegan Paul.

Gregory, M. and Malcolm, K. (1981) Generic situation and discourse phase: an approach to the analysis of children's talk. Applied Linguistics Research Working Group, Glendon College, York University, Toronto. Mimeo.

Gries, S. Th. (Forthcoming) *Quantitative Corpus Linguistics with R: A Practical Introduction*. New York: Routledge.

Gross, M. (1979) On the failure of generative grammar. *Language* 55(4): 859–85.

Gu, Y. G. (1999) Towards a model of situated discourse. In K. Turner (ed.), *The Semantics/Pragmatics Interface from Different Points of View*. Oxford: Elsevier. 150–78.

Gu, Y. G. (2002) Towards an understanding of workplace discourse - a pilot study for compiling a spoken Chinese corpus of situated discourse. In C. Candlin (ed.) (2002): 137–85.

Gutwinski, W. (1976) *Cohesion in Literary Texts: A Study of Some Grammatical and Lexical Features of English Discourse*. The Hague: Mouton (Janua Linguarum Series Minor 204).

Hajič, J., Böhmová, A., Hajičová, E. and Vidová-Hladká, B. (2000) The Prague Dependency Treebank: a three-level annotation scenario. In A. Abeillé (ed.), *Treebanks: Building and Using Parsed Corpora*. Amsterdam: Kluwer. 103–27.

Halliday, M. A. K. (1950) Some lexicogrammatical features of the dialects of the Pearl River Delta. Reprinted in *Collected Works,* vol. 8 (2006): 249–69.

Halliday, M. A. K. (1956) The linguistic basis of a mechanical thesaurus, and its application to English preposition classification. *Mechanical Translation* 3(3): 81–8. Reprinted in *Collected Works*, vol. 6 (2005): 20–36.

Halliday, M. A. K. (1959) *The Language of the Chinese "Secret History of the Mongols"*. Oxford: Blackwell (Publications of the Philological Society 17). Reprinted in *Collected Works*, vol. 8 (2006): 5–171.

Halliday, M. A. K. (1961) Categories of the theory of grammar. *Word* 17(3): 242–92. Reprinted in *Collected Works*, vol. 1 (2002): 37–94.

Halliday, M. A. K. (1963) The tones of English. *Archivum Linguisticum* 15(1): 1–28.

Halliday, M. A. K. (1964a) Syntax and the consumer. In C. I. J. M. Stuart (ed.), *Report of the Fifteenth Annual (First International) Round Table Meeting on Linguistics and Language*. Washington, DC: Georgetown University Press. 11–24. Reprinted in M. A. K. Halliday and J. R. Martin (eds), *Readings in Systemic Linguistics* (1981). London: Batsford. Reprinted in *Collected Works*, vol. 3 (2003): 36–49.

Halliday, M. A. K. (1964b) The linguistic study of literary texts. Reprinted in *Collected Works*, vol. 2 (2002): 5–22.

Halliday, M. A. K. (1966) Some notes on 'deep' grammar. *Journal of Linguistics* 2(1): 57–67.

Halliday, M. A. K. (1967) *Intonation and Grammar in British English*. The Hague: Mouton. (Janua Linguarum Series Practica 48).

Halliday, M. A. K. (1967–1968) Notes on transitivity and theme in English, Parts 1–3. *Journal of Linguistics* 3(1): 37–81; 3(2): 199–244; 4(2): 179–215. Reprinted in *Collected Works*, vol. 7 (2005): 5–153.

Halliday, M. A. K. (1970a) *A Course in Spoken English: Intonation*. London: Oxford University Press.

Halliday, M. A. K. (1970b) Language structure and language function. In J. Lyons (ed.), *New Horizons in Linguistics*. Harmondsworth: Penguin Books. Reprinted in *Collected Works*, vol. 1 (2002): 173–95.

Halliday, M. A. K. (1971a) Linguistic function and literary style: an enquiry into the language of William Golding's 'The Inheritors'. In S. Chatman (ed.).

Halliday, M. A. K. (1971b) Language in a social perspective. *Educational Review* 23(3). Reprinted in *Collected Works*, vol. 10 (2007): 43–64.

Halliday, M. A. K. (1972) Towards a sociological semantics. Urbino: Centro Internazionale di Semiotica e di Linguistica (Working Papers and Prepublications 14/C). Reprinted in M. A. K. Halliday (1973a). Reprinted in *Collected Works*, vol. 3 (2003): 323–54.

Halliday, M. A. K. (1973a) *Explorations in the Functions of Language*. London: Edward Arnold.

Halliday, M. A. K. (1973b) The functional basis of language. In M. A. K. Halliday (1973a). Reprinted in *Collected Works*, vol. 3 (2003): 298–322.

Halliday, M. A. K. (1973c) Towards a sociological semantics. In M. A. K. Halliday (1973a). Reprinted in *Collected Works*, vol. 3 (2003): 323–54.

Halliday, M. A. K. (1975a) *Learning How to Mean*. London: Edward Arnold.

Halliday, M. A. K. (1975b) Into the adult language. First published in M. A. K. Halliday (1975a). Reprinted in *Collected Works*, vol. 4 (2003): 157–96.

Halliday, M. A. K. (1975c) The social context of language development. First published in M. A. K. Halliday (1975a). Reprinted in *Collected Works*, vol. 4 (2003): 281–307.

Halliday, M. A. K. (1976a) English system networks. In G. R. Kress (ed.), *Halliday: System and Function in Language: Selected Papers*. London: Oxford University Press.

Halliday, M. A. K. (1976b) The teacher taught the student English: an essay in applied linguistics. In P. A. Reich (ed.), *The Second LACUS Forum 1975*. Columbia, SC: Hornbeam Press. Reprinted in *Collected Works*, vol. 7 (2005): 297–305.

Halliday, M. A. K. (1977a) Ideas about language. In M. A. K. Halliday, *Aims and Perspectives in Linguistics*. Applied Linguistics Association of Australia (Occasional Papers 1). 32–49.

Halliday, M. A. K. (1977b) Text as semantic choice in social contexts. In T. A. van Dijk and J. S. Petöfi (eds), *Grammars and Descriptions*. Berlin: W de Gruyter. Reprinted in *Collected Works*, vol. 2 (2002): 23–84

Halliday, M. A. K. (1978a) *Language as Social Semiotic: The Social Interpretation of Language and Meaning*. London and Baltimore: Edward Arnold and University Park Press.

Halliday, M. A. K. (1978b) Language as social semiotic. In M. A. K. Halliday, *Language as Social Semiotic: The Social Interpretation of Language and Meaning*. London: Arnold. 108–26.

Halliday, M. A. K. (1978c) Meaning and the construction of reality in early childhood. In H. L. Pick and E. Saltzman (eds), *Modes of perceiving and processing of information*. Hillsdale, NJ: Erlbaum. 67–96. Reprinted in *Collected Works*, vol. 4 (2003): 113–43.

Halliday, M. A. K. (1979a) Development of texture in child language. In T. Myers (ed.), *The Development of Conversation and Discourse*. Edinburgh: Edinburgh University Press. 72–87.

Halliday, M. A. K. (1979b) Modes of meaning and modes of expression: types of grammatical structure and their determination by different semantic functions. In D. G. J. Allerton, E. Carney and D. Holdcroft (eds), *Function and Context in Linguistic Analysis: Essays offered to William Haas*. Cambridge: Cambridge University Press. Reprinted in *Collected Works*, vol. 1 (2002): 196–218.

Halliday, M. A. K. (1980) Three aspects of children's language development: learning language, learning through language, learning about language. In Y. M. Goodman, M. M. Haussler and D. Strickland (eds), *Oral and Writen Language Development: Impact on Schools*. Newark, DE: International Reading Association. 7–19. Reprinted in *Collected Works*, vol. 4 (2003): 308–26.

Halliday, M. A. K. (1981a) Text semantics and clause grammar: some patterns of realization. In J. E. Copeland and P. W. Davis (eds): 31–59.

Halliday, M. A. K. (1981b) Text semantics and clause grammar: how is a text like a clause?. In *Collected Works*, vol. 1 (2002): 219–60.

Halliday, M. A. K. (1982) The de-automatization of grammar: from Priestley's 'An Inspector Calls'. In J. M. Anderson (ed.), *Language Form and Linguistic Variation: Papers Dedicated to Angus McIntosh*. Amsterdam: Benjamins. 129–59. Reprinted in *Collected Works*, vol. 2 (2002): 126–48.

Halliday, M. A. K. (1983) On the transition from child tongue to mother tongue. *Australian Journal of Linguistics* 3(2): 201–16. Reprinted in *Collected Works*, vol. 4 (2003): 209–26.

Halliday, M. A. K. (1984a) Language as code and language as behaviour: a systemic-functional interpretation of the nature and ontogenesis of dialogue. In M.A.K. Halliday, R. P. Fawcett, S. Lamb and A. Makkai (eds), *The Semiotics of Language and Culture Vol. 1*. London: Frances Pinter. 3–35.

Halliday, M. A. K. (1984b) A systemic-functional interpretation of the nature and ontogenesis of dialogue. Reprinted in *Collected Works*, vol. 4 (2003): 226–50.

Halliday, M. A. K. (1984c) On the ineffability of grammatical categories. Reprinted in *Collected Works,* vol. 1 (2002): 291–322.

Halliday, M. A. K. (1985a) *An Introduction to Functional Grammar*. London: Edward Arnold. 2nd edn, London and Melbourne: Arnold, 1994. 3rd edn (revised by C. M. I. M. Matthiessen), London: Arnold, 2004.

Halliday, M. A. K. (1985b) *Spoken and Written Language*. Geelong, Vic.: Deakin University Press. Reprinted in London: Oxford University Press, 1989.

Halliday, M. A. K. (1985c) Systemic background. In J. D. Benson and W. S. Greaves (eds) (1985a): 1–15.

Halliday, M. A. K. (1987) Spoken and written modes of meaning. In R. Horowitz and S. J. Samuels (eds), *Comprehending Oral and Written Language*. Orlando, Florida: Academic Press. Reprinted in *Collected Works*, vol. 1 (2002): 323–51.

Halliday, M. A. K. (1988a) On the language of physical science. In M. Ghadessy (ed.), *Registers of Written English: Situational Factors and Linguistic Features.* London and New York: Pinter Publishers. 162–78.

Halliday, M. A. K. (1988b) Poetry as scientific discourse: the nuclear sections of Tennyson's 'In Memoriam'. In D. Birch and L. M. O'Toole (eds). Reprinted in *Collected Works*, vol. 2 (2002): 149–67.

Halliday, M. A. K. (1991a) Corpus linguistics and probabilistic grammar. In K. Aijmer and B. Altenberg (eds): 30–43.

Halliday, M. A. K. (1991b) The place of dialogue in children's construction of meaning. In S. Stati, E. Weigand and F. Hundsnurscher (eds), *Dialoganalyse III. Referate der 3 Arbeitstagung.* Tubingen: Max Niemeyer Verlag. 417–30. Reprinted in *Collected Works*, vol. 4 (2003): 250–64.

Halliday, M. A. K. (1991c) Towards probabilistic interpretations. In E. Ventola (ed.): 39–61.

Halliday, M. A. K. (1991d) The notion of "context" in language education. In T. Lê and M. McCausland (eds). Reprinted with amendment in M. Ghadessy (ed.) (1999). Final version: Reprinted in *Collected Works*, vol. 9 (2007): 269–90.

Halliday, M. A. K. (1992a) Systemic grammar and the concept of a 'science of language'. *Waiguoyu* (Journal of Foreign Languages, Shanghai International Studies University) 2.

Halliday, M. A. K. (1992b) New ways of meaning: a challenge to applied linguistics. *Journal of Applied Linguistics* 6. Greek Applied Linguistics Association.

Halliday, M. A. K. (1992c) A systemic interpretation of Peking syllable finals. In P. Tench (ed.): 98–121.

Halliday, M. A. K. (1992d) How do you mean? In M. Davies and L. J. Ravelli (eds): 20–35. Reprinted in *Collected Works*, vol. 2 (2002): 352–68.

Halliday, M. A. K. (1992e) Language as system and language as instance: the corpus as a theoretical construct. In J. Svartvik (ed.) (1991): 65–77. Reprinted in *Collected Works*, vol. 6 (2005): 76–92.

Halliday, M. A. K. (1993a) Quantitative studies and probabilities in grammar. In M. Hoey (ed.), *Data, Description, Discourse: Papers on English Language in Honour of John McH. Sinclair [on his sixtieth birthday].* London: Harper Collins. 1–25.

Halliday, M. A. K. (1993b) Towards a language-based theory of learning. *Linguistics and Education* 5(2): 93–116. Reprinted in *Collected Works*, vol. 4 (2003): 327–352.

Halliday, M. A. K. (1993c) The act of meaning. In J. E. Alatis (ed.), *Language, Communication and Social Meaning: Georgetown University Round Table on Language and Linguistics.* Washington, DC: Georgetown University Press. Reprinted in *Collected Works*, vol. 3 (2003): 355–74.

Halliday, M. A. K. (1993d) Analysis of scientific texts in English and Chinese. Reprinted in *Collected Works*, vol. 8 (2006): 334–45.

Halliday, M. A. K. (1995a) Computing meaning: some reflections on past experience and present prospects. Paper presented to *PACLING 95, Brisbane, April 1995.* Reprinted in G. W. Huang and Z. Y. Wang (eds): 3–25. Reprinted in *Collected Works*, vol. 6 (2005): 239–67.

Halliday, M. A. K. (1995b) Language and the theory of codes. In A. Sadovnik (ed.): 127–44.

Halliday, M. A. K. (1995c) On language in relation to the evolution of human consciousness. In S. Allén (ed.), *Of Thoughts and Words: Proceedings of Nobel Symposium 92 "The relation between language and mind"*, Stockholm, August 8–12, 1994. Singapore, River Edge, NJ and London: Imperial College Press. 45–84. Reprinted in *Collected Works*, vol. 3 (2003): 390–432.

Halliday, M. A. K. (1995d) Fuzzy grammatics: a systemic functional approach to fuzziness in natural language. *Proceedings of 1995 IEEE International Conference on Fuzzy Systems*. Piscataway, NJ: IEEE. Reprinted in *Collected Works*, vol. 6 (2005): 213–38.

Halliday, M. A. K. (1996) On grammar and grammatics. In R. Hasan, C. Cloran and D. G. Butt (eds): 1–38. Reprinted in *Collected Works*, vol. 1 (2002): 384–417.

Halliday, M. A. K. (1998a) Things and relations: regrammaticising experience as technical knowledge. In J. R. Martin and R. Veel (eds): 185–235.

Halliday, M. A. K. (1998b) On the grammar of pain. *Functions of Language* 5.1. Reprinted in *Collected Works*, vol. 7 (2005): 306–37.

Halliday, M. A. K. (1998c) Language and knowledge: the 'unpacking' of text. In *Collected Works*, vol. 5 (2004): 24–48.

Halliday, M. A. K. (1999) Grammar and the construction of educational knowledge. In B. Asker, K. Hyland and M. Lam (eds), *Language Analysis, Description and Pedagogy*. Hong Kong: Language Centre, Hong Kong University of Science and Technology. 70–87. Reprinted in *Collected Works*, vol. 4 (2003): 353–72.

Halliday, M. A. K. (2000) Phonology past and present: a personal retrospect. *Folia Linguistica* XXXIV 1–2: 101–11.

Halliday, M. A. K. (2002) The spoken language corpus. In K. Aijmer and B. Altenberg (eds), *Proceedings of ICAME 2002: The Theory and Use of Corpora, Göteborg, May 22–26, 2002*. Amsterdam: Rodopi.

Halliday, M. A. K. (2002–2007) *Collected Works* vols. 1–10. Edited by J. J. Webster. London and New York: Continuum.
Volume 1 (2002) On Grammar
Volume 2 (2002) Linguistic Studies of Text and Discourse
Volume 3 (2003) On Language and Linguistics
Volume 4 (2003) The Language of Early Childhood
Volume 5 (2004) The Language of Science
Volume 6 (2005) Computational and Quantitative Studies
Volume 7 (2005) Studies in English Language
Volume 8 (2006) Studies in Chinese Language
Volume 9 (2007) Language and Society
Volume 10 (2007) Language and Education
China edition of Vols 1–10 published Beijing: Peking University Press, 2007.

Halliday, M. A. K. (2004a) On grammar as the driving force from primary to higher-order consciouness. In G. Williams and A. Lukin (eds): 15–44.

Halliday, M. A. K. (2004b) Representing the child as a semiotic being: (one who means). In J. A. Foley (ed.), *Language, Education and Discourse: Functional Approaches*. London: Continuum. 19–42.

Halliday, M. A. K. (2005a) On matter and meaning: the two realms of human experience. *Linguistics and the Human Sciences* 1(1): 59–82.

Halliday, M. A. K. (2005b) Introduction. In *Collected Works*, vol. 7 (2005): xii–xxx.

Halliday, M.A.K. (2006) Afterwords. In G. Thompson and S. Hunston (eds).
Halliday, M. A. K. (2008) *Complementarities in Language*. Beijing: The Commercial Press.
Halliday, M. A. K. and Greaves, W. S. (2008) *Intonation in the Grammar of English*. London and Oakville: Equinox.
Halliday, M. A. K. and Hasan, R. (1976) *Cohesion in English*. London: Longman (English Language Series 9).
Halliday, M. A. K. and Hasan, R. (1985) *Language, Context, and Text: Aspects of Language in a Social-semiotic Perspective*. Geelong, Vic.: Deakin University Press. Republished in (1989). Oxford: Oxford University Press.
Halliday, M. A. K. and James, Z. L. (1993) A quantitative study of polarity and primary tense in the English finite clause. In J. M. Sinclair, M. Hoey and G. Fox (eds): 32–66. Reprinted in *Collected Works*, vol. 6 (2005): 93–129.
Halliday, M. A. K. and Martin, J. R. (1993) *Writing Science: Literacy and Discursive Power*. London: Falmer (Critical Perspectives on Literacy and Education).
Halliday, M. A. K. and Matthiessen, C. M. I. M. (1999) *Construing Experience through Meaning: A Language-based Approach to Cognition*. London: Cassell. Study edition by Continuum, 2006.
Halliday, M. A. K., Gibbons, J. and Nicholas, H. (eds) (1990) *Learning, Keeping and Using Language: Selected Papers from the Eighth World Congress of Applied Linguistics, Sydney, August 16–21, 1987*. Amsterdam and Philadelphia: John Benjamins.
Halliday, M. A. K., McIntosh, A. and Strevens, P. (1964) *The Linguistic Sciences and Language Teaching*. London: Longman (Longman Linguistics Library).
Hammill, P. L. and Newcomer, D. D. (1997) *Test of Language Development –Primary*. 3rd edn, Bloomington, MN: Pearson Education.
Harré, R. (1983) *Personal Being: A Theory for Individual Psychology*. Oxford: Blackwell.
Harrison, C. and Young, L. (2004) Bureaucratic discourse: writing in the 'comfort zone'. In Y. Lynne and C. Harrison (eds): 231–46.
Hasan, R. (1964) *A Linguistic Study of Contrasting Features in the Style of Two Contemporary English Prose Writers*. Unpublished Ph.D. Thesis. Edinburgh: University of Edinburgh.
Hasan, R. (1968) Linguistics and the study of literature. *Etudes de Linguistique Appliquée* 5.
Hasan, R. (1971) Rime and reason in literature. In S. Chatman (ed.).
Hasan, R. (1973a) Measuring the length of a text. Mimeo.
Hasan, R. (1973b) Cohesive categories. Mimeo.
Hasan, R. (1973c) Code, register and social dialect. In B. Bernstein (ed.), *Class, Codes and Control, Vol 2: Applied Studies towards a Sociology of Language*. London: Routledge and Kegan Paul. 253–92. Reprinted in *Collected Works of Ruqaiya Hasan*, vol. 1 (2005): 160–93.
Hasan, R. (1975) The place of stylistics in the study of verbal art. In H. Ringbom (ed.), *Style and Text*. Amsterdam: Skriptor.
Hasan, R. (1978) Text in the systemic-functional model. In W. Dressler (ed.), *Current Trends in Text Linguistics*. Berlin: Walter de Gruyter. 228–46.
Hasan, R. (1979) On the notion of text. In J. S. Petöfi (ed.), *Text vs. Sentence: Basic Questions of Text Linguistics*. Hamburg: Helmut Buske Verlag.

Hasan, R. (1981) What's going on: a dynamic view of context in language. In J. E. Copeland and P. W. Davis (eds).
Hasan, R. (1984a) Coherence and cohesive harmony. In J. Flood (ed.), *Understanding Reading Comprehension: Cognition, Language and the Structure of Prose*. Newark, Delaware: International Reading Association. 181–219.
Hasan, R. (1984b) The nursery tale as a genre. In M. Berry, M. Subbs and R. Carter (eds), *Nottingham Linguistic Circular*, 13: 71–102 (Special Issue on Systemic Linguistics). Department of English: Nottingham University. Reprinted in R. Hasan (1996a): 51–72.
Hasan, R. (1985a) Meaning, context and text – fifty years after Malinowski. In J. D. Benson and W. S. Greaves (eds) (1985a): 15–50.
Hasan, R. (1985b) *Linguistics, Language and Verbal Art*. Geelong, Vic.: Deakin University Press. Reprinted in London: Oxford University Press, 1989.
Hasan, R. (1985c) The texture of a text. In M. A. K. Halliday and R. Hasan (eds): 70–96. Republished in (1989). Oxford: Oxford University Press.
Hasan, R. (1985d) The structure of a text. In M. A. K. Halliday and R. Hasan, (eds). Republished by Oxford University Press, 1989.
Hasan, R. (1988) The analysis of one poem: theoretical issues in practice. In D. Birch and L. M. O'Toole (eds).
Hasan, R. (1990) Semantic variation and sociolinguistics. *Australian Journal of Linguistics* 9(2): 221–76.
Hasan, R. (1991) Questions as a mode of learning in everyday talk. In T, Lê and M. McCausland (eds): 70–119.
Hasan, R. (1992a) Meaning in sociolinguistic theory. In K. Bolton and H. Kwok (eds), *Sociolinguistics Today: International Perspectives*. London: Routledge. 80–119.
Hasan, R. (1992b) Rationality in everyday talk: from process to system. In J. Svartvik (ed.): 122–307.
Hasan, R. (1992c) Speech genre, semiotic mediation and the development of higher mental functions. *Language Sciences* 14(4): 489–528.
Hasan, R. (1995a) On social conditions for semiotic mediation: the genesis of mind in society. In A. Sadovnik (ed.): 171–96.
Hasan, R. (1995b) The conception of context in text. In P. H. Fries and M. Gregory (eds): 183–283.
Hasan, R. (1996a) *Ways of Saying: Ways of Meaning: Selected Papers of Ruqaiya Hasan*. Edited by C. Cloran, D. G. Butt and G. Williams. London: Cassell (Open Linguistics Series).
Hasan, R. (1996b) Semantic networks: a tool for the analysis of meaning. In R. Hasan (1996a).
Hasan, R. (1999a) The disempowerment game: Bourdieu on language. *Linguistics and Education* 10(1). Reprinted in *Collected Works of Ruqaiya Hasan*, vol. 1 (2005): 277–336.
Hasan, R. (1999b) Speaking with reference to context. In M. Ghadessy (ed.): 219–328.
Hasan, R. (2004a) Analysing discursive variation. In L. Young and C. Harrison (eds).

Hasan, R. (2004b) The world in words: semiotic mediation, tenor and ideology. In G. Williams and A. Lukin (eds): 158–81.
Hasan, R. (2005) *Language, Society and Consciousness: Collected Works of Ruqaiya Hasan Vol. 1*. Edited by J. J. Webster. London and Oakville: Equinox.
Hasan, R. (In Press) Wanted a theory for integrated sociolinguistics. In *Collected Works of Ruqaiya Hasan Vol. 2*. London: Equinox.
Hasan, R. and Cloran, C. (1990) A sociolinguistic interpretation of everyday talk between mothers and children. In M. A. K. Halliday, J. Gibbons and H. Nicholas (eds): 67–99.
Hasan, R., Cloran, C. and Butt, D. G. (eds) (1996) *Functional Descriptions: Theory in Practice*. Amsterdam and Philadelphia: John Benjamins.
Hasan, R. and Fries, P. H. (eds) (1995) *On Subject and Theme: A Discourse Functional Perspective*. Amsterdam: Benjamins (Amsterdam Studies in the Theory and History of Linguistic Science).
Hasan, R. and Martin, J. R. (eds) (1989) *Language Development: Learning Language, Learning Culture. Meaning and Choice in Language*. Norwood, NJ: Ablex.
Hasan, R. and Williams, G. (eds) (1996) *Literacy in Society*. London: Longman (Applied Linguistics and Language Study).
Hasan, R., Cloran, C., Williams, G and Lukin, A. (2007) Semantic networks: the description of linguistic meaning in SFL. In R. Hasan, C. M. I. M. Matthiessen and J. J. Webster (eds): 697–738.
Hasan, R., Matthiessen, C. M. I. M. and J. J. Webster (eds) (2005, 2007) *Continuing Discourse on Language: A Functional Perspective Vols. 1 and 2*. London and Oakville: Equinox.
Hansen-Schirra, S. (2003) *The Nature of Translated Text - An Interdisciplinary Methodology for the Investigation of the Specific Properties of Translations*. Saarbrücken Dissertations in Computational Linguistics and Language Technology, Volume 13. Saarbrücken: German Research Center for Artificial Intelligence and Saarland University.
Hansen-Schirra, S. and Neumann, S. (2004) Linguistische Verständlichmachung in der juristischen Realität. In K. D. Lerch (ed.), *Recht Verstehen. Verständlichkeit, Missverständlichkeit und Unverständlichkeit von Recht*. Band 1. Schriftenreihe *Die Sprache des Rechts* der Berlin-Brandenburgischen Akademie der Wissenschaften. Berlin and New York: de Gruyter. 167–84.
Hansen-Schirra, S., Neumann, S. and Steiner, E. (2007) Cohesive explicitness and explicitation in an English-German translation corpus. *Languages in Contrast* 7(2): 241–65.
Haspelmath, M., Dryer, M. S., Gil, D. and Comrie, B. (eds) (2005) *The World Atlas of Language Structures*. Oxford: Oxford University Press.
Hatim, B. and Mason, I. (1990) *Discourse and the Translator*. London: Longman.
Hauser, M., Chomsky, N. and Fitch, W. T. (2002) The faculty of language: what is it, who has it, and how did it evolve?. *Science* 298(5598): 1569–79.
Herke-Couchman, M. (2006) *SFL, Corpus and the Consumer: An Exploration of Theoretical and Technological Potential*. Unpublished Ph.D. Thesis. Macquarie University, Sydney.
Hill, T. (1958) Institutional linguistics. *Orbis* 7(2): 441–55.

Hirst, W. (ed.) (1988) *The Making of Cognitive Science: Essays in Honor of George A. Miller.* Cambridge: Cambridge University Press.

Hjelmslev, L. (1943) *Omkring Sprogteoriens Grundlæggelse.* København: Akademisk Forlag. (English version. 1961 *Prolegomena to a Theory of Language.* Madison, Wisconsin: University of Wiscons.)

Hjelmslev, L. (1961) *Prolegomena to a Theory of Language* (Translated by F. J. Whitfield). Madison: University of Wiscons.

Hoey, M. (1991a) Another perspective on coherence and cohesive harmony. In E. Ventola (ed.): 385–414.

Hoey. M. (1991b) *Pattern of Lexis in Text.* Oxford: Oxford University Press.

Hoey, M. (2001) *Textual Interaction: An Introduction to Written Discourse Analysis.* London: Routledge.

Hoey, M. (2006) Language as choice: what is chosen?. In S. Hunston and G. Thompson (eds): 37–54.

Holland, A. L. (1998) Functional outcome assessment of aphasia following left hemisphere stroke. *Seminars in Speech and Language* 19(3): 249–60.

Honnibal, M. (2004a) *Adapting the Penn Treebank to Systemic Functional Grammar: Design, Creation and Use of a Metafunctionally Annotated Corpus.* BA Honours Thesis. Macquarie University, Department of Linguistics.

Honnibal, M. (2004b) Converting the Penn Treebank to Systemic Functional Grammar. *Proceedings of the Australasian Language Technology Workshop, December 2004, Sydney, Australia.*

Hood, S. and Forey, G. (2008) The interpersonal dynamics of call-centre interactions: co-constructing the rise and fall of emotion. *Discourse and Communication* 2(4): 389–409.

Hood, S. and Martin, J. R. (2007) Invoking attitude: the play of graduation in appraising discourse. In R. Hasan, C. M. I. M. Matthiessen and J. J. Webster (eds): 739–64.

Hori, M. (2006) Pain expressions in Japanese. In G. Thompson and S. Hunston (eds).

Horvath, B. and Eggins, S. (1995) Opinion texts in conversation. In P. H. Fries and M. J. Gregory (eds): 29–47.

Huang, G. W. and Wang, Z. Y. (eds) (2002) *Discourse and Language Functions.* Shanghai: Foreign Language Teaching and Research Press.

Huddleston, R. D., Hudson, R. A., Winter, E. and Henrici, A. (1968) *Sentence and Clause in Scientific English.* University College London: Communication Research Centre. (mimeo).

Hunston, S. and Thompson, G. (eds) (2000) *Evaluation in Text: Authorial Stance and the Construction of Discourse.* Oxford: Oxford University Press.

Hunston, S. and Thompson, G. (eds) (2006) *System and Corpus: Exploring Connections.* London: Equinox.

Hyland, K. (2002) Genre: language, context and literacy. *ARAL* 22: 113–35.

Hyon, S. (1996) Genre in three traditions: implications for ESL. *TESOL Quarterly* 30(4): 693–722.

Iedema, R. (1993) Legal English: discipline specific literacy and genre theory. *Australian Review of Applied Linguistics* 16(2): 86–122.

Iedema, R. (1995) Legal Ideology: the role of language in common law appellate judgments. *The International Journal for the Semiotics of Law* VIII 22: 21–36.

Iedema, R. (1996) *The Language of Administration*. (Write it right industry research report no. 3.) Sydney: NSW, Department of Education, Disadvantaged Schools Program Metropolitan East.

Iedema, R. (1997a) The language of administration: organizing human activity in formal institutions. In F. Christie and J. R. Martin (eds): 73–100.

Iedema, R. (1997b) The history of the accident news story. *Australian Review of Applied Linguistics* 20(2): 95–119.

Iedema, R. (1997c) *Interactional Dynamics and Social Change: Planning as Morphogenesis*. Ph.D. Thesis. Sydney University.

Iedema, R. (1998) Hidden meanings and institutional responsibility. *Discourse and Society* 9(4): 481–500.

Iedema, R. (2000) Bureaucratic planning and resemiotisation. In E. Ventola (ed.): 47–69.

Iedema, R. (2001) Analysing film and television. In T. van Leeuwen and C. Jewitt (eds): 183–204.

Iedema, R. (2003) *Discourses of Post-Bureaucratic Organization*. Amsterdam: Banjamins.

Iedema, R. (ed.) (2007) *The Discourse of Hospital Communication: Tracing Complexities in Contemporary Health Organizations*. London and New York: Palgrave Macmillan.

Iedema, R. and Degeling, P. (2001) From difference to divergence: the logogenesis of interactive tension. *Functions of Language* 8(1): 41–78.

Iedema, R. and Scheeres, H. (2003) From doing to talking work: renegotiating knowing, doing and identity. In C. Candlin and S. Sarangi (eds), *International Journal of Applied Linguistics* 24(3): 316–37.

Iedema, R., Feez, S. and White, P. R. R. (1994) *Media Literacy*. (Write it right industry research report no. 2.) Sydney: NSW, Department of Education, Disadvantaged Schools Program Metropolitan East. Reprinted in Sydney: NSW AMES 2008.

Jakobson, R. (1978) Realism in Art. In L. Matejka and K. Pomorska (eds).

Jakobson, R. (ed.) (1987) *Language in Literature*. Cambridge, Mass.: The Belknap Press of Harvard University Press.

Johnston T. (2004) W(h)ither the deaf community? Population, genetics, and the future of Australian sign language. *American Annals of Deaf* 148(5): 358–75.

Jordens, C. F. C., Little, M., Paul, P. and Sayers, E.-J. (2001) Life disruption and generic complexity: a social linguistic analysis of narratives of cancer illness. *Social Science and Medicine* 53: 1227–36.

Kaplan, E., Goodglass, H. and Weintraub, S. (1983) *The Boston Naming Test*. Philadelphia: Lippincott, Williams, and Wilkins.

Kappagoda, A. (2005) What people do to know: the construction of knowledge as a social-semiotic activity. In R. Hasan, C. M. I. M. Matthiessen and J. J. Webster (eds): 185–216.

Kasper, R. (1988) An experimental parser for systemic grammars. *Proceedings of the 12th International Conference on Computational Linguistics, Budapest, Association for Computational Linguistics*.

Kay, J., Lesser, R. and Coltheart, M. (1992) *Psycholinguistic Assessment of Language Processing in Aphasia*. Hove: Psychology Press.

Kay, M. and Röscheisen, M. (1993) Text-translation alignment. *Computational Linguistics* 19(1): 121–42.

Kaye, G. (1990) A corpus builder and real-time concordance browser for an IBM PC. In J. Aarts and W. Meijs (eds).

Kealley, D. J. (2007) *"I can't find a pulse but that's OK": Nursing in Context: A Systemic Functional Linguistic Examination of Nursing Practice*. Ph.D. Thesis. University of South Australia.

Kennedy, G. (1998) *An Introduction to Corpus Linguistics*. New York: Addison Wesley.

Kertesz, A. (1982) *Western Aphasia Battery*. New York: Grune and Stratton.

Kim, M. (2007) Using systemic functional text analysis for translator education: an illustration with a focus on textual meaning. *The Interpreter and Translator Trainer* 1(2): 223–46.

Kipp, M. (2001) Anvil - a generic annotation tool for multimodal dialogue. *Proceedings of the 7th European Conference on Speech Communication and Technology (Eurospeech), Aalborg, Denmark*.

Klein, D. and Manning, C. (2003) Accurate unlexicalized parsing. *Proceedings of the 41st Meeting of the Association for Computational Linguistics (ACL), Sapporo, Japan*.

Knox, J. S. (2007) Visual-verbal communication on online newspaper home pages. *Visual Communication* 6(1): 19–53.

Knox, J. S. (2008) Online newspapers and TESOL classrooms: a multimodal perspective. In L. Unsworth (ed.).

Knox, J. S. (In Press) Designing the news in an online newspaper: a systemic description. In A. Baldry and E. Montagna (eds), *Interdisciplinary Perspectives on Multimodality: Theory and Practice (Proceedings of the Third International Conference on Multimodality)*. Campobasso: Palladino.

Knox, J. S. and Patpong, P. (2008) Reporting bloodshed in Thai newspapers: a comparative case study of English and Thai. In E. Thomson and P. R. R. White (eds), *Communicating Conflict: Multilingual Case Studies of the Rhetoric of the News Media*. London: Continuum. 173–202.

Kress, G. and Hodge, R. (1979) *Language as Ideology*. London: Routledge and Kegan Paul.

Kress, G. and Hodge, R. (1988) *Social Semiotics*. London: Polity.

Kress, G. and van Leeuwen, T. (1996) *Reading Images: The Grammar of Visual Design*. London: Routledge.

Kress, G. and van Leeuwen, T. (2001) *Multimodal Discourse: The Modes and Media of Contemporary Communication*. London: Arnold.

Kuch, P. (1995) *Bruce Dawe*. Melbourne: Oxford University Press.

Labov, W. (1972a) *Language in the Inner City*. Philadelphia: University of Pennsylvania.

Labov, W. (1972b) *The Study of Language in Its Social Context, in Patterns of Language*. London: Cambridge University Press.

Lamb, S. M. (1999) *Pathways of the Brain: The Neurocognitive basis of Language*. Amsterdam and Philadelphia: John Benjamins.

Lamb, S. M. (2005) Language and brain: when experiments are unfeasible, you have to think harder. *Linguistics and the Human Sciences* 1(2): 151–76.

Lantolf, J. P. and Thorne, S. L. (2006) *Sociocultural Theory and the Genesis of Second Language Development*. Oxford: Oxford University Press.

Lappin, S. and Shieber, S. M. (2007) Machine learning theory and practice as a source of insight into universal grammar. *Journal of Linguistics* 43:1–34.

Lavid, J. (1997) Specifying the discourse semantics of grammatical theme for multi-lingual text generation: preliminary findings. *Revista de la Sociedad Española para el Procesamiento del Lenguaje Natural* 21: 57–79.

Lavid, J. (2000) Cross-cultural variation in multilingual instructions: a study of speech act realisation patterns. In E. Ventola (ed.).

Lavid, J. (2008) The grammar of emotion in English and Spanish: a corpus-based study. In E. Ventola and C. Jones (eds), *Field, Ideation and Experiential Representation: From Language to Multimodality*. London: Equinox.

Law, P. (1979) The poetry of Bruce Dawe. *Southerly* 2(39): 192–203.

Lê, T. and McCausland, M. (eds) (1991) *Language Education: Interaction and Development*. Tasmania: University of Tasmania.

Leech, G. N. (1974) *Semantics*. Harmondsworth: Penguin.

Lemke, J. L. (1984) *Semiotics and Education*. Toronto: Victoria University (Toronto Semiotic Circle Monographs, Working Papers and Prepublications 2).

Lemke, J. L. (1993) Discourse, dynamics and social change. *Cultural Dynamics* 6(1): 243–275.

Lemke, J. L. (1995) *Textual Politics: Discourse and Social Dynamics*. London: Taylor and Francis (Culture and Society/Critical Perspectives on Literacy and Education).

Lemke, J. L. (1998) Multiplying meaning: visual and verbal semiotics in scientific text. In J. R. Martin and R. Veel (eds): 87–113.

Lemme, M. L., Hedberg, N. L. and Bottenberg, D. F. (1984) Cohesion in narratives of aphasic adults. In R. H. Brookshire (ed.): 215–22.

Lewin, B., Fine, J. and Young, L. (2001) *Expository Discourse: A Genre Based Approach to Social Science Texts*. London: Continuum.

Liles, B., Duffy, R., Merritt, D. and Purcell, S. (1995) Measurement of narrative discourse in children with language disorders. *Journal of Speech and Hearing Disorders* 38: 415–25.

Lock, S. and Armstrong, L. (1997) Cohesion analysis of the expository discourse of normal, fluent aphasic and demented adults: a role in differential diagnosis? *Clinical Linguistics and Phonetics* 11: 299–317.

Lockwood, J., Forey, G. and Elias, N. (Forthcoming) Call centre communication: measurement processes in non-English speaking contexts. In D. Belcher (ed.), *English for Specific Purposes in Theory and Practice*. Michigan: Michigan University Press.

Lüdeling, A. and Kytö, M. (eds) (2008) *Corpus Linguistics. An International Handbook. Series: Handbücher zur Sprache und Kommunikationswissenschaft/ Handbooks of Linguistics and Communication Science*. Berlin: Mouton de Gruyter.

Lukin, A. (2003) *Examining Poetry: A Corpus Based Enquiry into Literary Criticism*. Ph.D. Thesis. Macquarie University, Sydney.

Lukin, A. and Webster, J. J. (2005) SFL and the study of literature. In R. Hasan, C. M .I. M. Matthiessen and J. J. Webster (eds): 413–56.

Maamouri, M., Bies, A., Buckwalter, T. and Mekki, W. (2004) The Penn Arabic Treebank: building a large-scale annotated arabic corpus. *Proceedings of the NEMLAR International Conference on Arabic Language Resources and Tools, Cairo, Egypt*.

Macken-Horarik, M. and Martin, J. R. (eds) (2003) *Negotiating Heteroglossia: Social Perspectives on Evaluation.* (Special Issue of *Text* 23.2).

Mahfouz, I. (2008) *Macro-textual Cues and Word Sense Disambiguation: A Symantico-syntactic Study to Build an Electronic Linguistic Database.* Unpublished Ph.D. Dissertation.

Mair, C. (1998) Corpora and the study of the major varieties of English: Issues and results. In H. Lindquist, S. Klintborg, M. Levin and M. Estling (eds), *The Major Varieties of English: Papers from MAVEN 97.* Växjö: Växjö Acta Wexionensia. 139–57.

Makkai, A. and Lockwood, D. (1973) *Readings in Stratificational Linguistics.* University, AL: Alabama University Press.

Malinowski, B. (1923) The problem of meaning in primitive languages. Supplement I to C. K. Ogden and I. A. Richards (eds), *The Meaning of Meaning.* New York: Harcourt Brace.

Malinowski, B. (1935) An ethnographic theory of language. *Coral Gardens and their Magic, Vol. II* (Part IV). London: Allen and Unwin.

Malinowski, B. (1944) *A scientific theory of culture and other essays.* Chapel Hill: University of North Carolina Press.

Manidis, M., McGregor, J., Herke, M., Matthiessen, C. M. I. M., Slade, D., McCarthy, S., Scheeres, H., Stein-Parbury, J., Dunston, R. and Iedema, R. (In Press) Patient safety in emergency departments: the critical role of communication in the patient experience. *Social Science and Medicine.*

Mann, W. C. (1984) A linguistic overview of the Nigel text generation grammar. In A. Manning, P. Martin and K. McCalla (eds), *The Tenth LACUS Forum.* Columbia: South Carolina Hornbeam Press.

Mann, W. C. and Matthiessen, C. M. I. M. (1985) Demonstration of the Nigel text generation computer program. In J. D. Benson and W. S. Greaves (eds) (1985b).

Mann, W. C. and Thompson, S. A. (eds) (1992) *Discourse Description: Diverse Linguistic Analyses of a Fund-raising Text.* Amsterdam: Benjamins (Pragmatics and Beyond, New Series, 16).

Mann, W. C., Matthiessen, C. M. I. M. and Thompson, S. A. (1992) Rhetorical structure theory and text analysis. In W. C. Mann and S. A. Thompson (eds): 39–78.

Manning, C. D. and Schütze, H. (1999) *Foundations of Statistical Natural Language Processing.* Cambridge, Mass.: MIT Press.

Marcus, M. P., Santorini, B. and Marcinkiewicz, M. A. (1993) Building a large annotated corpus of English: the Penn Treebank. *Computational Linguistics* 19 (2): 313–30.

Martin, J. R. (1983) Participant identification in English, Tagalog and Kâte. *Australian Journal of Linguistics* 3(1): 45–74.

Martin, J. R. (1985a) *Factual Writing: Exploring and Challenging Social Reality.* Geelong, Vic.: Deakin University Press. Republished in (1989). Oxford: Oxford University Press.

Martin, J. R. (1985b) Process and text: two aspects of human semiosis. In J. D. Benson and W. S. Greaves (eds) (1985a): 248–74.

Martin, J. R. (1992a) *English Text: System and Structure.* Amsterdam: Benjamins. Reprinted by Peking University Press, 2004.

Martin, J. R. (1992b) Macro-proposals: meaning by degree. In W. C. Mann and S. A. Thompson (eds): 359–95.

Martin, J. R. (1993) Life as a noun. In M. A. K. Halliday and J. R. Martin (eds): 221–67.

Martin, J. R. (1994) Macro-genres: the ecology of the page. *Network* 21: 29–52.

Martin, J. R. (1995a) More than what the message is about: English Theme. In M. Ghadessy (ed.): 223–58.

Martin, J. R. (1995b) Text and clause: fractal resonance. *Text* 15(1): 5–42.

Martin, J. R. (1996a) Evaluating disruption: symbolising theme in junior secondary narrative. In R. Hasan and G. Williams (eds): 124–71.

Martin, J. R. (1996b) Types of structure: deconstructing notions of constituency in clause and text. In E. H. Hovy and D. R. Scott (eds), *Computational and Conversational Discourse: Burning Issues - An Interdisciplinary Account*. Heidelberg: Springer (NATO Advanced Science Institute Series F - Computer and Systems Sciences, Vol. 151). 39–66.

Martin, J. R. (1998) Practice into theory: catalysing change. In S. Hunston (ed.), *Language at Work*. Clevedon: Multilingual Matters (British Studies in Applied Linguistics 13 [BAAL 13]). 151–67.

Martin, J. R. (1999) Modelling context: a crooked path of progress in contextual linguistics (Sydney SFL). In M. Ghadessy (ed.): 25–61.

Martin, J. R. (2000a) Beyond exchange: APPRAISAL systems in English. In S. Hunston and G. Thompson (eds): 142–75.

Martin, J. R. (2000b) Close reading: functional linguistics as a tool for critical analysis. In L. Unsworth (ed.): 275–303.

Martin, J. R. (2000c) Design and practice: enacting functional linguistics in Australia. *Annual Review of Applied Linguistics* 20: 116–26. (20th Anniversary Volume 'Applied Linguistics as an Emerging Discipline').

Martin, J. R. (2001a) A context for genre: modelling social processes in functional linguistics. In R. Stainton and J. Devilliers (eds), *Communication in Linguistics*. Toronto: GREF (Collection Theoria). 1–41.

Martin, J. R. (2001b) From little things big things grow: ecogenesis in school geography. In R. Coe, L. Lingard and T. Teslenko (eds), *The Rhetoric and Ideology of Genre: Strategies for Stability and Change*. Cresskill, NJ: Hampton Press. 243–71.

Martin, J. R. (2001c) Writing history: construing time and value in discourses of the past. In C. Colombi and M. Schleppergrell (eds), *Developing Advanced Literacy in First and Second Languages*. Mahwah, NJ: Erlbaum.

Martin, J. R. (2001d) Giving the game away: explicitness, diversity and genre-based literacy in Australia. In R. Wodak et al. (eds), *Functional Il/literacy*. Vienna: Verlag der Osterreichischen Akadamie der Wissenschaften. 155–74.

Martin, J. R. (2002) Blessed are the peacemakers: reconciliation and evaluation. In C. Candlin (ed.): 187–227.

Martin, J. R. (2003) Making history: grammar for interpretation. In J. R. Martin and R. Wodak (eds): 19–57.

Martin, J. R. (2004) Positive discourse analysis: power, solidarity and change. *Revista Canaria de Estudios Ingleses* 49.

Martin, J. R. (2007) Genre, ideology and intertextuality: a systemic functional perspective. *Linguistics and Human Sciences* 2(2): 275–98.
Martin, J. R. and Matthiessen, C. M. I. M. (1992) Systemic typology and topology. In F. Christie (ed.).
Martin, J. R. and Plum, G. (1997) Construing experience: some story genres. *Journal of Narrative and Life History* 7(1–4): 299–308. (Special Issue: *Oral Versions of Personal Experience: three decades of narrative analysis*; M Bamberg Guest Editor).
Martin, J. R. and Rose, D. (2003) *Working with Discourse: Meaning beyond the Clause*. London: Continuum. Reprinted in (2007) Peking University Press, 2nd edn.
Martin, J. R. and Rose, D. (2005) Designing literacy pedagogy: scaffolding democracy in the classroom. In R. Hasan, C. M. I. M. Matthiessen and J. J. Webster (eds): 251–80.
Martin, J. R. and Rose, D. (2008) *Genre Relations: Mapping Culture*. London and Oakville: Equinox.
Martin, J. R. and Stenglin, M. (2006) Materialising reconciliation: negotiating difference in a post-colonial exhibition. In T. Royce and W. Bowcher (eds), *New Directions in the Analysis of Multimodal Discourse*. Mahwah, NJ: Lawrence Erlbaum Associates. 215–38.
Martin, J. R. and Veel, R. (eds) (1998) *Reading Science: Critical and Functional Perspectives on Discourses of Science*. London and New York: Routledge.
Martin, J. R. and White, P. R. R. (2005) *The Language of Evaluation: Appraisal in English*. London: Palgrave. [Chinese translation in preparation for Peking University Press].
Martin, J. R. and Wodak, R. (eds) (2003) *Re/Reading the Past: Critical and Functional Perspectives on Time and Value* (Discourse Approaches to Politics, Society and Culture, 8). Amsterdam and Philadelphia: Benjamins.
Martin, P. (1979) In the matter of law v. Dawe: case for the defence. *Southerly* 39(4): 355–63.
Martinec, R. (1995) *Hierarchy of Rhythm in English Speech*. Ph.D. Thesis. Sydney University.
Martinec, R. (1998) Cohesion in action. *Semiotica* 120(1/2): 161–80.
Martinec, R. (2000a) Rhythm in multimodal texts. *Leonardo* 33(4): 289–97.
Martinec, R. (2000b) Types of process in action. *Semiotica* 130(3/4): 243–68.
Martinec, R. (2000c) Construction of identity in M. Jackson's 'Jam'. *Social Semiotics* 10(3): 313–29.
Martinec, R. (2001) Interpersonal resources in action. *Semiotica* 135(1/4).
Martinec, R.. (2005) Topics in multimodality. In R. Hasan, C. M. I. M. Matthiessen and J. J. Webster (eds): 157–81.
Mason, I. (2003) Text parameters in translation: transitivity and institutional cultures. In E. Hajicova, P. Sgall, Z. Jettmarova, A. Rothkegel, D. Rothfuß-Bastian and H. Gerzymisch-Arbogast (eds), *Textologie und Translation* (Jahrbuch Übersetzen und Dolmetschen 4/2). Tübingen: Narr. Reprinted in L. Venuti (ed.), 2004, *The Translation Studies Reader*. 2nd edn, London: Routledge. 470–81.
Matejka, L. and Pomorska, K. (eds) (1971) *Readings in Russian Poetics: Formalist and Structuralist Views*. Cambridge, Mass: MIT Press. Reprinted in (1978) Ann Arbor Mich: Michigan Slavic Publications.

Mathers, M. (2005) Some evidence for distinctive language use by children with Attention Deficit Hyperactivity Disorder. *Clinical Linguistics and Phonetics* 19(3): 215–25.

Matthiessen, C. M. I. M. (1987a) Notes on the organization of the environment of a text generation grammar. In G. Kempen (ed.), *Natural Language Generation* Dordrecht: Martinus Nijhof. 253–78.

Matthiessen, C. M. I. M. (1987b) *Notes on Akan Phonology: A Systemic Interpretation*. MS.

Matthiessen, C. M. I. M. (1988a) Representational issues in systemic functional grammar. In J. D. Benson and W. S. Greaves (eds), *Systemic Functional Perspectives on Discourse*. Norwood, NJ: Ablex. 136–75.

Matthiessen, C. M. I. M. (1988b) Semantics for a systemic grammar: the Chooser and Inquiry framework. In J. D. Benson, M. J. Cummings and W. S. Greaves (eds).

Matthiessen, C. M. I. M. (1993) Register in the round: diversity in a unified theory of register analysis. In M. Ghadessy (ed.) (1993a): 221–92.

Matthiessen, C. M. I. M. (1995a) Fuzziness construed in language: a linguistic perspective. *Proceedings of 1995 IEEE International Conference on Fuzzy Systems Piscataway*. NJ: IEEE.

Matthiessen, C. M. I. M. (1995b) *Lexicogrammatical Cartography: English Systems*. Tokyo: International Language Sciences Publishers.

Matthiessen, C. M. I. M. (1999) The system of TRANSITIVITY: an exploratory study of text-based profiles. *Functions of Language* 6(1): 1–51.

Matthiessen, C. M. I. M. (2001) The environment of translation. In E. Steiner and C. Yallop (eds).

Matthiessen, C. M. I. M. (2002a) Lexicogrammar in discourse development: logogenetic patterns of wording. In G. W. Huang and Z. Y. Wang (eds): 91–127.

Matthiessen, C. M. I. M. (2002b) Combining clauses into clause complexes: a multi-faceted view. In J. Bybee and M. Noonan (eds), *Complex Sentences in Grammar and Discourse: Essays in Honor of Sandra A. Thompson*. Amsterdam: Benjamins. 237–322.

Matthiessen, C. M. I. M. (2004) The evolution of language: a systemic functional exploration of phylogenetic phases. In G. Williams and A. Lukin (eds): 45–90.

Matthiessen, C. M. I. M. (2006) Frequency profiles of some basic grammatical systems: an interim report. In S. Hunston and G. Thompson (eds): 103–42.

Matthiessen, C. M. I. M. (2007a) The 'architecture' of language according to systemic functional theory: developments since the 1970s. In R. Hasan, C. M. I. M. Matthiessen and J. J. Webster (eds): 505–61.

Matthiessen, C. M. I. M. (2007b) Lexicogrammar in systemic functional linguistics: descriptive and theoretical developments in the 'IFG' tradition since the 1970s. In R. Hasan, C. M. I. M. Matthiessen and J. J. Webster (eds): 765–858.

Matthiessen, C. M. I. M. (In Press) Multisemiotic and context-based register typology: registerial variation in the complementarity of semiotic systems. In E. Ventola and A. J. Moya Guijarro (eds), *The World Shown and the World Told*. Houndmills: Palgrave Macmillan.

Matthiessen, C. M. I. M. and Bateman, J. A. (1991) *Text Generation and Systemic Linguistics: Experiences from English and Japanese.* London: Pinter.

Matthiessen, C. M. I. M. and Nesbitt, C. (1996) On the idea of theory-neutral descriptions. In R. Hasan, C. Cloran and D. G. Butt (eds): 39–85.

Matthiessen, C. M. I. M., Teruya, K. and Wu, C. (2008) Multilingual studies as a multi-dimensional space of interconnected language studies. In J. J. Webster (ed.): 146–220.

Matthiessen, C. M. I. M., Lukin, A., Butt, D. G., Cleirigh, C. and Nesbitt, C. (2005) Welcome to Pizza Hut: a case study of multistratal analysis. *Australian Review of Applied Linguistics* 19: 123–50.

Matthiessen, C. M. I. M., Zeng, L. C., Cross, M., Kobayashi, I., Teruya, K. and Wu, C. (1998) The Multex generator and its environment: application and development. *Proceedings of the International Generation Workshop '98, August 1998*, Niagara-on-the-Lake. 228–37.

McAndrew, J. (2003) *Ideology, Heteroglossia, and Systemic Functional Linguistics: An Analysis of a NSW Government Advertisement.* Ph.D. Thesis. Macquarie University.

McEnery, T. and Wilson, A. (1996) *Corpus Linguistics.* Edinburgh: Edinburgh University Press.

Melrose, R. (1996) *The Margins of Meaning: Arguments for a Postmodern Approach to Language and Text.* Amsterdam and Atlanta, GA: Rodopi.

Melrose, R. (2006) Protolanguage, mirror neurons, and the 'front-heavy' brain: explorations in the evolution and functional organization of language. *Linguistics and the Human Sciences* 2(1): 89–110.

Melzoff, A. N. and Moore, M. K. (1998) Infant intersubjectivity: broadening the dialogue to include imitation, identity and intention. In S. Bråten (ed.) (1998b): 47–62.

Miller, D. R. and Turci M. (eds) (2007) *Language and Verbal Art Revisited: Linguistic Approaches to the Study of Literature.* London: Equinox.

Mintigl, P. (2004) *Narrative Counselling: Social and Linguistic Processes of Change.* Amsterdam: Benjamins (Discourse Approaches to Politics, Society and Culture).

Mitchell, T. F. (1957) The language of buying and selling in Cyrenaica: a situational statement. *Hesperis* 26: 31–71. Reprinted in T. F. Mitchell (1975) *Principles of Neo-Firthian Linguistics.* London: Longman. 167–200.

Mohan, B. A. (1986) *Language and Content.* Reading, Mass.: Addison-Wesley.

Mortensen, L. (1992) A transitivity analysis of discourse in dementia of the Alzheimer's Type. *Journal of Neurolinguistics* 7: 309–24.

Mortensen, L. (2003) *Reconstructing the Writer: Acquired Brain Impairment and Letters of Community Membership.* Unpublished Ph.D. Thesis. Macquarie University, Sydney.

Mortensen, L. (2005) Grammatical complexity in letters written by people with acquired brain impairment. *Australian Review of Applied Linguistics* 19: 87–102.

Mukařovský, J. (1977) *The Word and Verbal Art.* New Haven: Yale University Press.

Müller, C. and Strube, M. (2001) MMAX: A tool for the annotation of multi-modal corpora. *Proceedings of the 2nd IJCAI Workshop on Knowledge and Reasoning in Practical Dialogue Systems, Seattle, USA.*

Munday, J. (2001) *Introducing Translation Studies: Theories and Applications.* London and New York: Routledge.

Murcia-Bielsa, S. (2000) The choice of directives expressions in English and Spanish instructions: a semantic network. In E. Ventola (ed.): 117–46.

Neale, A. (2006) Matching corpus data and system networks: using corpora to modify and extend the system networks for TRANSITIVITY in English. In S. Hunston and G. Thompson (eds): 143–63.

Nesbitt, C. (1994) *Construing Linguistic Resources: Consumer Perspective.* Ph.D. Thesis. University of Sydney.

Nesbitt, C. and Plum, G. (1988) Probabilities in a systemic-functional grammar: the clause complex in English. In R. P. Fawcett and D. Young (eds), *New Developments in Systemic Linguistics Vol. 2: Theory and Application.* London: Pinter. 6–38.

Neumann, S. (2003) *Textsorten und Übersetzen. Eine Korpusanalyse englischer und deutscher Reiseführer.* Frankfurt u.a.: Peter Lang Verlag. (Reihe SABEST Band 3.)

Neumann, S. and Hansen-Schirra, S. (2005) The CroCo Project: cross-linguistic corpora for the investigation of explicitation in translations. *Proceedings from the Corpus Linguistics Conference Series,* 1(1). ISSN 1747–9398 http://www.corpus.bham.ac.uk/PCLC.

Nicholas, M., Obler, L. K., Albert, M. L. and Helm-Estabrooks, N. (1985) Empty speech in Alzheimer's disease and fluent aphasia. *Journal of Speech and Hearing Research 28:* 405–10.

Ninio, A. and Bruner, J. (1978) The achievements and antecedents of labelling. *Journal of Child Language* 5: 1–15.

Nord, C. (2005) *Text Analysis in Translation: Theory, Methodology, and Didactic Application of a Model for Translation-oriented Text Analysis.* 2nd edn, Amsterdam and New York: Rodopi.

O'Donnell, M. (1994) *From theory to implementations: analysis and generation with systemic grammar.* Ph.D. Thesis. University of Sydney.

O'Donnell, M. (1995) From corpus to codings: semi-automating the acquisition of linguistic features. *Proceedings of the AAAI Symposium on Empirical Methods in Discourse Interpretation and Generation, Stanford, CA.*

O'Donnell, M. (2000) RSTTool 2.4 – a markup tool for rhetorical structure theory. *Proceedings of the International Natural Language Generation Conference (INLG), Mitzpe Ramon, Israel.*

O'Donnell, M. (2007) UAM Corpus Tools Manual. http://www.wagsoft.com/CorpusTool/UAMCorpusToolManualv1.2.pdf (last visited January 2008).

O'Donnell, M. and Bateman, J. A. (2005) SFL in computational contexts: a contemporary history. In R. Hasan, C. M. I. M. Matthiessen and J. J. Webster (eds): 343–82.

O'Halloran, K. L. (1999a) Interdependence, interaction and metaphor in multi-semiotic texts. *Social Semiotics* 9(3): 317–54.

O'Halloran, K. L. (1999b) Towards a systemic functional analysis of multisemiotic Mathematics texts. *Semiotica* 124(1/2): 1–29.

O'Halloran, K. L. (2000) Classroom discourse in Mathematics: a multisemiotic analysis. *Linguistics and Education* 10(3): 359–88. (Special Edition: *Language and Other Semiotic Systems in Education*).

O'Halloran, K. L. (2004) *Multimodal Discourse Analysis: Systemic Functional Perspectives*. London: Continuum (Open Linguistics Series).

O'Halloran, K. L. (2005) *Mathematical Discourse: Language, Symbolism and Visual Images*. London: Continuum.

O'Halloran, K. L. and Judd, K. (2002) Systemics 1.0. (CD ROM). Singapore: Singapore University Press.

O'Toole, L.M. (1982) *Structure, Style and Interpretation in the Russian Short Story*. New Haven: Yale University Press.

O'Toole, L. M. (1988) Henry Reed and what follows the 'Naming of Parts'. In D. Birch and L. M. O'Toole (eds).

O'Toole, L. M. (1994) *The Language of Displayed Art*. London: Leicester University Press (a division of Pinter).

O'Toole, L. M. (2001) Russian literary theory: from the Formalists to Lotman. In N. Cornwell (ed.), *The Routledge Companion to Russian Literature*. London and New York: Routledge.

O'Toole, L. M. and Shukman, A. (eds) (1975–1981) *Russian Poetics in Translation, Vols. 1–8*. Oxford: Holden Books Ltd.

O'Toole, L. M. and Shukman, A. (eds) (1977) *Russian Poetics in Translation, Vol. 4: Formalist Theory*. Oxford: Holdan Books Ltd.

Ochs, E, Schegloff, E. A. and Thompson, S. A. (eds) (1996) *Interaction and Grammar*. Cambridge: Cambridge University Press (Studies in Interactional Sociolinguistics 13).

Oldenburg (Torr), J. (1986) The transitional stage of a second child – 18months to 2 years. *Australian Review of Applied Linguistics* 9(1):123–35.

Oldenburg (Torr), J. (1990) Learning the language and learning through language in early childhood. In M. A. K. Halliday, J. Gibbons and H. Nicholas (eds): 27–38.

Oram, J., Fine, J., Okamoto, C. and Tannock, R. (1999) Assessing the language of children with Attention Deficit Hyperactivity Disorder. *American Journal of Speech - Language Pathology* 8: 72–80.

Ovadia, R. and Fine, J. (1995) A Functional analysis of intonation in Asperger's Syndrome. In J. Siegfried (ed.), *Therapeutic and Everyday Discourse as Behavior Change: Towards a Micro-analysis in Psychotherapy Process Research*. Norwood, NJ: Ablex. 491–510.

Pagano, A. S., Magalhães, C. M. and Alves, F. (2004) Towards the construction of a multilingual, multifunctional corpus: factors in the design and application of CORDIALL. *Tradterm*, São Paulo 10: 143–162.

Painter, C. (1984) *Into the Mother Tongue*. London: Pinter.

Painter, C. (1986) The role of interaction in learning to speak and learning to write. In C. Painter and J. R. Martin (eds) *Writing to Mean: Teaching Genres across the Curriculum*. (ALAA Occasional Papers no. 9) Applied Linguistics Association of Australia. 62–97.

Painter, C. (1989) Learning language: a functional view of language development. In R. Hasan and J. R. Martin (eds): 18–65.

Painter, C. (1991) *Learning the Mother Tongue*. 2nd edn, Geelong, Vic.: Deakin University Press.

Painter, C. (1996a) The development of language as a resource for thinking: a linguistic view of learning. In R. Hasan and G. Williams (eds): 50–85.

Painter, C. (1996b) Learning about learning: construing semiosis in the pre-school years. *Functions of Language* 3(1): 95–125.
Painter, C. (1999a) *Learning through Language in Early Childhood*. London: Continuum.
Painter, C. (1999b) Preparing for school: developing a semantic style for educational knowledge. In F. Christie (ed.): 68–87.
Painter, C. (2003a) Developing attitude: An ontogenetic perspective on APPRAISAL. In M. Macken-Horarik and J. R. Martin (eds), *Negotiating Heteroglossia: Social Perspectives on Evaluation*. Special Issue *Text* 23(2): 183–209.
Painter, C. (2003b) The use of a metaphorical mode of meaning in early language development. In A.-M. Simon-Vandenbergen, M. Taverniers and L. J. Ravelli (eds): 151–67.
Painter, C. (2004a) The development of language as a resource for learning. In C. Coffin, A. Hewings and K. O'Halloran (eds), *Applying English Grammar: Functional and Corpus Approaches*. London: Arnold, The Open University. 155–71.
Painter, C. (2004b) The 'interpersonal first' principle in child language development. In G. Williams and A. Lukin (eds): 137–57.
Painter, C. (2005) The concept of protolanguage in language development. *Linguistics and the Human Sciences* 1(2): 177–96.
Painter, C. (2007) Language for learning in early childhood. In F. Christie and J. R. Martin (eds): 131–55.
Painter, C., Derewianka, B. and Torr, J. (2007) From microfunction to metaphor: learning language and learning through language. In R. Hasan, C. M. I. M. Matthiessen and J. J. Webster (eds): 563–88.
Palmer, F. R. (ed.) (1968) *Selected Papers of J. R. Firth 1952–59*. London: Longmans (Longmans' Linguistics Library).
Pappas, C. C. (1985) The cohesive harmony and cohesive density of children's oral and written stories. In J. D. Benson and W. S. Greaves (eds) (1985b): 169–86.
Pappas, C. C. (1987) Exploring the textual properties of "proto-reading". In R. Steele and T. Threadgold (eds): 137–62.
Parsons, G. (1990) *Cohesion and Coherence: Scientific Texts – A Comparative Study*. Department of English Studies, University of Nottingham (Monographs in Systemic Linguistics 1).
Parsons, G. (1991) Cohesion and coherence: scientific texts. In E. Ventola (ed.): 415–30.
Patpong, P. (2006) *A systemic functional interpretation of Thai grammar: an exploration of Thai narrative discourse*. Unpublished Ph.D. Thesis. Macquarie University, Sydney.
Patten, T. (1988) *Systemic Text Generation as Problem Solving*. Cambridge: Cambridge University Press.
Paul, R. (2007) *Language Disorders from Infancy through Adolescence*. 3rd edn, St Louis, MO: Mosby Elsevier.
Pearce, J., Thornton, G. and Mackay, D. (1989) The programme in linguistics and English teaching, University College London, 1964–1971. In R. Hasan and J. R. Martin (eds): 329–83.
Pierrehumbert, J. B. (2001) Stochastic phonology. *Glot International* 5(6): 196–207.

Pierrehumbert, J. B. (2003) Probabilistic phonology: discrimination and robustness. In R. Bod, J. Hay and S. Jannedy (eds): 177–228.

Pike, K. L. (1982) *Linguistic Concepts: An Introduction to Tagmemics*. Lincoln: University of Nebraska Press.

Pinker, S. (1994) *The Language Instinct*. New York: William Morrow.

Plum, G. and Cowling, A. (1987) Some constraints on grammatical variables: tense choice in English. In R. Steele and T. Threadgold (eds): 281–305.

Poynton, C. (1985) *Language and Gender: Making the Difference*. Geelong, Vic.: Deakin University Press. Republished in (1989). London: Oxford University Press.

Prakasam, V. (1999) *Semiotics of Language, Literature and Culture*. New Delhi: Allied Publishers Limited.

Qiu, S. J. (1985) Transition period in Chinese language development. *Australian Review of Applied Linguistics* 8(1): 31–49.

Quirk, R., Greenbaum, S., Leech, G. and Svartvik, J. (1985) *A Comprehensive Grammar of the English Language*. London: Longman.

Rada, E. (1989) *Writing about Art: A Linguistic Consideration of Art History and Related Genres*. Ph.D. Thesis. Sydney University.

Ravelli, L. J. (1995) A dynamic perspective: implications for metafunctional interaction and an understanding of Theme. In R. Hasan and P. H. Fries (eds): 187–235.

Ravelli, L. J. (1996) Making language accessible: successful text writing for museum visitors. *Linguistics and Education* 8: 367–87.

Ravelli, L. J. (1998) The consequences of choice: discursive positioning in an art institutions. In A. Sanchez-Macarro and R. Carter (eds): 137–54.

Ravelli, L. J. (2000) Beyond shopping: constructing the Sydney Olympics in three-dimensional text. *Text* 20(4): 1–27.

Ravelli, L. J. (2006) *Museum Texts: Communication Frameworks*. London: Routledge.

Ravelli, L. J. (2007) Genre and the museum exhibition. *Linguistics and the Human Sciences* 2(2): 299–317.

Ravelli, L. J. and Ellis, R. A. (eds) (2004) *Analysing Academic Writing*. London: Continuum.

Rinner, S. and Weigert, A. (2006) From sports to the EU economy: integrating curricula through genre-based content courses. In H. Byrnes, H. D. Weger-Gunthrap and K. A. Sprang (eds), *Educating for Advanced Foreign Language Capacities: Constructs, Curriculum, Instruction, Assessment*. Washington, DC: Georgetown University Press. 136–51.

Ripich, D. and Terrell, B. (1988) Patterns of discourse cohesion and coherence in Alzheimer's Disease. *Journal of Speech and Hearing Disorders* 53: 8–15.

Roochnik, D. (1996) *Of Art and Wisdom: Plato's Understanding of Techne*. Pennsylvania: The Pennsylvania State University Press.

Rose, D. (1997) Science, technology and technical literacies. In F. Christie and J. R. Martin (eds): 40–72.

Rose, D. (1998) Science discourse and industrial hierarchy. In J. R. Martin and R. Veel (eds): 236–65.

Rose, D., McInnes, D. and Korner, H. (1992) *Scientific Literacy (Write it Right Literacy in Industry Research Project - Stage 1)*. Sydney: Metropolitan East Disadvantaged Schools Program. Reprinted in (2007) Sydney: NSW AMES.

Rothery, J. (1990) *Story Writing in Primary School: Assessing Narrative Type Genres*. Ph.D. Thesis. University of Sydney.
Rothery, J. and Stenglin, M. (1997) Entertaining and instructing: exploring experience through story. In F. Christie and J. R. Martin (eds): 231–63.
Rothery, J. and Stenglin, M. (2000) Interpreting literature: the role of appraisal. In L. Unsworth (ed.): 222–44.
Royce, T. D. and Bowcher, W. L. (eds) (2006) *New Directions in the Analysis of Multimodal Discourse*. Hillsdale, NJ: Lawrence Erlbaum.
Rundell, M. (1996) The corpus of the future, and the future of the corpus. Online. Internet. Available: http://www.ruf.rice.edu/~barlow/futcrp.html. 18 May 1998.
Sadovnik, A. (ed.) (1995) *Knowledge and Pedagogy: The Sociology of Basil Bernstein*. Norwood, NJ: Ablex (The David C Achin Series in Social and Policy Issues in Education).
Saffran, E. M., Sloan-Berndt, R. and Schwartz, M. (1989) The quantitative analysis of agrammatic production: procedure and data. *Brain and Language* 37: 440–79.
Sampson, G. (1995) *English for the Computer: The SUSANNE Corpus and Analytic Scheme*. Oxford: Oxford University Press.
Sánchez-Macarro, A. and Carter, R. (eds) (1998) *Linguistic Choice across Genres: Variation in Spoken and Written English*. Amsterdam: Benjamins (Amsterdam Studies in the Theory and History of Lingusitic Science 158).
Savage-Rumbaugh, S., Murphy, J., Sevcik, R., Brakke, K., Williams, S., and Duane R. (1993) *Language Comprehension in Ape and Child*. Monographs of the Society for Research in Child Development. Chicago: University of Chicago Press.
Savage-Rumbaugh, S., Shanker, S., and Talbot, T. (1998) *Apes, Language, and the Human Mind*. New York: Oxford University Press.
Schieffelin, B. B. and Ochs, E. (eds) (1986) *Language Socialization across Cultures*. (Studies in the Social and Cultural Foundations of Language 3). New York: Cambridge University Press.
Schiffrin, D., Tannen, D. and Hamilton, H. E. (2001) *The Handbook of Discourse Analysis*. Oxford: Blackwell.
Schleppegrell, M. J. and Colombi, M. C. (eds) (2002) *Developing Advanced Literacy in First and Second Languages: Meaning with Power*. Mahwah, NJ: Lawrence Erlbaum.
Schmid, H. (1994) Probabilistic part-of-speech tagging using decision trees. *Proceedings of International Conference on New Methods in Language Processing*. Manchester, UK.
Scott, M. (1996) *WordSmith Tools Manual*. Oxford: Oxford University Press.
Scott, M. (2004) *Wordsmith Tools*. Oxford: Oxford University Press
Scott, M. and Thompson, G. (eds) (2000) *Patterns of Text: In Honour of Michael Hoey*. Amsterdam and Philadelphia: John Benjamins.
Segerdahl, P., Fields, W. and Savage-Rumbaugh, S. (2005) *Kanzi's Primal Languge: The Cultural Initiation of Primates into Language*. Basingstoke and New York: Palgrave.
Semel, E. M., Wiig, E. H. and Secord, W. (1995) *Clinical Evaluation of Language Fundamentals*. San Antonio, TX: The Psychological Corporation.

Sherratt, S. (2007) Right brain damage and the verbal expression of emotion: a preliminary investigation. *Aphasiology* 21(3/4): 320–39.

Shklovsky, V. (1990 [1925]) *Theory of Prose*. Elmwood Park, IL: Dalkey Archive Press.

Shoebox (2008) The Linguist's Shoebox – Integrated data management and analysis for the field linguist. Tutorial and User's Guide. SIL, http://www.sil.org/computing/shoebox/index.html (last visited January 2008).

Shore, S. (2001) Teaching translation. In E. Steiner and C. Yallop (eds): 249–76.

Shum, M. S. K. (2006) Developing an approach for teaching subject specific genres in Chinese – the case of post-colonial Hong Kong. *Australian Review of Applied Linguistics* 29(1): 1–22.

Simon-Vandenbergen, A.-M., Taverniers, M. and Ravelli L. J. (eds) (2003) *Grammatical Metaphor: Views from Systemic Functional Linguistics*. Amsterdam and Philadelphia: John Benjamins.

Sinclair, J. M. (1986) Basic computer processing of long texts. In G. Leech and C. Candlin (eds), *Computers in English Language Teaching and Research*. Essex: Longman. 185–203.

Sinclair, J. M. and Coulthard, R. M. (1975) *Towards an Analysis of Discourse: The English Used by Teachers and Pupils*. London: Oxford University Press.

Sinclair, J. M., Hoey, M. and Fox, G. (eds) (1993) *Techniques of Description: Spoken and Written Discourse*. London: Routledge.

Sjölander, K. and Beskow, J. (2000) WaveSurfer - an open source speech tool. In B. Yuan, T. Huang and X. Tang (eds), *Proceedings of the 6th International Conference on Spoken Language Processing (ICSLP)*, Beijing, China.

Slade, D., Scheeres, H., Manidis, M., Matthiessen, C. M. I. M., Iedema, R., Herke, M., McGregor, J., Dustan, R. and Stein-Parbury, J. (2008) Emergency communication: the discursive challenges facing emergency clinicians and patients in hospital emergency departments. *Discourse and Communication* 2(3): 271–98.

Smith, B. (2008) *Intonational Systems and Register: A Multidimensional Exploration*. Ph.D. Thesis. Macquarie University.

Souter, C. (1990) Systemic-functional grammars and corpora. In J. Aarts and W. Meijs (eds).

Spencer, E., Packman, A., Onslow, M. and Ferguson, A. (2005) *Clinical Linguistics and Phonetics* 19(3): 191–201.

Stainton, R. and de Villiers, J. (eds) (2001) *Communication in Linguistics*. Toronto: GREF (Collection Theoria).

Steele, R. and Threadgold, T. (eds) (1987) *Language Topics: Essays in Honour of Michael Halliday, Vols. I and II*. Amsterdam: Benjamins.

Steiner, E. (1988) Language and music as semiotic systems: the example of a folk ballad. In J. D. Benson, M. J. Cummings and W. S. Greaves (eds): 393–441.

Steiner, E. (1991) *A Functional Perspective on Language, Action and Interpretation*. Berlin and New York: Mouton de Gruyter.

Steiner, E. (2004) *Translated Texts: Properties, Variants, Evaluations*. Frankfurt am Main and New York: Peter Lang.

Steiner, E. (2005a) Hallidayan thinking and translation theory – enhancing the options, broadening the range, and keeping the ground. In R. Hasan, C. M. I. M. Matthiessen and J. J. Webster (eds): 481–500.

Steiner, E. (2005b) The heterogeneity of individual languages as a translation problem. In H. Kittel, A. P. Frank, N. Greiner, T. Hermans, H. Koller, J. Lambert and F. Paul (eds), *Translation: An International Encyclopedia of Translation Studies.* Berlin and New York: Walter de Gruyter. 446–54.

Steiner, E. and Veltman, R. (1988) *Pragmatics, Discourse and Text: Some Systemically-inspired Approaches.* London: Pinter.

Steiner, E. and Yallop, C. (eds) (2001) *Exploring Translation and Multilingual Text Production: Beyond Content.* Berlin: Mouton de Gruyter.

Steiner, P. (1984) *Russian Formalism: A Metapoetics.* Ithaca: Cornell University Press.

Stevens, W. (1990 [1957]) *Opus Posthumous.* New York: Vintage Books.

Stillar, G. (1998) *Analyzing Everyday Texts: Discourse, Rhetoric and Social Perspective.* London: SAGE.

Striedter, J. (1989) *Literary Structure, Evolution, and Value: Russian Formalism and Czech Structuralism Reconsidered.* Cambridge, MA, and London: Harvard University Press.

Stuart-Smith, V. (2007) The hierarchical organization of text as conceptualised in rhetorical structure theory: a systemic functional perspective. *Australian Journal of Linguistics* 27(1): 41–62.

Svartvik, J. (ed.) (1990) *The London Corpus of Spoken English: Description and Research. Lund Studies in English 82.* Lund: Lund University Press.

Svartvik, J. (ed.) (1991) *Directions in Corpus Linguistics: Proceedings of Nobel Symposium 82, Stockholm, August 4–8, 1991.* Berlin: Mouton de Gruyter.

Taboada, M. (2000) Cohesion as a measure in generic analysis. In A. Melby and A. Lommel (eds), *LACUS Forum XXVI.* Fullerton, CA: The Linguistic Association of Canada and the United States. 35–49.

Taboada, M. (2001) Rhetorical relations in dialogue: a contrastive study. In C. L. Moder and A. Martinovic-Zic (eds), *Discourse across Languages and Cultures.* Amsterdam: Benjamins. (Typological Studies in Language).

Taglialatela, J., Rumbaugh, D., Savage-Rumbaugh, S., Benson, J. D. and Greaves, W. S. (2004) Language, apes, and meaning-making. In G. Williams and A. Lukin (eds), *Language Development: Functional Perspectives on Evolution and Ontogenesis.* London: Continuum.

Taylor, C. (2003) Multimodal transcription in the analysis, translation and subtitling of Italian films. *The Translator* 9(2): 191–205.

Taylor, C. and Baldry, A. (2001) Computer assisted text analysis and translation: a functional approach in the analysis and translation of advertising texts. In E. Steiner and C. Yallop (eds): 277–305.

Taylor Torsello, C. (1996) Theme as the interpreter's path indicator through the unfolding text. *The Interpreters Newsletter VII:* 113–49.

Taylor Torsello, C. (1997) Linguistics, discourse analysis and interpretation." In Gambier, Y., Gile, D. and Taylor, C. (eds), *Conference Interpreting: Current Trends in Research.* Amsterdam: John Benjamins. 167–86.

Tebble, H. (1999) The tenor of consultant physicians: implications for medical interpreting. *The Translator* 5(2): 179–200.

Teich, E. (1999) *Systemic Functional Grammar in Natural Language Generation: Linguistic Description and Computational Representation.* London: Cassell.

Teich, E. (2003) *Cross-linguistic Variation in System and Text. A Methodology for the Investigation of Translations and Comparable Texts.* Berlin and New York: De Gruyter.

Teich, E. and Fankhauser, P. (2004) Multiple perspectives on text using multiple resources: Experiences with XML processing. *Proceedings of LREC Workshop on XML-based richly annotated corpora, 4th Conference on Language Resources and Evaluation (LREC), Lisbon, May 2004.*

Teich, E. and Fankhauser, P. (2008) Characterizing genre: the case of scientific text. *Paper at the Meeting of the American Association for Corpus Linguistics (AACL), Provo, Utah, March 2008.*

Tench, P. (1990) *The Roles of Intonation in English Discourse.* Frankfurt: Peter Lang. (Forum Linguisticum 31).

Tench, P. (ed.) (1992) *Studies in Systemic Phonology.* London and New York: Pinter Publishers.

Tench, P. (1996) *The Intonation Systems of English.* London: Cassell.

Teruya, K. (2006) *A Systemic Functional Grammar of Japanese.* London: Continuum.

Teruya, K. (In Press) Grammar as a gateway into discourse: a systemic functional approach to SUBJECT, THEME, and logic. In H. Byrnes (ed.) (In Press).

Teruya, K., Akerejola, E., Andersen, T. H., Caffarel, A., Lavid, J., Matthiessen, C. M. I. M., Petersen, U. H., Patpong, P. and Smedegaard, F. (2007) Typology of MOOD: a text-based and system-based functional view. In R. Hasan, C. M. I. M. Matthiessen and J. J. Webster (eds): 859–920.

Teubert, W. (2005) My version of corpus linguistics. *International Journal of Corpus Linguistics* 10(1): 1–13.

Thibault, P. J. (1984) *Narrative Structure and Narrative Function in Vladimir Nabokov's Ada.* Unpublished Ph.D. Thesis. Sydney: University of Sydney.

Thibault, P. J. (1987) An interview with Michael Halliday. In R. Steele and T. Threadgold (eds): 599–627.

Thibault, P. J. (1991) *Social Semiotics as Praxis: Text Social Meaning Making and Nabokov's 'Ada'.* Minneapolis: University of Minnesota Press.

Thibault, P. J. (1997) *Rereading Saussure: The Dynamic of Signs in Social Life.* London and New York: Routledge.

Thibault, P. J. (2000) The dialogic integration of the brain in social semiosis: Edelman and the case for downward causation. *Mind, Culture and Activity* 7(4): 291–311.

Thibault, P. J. (2004a) *Brain, Mind, and the Signifying Body: An Ecosocial Semiotic Theory.* Foreword by M. A. K. Halliday. London and New York: Continuum.

Thibault, P. J. (2004b) *Agency and Consciousness in Discourse: Self-other Dynamics as a Complex System.* London and New York: Continuum.

Thibault, P. J. (2005a,b) What sort of minded being has language? Anticipatory dynamics, arguability and agency in a normatively and recursively self-transforming learning system, Parts 1 and 2. *Linguistics and the Human Sciences* 1(2): 261–335; 1(3): 355–401.

Thibault, P. J. (2005c) Brains, bodies, contextualizing activity and language: do humans (and bonobos) have a language faculty, and can they do without one?. *Linguistics and the Human Sciences* 1(1): 99–125.

Thibault, P. J. (2005d) The interpersonal gateway to the meaning of mind: unifying the inter- and intraorganism perspectives on language. In R. Hasan, C. M. I. M. Matthiessen and J. J. Webster (eds): 117–56.

Thibault, P. J. (with Benson, J. D. and Greaves, W. S.). (2005) Scientific report as contribution towards Project #2 – Savage-Rumbaugh, Fields, Segerdahl,

Thibault, Benson, and Greaves, *Experimental Investigations: The Effect of the Intentional Introduction of Forgiveness into a Pan/Homo Culture*. Funded by the Campaign for Forgiveness, Templeton Foundation (USA).

Thoma, C. (2006) *Combining Functional Linguistics and Skopos Theory. A Case Study of Greek Cypriot and British Folkales. European University Studies. Series XXI Linguistics. Vol. 295.* Frankfurt am Main: Peter Lang.

Thompson, J. (1996) *Conc: A Concordance Generator for the Macintosh.* Dallus: Summer Institute of Linguistics.

Thomson, E. and White, P. R. R. (eds) (2008) *News across Cultures: A Multilingual Study of the Mass Media Reporting of Conflict.* London: Continuum.

Thomson, J. (2000) *Textual Resources in the Narratives of Children with and without Language Disorder.* Unpublished Masters Thesis. The University of Newcastle, Australia.

Thomson, J. (2003) Clinical discourse analysis: one theory or many? *Advances in Speech Language Pathology* 5: 41–50.

Thomson, J. (2005) Theme analysis of narratives produced by children with and without Specific Language Impairment. *Clinical Linguistics and Phonetics* 19(3): 175–90.

Titscher, S., Meyer, M., Wodak, R. and Vetter, E. (2000) *Methods of Text and Discourse Analysis.* London: SAGE.

Togher, L. and Hand, L. (1998) Use of politeness markers with different communication partners: an investigation of five subjects with traumatic brain injury. *Aphasiology* 12(7/8): 491–504.

Togher, L., Hand, L. and Code, C. (1997) Analysing discourse in the traumatic brain injury population: telephone interactions with different communication partners. *Brain Injury* 11(3): 169–89.

Togher, L., McDonald, S., Code, C. and Grant, S. (2004) Training communication partners of people with traumatic brain injury: a randomised controlled trial. *Aphasiology* 18(4): 313–35.

Toolan, M. (1998) *Language in Literature: An Introduction to Stylistics.* London: Hodder Arnold.

Toolan, M. (2001) *Narrative: A Critical Linguistic Introduction.* 2nd edn, New York: Routledge.

Toolan, M. (ed.) (1992) *Language, text and context: essays in stylistics.* London and New York: Routledge.

Torr, J. (1997) *From Child Tongue to Mother Tongue: A Case Study of Language Development in the First Two and a Half Years* (Monographs in Systemic Linguistics no.) Dept. of Engish Studies, University of Nottingham, Nottingham. First produced as a PhD thesis, University of Sydney under the name Oldenburg.

Torr, J. (1998) The development of modality in pre-school years: language as a vehicle for understanding possibilities and obligations in everyday life. *Functions of Language* 5(2): 157–78.

Torr, J. and Simpson, A. (2003) The emergence of grammatical metaphor: Literacy-oriented expressions in the everyday speech of young children. In A.-M. Simon-Vandenbergen, M. Taverniers and L. J. Ravelli (eds): 169–83.

Trevarthen, C. (1974) Conversations with a two-month old. *New Scientist* (1974, May 2): 230–5.

Trevarthen, C. (1979) Communication and cooperation in early infancy: a description of primary intersubjectivity. In M. Bullowa (ed.), *Before Speech: The Beginning of Interpersonal Communication*. Cambridge: Cambridge University Press. 321–47.

Trevarthen, C. (1987) Sharing making sense: intersubjectivity and the making of an infant's meaning. In R. Steele and T. Threadgold (eds): 177–99.

Trevarthen, C. (1993) The function of emotions in early infant communication and development. In J. Nadel and L. Camaioni (eds), *New Perspectives in Early Communicative Development*. London: Routledge. 48–81.

Trevarthen, C. (1998) The concept and foundations of infant intersubjectivity. In S. Bråten (ed.) (1998b): 15–46.

Tucker, G. H. (1996) So grammarians haven't the faintest idea: reconciling lexis-oriented and grammar-oriented approaches to language. In R. Hasan, C. Cloran and D. G. Butt (eds).

Tucker, G. H. (1998) *The Lexicogrammar of Adjectives: A Systemic Functional Approach to Lexis*. London: Cassell.

Tucker, G. H. (2007) Between grammar and lexis: towards a systemic functional account of phraseology. In R. Hasan, C. M. I. M. Matthiessen and J. J. Webster (eds): 953–77.

Tynyanov, J. (1978) On literary evolution. In L. Matejka and K. Pomorska (eds).

UIMA (2007) UIMA Documentation Overview, Version 2.2.1–incubation. The Apache Software Foundation, http://incubator.apache.org/uima/downloads/releaseDocs/2.2.1–incubating/docs/html/index.html (last visited January 2008).

Unsworth, L. (1997) Scaffolding reading of science explanations: accessing the grammatical and visual forms of specialized knowledge. *Reading* 31(3): 30–42.

Unsworth, L. (1998) "Sound" explanations in school science: a functional linguistics perspective on effective apprenticing texts. *Linguistics and Education* 9(2): 199–226.

Unsworth, L. (ed.) (2000) *Researching Language in Schools and Communities: Functional Linguistic Perspectives*. London: Cassell.

Unsworth, L. (2006) *E-literature for Children: Enhancing Digital Literacy Learning*. London: Routledge.

Unsworth L. (ed.) (2008) *Multimodal Semiotics: Functional Analysis in Contexts of Education*. London: Continuum.

Ure, J. (1971) Lexical density and register differentiation. In G. E. Perren and J. L. M. Trim (eds), *Applications of Linguistics: Selected Papers of the Second International Congress of Applied Linguistics, Cambridge 1969*. Cambridge: Cambridge University Press.

Ure, J. and Ellis, J. (1974) Register in descriptive linguistics and linguistic sociology. In O. Uribe-Villegas (ed.), *Issues in Sociolinguistics*. The Hague: Mouton.

van Dijk, T. A. (1977) *Text and Context: Explorations in the Semantics and Pragmatics of Discourse*. London: Longman.

van Dijk, T. A. (ed.) (1985) *Handbook of Discourse Analysis*. New York: Academic Press.

van Dijk, T. A. (ed.) (1997) *Discourse: A Multidisciplinary Introduction*. London: Sage.

van Dijk, T. A. (2001) Critical discourse analysis. In D. Tannen, D. Schiffrin and H. Hamilton (eds), *Handbook of Discourse Analysis*. Oxford: Blackwell. 352–71.

van Leeuwen, T. (1985) Persuasive speech: the intonation of the live radio commercial. *Australian Journal of Communication* 7: 25–35.
van Leeuwen, T. (1992) Rhythm and social context. In P. Tench (ed.): 231–62.
van Leeuwen, T. (1996) The representation of social actors. In C. Caldas-Coulthard and M. Coulthard (eds): 32–70.
van Leeuwen, T. (1999) *Speech, Music, Sound*. London: Macmillan.
van Leeuwen, T. and Humphrey, S. (1996) On learning to look through a geographer's eyes. In R. Hasan and G. Williams (eds): 29–49.
van Leeuwen, T. and Jewitt, C. (2001) *Handbook of Visual Analysis*. London: Sage.
Vandenbergen, A.-M., Taverniers, M. and Ravelli, L. J. (eds) (2003) *Grammatical Metaphor: Views from Systemic Functional Linguistics*. Amsterdam: John Benjamins.
Varela, F. J., Thompson, E. and Rosch, E. (1991) *The Embodied Mind: Cognitive Science and Human Experience*. Cambridge, MA: The MIT Press.
Veel, R. (1997) Learning how to mean - scientifically speaking: apprenticeship into scientific discourse in the secondary school. In F. Christie and J. R. Martin (eds): 161–95.
Veel, R. (1998) The greening of school science: ecogenesis in secondary classrooms. In J. R. Martin and R. Veel (eds): 114–51.
Veel, R. (1999) Language, knowledge and authority in school mathematics. In F. Christie (ed.): 185–216.
Veel, R. and Coffin, C. (1996) Learning to think like an historian: the language of secondary school history. In R. Hasan and G. Williams (eds): 191–231.
Veloso, F. O. D. (2006) *Never Awake a Sleeping Giant...: A Multimodal Analysis of Post 9–11 Comic Books*. Ph.D. Thesis. Universidade Federal de Santa Catarina.
Ventola. E. (1987) *The Structure of Social Interaction: A Systemic Approach to the Semiotics of Service Encounters*. London: Pinter.
Ventola, E. (ed.) (1991) *Functional and Systemic Linguistics: Approaches and Uses*. Berlin: Mouton de Gruyter (Trends in Linguistics: studies and monographs 55).
Ventola, E. (1998) Interpersonal choices in academic work. In A. Sánchez-Macarro and R. Carter (eds): 117–36.
Ventola, E. (1999) Semiotic Spanning at Conferences: cohesion and coherence in and across conference papers and their discussions. In W. Bublitz, U. Lenk and E. Ventola (eds), *Coherence in Spoken and Written Discourse: How to Create It and How to Describe It*. Amsterdam: Benjamins. 101–25.
Ventola, E. (ed.) (2000) *Discourse and Community: Doing Functional Linguistics*. Tübingen: Günter Narr Verlag.
Ventola, E. and Mauranen, A. (eds) (1995) *Academic Writing: Intercultural and Textual Issues*. Amsterdam: John Benjamins.
Ventola, E. and Moya Guijarro, A. J. (eds) (In Press) *The World Shown and the World Told*. Houndmills: Palgrave Macmillan.
Ventola, E, Charles, C. and Kaltenbacher, M. (eds) (2004) *Perspectives on Multimodality*. Amsterdam: Benjamins.
Vygotsky, L. S. (1962) *Though and Language*. Translated and Edited by E. Henfmann and G. Vakar. Cambridge, MA: MIT Press.
Vygotsky, L. S. (1986) *Thought and Language*. In A. Kozulin (Ed. and Trans.). Cambridge, MA: MIT Press.
Wallace-Crabbe, C. (1976) Bruce Dawe's inventiveness. *Meanjin* 35(1): 94–101.

Wang, X. Y. (2008) *Clause Boundary Shifts in Interpreting: Chinese-English.* MA Thesis. Macquarie University, Linguistics Department.

Webster, J. J. (1993) Text processing using the functional grammar processor (FGP). In M. Ghadessy (ed.) (1993a).

Webster, J. J. (1995) Studying thematic development in on-line help documentation using the Functional Semantic Processor. In M. Ghadessy (ed.): 259–71.

Webster, J. J. (1998) The poet's language: foregrounding in Edwin Thumboo's 'Gods can die'? *World Englishes* 17(3): 359–68.

Webster, J. J. (2001) Thumboo's *David*. In C. K. Tong, A. Pakir, Ban Kah Choon and R. B. H. Goh (eds), *Ariels: Departures and Returns. Essays for Edwin Thumboo.* Oxford: Oxford University Press.

Webster, J. J. (ed.) (2008) *Meaning in Context: Implementing Intelligent Applications of Language Studies.* London and New York: Continuum.

Webster, J. J. and Kit, C. (1995) Computational analysis of Chinese and English texts with the Functional Semantic Processor and the C-LFG Parser. *Journal of Literary and Linguistic Computing* 10(3): 203–11. Oxford: Oxford University Press.

Weinreich, U., Labov, W. and Herzog, M. I. (1968) Empirical foundations for a theory of language change. Reprinted from *Directions for Historical Linguistics: A Symposium.* Austin: University of Texas Press. 95–188.

White, P. R. R. (1997) Death, disruption and the moral order: the narrative impulse in mass 'hard news' reporting. In F. Christie and J. R. Martin (eds): 101–33.

White, P. R. R. (1998) Extended reality, proto-nouns and the vernacular: distinguishing the technological from the scientific. In J. R. Martin and R. Veel (eds): 266–96.

White, P. R. R. (2000) Dialogue and inter-subjectivity: reinterpreting the semantics of modality and hedging. In M. Coulthard, J. Cotterill and F. Rock (eds), *Working With Dialogue.* Tubingen: Neimeyer. 67–80.

Whitelaw, C., Patrick, J. and Herke-Couchman, M. (2006) Identifying Interpersonal Distance using Systemic Features. In J. Shanahan, Y. Qu and J. Wiebe (eds), *Computing Attitude and Affect in Text: Theory and Applications.* Berlin and New York: Springer. 199–214.

Whorf, B. (1956) *Language, Thought, and Reality: Selected Writings.* (Edited by J. Carrol). Cambridge, MA: MIT Press.

Wignell, P. (2007) *On the Discourse of Social Science.* Darwin: Charles Darwin University Press.

Wignell, P., Martin, J. R. and Eggins, S. (1990) The discourse of geography: ordering and explaining the experiential world. *Linguistics and Education* 1(4): 359–92. Republished in M. A. K. Halliday and J. R. Martin (1993): 136–65.

Williams, G. (1995) *Joint Book Reading and Literacy Pedagogy: A Socio-semantic Examination.* Unpublished Ph.D. Dissertation. Macquarie University: Department of Linguistics. / Volume 1. CORE. 19(3). Fiche 2 B01– Fiche 6 B01.

Williams, G. (1996) *Joint BooK Reading and Literacy Pedagogy: A Socio-semantic Examination.* Volume 2. CORE. 20(1). Fiche 3 B01– Fiche 8 E10.

Williams, G. (1999) The pedagogic device and the production of pedagogic discourse: a case example in early literacy education. In F. Christie (ed.): 88–122.

Williams, G. (2000) Children's literature, children and uses of language description. In L. Unsworth. (ed.): 111–29.
Williams, G. (2001) Literacy pedagogy prior to schooling: relations between social positioning and semantic variation. In A. Morais, H. Baillie and B.Thomas (ed.), *Towards a Sociology of Pedagogy: The Contribution of Basil Bernstein to Research*. New York: Peter Lang.
Williams, G. (2005a) Language, brain, culture. *Linguistics and the Human Sciences* 1(3): 147–50.
Williams, G. (2005b) Grammatics in school. In R. Hasan, C. M. I. M. Matthiessen and J. J. Webster (eds): 281–310.
Williams, G. (ed.) (2005c) *Linguistics and the Human Sciences Vol. 1.2* (thematic issue on relations between language and brain function).
Williams, G. and Lukin, A. (eds) (2004) *The Development of Language: Functional Perspectives on Species and Individuals*. London and New York: Continuum.
Wu, C. (2000) *Modelling Linguistic Resources: A Systemic Functional Approach*. Ph.D. Thesis. Macquarie University.
Wu, C. and Fang, J. (2007) The semiotics of university introductions in Australia and China. In L. Barbara and T. Sardinha (eds), *Proceedings of the 33rd International Systemic Functional Congress (PUCSP, São Paulo, Brazil)*. Online publication available at http://www.pucsp.br/isfc. ISBN 85-283-0342-X. 568–591.
Yang, A. (1989) Cohesive chains and writing quality. *Word* 40(1–2): 235–54.
Young, L. and Harrison, C. (eds) (2004) *Systemic Functional Linguistics and Critical Discourse Analysis: Studies in Social Change*. London and New York: Continuum.
Youse K. M. and Coelho, C. A. (2005) Working memory and discourse production abilities following closed-head injury. *Brain Injury* 19(12): 1001–9.

Index

aphasia 10, 17, 143, 145, 147–8, 150–2, 248
  aphasic 144–7, 151
appraisal 25, 36–7, 57, 65, 67–8, 96, 118, 151–2, 157, 162, 199, 217–18, 232, 248
Armstrong, E. 10, 20, 40, 143, 145–6, 151–2, 163, 189

Baldry, A. 36, 86, 162, 223, 226
Bateman, J. 14, 19, 22, 42–3, 58, 68, 124, 132, 161, 224
Benson, J.D. 9, 104, 106–7, 111, 154, 157, 161, 196–7, 227
Bernstein, B. 14–15, 36, 39, 83, 91, 171, 176, 179
biological 23, 45–6, 109–10, 112
bonobo(s) 9, 105–12, 238, 289
Bowcher, W.L. 28, 42, 162, 181, 185, 187, 189
brain 19, 60, 74, 77–8, 82, 88, 108, 109–11, 145, 149, 151–2, 188, 198, 208–9, 212, 242, 248, 254

Cantonese 1–2, 128
causal 95, 98, 100, 147, 161, 191, 236
  causation 62, 105, 161, 191
Chinese 1–2, 6–8, 33, 41, 78, 103, 131, 142, 160, 217–18, 220, 222
Chomsky, N. 104
  Chomskyan 168, 195–6, 227
Christie, F. 15, 19–20, 32, 36, 38–9, 43, 159, 163–4
cline of instantiation 12, 25–6, 28–9, 32, 41, 45–8, 50, 52, 54, 57, 82, 128, 131, 231
Cloran, C. 20, 83, 98–9, 128, 158, 161–2, 167, 170, 178, 181, 187, 189

cognition 104, 161
  cognitive 8, 15, 18–19, 37, 88, 100, 109–12, 120, 152, 197, 248
coherence 145, 158
cohesion, cohesive 7, 25, 85, 113, 118, 145–6, 154–8, 164–5, 186, 199, 201, 211–12, 229, 241, 248
computational 9–10, 12, 14–15, 18–19, 21–2, 28–30, 51–3, 58, 67–8, 83, 113–15, 122, 124–6, 128, 133–4, 142, 218, 226, 229, 247–50, 252
concordance(s) 10, 115, 121–2, 124, 128, 133, 135–8, 141, 223, 249–50
  concordancer 53, 136, 224
consciousness 5, 95, 99, 106, 207, 239
construal 3–4, 74, 77, 81, 96, 98, 100–2, 106, 173, 181, 201, 236, 253
  construe 1, 3–5, 79–80, 83, 98, 101, 145, 170, 173, 211, 236
conversation 29, 32, 37, 54, 88, 93, 97, 99, 101–2, 144, 149, 150–1, 155–7, 161–2, 178–80
  conversational 106, 148, 162, 187
corpus 2, 10, 21–2, 28, 46, 52–4, 66, 69–70, 99, 102, 115–16, 118, 121–2, 124–42, 160, 164, 222–3, 227, 229, 249, 252
Coulthard, M. 20, 40, 156, 164
culture(s) 17, 25, 28–9, 44, 46, 48–9, 78, 98, 103–4, 107–8, 111, 159, 167–71, 181, 185, 188, 195, 197–8, 206, 214, 240
  cultural 9, 18–24, 27, 38, 45, 47, 99, 107–8, 110–12, 153–4, 169, 171, 188, 191–4, 199, 201, 206, 214–15
Cummings, M.J. 195–7, 227

Darwin, C. 198
deixis 66–7, 79, 94, 195
delicacy 13, 28, 50, 57, 62, 68–9, 79–80, 133, 186, 231–2
Derewianka, B. 78, 88, 101–2
diachronic 167–8, 171, 174, 246
dialect(-al)/(s) 17, 107, 128, 171, 193, 246, 249
dialogue 19, 22, 40, 76, 94, 97, 124, 156, 161, 166, 179, 247
discourse
　analysis 9, 18, 20–1, 25–6, 33, 104, 113, 128, 154, 160, 162, 164, 175, 179, 181, 197, 227, 246
　semantics 106, 161, 164
　structure 156–7

educational linguistics 10, 20, 30, 36, 38–9, 43, 47, 159
ellipsis 155–6, 164–5, 241
English 2, 7–8, 20–1, 26, 33, 35–6, 38, 41–2, 51–2, 66–70, 73–81, 85, 87–9, 105–7, 112, 114, 116, 118, 120, 128–31, 142, 155, 160–4, 188, 196–8, 219–20, 223, 225–8, 232, 237
ergative 80, 232
experiential 5–7, 25, 31, 66–7, 71–2, 80, 85, 157–9, 163, 165, 189, 201, 211, 231–2, 234–5, 253

Fawcett, R.P. 19, 64, 68, 187, 227
Firth, J.R. 10, 13, 52, 59, 63–5, 70, 72, 82, 154–5, 166–8, 175–6, 180–1, 188, 193, 214
　Firthian 13, 43, 83, 181, 196
Fries, P.H. 2, 36, 154, 157, 161, 165, 196–7
functional
　analysis 42, 118, 134–5
　description(s) 54, 56, 160
　grammar 10, 164, 195, 225, 228
　linguistics 10, 12, 14–15, 34–5, 40, 43, 48, 51, 55, 59, 61, 63, 128, 142, 154, 166, 196
　metatheory 9, 51–2
　theory 9, 12, 41, 51–2, 64, 70, 158, 166

genre(s) 10, 39–40, 47, 102, 129, 147, 154, 158–64, 179, 182, 189–90, 195, 197–8, 214, 225, 229, 237, 240, 246, 249
German 35, 42, 117–18, 131, 160, 226
grammar 2–7, 10, 14, 17, 28, 51, 54, 64, 67–8, 70–8, 80–3, 85, 94, 101, 106, 122, 128–9, 136, 142, 147, 154, 158, 160, 163–4, 173, 180–1, 189, 195, 199–201, 205, 217, 224–5, 228, 230, 232, 234–5, 237, 244, 252–3
grammatical
　cohesion 155
　intricacy 76–7, 147, 152
　metaphor 3–4, 75, 78, 88, 91, 98, 101–3, 161, 245
grammatics 3, 80, 157, 180–1, 217–18, 230
Greaves, W.S. 26, 70, 73, 76, 82, 106–7, 111, 154, 157, 196–7, 227
Gregory, M. 31, 57, 154, 162, 166, 189, 196, 227

Halliday, M.A.K. 1–23, 26, 28, 32–3, 36–7, 41, 43, 45, 48, 50–60, 64, 67, 69–76, 81–3, 86–103, 109, 111, 113–14, 128, 131–2, 144–5, 149, 154–77, 181–3, 185, 187–9, 193–202, 218, 224–6
Hasan, R. 9–10, 14–15, 19–20, 24, 28, 31, 33–4, 37–8, 43, 54, 57, 61–2, 64, 83, 86, 98–9, 113, 128, 145, 149, 154–5, 157–8, 161–2, 164–7, 170, 174–91, 194–6, 198, 200, 214
Hjelmslev, L. 2, 48, 52, 63–4, 74, 170, 196, 236
Hoey, M. 52, 113, 158, 164, 227
hyponomy 79, 155, 157, 241
hypotactic, hypotaxis 67, 71, 76, 155, 202, 223, 234–5

ideational 5–7, 37, 62, 67, 85, 91, 94, 97, 100–1, 106, 144, 152, 157, 159–62, 165, 172–4, 201, 204, 231, 237, 241, 245, 253
interrogative 209–11
intersubjective(-ity) 7, 19, 157, 257

intertextuality 247
intonation 14, 26–8, 54, 68, 80, 91, 94, 120, 124, 235, 242–3
Italian 35, 42

Japanese 131, 160, 217, 220, 222

Kanzi 105–12

Labov, W. 168, 171
Lamb, S.M. 64, 197
language
  child 88, 93, 145, 201
  English 38, 129, 225–6, 228
  human 22, 106, 108, 112, 173–4, 253
  natural 5, 21–2, 128, 141, 214, 250
langue 168, 174, 188
Lemke, J.L. 82, 159, 162, 188, 227
lexical 13, 41, 71–8, 83–4, 90–3, 100–1, 113, 117, 124, 129, 133–7, 142, 145–6, 148, 151–2, 155–8, 185, 222–3, 241, 245, 250
lexicogrammar 5, 12–13, 15, 24, 27–8, 50, 52–3, 62, 64, 66–7, 71, 73–6, 80, 82–3, 86, 99, 106, 156–7, 169–70, 173–5, 180–1, 188, 196, 198–9, 201, 205, 231, 236–7, 239, 245–6
  lexicogrammatical 6, 10, 74, 84, 106, 134, 145, 150, 152, 170, 173–4, 181–2, 194, 199, 202–3, 244, 246, 248
lexis 28, 73–5, 81, 83, 94, 128, 136, 205, 207, 225, 244
linguistic
  analysis 7, 10, 115, 133–5, 148, 214, 248
  computing 22, 30, 52, 113–14, 124–6, 250–1
  system 17, 22, 48, 54, 69, 81, 96, 98, 102, 131, 145, 197, 240
  theory 9, 59–60, 64, 83, 113, 171, 174, 188, 201
linguistics
  applied 35, 37, 61, 228
  artistic 30, 34
  clinical 20, 29–30, 35, 40
  computational 21–2, 30, 83, 122, 124, 226, 250

corpus 10, 21–2, 28, 52, 124–6, 128
educational 10, 20, 30, 36, 38–9, 43, 47, 159
epistemological 30, 36
forensic 30, 33, 40, 252
functional 10, 12, 14–15, 34–5, 40, 43, 48, 51, 55, 59, 61, 63, 128, 142, 154, 166, 196
literacy 29–30, 38, 78, 102, 218, 225, 227–8
literary 17, 29–30, 33–4, 37–8, 57, 82–3, 124, 157, 189–90, 193, 196–8, 207, 219, 244, 249
logical 5, 25, 71–2, 85, 94, 115, 146–7, 159, 165, 201, 231–2, 234–5, 253

Malinowski, B. 15, 22, 43–5, 83, 166, 176, 187
Martin, J.R. 9–10, 15, 19–20, 23, 25–6, 28, 31–2, 34, 36–9, 42–3, 45, 48, 57, 62, 64, 67, 72, 74, 79, 83, 125, 154, 156–9, 161–5, 167, 175, 181–2, 187, 189, 207, 218, 224, 228
Martinec, R. 14, 28, 42, 86, 160, 162
Matthiessen, C.M.I.M. 8–9, 12, 14–15, 19, 21, 23, 26, 28–9, 32, 36–7, 39, 42–3, 48–52, 57–8, 60–2, 64–5, 67–8, 70–1, 73, 79, 83, 86, 95, 97, 102, 128, 131–3, 144, 158, 160–1, 165, 167, 170, 187, 222, 224–5, 228
meaning potential 5, 8, 14, 41–2, 46, 60, 63, 65, 69, 83, 91, 99, 131, 173, 193, 206
meaning-making 72, 97, 107, 112, 238
media 14, 25, 29–30, 32, 34–7, 43, 48, 159, 162–3, 225
metafunction(s), metafunctional 5–7, 25–6, 39, 50, 57, 61–2, 67–8, 71–4, 79, 85, 87, 94–5, 97–8, 102–3, 106, 118, 120, 145, 155–7, 160, 162, 165, 172–4, 198–9, 201–2, 231, 234–7, 245, 248, 251, 253
metaphor(-ical) 3–4, 46, 61, 75, 77–9, 83, 87–8, 91, 96, 101–3, 161, 193, 207, 229, 239, 244–5

298

Index

modality(-ies) 7, 9–10, 65–6, 85, 95, 107, 124, 148–9, 162, 164, 173, 197, 199, 208, 232, 238, 247–8
mode 7, 10, 23, 29, 31, 42–8, 57, 60, 72, 77, 83, 91, 99, 107, 154, 159–60, 162, 166, 169, 171–2, 176–80, 182, 224, 228, 233, 239–40, 242
multimodal(-ity) 14–15, 35, 43, 58, 86, 187, 189, 221, 223, 225–6, 238, 247
multisemiotic 20, 29–30, 34, 41–3, 47, 114

narrative(s) 29, 33, 38, 40, 42, 82, 96, 111, 146, 157, 162–3, 176, 207, 246
Nigel 14, 88–9, 91, 93–4, 96, 100
nominal 4, 6, 65–7, 71, 76–7, 79, 101–2, 148, 152, 155, 158, 161, 195, 202, 235–6
noun(s) 3–4, 78, 101, 121, 144, 156, 245

ontogenesis, ontogenetic 77, 88–9, 94–5, 97–100, 102, 106, 167

Painter, C. 9, 15, 77–8, 87–9, 93–102, 167
paradigmatic 10, 22, 62–4, 66, 89, 131, 172–3, 182, 231–2, 234
paratactic, parataxis 67, 71, 76, 155, 234–5
parole 167–8, 170–1, 174, 177, 188
parser, parsing 22, 53–4, 58, 83, 118–19, 121–2, 134–5, 249–50
passive 82, 140–1, 203, 205
phonetics 13–14, 16–17, 24, 27–8, 50, 62, 80, 82, 145, 169–70, 188, 231, 236
  phonetic 1–2, 27, 124, 171, 242, 248
phonological 5, 14, 27, 57, 64–7, 70–1, 80, 90–3, 102, 124, 143, 160, 170, 194, 230, 232, 235, 237
phonology 13–15, 22, 24, 26–8, 50, 54, 57, 62, 64, 66–7, 70–1, 73, 80, 82, 89, 94, 122, 160, 169–70, 174, 181, 188, 196, 230–9, 242, 252–3
poetry 33, 192, 196, 198, 207
probabilistic, probability 15, 22, 57, 69, 97, 113, 132, 135, 193, 208, 229, 244, 252
prosodic, prosody 26, 54, 67, 72, 157, 174, 232, 234, 242–3

protolanguage, protolinguistic 62, 78–9, 88–92, 94, 96, 98–9, 101–2, 239, 253

quantitative 73, 99, 128–9, 160, 194, 244, 246

rank 28, 45, 52, 62–73, 76, 80, 85, 134, 158, 229, 231–3, 234, 237
  rankshifted 75, 231
recursion, recursive 104, 106–8, 110, 150, 182
referential 78, 104, 144, 153, 156, 167, 185, 239, 241
register, registerial 10, 12, 17, 24–5, 27–33, 35–6, 38–43, 46–8, 52–3, 57, 75, 98, 122, 125, 131–2, 154, 157–62, 164, 167, 169, 171, 177–8, 181, 186–7, 189, 191, 193–5, 225, 229, 237, 240, 246, 252
representational 92, 108–11, 226
rhetorical 32, 161–2, 199, 201, 211, 217, 223, 237, 246
rhyme 63, 70, 235
rhythm(ic) 26–8, 54, 73, 160, 235, 237, 242–3

Saussure, F. 63, 167–8, 188, 198, 214
Savage-Rumbaugh, S. 105–6, 111
semantic
  consequences 10, 192, 200–1, 211
  networks 14, 161, 164
  relations 165, 191, 235
  system 5, 14, 19, 98, 156, 195
  variation 83, 99
semantics 5, 10, 13–15, 17, 24, 27–8, 37, 50, 53–4, 62, 64, 78, 82–3, 86, 94, 96, 101, 104, 106, 114, 149, 156, 161, 164, 168–70, 174, 182, 188–9, 191, 193, 196, 201, 219, 225, 228, 231, 236, 238–40, 245–6
semiotic system(s) 5, 12–15, 19, 23–4, 44–50, 55, 57, 60, 62, 64, 89, 95, 162, 164, 188, 233, 238
semiotics 9, 18–20, 78, 104, 196, 219
semogenesis, semogenic 8, 60, 64, 74, 80, 102, 238–9
Sinclair, J.M. 128, 156, 189

social
  class 83, 98–9, 161
  context(s) 10, 37, 60, 87, 154, 156, 158–9, 164–5, 174–5
  process 24, 74, 95, 98, 159, 166, 171, 179, 236
  relationships 1, 5, 47, 62, 74, 152, 236, 244
  semiotic 9, 18–20, 99, 181
  system(s) 23, 43, 46, 48
sociolinguistics 17–18, 167, 174
speech
  function(s) 65, 94–5, 150–2, 161, 208–11, 248
  pathology 15, 38, 40, 143
spoken
  discourse 26, 77, 164
  English 105, 107
  language 26, 75–6
  model(s) 42–3
stylistics 29–30, 33–4, 82–3, 192–8, 245
  stylistic analysis 10, 190–215
syllable 14, 63, 67–8, 70, 72–3, 235, 237
synonomy 155, 157, 241
syntax 64, 73–4, 104–5, 107–8, 110
  syntactic 6, 105, 114–15, 118, 121–2, 143, 195, 250–1
syntagm, syntagmatic 22, 62–4, 70–2, 117, 172–3, 229, 231, 234–6
systemic
  functional 9–10, 12–15, 19–20, 22–5, 28, 33–8, 40–3, 45–6, 48, 51–2, 54–7, 59, 61, 63–4, 70, 82, 115, 118, 122, 125, 128, 131, 134–5, 137, 141–2, 154, 166, 193, 225
  phonology 57
  potential 6, 52, 67, 71, 131, 134, 233

Teruya, K. 23, 26, 29, 49, 128
textual
  meaning 6, 146, 154, 157, 159–60, 173
  metafunction 25, 39, 94, 102, 155, 214
Thibault, P. 9, 19–20, 22, 34, 86, 104, 107–8, 111–12, 157, 162, 197–8
transitivity 7, 65–7, 81, 85, 93–5, 131, 134, 147–8, 173, 196, 201–2, 204, 223, 241, 248

Unsworth, L. 15, 34, 38, 43, 162–4

Ventola, E. 37, 42–3, 149, 154, 156, 159, 162–3, 182
verbal
  action 176, 178–9, 183–5
  art 33–4, 57, 178, 191–2, 195–9, 206, 214–15
  group 68, 71, 148, 155, 235
Vygotsky, L.S. 19, 96–7

written
  discourse 77, 147, 152, 239–40
  language 14, 81, 101–2